D1523922

MEASUREMENT ERROR
and RESEARCH DESIGN

Dedicated to

Sidanth,
Deepa,
Amma (Mother),
&
Appa (Father)

For being my best friends

MEASUREMENT ERROR
and RESEARCH DESIGN

Madhu Viswanathan
University of Illinois, Urbana-Champaign

SAGE Publications
Thousand Oaks ▪ London ▪ New Delhi

For information:

 Sage Publications, Inc.
2455 Teller Road
Thousand Oaks, California 91320
E-mail: order@sagepub.com

Sage Publications Ltd.
1 Oliver's Yard
55 City Road
London EC1Y 1SP
United Kingdom

Sage Publications India Pvt. Ltd.
B-42, Panchsheel Enclave
Post Box 4109
New Delhi 110 017 India

Printed in the United States of America.

Library of Congress Cataloging-in-Publication Data

Viswanathan, Madhu.
Measurement error and research design / by Madhu Viswanathan; foreword by Richard Bagozzi.
      p. cm.
Includes bibliographical references and index.
ISBN 1-4129-0642-3 (pbk.)
    1. Social sciences—Research—Methodology.
2. Measurement. I. Title.
H62.V54 2005
001.4′2—dc22

                                        2004022908

This book is printed on acid-free paper.

05 06 07 08 09 10 9 8 7 6 5 4 3 2 1

Acquisitions Editor:	Lisa Cuevas Shaw
Editorial Assistant:	Margo Crouppen
Production Editor:	Tracy Alpern
Copy Editor:	Liann Lech
Typesetter:	C&M Digitals (P) Ltd.
Indexer:	Gloria Tierney
Cover Designer:	Glenn Vogel
Cover Concept:	Sidanth Madhubalan

Contents

Foreword

Theory and method have been treated typically as distinct aspects of science in the basic and applied social sciences. This can be seen in three senses. Academic researchers tend to see themselves as either theorists or substantive inquirers on one hand, or as methodologists on the other hand. Coursework is segregated into theory or methods classes. And fields of inquiry promote a favorite method to test their theories with alternative methods given secondary status, if treated at all. All too often, the net result is theories that are tested inadequately or are tested in narrow ways or methods in search of applications to phenomena without proper attention given to the mechanisms behind, and boundary conditions of, the theories and phenomena under investigation. We lack a dialogue between theorists and methodologists and a balance between conceptual and empirical foundations of research so as to promote valid and useful scientific knowledge.

Madhu Viswanathan presents a thoroughly integrative and original approach to the theory-method gap in contemporary basic social science and applied research. The central theme of the book, which is grounded in the best of technical and philosophical practice, is that measurement is at the heart of scientific research, and researchers must be mindful of measurement error as they test theories and search for valid empirical evidence.

Viswanathan provides a subtle, scientifically grounded framework for the conduct and interpretation of empirical research. Special attention is given to the conceptualization of measurement error and decomposition of it into unique components. He meticulously shows us how to identify and correct for measurement error with the aim of better designing measures and methods. His analytical framework for measure development and validation, summarized in Chapter 5, is a contribution of far-ranging import and one that is sure to guide researchers for years to come and accelerate the generation of new knowledge in the fields it informs.

This is a splendid book as well for students in the sense of constantly reinforcing technical learning with concrete examples. Moreover, the presentation explicitly links measurement to broader methodological, philosophical, and interpretive issues, a feature missing in contemporary methodological books.

In sum, Viswanathan takes us on a journey of discovery where measurement is shown to fundamentally link our ideas and speculations found in our theories to empirical evidence as manifested in the world of experience. In the process, we reach a new level of scientific maturity and come ever closer to achieving things heretofore beyond our grasp.

Richard P. Bagozzi
Rice University

Preface

Accurate measurement is central to scientific research. Minimizing measurement error is a central goal in empirical research. Reliability and validity are considered the foundations of measurement because they represent attempts to reduce measurement error. Although it is impossible to eliminate all errors, it is possible to use a fuller understanding of measurement error in designing research, analyzing and interpreting data, and acknowledging limitations. This book evolved from teaching a research methods course at the doctoral level and research courses at the undergraduate and graduate levels at the University of Illinois, Urbana–Champaign, for more than a decade. It is written for present and future empirical researchers in the social sciences. This book will show how researchers can identify and correct for error in the process of developing measures, using measures in substantive studies, and designing methods. Through an understanding of the issues involved in measuring one "thing," this book lays a foundation for understanding the issues inherent in measuring many "things" (i.e., in designing research methods).

In describing the approach taken in this book, it is useful to understand what this book is not. This book is not a primer on statistical analyses in measurement. Basic statistical analyses are described and illustrated throughout, but the reader interested in a thorough treatment of this subject matter should perhaps look elsewhere. This book does not provide exhaustive coverage of recent measurement techniques, such as generalizability and item response theory. This book is not a comprehensive primer on measurement theory; classics on this topic are available elsewhere. Rather, this book takes an approach that is different from current and past offerings in this area.

This book is organized around the meaning of measurement error. It begins with a brief overview of measurement principles that is supplemented with many examples to provide necessary background to the reader. The book then explores the meaning of measurement error, the different sources that could cause different types of measurement error, the nature of responses that would characterize each type of error, and the pattern of empirical outcomes that would be observed. Various sources of error lead to different types of error, which are reflected in response patterns that are assessed through empirical procedures. A detailed examination of this interplay provides the foundation for this book. Such an approach provides guidance in developing and editing items and measures and designing methods. It is also useful in analyzing data and interpreting empirical results in light of measures and methods used.

This book attempts to answer many questions: What is measurement? What are the steps in the measure development process? What is the meaning of measurement error? What are the types of measurement error? What are the causes of each type of error? What are the response patterns that follow from each type of error? What are the effects of each type of error on empirical outcomes? Given the understanding obtained from these questions, how can error be minimized in the design of items? Of measures? Of methods? How can innovative design and analyses be used to minimize error in the design of items? Of measures? Of methods? How do measures differ or how can measures be classified? How should different types of measures be developed, validated, and used? What are examples of measures and measurement across the disciplines? What are the implications of understanding measurement error for research design and analysis—that is, for using existing measures in research designs? For structural equation modeling? For measurement in applied research? How does an understanding of measurement error enhance the design of experiments and surveys? What is the role of measurement in science? And finally, what are the orientations underlying the material in this book?

This book is of particular value in designing measures and methods in the social sciences. It delves into the "soft," intangible aspects of research design that the researcher confronts constantly when designing items, measures, and methods. Other books on measurement typically have presented a more statistical orientation or an orientation toward measurement theory. Although these approaches are invaluable, this book was motivated by the lack of literature that enhances understanding of measurement error, its sources, and its effects. Through the understanding provided here, the aim is to enhance the *design* of research, both of measures and of methods.

For the budding researcher, this book will facilitate understanding of the basic principles of measurement required to design measures and methods for empirical research. For the experienced researcher, this book will provide an in-depth analysis and discussion of the essence of measurement error and procedures to minimize it, as well as the interrelationship between measurement and research design. This book aims to "push the envelope" by handling a host of issues in measurement heretofore not discussed explicitly. If the reader has no intention of developing a measure, the principles covered here are very relevant for *using* existing measures in empirical methods and in the design of research methods. A variety of issues of relevance to research methodology in day-to-day research are also discussed.

The unique treatment of measurement error in this book should become evident in the first few pages. Depth of understanding of measurement error is provided through the treatment of the subject matter at a nuts-and-bolts level with numerous concrete examples of errors and empirical procedures. The need for this book arose from the nature of treatment of measurement error in the literature primarily in terms of empirical analyses without sufficiently in-depth conceptual examination of measurement error. The approach taken here is to subject measurement procedures and measurement error to the same conceptual and operational examination that is involved in conceptualizing and operationalizing any construct. In other words, measurement error involved in operationalizing the concepts of measurement error in traditional empirical procedures is examined here! Hence, the level of treatment of subject matter traverses the linkage between conceptual notions of error and patterns of responses. Numerous examples of measures from a variety of disciplines are discussed to provide the reader with concrete instances and to stimulate creative measure development. Many figures, tables, and exhibits are used to illustrate concepts, procedures, and empirical outcomes. This book is also unique in using a measurement framework to examine a variety of issues in research methodology, both quantitative and qualitative. This book is about the design of measures and methods through understanding measurement error. In this context, statistical procedures are discussed at an intuitive level rather than in distant terms. Numbers analyzed through statistical procedures can be precise, concrete, and sometimes illusive. What numbers mean and where they came from is a central focus in this book.

A figure provides an overview of the chapters. Chapter 1 is an introduction to measurement that covers current knowledge in a succinct form with extensive use of examples. Chapter 2 provides a detailed discussion of measurement error and develops a taxonomy of measurement errors. The aim here is to provide clear understanding of types of measurement error. Chapter 3 develops a taxonomy of different sources of measurement error based on a detailed review of literature in the social sciences and cross-listed with a taxonomy of measurement errors. Thus, this chapter relates common error sources to errors, providing researchers with a framework to consider sources of error and their effects. Chapter 4 discusses traditional empirical procedures used in assessing reliability and dimensionality in terms of the types of measurement errors that are captured by these procedures. Using Chapters 2–4 as a basis, Chapter 5 presents guidelines for identifying and correcting for measurement error. Chapter 6 presents some innovative design and analyses, in light of earlier chapters, that can be used to identify error.

Chapters 1–6 provide the basic foundation in measurement. Chapters 7–8 expand the discussion to several issues. Chapter 7 discusses how measures differ and how they can be classified, covering issues in measurement that lack coverage in the literature but are faced by researchers in day-to-day research. Fundamental differences in the nature of measures have implications for their development, validation, and usage. Chapter 8 provides examples of measures and measurement from a range of disciplines that will assist researchers in thinking outside the box.

The book then moves from discussing measurement as measuring a single measure to measurement as developing an entire research method where several variables are measured. The discussion moves from issues pertaining to measurement as in the operationalization of a single construct to measurement as in the operationalization of a complete research method. For example, a survey method could be thought of as a set of measures that involves measuring one thing (where issues such as item wording and response scale formats are germane) as well as measuring many things (where issues such as sequencing of measures are germane). An experiment involves manipulating independent variables (i.e., generating levels of measurement) and measuring dependent variables. Chapters 9–11 broaden the discussion to cover issues in research design and, more broadly, research methodology, using measurement concepts as the basic building blocks.

Chapter 9 discusses the implications of understanding measurement error for research design and analysis—that is, the use of existing measures in research designs and the use of structural equation modeling in data analysis— as well as for applied research. Chapter 10 uses the foundation of measurement to discuss issues in research methods such as designing experiments and surveys. Chapter 11 provides a broad discussion of the role and nature of measurement in scientific research. Chapter 12 summarizes the orientations of the book.

For the reader unfamiliar with the measurement literature, Chapter 1 is an ideal place to start. For the reader more familiar with measurement, Chapter 1 could be skimmed. The initial chapters, specifically Chapters 1–5, develop terminology and present detailed examples of a few measures that are used in later chapters. However, several of the subsequent chapters could be read independently, such as Chapter 8 on examples of measures.

Chapter 1
What is measurement? What are the steps in the measure development process?

Chapter 2
What is the meaning of measurement error? What are the types of measurement error?
What are the response patterns that follow from each type of error?

Chapter 3
What are some common sources of each type of error?

Chapter 4
What are the effects of each type of error on empirical outcomes in psychometric
procedures?

Chapter 5
How can error be identified and corrected for in developing measures?

Chapter 6
How can error be identified and corrected through innovative
design and analysis?

Chapter 7
How do measures differ or how can they be classified?

Chapter 8
How can examples of measures and measurement from across disciplines
provide creative ideas on developing measures?

Chapter 9
What are the implications of understanding measurement error for using measures in research
design? For structural equation modeling? For measurement in applied research?

Chapter 10
How does understanding measurement error enhance
methodological design of experiments and surveys?

Chapter 11
What is the role of measurement in science?

Chapter 12
What are the orientations underlying the material in this book?

Wherever possible, data are presented from my own work, and data sets and instructions are available at the Web site for this book (http://www .sagepub.com/viswanathan). Suggestions for using this book in courses are also provided at the Web site http://www.business.uiuc.edu/~madhuv/msmt .html.

I have tried to appropriately cite past literature, old and new, and to give due credit. However, the measurement and methodology literature is vast and spans a long period of time. Despite my best efforts, I hope there are no oversights. I have also sometimes employed the adjective "methodological" in a narrower sense than suggested in dictionaries, for lack of a better descriptor, although I have employed the noun "methodology" more appropriately. In closing, I hope this book delivers what is promised here.

Acknowledgments

A book of this sort can rarely be the work of one person. Many people have contributed to its writing. In a broader sense, I have been truly fortunate to benefit from the encouragement and support of many individuals. The names of some of these individuals are listed at the end of the acknowledgments.

This book evolved from teaching a research methods course at the doctoral level and research courses at the undergraduate and graduate levels at the University of Illinois, Urbana-Champaign, for more than a decade. I have learned from many students who contributed to discussions in these classes over the years. Several doctoral students at Illinois contributed directly to this book. Hila Riemer, Tianjiao Qiu, and Carlos Torelli devoted considerable effort to the illustrations and references in the book. Ashok Lalwani, Kyoungmi Lee, Hila Riemer, Kevin Rock, and Linda Tuncay provided helpful comments on earlier drafts of chapters of the book. I also thank my present and past colleagues in the marketing area, the Department of Business Administration, and the College of Business for their encouragement and support. I hope this effort is fitting and worthy of the great interdisciplinary traditions of the University of Illinois, where I have had the opportunity to learn from and work with great scholars such as the late Seymour Sudman. I especially thank Sheila Loudermilk at the Department of Business Administration, who tirelessly typed many parts of the manuscript. In characteristic fashion, she went through drafts with attention to the most minute of details.

I thank Sage Publications for this unique opportunity. Lisa Cuevas, the acquisitions editor, provided thoughtful and professional guidance and encouragement at every stage of the publication process, essentially making the entire authorship experience most enjoyable. I thank Liann Lech for her careful and thorough efforts in copyediting the manuscript. Tracy Alpern, the production editor, enabled a timely, efficient, and responsive process that readied the manuscript for publication. I thank Margo Crouppen and Janet Foulger for their efforts in the publication process. Several reviewers of the proposal and manuscript provided helpful comments that enabled important improvements: Robert DeVellis, University of North Carolina; Richard Netemeyer, University of Virginia; Arturo Olivarez, Texas Tech University; Richard Sudweeks, Brigham Young University; Dennis Jackson, University of Windsor; and Dougal Hutchison, National Foundation for Educational Research.

James Anderson, Northwestern University; Joe Cote, Washington State University; James Hess, University of Houston; Ujwal Kayande, Pennsylvania State University; Terry Shimp, University of South Carolina; and Brian Wansink, University of Illinois, provided comments on a paper that forms the basis for a chapter.

I especially thank Rick Bagozzi for providing me with invaluable advice and encouragement. He has written the foreword to this book, an overwhelming gesture that made the entire endeavor worthwhile.

I consider two individuals to be my mentors and role models in academics. They have had considerable influence in developing my interests in measurement and research design to the point of writing a book. Terry Childers, my dissertation advisor at the University of Minnesota, taught an excellent seminar in the area of measurement during my doctoral education. He was influential in developing my early interests in this area. He has encouraged my endeavors for almost two decades now, since my early days as a befuddled doctoral student. Kent Monroe, my senior colleague at the University of Illinois, had the vision more than a decade ago to ask me to teach a doctoral-level course on measurement and research methods. This experience has culminated in my writing this book. I cannot express in words what his support and guidance over the years have meant to me.

This book is dedicated to four people who are the best friends one could ask for. I count my son, Sidanth, as my best friend. He is everything a parent could dream of in a child and the biggest source of joy in my life. I have learned immensely from his wisdom, goodness, talent, and drive. My wife, Deepa, with her characteristically quiet, constant, and unconditional support, encouraged me during all the times of soul-searching. She has enabled my endeavors by taking care of the important things in life that are often unnoticed or underappreciated. What I have learned from my parents, who have been role models of excellence in all their endeavors, is immeasurable. I count them among my best friends, ever-supportive and proud of their son's endeavors.

Thank you!

Ramesh Arunachalam
Terry Childers
Rosy Diwakar
V. N. Diwakar
Chinnammal Dorairajan
S. E. Dorairajan
Kanchana Dore
Shantanu Dutta
Manoj Hastak
Curtis Haugtvedt
R. Jaikumar
Meera Krishnamurthy
T. S. Krishnamurthy
Kausalya Madavan
Deepa Madhubalan
Sidanth Madhubalan
Krishnanand Maillacheruvu
Kent Monroe
Radha Nagaraj
T. S. Nagarajan
T. V. Narayanan
T. T. Narendran
Rajeswari Niranjan

Atul Prasad
Shashikala Raghunathan
Kalpana Rao
Malathy
    Lakshmana Rao
V. N. Lakshmana Rao
Jose Antonio Rosa
C. S. Sivaraman
Jaya Sitaram
Shashidhar Sitaram
Vijayan Sitaram
Alamelu Srinivasan
C. R. Srinivasan
Ganesh Subramaniam
L. Subramanian
Padma Subramanian
T. K. Subramanian
Subbaraman Vaidyanathan
Anita Viswanathan
Mahesh Viswanathan
Niranjan Viswanathan
Saradha Viswanathan
S. D. Viswanathan

1

What Is Measurement?

Overview

This chapter covers the basics of measurement. The chapter aims to provide understanding of measurement and measure development procedures currently discussed in the literature. Measurement error is introduced, and the steps in the measure development process and empirical procedures to assess error are described. The chapter uses many examples based on data to illustrate measurement issues and procedures. Treatment of the material is at an intuitive, nuts-and-bolts level with numerous illustrations.

The chapter is not intended to be a statistics primer; rather, it provides sufficient bases from which to seek out more advanced treatment of empirical procedures. It should be noted that many issues are involved in using appropriately the statistical techniques discussed here. The discussion in this chapter aims to provide an introduction to specific statistical techniques, and the references cited here provide direction for in-depth reading.

What Is Measurement Error?

Measurement is essential to empirical research. Typically, a method used to collect data involves measuring many things. Understanding how any one thing is measured is central to understanding the entire research method. Scientific measurement has been defined as "rules for assigning numbers to objects in such a way as to represent quantities of attributes" (e.g., Nunnally, 1978, p. 3). Measurement "consists of rules for assigning symbols to objects so as to (1) represent quantities of attributes numerically (scaling) or (2) define whether the objects fall in the same or different categories with respect to a given attribute (classification)" (Nunnally & Bernstein, 1994, p. 3).[1] The attributes of objects, as well as people and events, are the underlying concepts that need to be measured. This element of the definition of measurement highlights the importance of finding the most appropriate attributes to study in a research area. This element also emphasizes understanding what these attributes really mean, that is, fully understanding the underlying concepts being measured. Rules refer to everything that needs to be done to measure something, whether measuring brain activity, attitude toward an object, organizational emphasis on research and development, or stock market performance. Therefore, these rules include a range of things that occur during the data collection process, such as how questions are worded and how a measure is administered. Numbers are central to the definition of measurement for several reasons: (a) Numbers are standardized and allow communication in science, (b) numbers can be subjected to statistical analyses, and (c) numbers are precise. But underneath the façade of precise, analyzable, standardized numbers is the issue of accuracy and measurement error.

The very idea of scientific measurement presumes that there is a thing being measured (i.e., an underlying concept). A concept and its measurement can be distinguished. A measure of a concept is not the concept itself, but one of several possible error-filled ways of measuring it.[2] A distinction can be drawn between conceptual and operational definitions of concepts. A conceptual definition describes a concept in terms of other concepts (Kerlinger, 1986; Nunnally, 1978). For instance, stock market performance is an abstract notion in people's minds. It can be defined conceptually in terms of growth in value of stocks; that is, by using other concepts such as value and growth. An operational definition describes the operations that need to be performed to measure a concept (Kerlinger, 1986; Nunnally, 1978). An operational definition is akin to rules in the definition of measurement discussed earlier in the chapter, and refers to everything that needs to be done to measure something. The Dow Jones average is one measure of stock market performance. This operational definition involves tracking the stock value of a specific set of companies. It is by no means a perfect measure of stock market performance. It is one error-filled way of measuring the concept of stock market performance.

The term *construct* is used to refer to a concept that is specifically defined for scientific study (Kerlinger, 1986). In *Webster's New World Dictionary*, *construct* means "to build, form or devise." This physical meaning of the word *construct* is similar to the scientific meaning: Constructs are concepts devised or built to meet scientific specifications. These specifications include precisely defining the construct, elaborating on what it means, and relating it to existing research. Words that are acceptable for daily conversation would not fit the specifications for science in terms of clear and precise definitions. "I am going to study what people think of catastrophic events" is a descriptive statement that may be acceptable at the preliminary stages of research. But several concepts in this statement need precise description, such as "think of," which may separate into several constructs, and "catastrophe," which has to be distinguished from other descriptors of events. Scientific explanations are essentially words, and some of these words relate to concepts. Constructs are words devised for scientific study.[3] In science, though, these words need to be used carefully and defined precisely.

When measuring something, error is any deviation from the "true" value, whether it is the true value of the amount of cola consumed in a period of time, the level of extroversion, or the degree of job satisfaction.[4] Although this true value is rarely known, particularly when measuring psychological variables, this hypothetical notion is useful to understand measurement error inherent in scientific research. Such error can have a pattern to it or be "all over the place." Thus, an important distinction can be drawn between consistent (i.e., systematic) error and inconsistent (i.e., random) error (Appendix 1.1). This distinction highlights two priorities in minimizing error. One priority is to achieve consistency,[5] and the second is to achieve accuracy.

Simple explanations of random and systematic error are provided below, although subsequent discussions will introduce nuances. Consider using a weighing machine in a scenario where a person's weight is measured twice in the space of a few minutes with no apparent change (no eating and no change in clothing). If the weighing machine shows different readings, there is *random error* in measurement. In other words, the error has no pattern to it and is inconsistent. Alternatively, the weighing machine may be off in one direction, say, consistently showing a reading that is 5 pounds higher than the accurate value. In other words, the machine is consistent across readings with no apparent change in the weight being measured. Such error is called *systematic error* because there is a consistent pattern to it. It should be noted, though, that on just one reading, the nature of error is not clear. Even if the true value is independently known through some other method, consistency still cannot be assessed in one reading. Multiple readings suggest the inconsistent or consistent nature of any error in the weighing machine, provided the weight of the target person has not changed. Similarly, repetition either across time or across responses to similar items clarifies the consistent or inconsistent nature of error in empirical measurement, assuming the phenomenon across time is unchanged.

If the weighing machine is "all over the place" in terms of error (i.e., random), conclusions cannot be drawn about the construct being measured. Random error in measures attenuates relationships (Nunnally, 1978); that is, it restricts the ability of a measure to be related to other measures. The phrase "all over the place" is, in itself, in need of scientific precision, which will be provided in subsequent pages. Random error has to be reduced before proceeding with any further analyses. This is not to suggest no random error at all, but just that such error should be reasonably low. Certainly, a viable approach is to collect multiple observations of such readings in the hope that the random errors average out. Such an assumption may work when random errors are small in magnitude and when the measure actually captures the construct in question. The danger here, though, is that the measure may not capture any aspect of the intended construct. Therefore, the average of a set of inaccurate items remains inaccurate. Measures of abstract concepts in the social sciences, such as attitudes, are not as clear-cut as weighing machines. Thus, it may not be clear if, indeed, a construct, such as an attitude, is being captured with some random error that averages out. The notion that errors average out is one reason for using multiple items, as discussed subsequently.

Measures that are relatively free of random error) are called *reliable* (Nunnally, 1978). There are some similarities between the use of reliability in measurement and the common use of the term. For example, a person who is reliable in sticking to a schedule is probably consistently on time. A reliable friend is dependable and predictable, can be counted on, and is consistent. However, there are some differences as well. A reliable person who is consistent but always 15 minutes late would still be reliable in a measurement context. Stated in extreme terms, reliability in measurement actually could have nothing to do with accuracy in measurement, because reliability relates only to consistency. Without some degree of consistency, the issue of accuracy may not be germane. If a weighing machine is all over the place, there is not much to be said about its accuracy. Clearly, there are shades of gray here in that some small amount of inconsistency is acceptable. Waiting for perfect consistency before attempting accuracy may not be as efficient or pragmatic as achieving reasonable consistency and approximate accuracy. Perfect consistency may not even be possible in the social sciences, given the inherent nature of phenomena being studied.

Whether a measure is accurate or not is the realm of *validity,* or the degree to which a measure is free of random and systematic error (Nunnally, 1978). If the weighing machine is consistent, then whether it is accurate becomes germane. If the weighing machine is consistent but off in one direction, it is reliable but not valid. In other words, there is consistency in the nature of error. To say a measure is accurate begs the question, "Accurate in doing what?" Here, validity refers to accuracy in measuring the intended construct.[6]

Random and systematic errors are the two types of errors that are pervasive in measurement across the sciences. Low reliability and low validity have consequences. Random error may reduce correlations between a measure and other variables, whereas systematic error may increase or reduce correlations between two variables. A brief overview of the measure development process is provided next. The purpose here is to cover the basic issues briefly to provide a background for more in-depth understanding of types of measurement error. However, the coverage is markedly different from treatment elsewhere in the literature. Presentation is at a level to enable intuitive understanding. Statistical analyses are presented succinctly with many illustrations and at an intuitive level.

Overview of Traditional Measure Development Procedures

A number of steps have been suggested in the measure development process (Churchill, 1979; Gerbing & Anderson, 1988) that are adapted here and discussed.[7] As in many stepwise processes, these steps are often blurred and iterative. The process is illustrated in Figure 1.1. The steps in the process emphasize that traversing the distance from the conceptual to the operational requires a systematic process. Rather than consider a concept and move directly to item generation, and use of a resulting measure, the distance between the conceptual and the operational has to be spanned carefully and iteratively.

Conceptual and Operational Definitions

The very idea of measurement suggests an important distinction between a concept and its measurement. Hence, the literature distinguishes between conceptual and operational definitions of *constructs* (i.e., concepts specifically designed for scientific study) (Kerlinger, 1986). Scientific research is about constructing abstract devices; nevertheless, the term *construct* is similar in several respects to constructing concrete things. In developing

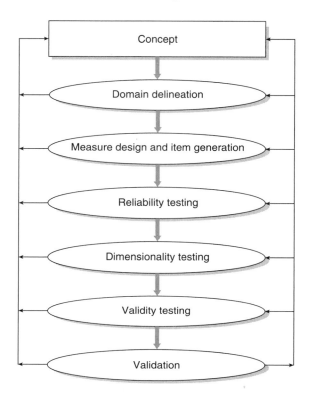

Figure 1.1   Steps in the Measure Development Process

constructs, the level of abstraction is an important consideration. If constructs are too concrete, then they are not as useful for theoretical generalization, although their measurement may be more direct. If constructs are too abstract, their direct measurement is difficult, although such constructs can be used for developing medium-level constructs that are measurable. For example, Freud's concepts of id and superego may not be directly measurable (not easily, anyway), yet they can be used to theorize and derive medium-level constructs. On the other hand, a construct, such as response time or product sales, is more concrete in nature but lacks the explanatory ability of a more abstract construct. Response time is often of interest in cognitive psychology in that it is an indicator of an underlying construct, such as cognitive effort. By itself, response time may not have the same level of theoretical importance.

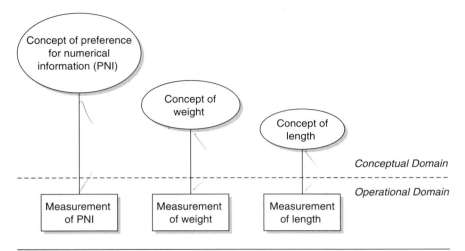

Figure 1.2   Distances Between Conceptual and Operational Domain for Physical and Psychological Constructs and Measures

As the abstractness of a construct increases, the distance between the conceptual and the operational definitions increases (Figure 1.2). Other than a few dimensions such as length (for short distances, not for astronomical ones!) and time (at least in recent times, an issue that will be revisited in a subsequent chapter), the operational definition or measure of a construct is indirect (e.g., weight or temperature) (Nunnally, 1978). For example, length can be defined conceptually as the shortest distance between two points. Measurement of length follows directly, at least for short lengths. The same could be said for time. However, weight or temperature involve more abstract conceptual definitions, as well as larger distances between the conceptual and the operational. Measurement is more indirect, such as through the expansion of mercury for temperature, that is, a correlate of temperature, or gravitational pull on calibrated weights for weight.

In moving to the social sciences, the distance between the conceptual and the operational can be large, for example, in measuring attitudes toward objects or issues. Larger distances between the conceptual and the operational have at least two implications. As the distance increases, so, too, do measurement error and the number of different ways in which something can be measured (Figure 1.3). This is akin to there being several ways of getting to a more distant location, and several ways of getting lost as well!

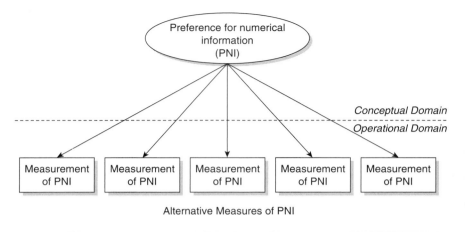

Figure 1.3   Distance Between the Conceptual and the Operational, Potential
Operationalizations and Error

Preference for numerical information, or PNI, is used as a sample construct in this chapter. This construct relates to an enduring proclivity toward numbers across several contexts, a relatively abstract construct. In contrast, a less abstract construct may be consumers' preference for numerical information or employees' preference for numerical information, essentially restricting the context of the construct (Figure 1.4). These context-specific constructs may be at a level of abstraction that is useful in deriving theoretical generalizations. In contrast, consider usage of calorie information as a construct (Figure 1.5). Here, the numerical context is further restricted. Although this construct may be useful in the realm of consumption studies, it is relatively concrete for purposes of understanding the use of numerical information in general. The point is that there is less theoretical generalization across different domains when a construct is relatively concrete. Abstract constructs allow for broader generalization. Suppose that a basic preference for numerical information is expected to cause higher performance in numerically oriented tasks. From the perspective of understanding numerical information, this is an argument at an abstract level with broader generalization than one linking usage of calorie information to, say, performance in choosing a brand of cereal. In fact, a modified form of the latter scenario of calorie information and choice of cereals may be a way to test the former scenario involving preference for numerical information and performance in numerically oriented tasks. But such an empirical test would

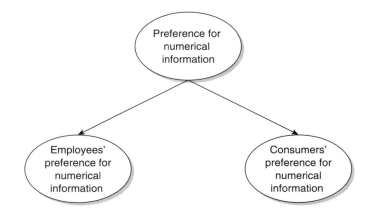

Figure 1.4   Levels of Abstractness of Constructs

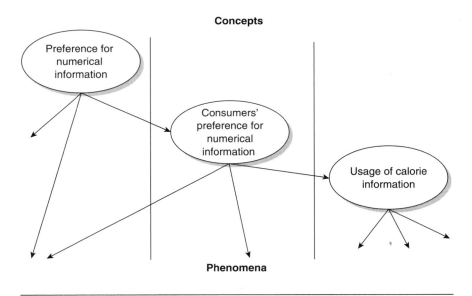

Figure 1.5   Abstractness of Constructs

have to be developed by carefully deriving ways of measuring the concepts being studied and choosing the best way to operationalize them. Empirical tests in specific, narrow contexts ideally should be developed from broader theoretical and methodological considerations, thereby choosing the best setting in which a theory is tested.

In conceptually defining a construct, it should be sufficiently different from other existing constructs. In other words, the construct should not be redundant and should make a sizable contribution in terms of explanatory power. Conducting science requires linking the work to past knowledge. Existing research is an important guide in defining a construct. The words that are used to define a construct have to communicate to a larger scientific audience. Defining constructs in idiosyncratic fashion that are counter to their use in the extant literature precludes or hinders such communication. This is not to preclude the redefinition of existing constructs. In fact, it is necessary to their constantly evaluate construct definitions. However, the point being made here is that redefinitions should be supported with compelling rationale. Existing theory in the area should be used to define a construct to be distinct from other constructs. The distinction should warrant the creation of a new construct. Thus, the hurdle for the development of new constructs is usually high. Conceptually rich constructs enable theoretical generalizations of importance and interest to a discipline.

The distance between the conceptual and operational can also lead to confounding between measurement and theory. Sometimes, discussions of conceptual relationships between constructs and hypotheses about these relationships may confound constructs with their operationalizations, essentially mixing two different levels of analysis (e.g., arguing for the relationship between PNI and numerical ability on the basis of specific items of the PNI scale, rather than at a conceptual level). This highlights the need to keep these two levels of analysis separate while iterating between them in terms of issues, such as conceptual definitions of constructs and rationale for conceptual relationships between constructs. Iterative analysis between these two levels is common and necessary; however, a clear understanding and maintenance of the distinction is critical. Alternatively, measures that aim to assess a specific construct may indeed assess a related construct, either an antecedent or an outcome (say, preference for numerical information measuring numerical ability or preference for qualitative information), thereby confounding constructs. Constructs may also have multiple dimensions, each with a different relationship with other constructs (say, usage of numbers and enjoyment of numbers, with the former having a stronger relationship with a measure of numerical ability) and that may need to be clarified. Such clarification often occurs as research in an area progresses and theoretical sophistication leads to sophistication in measurement and vice versa.

Domain Delineation

The next step in the process of developing a measure of a construct is to delineate its domain (Churchill, 1979; DeVellis, 1991). This step involves explicating what the construct is and is not. Related constructs can be used to explain how the focal construct is both similar to and different from them. This is also a step where the proposed dimensionality of the construct is described explicitly. For instance, a measure of intelligence would be explicated in terms of different dimensions, such as quantitative and verbal intelligence. The domain of the construct is described, thus clearly delineating what the construct is and is not. At its core, this step involves understanding what is being measured by elaborating on the concept, *before the measure is designed and items in the measure are generated.* Careful domain delineation should precede measure design and item generation as a starting point. This argument is not intended to preclude iterations between these two steps; iterations between measure design and item generation, and domain delineation are invaluable and serve to clarify the domain further. Rather, the point is to consider carefully what abstract concept is being measured as a starting point before attempting measure design and item generation and iterating between these steps. Collecting data or using available data without attention to underlying concepts is not likely to lead to the development of knowledge at a conceptual level.

The goal of domain delineation is to explicate the construct to the point where a measure can be designed and items can be generated. Domain delineation is a step in the conceptual domain and not in the operational domain. Therefore, different ways of measuring the construct are not considered in this step. Domain delineation precedes such consideration to enable fuller understanding of the construct to be measured. Several issues should be considered here, including using past literature and relating the construct to other constructs. In other words, the construct has to be placed in the context of existing knowledge, thus motivating its need and clarifying its uniqueness. The construct should be described in different ways, in terms of what is included and what is *not* included by the domain. Such an approach is an effective way of clarifying a construct and distinguishing it from related constructs. For example, preference for numerical information has to be clearly differentiated from numerical ability. This is similar to clarifying the exact meaning of related words, whether it is *happiness* versus *contentment, bluntness* versus *honesty,* and so on. In fact, if anything, scientific research can be distinguished in terms of the precision with which words are used, all the more so with words that denote constructs, the focus of scientific inquiry. Just as numbers are used in scientific measurement because they are standardized and they facilitate communication, words should be used to convey precise meaning in order to facilitate communication. Incisive conceptual thinking, akin to using a mental scalpel, should carefully clarify, distinguish, and explicate constructs well before data collection or even measure development is attempted. Such thinking will also serve to separate a construct from its antecedents and effects. A high hurdle is usually and appropriately placed in front of new constructs in terms of clearly distinguishing them from existing constructs.

A worthwhile approach to distinguishing related constructs is to construct scenarios where different levels of each construct coexist. For instance, if happiness and contentment are two related constructs, constructing examples where different levels of happiness versus contentment coexist can serve to clarify the domain of each at a conceptual level as well, distinguishing a construct from what it is not and getting to the essence of it conceptually. The process of moving between the conceptual and the operational can clarify both.

The continuous versus categorical nature of the construct, as well as its level of specificity (e.g., too broad vs. too narrow; risk aversion vs. financial risk aversion or physical risk aversion; preference for numerical information vs. consumers' preference for numerical information) need to be considered. Constructs vary in their level of abstractness, which should be clarified in domain delineation. The elements of the domain of the construct need to be explicated (e.g., satisfaction, liking, or interest with regard to, say, a construct relating to preference for some type of information). The purpose here is to carefully understand what exactly the domain of the construct covers, such as tendencies versus attitudes versus abilities. Visual representation is another useful way of thinking through the domain. An iterative process where items are developed at an operational level can, in turn, help in domain delineation as well by concretizing the abstract domain.

Domain delineation is an important step that enables understanding the conceptual as it relates to the operational. Delineation may well change the conceptual definition. Such iteration is common in measure development. The key is to allow sufficient iteration to lead to a well-thought-out measurement process. Domain delineation may help screen out constructs that are too broad or narrow. If constructs are too abstract, intermediate-level constructs may be preferable. Figure 1.6 illustrates a narrow versus broad operationalization of the domain of preference for numerical information. Figure 1.6 also illustrates how domain delineation can facilitate item generation by identifying different aspects of the domain. Thus, during the

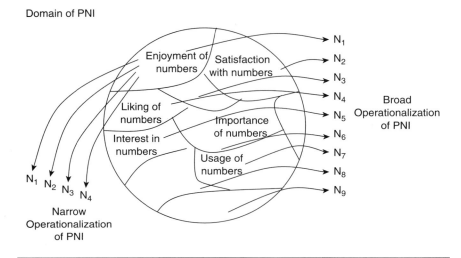

Figure 1.6   Domain Delineation and Item Generation

subsequent step of item generation, items can be generated to cover aspects such as enjoyment and importance. In this way, the distance between the conceptual and the operational is bridged.

Domain delineation is demonstrated using an example of the preference for numerical information (PNI) scale (Exhibit 1.1). Several points are noteworthy. First, PNI is distinguished from ability in using numerical information, and several aspects of preference are discussed. PNI is also distinguished from statistics and mathematics. In addition, PNI is described in terms of its level of abstraction in being a general construct rather than specific to a context such as consumer settings or classroom settings. In this respect, it can be distinguished from other scales such as attitude toward statistics and enjoyment of mathematics. The distinctive value of the PNI construct is thus illustrated by showing that it is a unique construct that is different from potentially related constructs, and that it has the potential to explain important phenomena. As discussed earlier, any proposed new construct has to answer the "So what?" question. After all, any construct can be proposed and a measure developed. There are different ways of motivating a construct: The PNI scale is motivated in a more generic way because of lack of existing theory, but alternatively, a scale could be motivated by placing it in the context of past theory or by identifying a gap in past theory.

The errors discussed earlier are illustrated using data from a published scale, the preference for numerical information scale (Viswanathan, 1993). Preference for numerical information is defined as *a preference or proclivity toward using numerical information and engaging in thinking involving numerical information*. Several aspects of this definition need to be noted. First, the focus is on preference or proclivity rather than ability, because the aim here is to focus on *attitude* toward numerical information. Second, the focus is solely on numerical information, rather than on domains such as statistics or mathematics, in order to isolate numerical information from domains that involve the use of such information. Third, PNI is conceptualized as a broad construct that is relevant in a variety of settings by using a general context rather than a specific context such as, say, an academic setting.

Item Generation

Items were generated for the PNI scale in line with an operationalization of the definition of the construct. As mentioned earlier, three aspects of importance in the definition are the focus on preference or proclivity, the focus on numerical information, and the use of a general rather than a specific context. The domain of the construct was operationalized by using parallel terms that represent numerical information, such as *numbers, numerical information,* and *quantitative information.* Proclivity or preference for numerical information was operationalized using a diverse set of elements or aspects, such as the extent to which people enjoy using numerical information (e.g., "I enjoy work that requires the use of numbers"), liking for numerical information (e.g., "I don't like to think about issues involving numbers"), and perceived need for numerical information (e.g., "I think more information should be available in numerical form"). Other aspects were usefulness (e.g., "Numerical information is very useful in everyday life"), importance (e.g., "I think it is important to learn and use numerical information to make well informed decisions"), perceived relevance (e.g., "I don't find numerical information to be relevant for most situations"), satisfaction (e.g., "I find it satisfying to solve day-to-day problems involving numbers"), and attention/interest (e.g., "I prefer not to pay attention to information involving numbers"). The use of information in a general rather than a specific context was captured by wording items to be general ("I prefer not to pay attention to information involving numbers") rather than specific to any context.

A pool of 35 items was generated in line with the operationalization described above in the form of statements with which a respondent could agree or disagree to varying degrees. These items were generated to cover the range of aspects of preference for numerical information listed above (such as satisfaction and usefulness). A total of 20 items were chosen from this pool and inspected in terms of content for coverage of these different aspects, usage of different terms to represent numerical information, and generality of context. The items were also chosen such that an equal number were positively or negatively worded with respect to preference for numerical information. The response format was a 7-point scale labeled at the extremes as *strongly agree* and *strongly disagree.*

Items of the PNI Scale

		Strongly Disagree				Strongly Agree		
1.	I enjoy work that requires the use of numbers.	1	2	3	4	5	6	7
2.	I find information easy to understand if it does not involve numbers.	1	2	3	4	5	6	7
3.	I find it satisfying to solve day-to-day problems involving numbers.	1	2	3	4	5	6	7
4.	Numerical information is very useful in everyday life.	1	2	3	4	5	6	7
5.	I prefer not to pay attention to information involving numbers.	1	2	3	4	5	6	7
6.	I think more information should be available in numerical form.	1	2	3	4	5	6	7
7.	I don't like to think about issues involving numbers.	1	2	3	4	5	6	7
8.	Numbers are not necessary for most situations.	1	2	3	4	5	6	7
9.	Thinking is enjoyable when it does not involve quantitative information.	1	2	3	4	5	6	7
10.	I like to make calculations using numerical information.	1	2	3	4	5	6	7
11.	Quantitative information is vital for accurate decisions.	1	2	3	4	5	6	7
12.	I enjoy thinking based on qualitative information.	1	2	3	4	5	6	7
13.	Understanding numbers is as important in daily life as reading or writing.	1	2	3	4	5	6	7
14.	I easily lose interest in graphs, percentages, and other quantitative information.	1	2	3	4	5	6	7
15.	I don't find numerical information to be relevant for most situations.	1	2	3	4	5	6	7
16.	I think it is important to learn and use numerical information to make well-informed decisions.	1	2	3	4	5	6	7
17.	Numbers are redundant for most situations.	1	2	3	4	5	6	7
18.	Learning and remembering numerical information about various issues is a waste of time.	1	2	3	4	5	6	7
19.	I like to go over numbers in my mind.	1	2	3	4	5	6	7
20.	It helps me to think if I put down information as numbers.	1	2	3	4	5	6	7

EXHIBIT SOURCE: Adapted from Viswanathan, M., Measurement of individual differences in preference for numerical information, in *Journal of Applied Psychology*, 78(5), 741–752. Copyright © 1993. Reprinted by permission of the American Psychological Association.

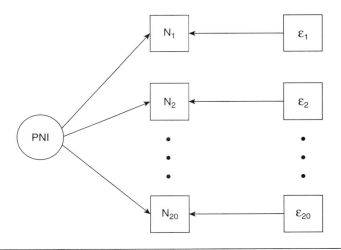

Figure 1.7   Visual Representation for PNI of Latent Construct, Items, and Error

Measure Design and Item Generation

Measure design and item generation follows domain delineation as illustrated for the PNI scale (Exhibit 1.1). Before specific items can be generated, the design of the measure needs to be determined. Important here is the need to think beyond measures involving agreement-disagreement with statements, and also beyond self-report measures. Measures can range from observational data to behavioral inventories. Later in the book, a variety of measures from different disciplines are reviewed to highlight the importance of creative measure design. The basic model that relates a construct to items in a measure is shown in Figure 1.7. A latent construct causes responses on items of the measure. The items are also influenced by error. The error term is the catch-all for everything that is not the construct.

Redundancy is a virtue during item generation, with the goal being to cover important aspects of the domain. Even trivial redundancy—that is, minor grammatical changes in the way an item is worded—is acceptable at this stage (DeVellis, 1991). Measure development is inductive in that the actual effects of minor wording differences are put to empirical test, and items that pass the test are retained. It is impossible to anticipate how people may respond to each and every nuance in item wording. Therefore, items are tested by examining several variations. All items are subject to interpretation. The aim is to develop items that most people in the relevant population would interpret in a similar fashion. Generic recommendations to enable such interpretation include avoiding ambiguous, lengthy, complex, or double-barreled items. Items also should not be worded to be extreme (e.g., I hate numbers), as discussed subsequently.

Unit of analysis is another consideration in item development (Sirotnik, 1980). For instance, items designed to capture individual perceptions about self versus other versus groups suggest different types of wording. Items such as "My workplace is friendly" versus "My colleagues view our workplace as being friendly" versus "Our work group views our workplace as friendly" capture different perceptions—an individual's perception of the workplace, colleagues' perceptions of the workplace (as measured by an individual's perception of these perceptions), and the group's perceptions of the workplace (as measured by an individual's perception of these perceptions), respectively.

Level of abstraction is an important consideration with item generation. Items vary in their level of abstractness. For instance, items could be designed at a concrete level about what people actually do in specific situations versus at a more abstract level in terms of their attitudes. On one hand, concrete items provide context and enable respondents to provide a meaningful response (say, a hypothetical item on the PNI scale such as, "I use calorie information on packages when shopping"). On the other hand, items should ideally reflect the underlying construct and not other constructs, the latter being a particular problem when it occurs for a subset of items, as discussed later. Because PNI is a more global construct that aims to cover different contexts, including the consumer context, an item specific to the consumer context may not be appropriate when other items are at a global level. Such an item also does not parallel other items on the PNI scale that are more global in their wording, the point being that the wording of items should be parallel in terms of level of abstraction. A different approach may well identify specific subdomains (e.g., social, economic) and develop items that are specific to each such subdomain. Thus, the subdomains are based on contexts where preference for numerical information plays out. In such an approach, items at the consumer level may be appropriate. Each of these subdomains essentially would be measured separately, the issue of items worded to be parallel in terms of the level of abstraction being germane for each subdomain. Another approach is to divide up the domain into subdomains, such as enjoyment of numbers and importance of numbers; that is, in terms of the different aspects of preference. Each subdomain could be conceptualized as a separate dimension and items developed for each dimension. Of course, the hypothesized dimensionality has to be tested empirically.

A large pool of items is important, as are procedures to develop a large pool. Several procedures can be employed to develop a pool of items, such as asking experts to generate items and asking experts or respondents to evaluate items in the degree to which they capture defined constructs (Haynes, Richard, & Kubany, 1995). There may be a temptation to quickly put together a few items because item generation seems intuitive in the social sciences. However, the importance of systematic procedures as a way to develop a representative set or sample of items that covers the domain of the construct cannot be overemphasized. These procedures, which take relatively small additional effort in the scheme of things, can greatly improve the chances of developing a representative measure. Moreover, it should be noted that item generation is an iterative process that involves frequently traversing the pathways between the conceptual and the operational. If many items are quickly put together in the hope that errors average out, the average may be of fundamentally inaccurate items, and therefore not meaningful.

The procedures discussed so far relate to the content validity of a measure, that is, whether a measure adequately captures the content of a construct. There are no direct empirical measures of content validity, only assessment based on whether (a) a representative set of items was developed and (b) acceptable procedures were employed in developing items (Nunnally, 1978). Hence, assessment of content validity rests on the explication of the domain and its representation in the item pool. The proof of the pudding is in the procedures used to develop the measure rather than any empirical indicator. In fact, indicators of reliability can be enhanced at the expense of content validity by representing one or a few aspects of the domain (as shown through narrow operationalization in Figure 1.6) and by trivial redundancies among items. An extreme scenario here is, of course, repetition of the same item, which likely enhances reliability at the expense of validity.

Internal Consistency Reliability

After item generation, measures typically are assessed for internal consistency reliability, and items are deleted or modified. Internal consistency frequently is the first empirical test employed and assesses whether items within a set are consistent with each other, that is, covary with each other. Internal consistency procedures assess whether a set of items fits together or belongs together. Responses are collected on a measure from a sample of respondents. Intercorrelations among items and correlations between each item and the total score are used to purify measures, using an overall indicator of internal consistency reliability, coefficient alpha (Cronbach, 1951).

Illustrative descriptions are provided using the PNI scale (Exhibit 1.2). Means for the items in the PNI scale are shown. Means close to the middle of the scale are desirable to allow for sufficient variance and the ability to covary with other items. If an item does not vary, it cannot covary, and measurement is about capturing variation as it exists. (A parallel example is in experimental design, where, say, the dependent variable is recall of information shown earlier, wherein either one or two pieces of information could be shown leading to very high recall and small variance, or a hundred pieces of information shown leading to very low recall and small variance. In both instances, lack of variation precludes appropriate tests of hypotheses.) As an illustration, Item 18 in Exhibit 1.2 (Learning and remembering numerical information about various issues is a waste of time) has a mean of 5.24; it was subsequently found to have low item-to-total correlations in some studies and replaced. The item is worded in somewhat extreme terms, referring to "waste of time." This is akin to having items with words such as "never" or "have you ever" or "do you hate." Items 4 and 5 are additional examples relating to usefulness of numbers and not paying attention to numbers. Item 17 relates to numbers being redundant for most situations—perhaps another example of somewhat extreme wording. An important issue here is that the tone of the item can lead to high or low means, thus inhibiting the degree to which an item can vary with other items. The item has to be valenced in one direction or the other (i.e., stated positively or negatively with respect to the construct in question) to elicit levels of agreement or disagreement (because disagreement with a neutral statement such as "I neither like nor dislike numbers" is ambiguous). However, if it is worded in extreme terms (e.g., "I hate . . ."), then item variance may be reduced. Therefore, items need to be moderately valenced. The name of the game is, of course, variation, and satisfactory items have the ability to vary with other items. Scale variance is the result of items with relatively high variance that covary with other items. This discussion is also illustrative of the level of understanding of the relationship between item characteristics and empirical results that is essential in measure development. Designers of measures, no matter how few the items, have to do a lot more than throw some items together.

Item-to-total correlations are typically examined to assess the extent to which items are correlated with the total. As shown in Appendix 1.1, a matrix of responses is analyzed in terms of the correlation between an item and the total score. The matrix shows individual responses and total scores. The degree to which an individual item covaries with other items can be assessed in a number of ways, such as through examining intercorrelations between items or the correlation between an item and the total scale. Items

(Text continues on page 24)

Exhibit 1.2   Internal Consistency of PNI Scale

Analysis of 20-Item PNI Scale

Results for the 20-item PNI scale (Viswanathan, 1993) are presented below for a sample of 93 undergraduate students at a midwestern U.S. university. Means and standard deviations can be examined. Extreme means or low standard deviations suggest potential problems, as discussed in the chapter.

		Mean	*Std. Dev.*
1.	N1	4.3407	2.0397
2.	N2	3.7253	1.9198
3.	N3	4.3956	1.9047
4.	N4	5.2747	1.6304
5.	N5	5.3297	1.3000
6.	N6	3.9890	1.6259
7.	N7	5.0000	1.6063
8.	N8	4.7363	1.6208
9.	N9	4.3516	1.6250
10.	N10	4.5495	1.9551
11.	N11	5.0769	1.3269
12.	N12	3.4286	1.3755
13.	N13	5.0989	1.3586
14.	N14	4.3297	1.7496
15.	N15	4.8571	1.2163
16.	N16	5.0769	1.3600
17.	N17	5.0220	1.2109
18.	N18	5.2418	1.1489
19.	N19	3.7033	1.7670
20.	N20	4.2527	1.9096

The average interitem correlation provides an overall indicator of the internal consistency between items. It is the average of correlations between all possible pairs of items in the 20-item PNI scale.

Average interitem correlation = .2977

Item-to-total statistics report the correlation between an item and the total score, as well as the value of coefficient alpha if a specific item were deleted. Items with low correlations with the total score are candidates for deletion. Item 12 actually has a negative correlation with the total score and should be deleted. It should be noted that all analyses are after appropriate reverse scoring of items such that higher scores reflect higher PNI.

Item-Total Statistics

	Corrected Item-Total Correlation	Alpha If Item Deleted
N1	.7736	.8839
N2	.3645	.8975
N3	.7451	.8857
N4	.5788	.8911
N5	.4766	.8939
N6	.6322	.8896
N7	.7893	.8853
N8	.4386	.8949
N9	.4781	.8938
N10	.7296	.8861
N11	.4843	.8937
N12	−.3603	.9143
N13	.5073	.8931
N14	.6287	.8895
N15	.4617	.8943
N16	.6095	.8904
N17	.5301	.8927
N18	.3947	.8958
N19	.5323	.8924
N20	.6281	.8894

Coefficient alpha is the overall indicator of internal consistency as explained in the chapter.

Alpha = .8975   Standardized item alpha = .8945

The analysis was repeated after deleting Item 12.

Analysis After Deletion of Item 12 (19-item version)
Average interitem correlation = .3562

Item-Total Statistics

	Corrected Item-Total Correlation	Alpha If Item Deleted
N1	.7705	.9043
N2	.3545	.9160
N3	.7479	.9052
N4	.5834	.9097
N5	.4823	.9121
N6	.6219	.9088
N7	.7889	.9047

(Continued)

Item-Total Statistics

N8	.4432	.9131
N9	.4811	.9122
N10	.7299	.9056
N11	.5071	.9115
N13	.5175	.9113
N14	.6373	.9083
N15	.4672	.9124
N16	.6237	.9088
N17	.5306	.9111
N18	.3950	.9138
N19	.5381	.9109
N20	.6339	.9084

Alpha = .9143   Standardized item alpha = .9131

The analysis is repeated after deleting another item, Item 2, which has a relatively low item-to-total correlation.

Analysis After Deletion of Item 2 (18-item version)
Average interitem correlation = .3715

Item-Total Statistics

	Corrected Item-Total Correlation	Alpha If Item Deleted
N1	.7650	.9063
N3	.7442	.9069
N4	.6025	.9111
N5	.4806	.9140
N6	.6144	.9108
N7	.7916	.9062
N8	.4417	.9151
N9	.4589	.9147
N10	.7290	.9073
N11	.5298	.9129
N13	.5277	.9129
N14	.6453	.9098
N15	.4726	.9142
N16	.6307	.9104
N17	.5156	.9132
N18	.3829	.9159
N19	.5405	.9128
N20	.6374	.9101

Alpha = .9160   Standardized item alpha = .9141

The effect of the number of items in a scale on reliability is noteworthy. Below, 10- and 5-item versions of the PNI scale are presented.

Analysis of 10- and 5-Item Versions of the PNI Scale
Reliability Analysis—10-item version
Average interitem correlation = .3952

Item-Total Statistics

	Corrected Item-Total Correlation	*Alpha If Item Deleted*
N1	.7547	.8411
N2	.3885	.8723
N3	.7489	.8424
N4	.5212	.8611
N5	.4872	.8634
N6	.5702	.8575
N7	.8033	.8402
N8	.3696	.8718
N9	.4761	.8643
N10	.7521	.8417

Alpha = .8688   Standardized item alpha = .8673

Reliability Analysis—5-Item Version
Average interitem correlation = .3676

Item-Total Statistics

	Corrected Item-Total Correlation	*Alpha If Item Deleted*
N1	.7016	.6205
N2	.3189	.7705
N3	.6888	.6351
N4	.4648	.7198
N5	.4357	.7298

Alpha = .7475   Standardized item alpha = .7440

that are internally consistent would have high correlation with the total score. Consider a scale that is assumed to consist of a number of internally consistent items. The higher an individual's response on a particular item, the higher the individual's response is likely to be on other items in the scale, and the higher the individual's total score. A person high on PNI would be expected to have a high total score as well as high scores on individual items (once the items have been reverse scored so that higher values reflect higher PNI; for instance, an item such as "I don't like numbers" would be reverse scored so that a response of a 7 is equivalent to a 1, and so on). Items with low correlations with the total score are deleted or modified. Such items are assumed to be lacking internal consistency. They do not covary or are not consistent with the total score or with other items.

Item 12 (Exhibit 1.2 and Figure 1.8) is instructive in that it has a negative correlation with the total score after reverse scoring. The item pertains to qualitative information and is employed here on the assumption that higher PNI may be associated with lower preference for qualitative information. In other words, rather than directly capture preference for numerical information, the item is premised on a contingent relationship between PNI and preference for qualitative information. In fact, for some individuals, high preferences for both types of information may coexist. The key lesson here is the importance of directly relating items to the constructs being measured. Essentially, the item confounds constructs it purports to measure. The negative correlation may also have been the result of some respondents misreading the term *qualitative* as *quantitative*. It should be noted here that the item was appropriately reverse-scored before data analyses, including computing correlations.

Another example from a different research area is illustrative. Consider a measure that attempts to capture the type of strategy a firm adopts in order to compete in the marketplace. A strategy may consist of many different aspects, such as emphasis on new product development and emphasis on research and development. Therefore, self-report items could be generated to measure strategy regarding emphasis on research and development and emphasis on new product development (e.g., "We emphasize new product development to a greater degree than our competition," with responses ranging from *strongly disagree* to *strongly agree*). Suppose also that there is an empirical relationship between the type of environment in which firms operate (e.g., uncertain environments) and the type of strategy in which firms engage; that is, in uncertain environments, firms tend to invest in research and development and new product development. Then, an item generated to measure strategy about how uncertain the environment is (e.g., "Our company operates in an uncertain environment," with

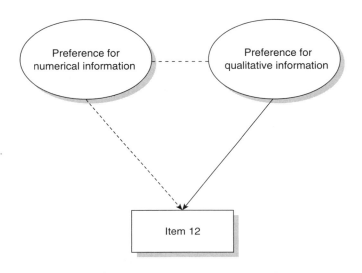

Figure 1.8   Indirect Versus Direct Measurement of Constructs

responses from *strongly disagree* to *strongly agree*) attempts to tap into strategy on the basis of a contingent relationship between the type of strategy and the type of environment. Such an item assumes that firms adopt a particular strategy in a certain environment. As far as possible, items should be developed to directly assess the construct they aim to measure. Otherwise, substantive relationships between constructs are confounded with measures of single constructs. Subtler issues arise depending on the type of indicator that is being developed, as discussed subsequently. Direct measurement does not imply repetitive, similar items. Any item typically captures a construct in some context. Creative measurement (and perhaps interesting items from the respondents' perspective) involves different ways of capturing a construct in different contexts. A key point to note is that ideally, items should not confound constructs but rather use contexts in which the focal construct plays out.

Coefficient alpha is an indicator of the internal consistency reliability of the entire scale. A goal in internal consistency procedures is to maximize *coefficient alpha,* or the proportion of variance attributable to common sources (Cronbach, 1951; DeVellis, 1991). Items are deleted on this basis to achieve a higher coefficient alpha, and this process is repeated until the marginal gain in alpha is minimal. Beyond a point, the marginal increase in alpha may not warrant additional deletion of items. In fact, items with moderate correlations with the total may be retained if they capture some unique aspect of the domain not captured by other items. The average interitem correlation, along with coefficient alpha, provides a summary, and researchers have suggested that its ideal range is between 0.2 and 0.4 (Briggs & Cheek, 1988). The rationale for this guideline is that relatively low correlations suggest that a common core does not exist, whereas relatively high correlations suggest trivial redundancies and a narrow operationalization of one subdomain of the overall construct. For example, for the PNI scale, if all the correlations in Exhibit 1.2 between items are close to 1, this may suggest that all the items in the measure capture only some narrow aspect of the domain of the construct. This could happen if items are merely repetitions of each other with trivial differences. In addition to item deletion on purely empirical grounds, the nature of the item needs to be taken into account. If an item has moderate correlation with the total score, yet captures some unique aspect of a construct not captured by other items, it may well be worth retaining. This is not to maximize reliability but rather to trade off reliability to increase validity, an issue to be discussed subsequently. Purely empirical or purely conceptual approaches are not sufficient in measure development and validation. The iteration between empirical results and conceptual examination is essential.

The definition and computation of coefficient alpha are discussed below (adapted from DeVellis, 1991). Exhibit 1.2 presents coefficient alpha for several versions of the PNI scale. The computation of coefficient alpha is illustrated in Appendix 1.1. A variance covariance matrix is shown for a three-item scale. Considering extreme scenarios in internal consistency is useful in clarifying the typical scenarios that fall in the middle. It is possible that none of the items covaries with each other (i.e., all nondiagonal items are zero). It is also possible that all items covary perfectly with each other (i.e., a correlation of 1 and covariances depending on the unit of measurement). Coefficient alpha is the proportion of total variance that is due to common sources. (Note the plural "sources" for subsequent discussion in factor analysis.) Variation attributable to common sources is indicated by covariances between items. The correction term in Appendix 1.1 standardizes alpha values from 0 to 1 (i.e., 0 and 1, respectively) for the extreme scenarios above. A simple example using three items with perfect intercorrelations illustrates the need for a correction term.

How does coefficient alpha measure reliability (where reliability is the minimization of random error)? Coefficient alpha is the proportion of variance attributable to common sources. These common sources are presumably the construct in question, although this remains to be demonstrated. These common sources have to be assumed to be the construct in question for the moment. Anything not attributable to common sources is assumed to be random error, that is, variation that is not systematically related to the common core that items share. The proportion of variance attributable to common sources represents the square of a correlation; hence, the unit of reliability is the square of the correlation between the scale and the true score. The unit of relevance for reliability is variance, the square of the correlation between a measure and a hypothetical true score.

A qualification is noteworthy here. Internal consistency reliability is essentially about the degree to which a set of items taps into some common sources of variance, presumably the construct being measured. The basic premise here in deleting items that are inconsistent based on their lack of correlation with the total scale is that most of the items in the scale tap into this basic construct. However, whether the scale indeed taps into the construct in question is determined subsequently through procedures for assessing validity. Hence, it is quite possible that a small number of items being deleted indeed represent the construct in question, whereas the majority of items retained tap into an unintended construct. This issue highlights the importance of examining items both conceptually and empirically in conjunction.

As the number of items in a scale increases, coefficient alpha increases. (Exhibit 1.2 reports alphas for 5-, 10-, and 20-item versions.) Why is this happening?[8] Note that this would happen even if the best five items on the basis of item-to-total correlation in the scale are used and compared with the 20-item scale. The mathematical answer to this question is that as the number of items increases, the number of covariance terms $(k^2 - k)$ increases much faster than the number of variance terms (k). As the number of items increases, the number of ways in which items covary increases at an even more rapid rate (e.g., if the number of items is 2, 3, 4, 5, 6, 7, 8, 9, and 10, the number of covariance terms is 2, 6, 12, 20, 30, 42, 56, 72, and 90, respectively). But what does this mean intuitively? As the number of items increases, so does the number of ways in which they covary with each other and contribute to a total score with a high degree of variation. Each item covaries with other items and captures aspects of the domain.

During this stage of measure development, the emphasis is on tapping into common sources, presumably the underlying construct. Whether the common sources are multiple sources or a single source is in the purview of dimensionality. However, whether the common sources that are reliably measured are the construct in question is in the purview of validity. Of course, whether any aspect of the true score is captured is an issue in the realm of validity. It is possible that the items in a measure capture no aspect of a construct. In summary, internal consistency assesses whether items covary with each other or belong together and share common sources. The word *sources* is noteworthy because dimensionality addresses the question of the exact number of distinguishable sources. Hence, internal consistency is a distinct form of reliability that hinges on items sharing a common core, presumably the construct in question. Reliability procedures attempt to assess the common variance in a scale. Internal consistency assesses the degree to which items covary together or are consistent with each other. In other words, if a person has a high score on one item, that person should have a high score on another item as well, items being scored such that higher values on them denote higher values on the underlying construct. Dimensionality, as discussed subsequently, assesses whether the common core in question is, indeed, a single core, or if multiple factors reflect the hypothesized number of dimensions with items loading onto their specified factors and covarying more closely within a factor than across. A factor at an empirical level is formed by a subset or combination of items that covary more closely with each other than with other items.

Test-Retest Reliability

Internal consistency reliability is often supplemented with test-retest reliability. Typically, the same scale is administered twice with an interval of a few weeks, with recommendations ranging anywhere from 4 to 6 weeks and higher. More importantly, the interval has to fit the specific research study in terms of allowing sufficient time to minimize recall of responses in the previous administration, just as the weighing machine in the example earlier in the chapter does not have memory of the previous weighing. The logic of test-retest reliability is simply that individuals who score higher (or lower) in one administration should score higher (or lower) in the second, or vice versa. In other words, the ordering of scores should be approximately maintained. A key assumption of test-retest reliability is that the true score does not change between test and retest. For instance, in the weighing machine example, the person does not eat or change clothes before being weighed again. In a sense, test-retest reliability represents a one-to-one correspondence with the concept of reliability, which is centered on replicability. Assessment of reliability involves asking a question: If the measure were repeated, would similar (i.e., consistent) scores be obtained? Test-retest reliability offers direct evidence of such consistency. Internal consistency reliability treats different items as replications of a measure.

Scales (e.g., the PNI scale) are evaluated by examining the overall test-retest correlation. The computation of test-retest reliability is shown in Figure 1.9. As shown in the figure, test-retest reliability is, indeed, the test-retest correlation itself, the square of the hypothetical correlation between a measure and

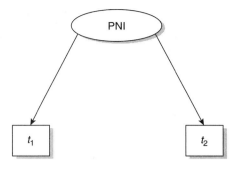

Figure 1.9   Computation of Test-Retest Reliability Formula

t_1 = Score at test at Time 1

t_2 = Score at retest at Time 2

$r_{t_1 T}$ = Correlation between score at Time 1 and true score

$r_{t_2 T}$ = Correlation between score at Time 2 and true score

$r_{t_1 t_2}$ = Test-retest correlation

$r_{t_1 T} \cdot r_{t_2 T} = r_{t_1 t_2}$

$r_{t_1 T}^2 = r_{t_1 t_2}$

$r_{t_1 T}^2$ = Proportion of variance attributable to true score

Test-retest reliability = Test-retest correlation

the true score. Individual items could also be examined by this criterion and deleted on this basis. Details for the PNI scale are presented (Exhibit 1.3). Noteworthy here is that some items may perform well on test-retest reliability but not on internal consistency, or vice versa, an issue discussed subsequently. Item 8, for example, has a high item-to-total correlation yet a low test-retest correlation for both the 1-week and 12-week intervals. This could be due to a variety of factors. Inconsistent administration across test and retest or distracting settings could cause low test-retest correlation. Similarly, item wording in Item 8, "Numbers are not necessary for most situations," may lead to inconsistent interpretations or inconsistent responses across time depending on the "situations" that respondents recall in responding to the item. Means at test versus retest can also be examined.

Dimensionality—Exploratory Factor Analysis

Reliability through internal consistency assesses whether a set of items is tapping into a common core as measured through the degree to which they

Exhibit 1.3   Test-Retest Reliability of a Modified PNI Scale

The PNI scale was administered to 106 undergraduate students at a midwestern U.S. university twice with an interval of 1 week (Viswanathan, 1993). Longer intervals should be used, and the PNI scale has been assessed for test-retest reliability using a 12-week interval (Viswanathan, 1994).

The following are new items that replaced items from the original scale:

2. I think quantitative information is difficult to understand.

12. I enjoy thinking about issues that do not involve numerical information.

18. It is a waste of time to learn information containing a lot of numbers.

Test-Retest Correlations

	1-week interval	*12-week interval*
Total scale	.91**	.73**
Item 1	.87**	.69**
Item 2	.50**	.46**
Item 3	.74**	.52**
Item 4	.62**	.30**
Item 5	.56**	.42**
Item 6	.66**	.56**
Item 7	.65**	.66**
Item 8	.28**	.00
Item 9	.74**	.42**
Item 10	.76**	.73**
Item 11	.58**	.30**
Item 12	.56**	.31**
Item 13	.60**	.39**
Item 14	.60**	.60**
Item 15	.46**	.50**
Item 16	.64**	.45**
Item 17	.42**	.39**
Item 18	.35**	.25**
Item 19	.74**	.56**
Item 20	.60**	.54**
Mean score at test	4.64	4.64
Mean score at retest	4.62	4.56

**p < .01.

covary with each other. But whether the common core consists of a specific set of dimensions is in the realm of dimensionality, assessed through factor analysis. At the outset, it should be noted that there are many issues involved in using factor analysis appropriately; the references cited here provide direction for in-depth reading. This discussion aims to provide an introduction to the topic.

Factor analysis is an approach in which variables are reduced to combinations of variables, or factors (Comrey & Lee, 1992; Hair, Anderson, Tatham, & Black, 1998). The assumption in performing factor analysis on a set of items is that an underlying factor or set of factors exists that is a combination of individual items. A correlation matrix for all items in a scale may offer some indication of the outcome of factor analysis and is well worth examining. When subsets of items have sizably higher correlations among each other and lower correlations with items outside of the subset, these items are likely to form a factor. For example, if there are two distinct factors, the matrix of correlations would have two distinct subsets of items with high correlations within items from the same subset and lower correlations among items from different subsets. At an intuitive level, this suggests that if a respondent provided a high (low) rating in response to an item, he or she was more likely to provide a high (low) rating in response to another item within the subset rather than across subsets. Items in a subset or items that belong in a factor covary more closely than do items from different factors. What each factor is has to be determined by the researcher. For example, two factors may be found among items just based on whether they are positively worded or negatively worded. Responses to positively worded items may covary among each other to a much greater degree than they do with negatively worded items. A set of ratings of attributes of grocery stores (e.g., location, times of operation, aisle space, etc.) may reduce to a couple of factors such as atmosphere and convenience. Similarly, ratings of automobiles on attributes such as shoulder room, gas mileage, and so on may reduce to underlying factors such as comfort, safety, and economy. In these examples, factor analysis can be used to understand what consumers are really looking for. Thus, when appropriately used by the researcher, factor analysis can provide insight into responses at the item level (e.g., why someone likes a grocery store in terms of underlying abstract factors, such as convenience, based on responses to concrete items such as checkout speed and location). Clearly, the results of factor analysis reflect the set of items and the content covered, that is, the questions asked and the aspects on which data were collected to begin with. Potential factors are precluded if items exclude specific subdomains.

For a subset to rise to the level of a factor, both empirical outcomes and conceptual examination have to be taken into account. In a sense, when items are generated to represent the domain of a construct, each subdomain may separate into a distinct factor. At an extreme, each item could be considered a separate factor. But such an approach is both an extremely inefficient way of conducting scientific research and very unlikely to lead to conceptually rich theory and abstract generalizations. In practice, whether a set of items rises to the level of a factor has to be determined by both empirical outcomes and conceptual examination of items.

Factor analysis results include correlations or loadings between individual items and factors. If a single factor is expected, then this is likely to be the first factor, with item correlations or loadings for this factor being high. The construct in question, rather than incidental factors being measured, is likely to be dominant and explain the most variation. Individual items can be evaluated by assessing their loading or correlation with the factor considered to represent the overall construct.

Another distinction in factor analysis is in using principal component analysis and common factor analysis (Hair et al., 1998). Essentially, variance for each item can be divided into error variance, specific variance, and common variance shared with other items. In other words, responses to each item reflect some error, some content unique to the item, and some content shared with other items. An item on the PNI scale has some content unique to the item and some content, presumably preference for numerical information, shared with other items. The content unique to an item would depend on the specific context of the item and the wording. In a narrow sense, the item is a measure of some unique and likely very concrete "thing." If one item on the PNI scale is influenced by social desirability in wording and others are not, then social desirability contributes to unique content in an item that does not covary with other items. Each item also has unique content in the way it is worded. Principal components analysis uses all the variance available and is a pure data reduction technique, whereas common factor analysis uses only the common variance shared by variables and is more appropriate for conceptually driven examination of the data. The nature of factor extraction that is meaningful for scales with a common core is one that works off the common variance across items rather than one that is a pure data reduction technique (e.g., principal component analysis). This is because such common variance shared among items reflects the conceptual meaning of a factor that relates to an underlying construct. Using a pure data reduction technique that takes advantage of all variation and chance correlations is inconsistent with the goal of capturing conceptual meaning shared across items within a factor.

In performing common factor analysis, the communality of each item is estimated, which is an indicator of the variance in each item that is shared with other items (Hair et al., 1998; see also Appendix 1.1). Every item has variance, but not all of it is shared with other items or is reflected in covariance between an item and other items. Only the shared portion of an item's variance is employed in common factor analysis. Such an approach corresponds to the conceptualization of a measure as consisting of items that share content. An approach that uses all the variance in an item regardless of such variance being shared is akin to a pure data reduction technique that capitalizes on available variance rather than isolating shared variance.

The results of factor analysis include the number of factors extracted and the variance explained by each factor. Appendix 1.1 presents simple illustrations of exploratory factor analysis. In unrotated factor analysis, the first factor represents the best linear combination of items, the second factor the second best, and so on (Hair et al., 1998). The second factor should be based on the remaining variance after extraction of the first factor in order to be orthogonal to it (i.e., mathematically independent factors or no correlations between factors) (Hair et al., 1998). Unrotated factor matrices are rotated to improve interpretation of the loadings of items on factors. Rotation involves turning the axes on their origin and can lead to improved interpretation of results (Figure 1.10). Rotation redistributes variance from earlier to later factors, whereas earlier factors usually explain considerable variance in unrotated factor analysis. Rotation can be orthogonal or oblique. In oblique rotation, factors may be correlated to each other (Figure 1.10).[9] The purpose of rotation is to facilitate interpretation of factors by simplifying loadings to be closer to 1 or 0. Different types of rotations serve different purposes, each with its limitations. Varimax rotation is one such approach often used when multiple dimensions are anticipated. This type of rotation may be particularly useful when multiple dimensions are present. However, such an approach may lead to multiple factors even when there is a single underlying dimension.

In factor analysis, a judgment has to be made as to the number of meaningful factors underlying the data by comparing the percentage of variance explained by each extracted factor (reflected in eigenvalues) in light of expectations. For instance, a dominant factor would be indicated by the first factor having a much higher eigenvalue (or percent of variance explained) than the second factor. The noteworthy point here is that not all extracted factors are meaningful, and several approaches are used to assess the number of meaningful factors. In essence, the relative variances explained by each factor are compared in deciding how many factors to retain. A scree test plots the variance explained by each factor to identify discontinuities in terms of a drop-off in variance explained (Hair et al., 1998). Later factors are generally thought to contain a higher degree of unique variance (Hair et al., 1998).

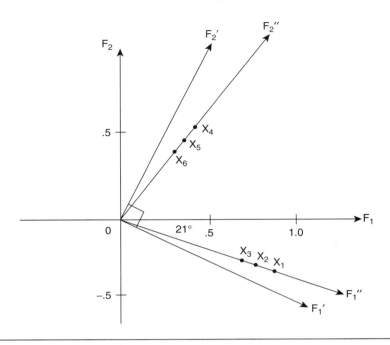

Figure 1.10   Orthogonal Factor Rotation

F_1 and F_2 = orthogonal factors (axes) before rotation;

F_1' and F_2' = orthogonal factors after varimax rotation;

F_1'' and F_2'' = oblique factors after Direct Oblimin rotation. The angle between the two is 66.42 degrees

SOURCE: Kim, J-O., & Mueller, C., *Introduction to factor analysis: What it is and how to do it*, p. 57, copyright © 1978. Reprinted by permission of Sage Publications, Inc.

The scree test plots factors in their order of extraction by eigenvalues (Figure 1.11). Such a plot is usually vertical to begin with and then becomes horizontal, the point at which this occurs being the cutoff for the maximum number of factors to extract. Another approach is to consider any factor with an eigenvalue greater than 1, suggesting that the factor explains more variance than any individual item (Hair et al., 1998).[10]

It should be noted that coefficient alpha and internal consistency relate to whether there are common underlying sources, the plural being the key here, and should not be used to make inferences about the dimensionality of a construct. This is illustrated using an example where there are clearly two factors, but coefficient alpha is extremely high (Figure 1.12). Whether there is one or a specific number of underlying sources is in the realm of dimensionality and factor analysis.

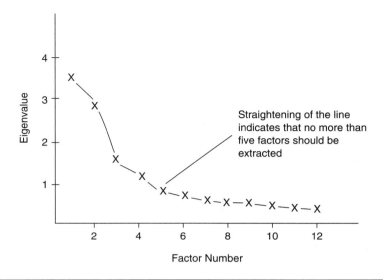

Figure 1.11   Eigenvalue Plot for Scree Test Criterion

SOURCE: Kim, J-O., & Mueller, C., *Introduction to factor analysis: What it is and how to do it*, p. 45, copyright © 1978. Reprinted by permission of Sage Publications, Inc.

Dimensionality analyses for the PNI scale are presented in Exhibit 1.4.[11] Key indicators here at this exploratory stage include the variance explained by a dominant factor and factor loadings of individual items. It should be noted that some items have medium to low loadings with the first factor, whereas other items have high loadings with the first factor and high loadings with other factors as well. What are these other factors? They could represent some content domain or some wording or methodological aspect of the measure that is shared by a subset of items. For example, items worded such that higher scores suggest higher PNI (i.e., positively worded items) may be more closely related with each other than with items worded such that lower scores suggest higher PNI (i.e., negatively worded items). Rotated factor analysis can serve to simplify matrices.

Dimensionality—Confirmatory Factor Analysis and Structural Equation Modeling

Exploratory factor analysis provides initial evidence of dimensionality, but confirmatory factor analysis is required for conclusive evidence.

Hypothetical correlation matrix for a 20-item scale with two factors comprising Items 1–10 and Items 11–20, respectively.

1	.9	.9	.9	.9	.9	.9	.9	.9	.9	0	0	0	0	0	0	0	0	0	0
.9	1	.9	.9	.9	.9	.9	.9	.9	.9	0	0	0	0	0	0	0	0	0	0
.9	.9	1	.9	.9	.9	.9	.9	.9	.9	0	0	0	0	0	0	0	0	0	0
.9	.9	.9	1	.9	.9	.9	.9	.9	.9	0	0	0	0	0	0	0	0	0	0
.9	.9	.9	.9	1	.9	.9	.9	.9	.9	0	0	0	0	0	0	0	0	0	0
.9	.9	.9	.9	.9	1	.9	.9	.9	.9	0	0	0	0	0	0	0	0	0	0
.9	.9	.9	.9	.9	.9	1	.9	.9	.9	0	0	0	0	0	0	0	0	0	0
.9	.9	.9	.9	.9	.9	.9	1	.9	.9	0	0	0	0	0	0	0	0	0	0
.9	.9	.9	.9	.9	.9	.9	.9	1	.9	0	0	0	0	0	0	0	0	0	0
.9	.9	.9	.9	.9	.9	.9	.9	.9	1	0	0	0	0	0	0	0	0	0	0
0	0	0	0	0	0	0	0	0	0	1	0	0	0	0	0	0	0	0	0
0	0	0	0	0	0	0	0	0	0	.9	1	.9	.9	.9	.9	.9	.9	.9	.9
0	0	0	0	0	0	0	0	0	0	.9	.9	1	.9	.9	.9	.9	.9	.9	.9
0	0	0	0	0	0	0	0	0	0	.9	.9	.9	1	.9	.9	.9	.9	.9	.9
0	0	0	0	0	0	0	0	0	0	.9	.9	.9	.9	1	.9	.9	.9	.9	.9
0	0	0	0	0	0	0	0	0	0	.9	.9	.9	.9	.9	1	.9	.9	.9	.9
0	0	0	0	0	0	0	0	0	0	.9	.9	.9	.9	.9	.9	1	.9	.9	.9
0	0	0	0	0	0	0	0	0	0	.9	.9	.9	.9	.9	.9	.9	1	.9	.9
0	0	0	0	0	0	0	0	0	0	.9	.9	.9	.9	.9	.9	.9	.9	1	.9
0	0	0	0	0	0	0	0	0	0	.9	.9	.9	.9	.9	.9	.9	.9	.9	1

$$\alpha = \frac{K}{K-1} \cdot \left(\frac{K\bar{r}}{1 + (K-1) \cdot \bar{r}} \right)$$

$$\bar{r} = \frac{100 \times 0 + 90 \times .9}{190} = 0.426$$

$$\alpha = \frac{20}{20-1} \cdot \left(\frac{20 \cdot (0.426)}{1 + 19 \cdot (0.426)} \right)$$

$$= 0.986$$

Figure 1.12   Coefficient α Versus Factor Analysis

Exploratory factor analysis assumes that all items are related to all factors, whereas confirmatory factor analysis imposes a more restrictive model where items have prespecified loadings with certain factors that also may be

Exhibit 1.4   Exploratory Factor Analysis of the 20-Item PNI Scale

Results for the original 20-item PNI scale are presented below for the same sample as in Exhibit 1.2 (Viswanathan, 1993). Correlations between items provide clues to the likely factor structure that may underlie the data. Below, the factor matrix is presented and is the result of exploratory factor analysis. The correlation between each item and each factor is presented here. A useful way to examine such a matrix is by highlighting the high loadings that each item has on one or more factors. Here, many items have their highest loading on the first factor.

Factor Matrix

	Factor 1	Factor 2	Factor 3	Factor 4
N1	.79874	.13506	−.01212	−.09337
N2	.36629	.25747	.27185	.10054
N3	.77987	.27999	−.14529	−.12853
N4	.63339	−.22174	−.29342	.00671
N5	.54453	−.02839	−.03588	.56900
N6	.63067	.21084	.10678	−.00046
N7	.81937	.07605	.03373	.28493
N8	.47641	−.32387	.11877	.01884
N9	.45266	.15707	.05986	.10623
N10	.72986	.21385	−.33176	−.08889
N11	.57628	−.47323	−.27856	.06503
N12	−.31912	.17510	.16366	.10411
N13	.55337	−.24397	.05221	−.23473
N14	.67780	.11840	.09128	−.27664
N15	.51572	−.28529	.30472	−.08219
N16	.67509	−.29761	.00241	−.14682
N17	.57455	−.12036	.56461	.04140
N18	.42251	.15295	.41612	−.05502
N19	.58197	.44522	−.22408	−.06153
N20	.66761	−.08386	−.17123	.13250

The communality of each variable, or the variance it shares with other variables, is reported below.

Variable	Communality
N1	.66510
N2	.28447
N3	.72421
N4	.53649
N5	.62237
N6	.45359

(Continued)

Exhibit 1.4 (Continued)

N7	.75948
N8	.34632
N9	.24444
N10	.69640
N11	.63786
N12	.17012
N13	.42356
N14	.55830
N15	.44697
N16	.56587
N17	.66510
N18	.37809
N19	.59091
N20	.49961

Eigenvalues and percent of variance explained by each factor is presented below. Such information is used to decide on the number of meaningful factors as discussed in the chapter.

Factor	Eigenvalue	Pct. of Var.	Cum. Pct.
1	7.32600	36.6	36.6
2	1.17967	5.9	42.5
3	1.13261	5.5	48.0
4	0.66097	3.3	51.3

related to each other. Exploratory factor analysis uses a general model *no matter what the substantively motivated constraints are*. Confirmatory factor analysis allows more precise specification of the relationship between items and factors.

It should be emphasized strongly that, although exploratory factor analysis can be used in preliminary stages of measure development, it should be followed up with confirmatory factor analysis (Gerbing & Anderson, 1988). Confirmatory factor analysis tests carefully specify models of the relationship between items and factors (Gerbing & Anderson, 1988). Confirmatory factor analysis also provides overall indexes of fit between the proposed model and the data, which range in value from 0 to 1. Exploratory factor analysis employs more of a shotgun approach by allowing all items to be related with all factors (Figure 1.13).

Exploratory Factor Analysis

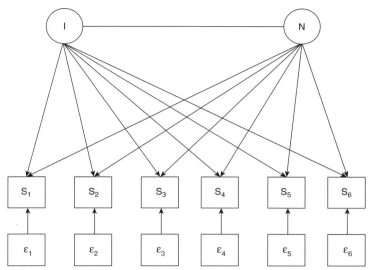

Confirmatory Factor Analysis

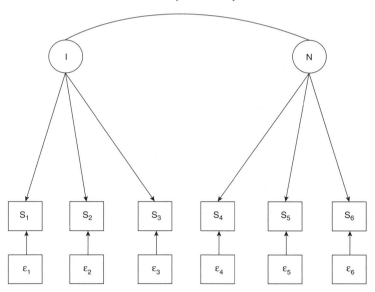

Figure 1.13   Confirmatory Factor Analysis Versus Exploratory Factor Analysis for the Speech Quality Scale

NOTES: I = Intelligibility factor of speech quality; N = Naturalness factor of speech quality; S_{1-3} = Items for intelligibility; S_{4-6} = Items for naturalness.

Whereas exploratory factor analysis considers internal consistency among items of a measure, confirmatory factor analysis considers external consistency across items of different measures or dimensions (Gerbing & Anderson, 1988). As shown in Figure 1.13 and illustrated in Appendix 1.1, the relationship between items from different dimensions is exclusively through the relationship between the dimensions. Therefore, external consistency is assessed by comparing the observed correlation between two items of different dimensions or constructs with the predicted correlation that arises out of the hypothesized relationship between items and measures. Confirmatory factor analysis applies the criterion of external consistency wherein relationships between items across factors are assessed (Appendix 1.1). In essence, the observed correlations between items are compared to the hypothesized correlations in light of the specified model. Moreover, overall fit indexes can be computed with confirmatory factor analysis. Residuals between items denote the degree to which observed relationships deviate from hypothesized relationships. A positive residual between two items suggests that the model underpredicts the relationship between two items and vice versa.

Confirmatory factor analysis is demonstrated using a speech quality scale (Exhibit 1.5). Confirmatory factor analysis allows isolation of items that measure multiple factors that are of substantive importance (see Appendix 1.1 for simplified illustration and Figures 1.13 and 1.14). In a multidimensional measure, each item ideally should measure only one dimension. Two items measuring different dimensions may have an unduly large relationship, suggesting that they are influenced by a common factor, perhaps one of the factors being measured or a different factor. If only one item is influenced by an additional unknown factor, that is usually tolerable. In fact, all items will probably have some unique variance. However, items that measure more than one substantive factor have to be identified and deleted. For instance, in Figure 1.14, reproduced from Gerbing and Anderson (1988), Items 4 and 7 measure more than one factor.

Confirmatory factor analysis falls under the broader umbrella of structural equation modeling (SEM). The caution about appropriate use of statistical techniques and the introductory nature of the material covered here should be reemphasized for structural equation modeling. Structural equation modeling combines econometric and psychometric approaches by simultaneously assessing structural and measurement models; the former deals with relationships between constructs, whereas the latter deals with relationships between constructs and their measures (Figure 1.15). In a typical econometric approach, such as regression, each measure is entered into the analysis without accounting for measurement error. For example,

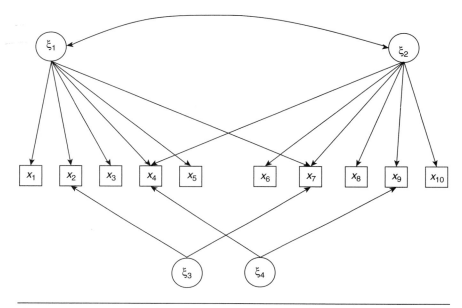

Figure 1.14   Example of Confirmatory Factor Analysis

SOURCE: Adapted from Gerbing, D. W., & Anderson, J. C. An updated paradigm for scale development incorporating unidimensionality and its assessment, in *Journal of Marketing Research*, 25(5), pp. 186–92, copyright © 1988. Reprinted by permission of the American Marketing Association.

NOTE: ξ_1 and ξ_2 are two moderately correlated factors. x_{1-5} and x_{6-10} are indicators for ξ_1 and ξ_2, respectively. ξ_3 and ξ_4 are additional factors that provide a source of common covariance for two pairs of items across two sets.

considerable random error in one or more measures in regression may decrease the observed relationship between two measures. Nevertheless, the observed relationship is assumed to reflect the true relationship between constructs. SEM combines the econometric and psychometric traditions to evaluate relationships between constructs while accounting for measurement error. At the measurement level, the advantage of SEM is in terms of specifying a precise model and testing it using confirmatory factor analysis (Figure 1.16). At the theoretical level, SEM allows assessment of relationships between constructs while accounting measurement error. For instance, as discussed earlier, random error and unreliability reduce the ability of a measure to correlate with other measures. SEM estimates the relationship between two constructs while taking into account the degree of reliability of their measures.

(Text continues on page 58)

Exhibit 1.5   Confirmatory Factor Analysis on the Speech Quality Scale

The quality of text-to-speech (TTS) systems can be assessed effectively only on the basis of reliable and valid listening tests. The method for these tests must be rigorous in voice sample presentation, respondent selection, and questionnaire preparation. These tests involve preparing several samples of synthesized output from multiple TTS systems, randomizing the system-sentence combinations, and asking listeners to score each output audio. Johnston (1996) notes that opinion tests of speech quality are the basis of speech quality assessment. The Mean Opinion Scale (MOS) has been the recommended measure of text-to-speech quality (ITU-T Recommendation, 1994). It consists of seven 5-point scales that assess overall impression, listening effort, comprehension problems, articulation, pronunciation, speaking rate, and pleasantness (Lewis, 2001). Items in this scale are presented in the Exhibit 1.5 Figure.

Past research lacks explication of the factors or dimensions of speech quality. Moreover, past research employed exploratory factor analysis to assess factor structure, a procedure appropriate at preliminary stages of measure development that needs to be followed up with testing using confirmatory factor analysis. An item in the MOS asks the respondent to rate the overall quality of the synthesized speech clip on a scale from 1 to 5 (Exhibit 1.5 Figure). The other items relate to various aspects of synthetic speech such as listening effort, pronunciation, speed, pleasantness, naturalness, audio flow, ease of listening, comprehension, and articulation (Exhibit 1.5 Figure). Responses are gathered on the 5-point scales with appropriate phrase anchors. The MOS combines an item on overall sound quality with other items that are more specific and relate to different facets of speech quality.

Several issues are noteworthy with respect to the MOS. At a conceptual level, a central issue is the factor structure of the domain of speech quality. A factor is essentially a linear combination of variables (Hair et al., 1998). In this context, factor analysis is conducted to assess the number of factors that are extracted and to assess the degree to which items correlate with specific factors. In terms of dimensionality, a variety of different results have been reported using exploratory factor analysis, including two factors referred to as intelligibility and naturalness and a separate speaking rate item (Kraft & Portele, 1995; Lewis, 2001) and one factor (Sonntag, Portele, Haas, & Kohler, 1999). More recently, Lewis suggested a revised version of the MOS with modified 7-point response scales. Results suggested two factors, with the speaking rate item loading on the intelligibility factor. Moreover, past research has typically employed exploratory factor analysis and has not followed up with subsequent confirmatory factor analysis, as recommended in the psychometric literature (Gerbing & Anderson, 1988). Confirmatory factor analysis offers a test of factor structure by testing specific models and providing overall indexes of fit.

Also lacking in past research is an explication of the domain of the speech quality construct through a description of underlying factors such as intelligibility. Such conceptual examination should ideally precede item generation and empirical assessment. Intelligibility is related to the extent to which words and sentences can be

(Continued)

Exhibit 1.5 Figure   Speech Quality Scale*

Overall Impression	Listening Effort	Pronunciation
How do you rate the quality of the audio you just heard? ○ Excellent ○ Good ○ Fair ○ Poor ○ Very poor	How would you describe the effort you were required to make in order to understand the message? ○ Complete relaxation possible; no effort required ○ Attention necessary; no appreciable effort required ○ Moderate effort required ○ Considerable effort required ○ No meaning understood with any feasible effort	Did you notice anomalies in pronunciation? ○ No ○ Yes, but not annoying ○ Yes, slightly annoying ○ Yes, annoying ○ Yes, very annoying

Speaking Rate	Pleasantness	Naturalness	Audio Flow
The average speed of delivery was: ○ Just right ○ Slightly fast or slightly slow ○ Fairly fast or fairly slow ○ Very fast or very slow ○ Extremely fast or extremely slow	How would you describe the pleasantness of the voice? ○ Very pleasant ○ Pleasant ○ Neutral ○ Unpleasant ○ Very unpleasant	How would you rate the naturalness of the audio? ○ Very natural ○ Natural ○ Neutral ○ Unnatural ○ Very unnatural	How would you describe the continuity or flow of the audio? ○ Very smooth ○ Smooth ○ Neutral ○ Discontinuous ○ Very discontinuous

Ease of Listening	Comprehension Problems	Articulation	Acceptance
Would it be easy or difficult to listen to this voice for long periods of time? ○ Very easy ○ Easy ○ Neutral ○ Difficult ○ Very difficult	Did you find certain words hard to understand? ○ Never ○ Rarely ○ Occasionally ○ Often ○ All of the time	Were the sounds in the audio distinguishable? ○ Very clear ○ Clear ○ Neutral ○ Less clear ○ Much less clear	Do you think that this voice can be used for an interactive telephone or wireless hand-held information service system? ○ Yes ○ No

*Items 1 to 9 of the scale described in the text refer to the consecutive items from listening effort to articulation.

(Continued)

understood; therefore, items should tap into factors that assess listening effort, pronunciation, speaking rate, comprehension problems, and articulation (Exhibit 1.5 Figure). These are aspects of speech that contribute to intelligibility. Therefore, contrary to results that suggest that speaking rate is a separate factor, it belongs conceptually in the intelligibility factor. Naturalness relates to the degree to which speech is similar to natural human speech; hence, items such as naturalness, ease of listening, pleasantness, and audio flow are relevant (see Exhibit 1.5 figure). These are impressions about the speech and the feeling it engenders in respondents. This should be contrasted with specific aspects of respondents' cognition, such as speaking rate, listening effort, and pronunciation. Thus, conceptually, intelligibility and naturalness relate to specific cognitions about aspects of the speech versus broader impressions and feelings about the speech, respectively. Central here from a procedural viewpoint is the importance of explicating the domain of speech quality prior to testing through confirmatory factor analysis.

Another issue with the MOS is the inclusion of an item that is global in nature—assessing overall speech quality—with other items that are more specific to aspects of speech quality, such as articulation and pronunciation. Such an approach is problematic; the scale should consist of either global items or specific items. The global

Exhibit 1.5   Table Results for Confirmatory Factor Analysis on Speech Quality Scale

Dataset	1		2		3		4		5		6	
No. of factors	1	2	1	2	1	2	1	2	1	2	1	2
n	128	128	128	128	128	128	128	128	128	128	128	128
df	27	26	27	26	27	26	27	26	27	26	27	26
Chi-square	72.8	39.1*	49.5	38.3^*	118.2	57.6*	102.8	64.3*	88.0	52.8*	78.3	49.2*
NFI	0.95	0.97	0.96	0.97	0.90	0.95	0.90	0.94	0.92	0.95	0.94	0.97
NNFI	0.96	0.99	0.98	0.99	0.89	0.96	0.90	0.95	0.92	0.96	0.95	0.98
CFI	0.97	0.99	0.98	0.99	0.92	0.97	0.92	0.96	0.94	0.97	0.96	0.98
IFI	0.97	0.99	0.98	0.99	0.92	0.97	0.92	0.96	0.94	0.97	0.96	0.98
SRMR	0.06	0.04	0.05	0.04	0.08	0.06	0.07	0.06	0.07	0.05	0.05	0.05

NOTES: ^ $p > .05$; $p < .05$ for all other chi-square values. *Chi-square values of 1- versus 2-factor models significantly different at .05 level. n = sample size; df = degrees of freedom; NFI = normed fit index; NNFI = non-normed fit index; CFI = comparative fit index; IFI = incremental fit index; SRMR = standardized root mean square residual. The results for the 3-factor model ($df = 24$) with speaking rate as a separate item were identical to those for the 2-factor model with the following exceptions: Dataset 1: Chi-square = 39.0, NNFI = 0.98; Dataset 2: Chi-square = 36.5; Dataset 3: Chi-square = 57.4; Dataset 4: Chi-square = 64.2, NNFI = 0.94; Dataset 6: Chi-square = 47.6, NNFI = 0.97.

approach essentially asks for overall impressions of speech quality, whereas the specific approach has items representing different aspects of speech quality. For example, if different items relate to different factors such as intelligibility and naturalness, then a global item would relate to both factors, being broader than either. In fact, this argument is supported by inconsistent results that have been obtained. Although this global item was thought to belong to the naturalness factor, Lewis (2001) unexpectedly found that it related to the intelligibility factor. All of these issues were examined through confirmatory factor analysis.

One hundred and twenty-eight employees of a U.S. company rated six systems on the single item on overall speech quality, the 9-item speech quality scale, and the single item on system acceptability. Because each respondent rated more than one system and the purpose here was to generate independent observations within a dataset, each dataset analyzed related to independent responses to a particular system. Moreover, some systems were slightly different across subsets of respondents. Therefore, the first step was to identify datasets of responses to exactly the same system. This led to four data sets of 64 respondents, each rating identical systems. These four datasets provided the best quality of data of independent observations of identical systems. Six more datasets provided 128 independent observations; however, the systems rated varied slightly across respondents. Sample sizes for these datasets met some of the criteria in past research for factor analysis (i.e., greater than five times the number of items [> 45], or greater than 100 in the case of the larger datasets [Iacobucci, 1994]), although more stringent criteria have been suggested as a function of factors such as the communality of items (MacCallum, Widaman, Zhang, & Hong, 1999). Given the high communality of items of speech quality, less stringent criteria appear to be appropriate here.

Several models were tested through confirmatory factor analysis. Several points are noteworthy with the overwhelming pattern of results. First, the overall levels of fit of both 1- and 2-factor models (i.e., Items 1, 2, 3, 8, and 9 on intelligibility and Items 4, 5, 6, and 7 on naturalness in Exhibit 1.5 Figure) are satisfactory by accepted (e.g., > 0.90) (Bagozzi & Yi, 1988; Bentler & Bonnet, 1980) and even by conservative norms (e.g., > 0.95) (Hu & Bentler, 1998). All individual items had significant loadings on hypothesized factors. Whereas the 2-factor model improved on the 1-factor model, the 1-factor model had a high level of fit. These results suggest that both 1- and 2-factor formulations of the 9-item scale are strongly supported through confirmatory factor analysis. Contrary to the notion that the item on speaking rate loads on a separate factor, here, speaking rate appears to be a part of the intelligibility factor. An alternative model with speaking rate as a separate factor did not improve on the 2-factor fit indexes, although fit levels were so high as to allow little or no room for improvement. A model with speaking rate loading on the intelligibility factor led to superior fit as opposed to a model with speaking rate loading on the naturalness factor, consistent with the argument that speaking rate loads primarily on the intelligibility factor.

(Continued)

(Continued)

Exploratory factor analysis is more of a shotgun approach, where all items can be related to all factors. Confirmatory factor analysis can be used to carefully specify the relationship between items and factors, and between factors. Overall fit indexes can be computed, and alternative models can be compared.

Input and Output From LISREL 8.5
for Confirmatory Factor Analysis

The program statements for confirmatory factor analysis are shown below. The first line states the number of input variables, the number of observations, the number of factors, and the nature of the matrix (i.e., a covariance matrix). The second line specifies the labels for the variables. This is followed by the covariance matrix and the model statement specifying nine variables, one factor, and the label for the factor.

```
DA NI = 9  MA = KM  NO = 128
LA

s1 s2 s3 s4 s5 s6 s7 s8 s9
KM

1.000000
0.595594   1.000000
0.478988   0.375190   1.000000
0.636631   0.448744   0.401614   1.000000
0.614881   0.567760   0.348624   0.756280   1.000000
0.618288   0.546916   0.410717   0.642101   0.722303   1000000
0.647556   0.523697   0.398602   0.783353   0.798083   0.731203
1.000000
0.582192   0.534391   0.378980   0.398120   0.349791   0.401245
0.394849   1.000000
0.628814   0.561461   0.359818   0.647491   0.651060   0.624736
0.663076   0.483979   1.000000

MO NX = 9  NK = 1  LX = FR  PH = ST
LK
sq

OU
```

Edited results are shown below.

```
DA NI = 9 NO = 128 NG = 1 MA = CM
SE
1 2 3 4 5 6 7 8 9 /
MO NX = 9 NK = 1 LX = FU, FI PH = SY, FR TD = DI, FR
LK
sq
FI PH(1,1)
FR LX(1,1) LX(2,1) LX(3,1) LX(4,1) LX(5,1) LX(6,1) LX(7,1) LX(8,1) LX(9,1)
VA 1.00 PH(1,1)
PD
OU ME = ML RS XM
```

TI DA NI = 9 NO = 128

Number of Input Variables 9
Number of Y - Variables 0
Number of X - Variables 9
Number of ETA - Variables 0
Number of KSI - Variables 1
Number of Observations 128

TI DA NI = 9 NO = 128

Covariance Matrix

	s1	s2	s3	s4	s5	s6
s1	1.00					
s2	0.60	1.00				
s3	0.48	0.38	1.00			
s4	0.64	0.45	0.40	1.00		
s5	0.61	0.57	0.35	0.76	1.00	
s6	0.62	0.55	0.41	0.64	0.72	1.00
s7	0.65	0.52	0.40	0.78	0.80	0.73
s8	0.58	0.53	0.38	0.40	0.35	0.40
s9	0.63	0.56	0.36	0.65	0.65	0.62

Covariance Matrix

	s7	s8	s9
s7	1.00		
s8	0.39	1.00	
s9	0.66	0.48	1.00

(Continued)

(Continued)

TI DA NI = 9 NO = 128

Parameter Specifications

LAMBDA-X

```
         sq
         ----------
s1       1
s2       2
s3       3
s4       4
s5       5
s6       6
s7       7
s8       8
s9       9
```

THETA-DELTA

s1	s2	s3	s4	s5	s6
10	11	12	13	14	15

THETA-DELTA

s7	s8	s9
16	17	18

TI DA NI = 9 NO = 128

Number of Iterations = 9

LISREL Estimates (Maximum Likelihood)
Loadings of each item on the factor are listed below with associated standard errors and t-values.

LAMBDA-X

```
         sq
         ----------
s1       0.77
         (0.08)
         10.11
```

---

s2	0.65				
	(0.08)				
	8.08				
s3	0.48				
	(0.09)				
	5.63				
s4	0.84				
	(0.07)				
	11.54				
s5	0.87				
	(0.07)				
	12.13				
s6	0.81				
	(0.07)				
	10.94				
s7	0.89				
	(0.07)				
	12.61				
s8	0.52				
	(0.08)				
	6.15				
s9	0.77				
	(0.08)				
	10.19				

PHI

```
        sq
     ----------
        1.00
```

THETA-DELTA

	s1	s2	s3	s4	s5	s6
	0.41	0.57	0.77	0.29	0.25	0.34
	(0.06)	(0.08)	(0.10)	(0.04)	(0.04)	(0.05)
	7.21	7.58	7.81	6.71	6.38	6.96

(Continued)

(Continued)

THETA-DELTA

s7	s8	s9
0.21	0.73	0.40
(0.04)	(0.09)	(0.06)
6.02	7.78	7.19

Squared Multiple Correlations for X - Variables

s1	s2	s3	s4	s5	s6
0.59	0.43	0.23	0.71	0.75	0.66

Squared Multiple Correlations for X - Variables

s7	s8	s9
0.79	0.27	0.60

Various goodness-of-fit indexes are presented below.
Goodness of Fit Statistics

Degrees of Freedom = 27
Minimum Fit Function Chi-Square = 72.82 (P = 0.00)
Normal Theory Weighted Least Squares Chi-Square = 87.95 (P = 0.00)
Estimated Non-Centrality Parameter (NCP) = 60.95
90 Percent Confidence Interval for NCP = (36.28 ; 93.23)

Minimum Fit Function Value = 0.57
Population Discrepancy Function Value (F0) = 0.48
90 Percent Confidence Interval for F0 = (0.29 ; 0.73)
Root Mean Square Error of Approximation (RMSEA) = 0.13
90 Percent Confidence Interval for RMSEA = (0.10 ; 0.16)
P-Value for Test of Close Fit (RMSEA < 0.05) = 0.00

Expected Cross-Validation Index (ECVI) = 0.98
90 Percent Confidence Interval for ECVI = (0.78 ; 1.23)
ECVI for Saturated Model = 0.71
ECVI for Independence Model = 6.10

Chi-Square for Independence Model with 36 Degrees of Freedom = 756.24
Independence AIC = 774.24
Model AIC = 123.95
Saturated AIC = 90.00

Independence CAIC = 808.91
Model CAIC = 193.29
Saturated CAIC = 263.34

Normed Fit Index (NFI) = 0.90
Non-Normed Fit Index (NNFI) = 0.92
Parsimony Normed Fit Index (PNFI) = 0.68
Comparative Fit Index (CFI) = 0.94
Incremental Fit Index (IFI) = 0.94
Relative Fit Index (RFI) = 0.87

Critical N (CN) = 82.91

Root Mean Square Residual (RMR) = 0.061
Standardized RMR = 0.061
Goodness of Fit Index (GFI) = 0.87
Adjusted Goodness of Fit Index (AGFI) = 0.78
Parsimony Goodness of Fit Index (PGFI) = 0.52

TI DA NI = 9 NO = 128

Fitted Covariance Matrix

	s1	s2	s3	s4	s5	s6
s1	1.00					
s2	0.50	1.00				
s3	0.37	0.32	1.00			
s4	0.65	0.55	0.41	1.00		
s5	0.67	0.57	0.42	0.73	1.00	
s6	0.62	0.53	0.39	0.68	0.70	1.00
s7	0.68	0.58	0.43	0.74	0.77	0.72
s8	0.40	0.34	0.25	0.44	0.45	0.42
s9	0.60	0.50	0.37	0.65	0.67	0.63

Fitted Covariance Matrix

	s7	s8	s9
s7	1.00		
s8	0.46	1.00	
s9	0.69	0.40	1.00

(Continued)

(Continued)

Fitted Residuals

	s1	s2	s3	s4	s5	s6
	-----	-----	-----	-----	-----	-----
s1	0.00					
s2	0.09	0.00				
s3	0.11	0.06	0.00			
s4	−0.01	−0.10	0.00	0.00		
s5	−0.05	0.00	−0.07	0.03	0.00	
s6	−0.01	0.02	0.02	−0.04	0.02	0.00
s7	−0.03	−0.06	−0.03	0.04	0.03	0.01
s8	0.18	0.19	0.13	−0.04	−0.10	−0.02
s9	0.03	0.06	−0.01	0.00	−0.02	0.00

Fitted Residuals

	s7	s8	s9
	-----	-----	-----
s7	0.00		
s8	−0.07	0.00	
s9	−0.02	0.08	0.00

Summary Statistics for Fitted Residuals

Smallest Fitted Residual = −0.10
Median Fitted Residual = 0.00
Largest Fitted Residual = 0.19

Stemleaf Plot

−1|00
−0|7765
−0|44332221110000000000000
0|12223334
0|6689
1|13
1|89

The standardized residuals between pairs of variables are useful to examine. For example, the residual between Items 1 and 8 is positive and high, whereas the residual between Items 2 and 4 is negative and high. It should be noted that Items 4, 5, 6, and 7 form the naturalness factor, and Items 1, 2, 3, 8, and 9 form the intelligibility factor. In a 1-factor model, these residuals are consistent with two underlying factors. Items 1, 2, 3, 8, and 9 tend to have large negative residuals or small residuals with Items 4, 5, 6, and 7. Residuals within each set of items tend to be positive.

Standardized Residuals

	s1	s2	s3	s4	s5	s6
s1	—					
s2	2.37	—				
s3	2.30	1.06	—			
s4	−0.37	−3.08	−0.11	—		
s5	−2.25	0.08	−2.05	1.57	—	
s6	−0.22	0.49	0.45	−1.71	0.94	—
s7	−1.70	−2.14	−0.97	2.40	2.11	0.64
s8	4.00	3.52	1.96	−1.07	−3.07	−0.53
s9	1.05	1.45	−0.30	−0.09	−0.85	−0.11

Standardized Residuals

	s7	s8	s9
s7	—		
s8	−2.27	—	
s9	−1.14	1.80	—

Summary Statistics for Standardized Residuals

Smallest Standardized Residual = −3.08
Median Standardized Residual = 0.00
Largest Standardized Residual = 4.00

Stemleaf Plot

− 3|11
− 2|3311
− 1|77110
− 0|85432111000000000
0|14569
1|11468
2|01344
3|5
4|0
Largest Negative Standardized Residuals
Residual for s4 and s2 −3.08
Residual for s8 and s5 −3.07
Largest Positive Standardized Residuals
Residual for s8 and s1 4.00
Residual for s8 and s2 3.52

(Continued)

(Continued)

Edited results for a 2-factor model are presented below for the same data.

MO NX = 9 NK = 2 PH = ST

LK

sq1 sq2

FR LX(1,1) LX(2,1) LX(3,1) LX(4,2) LX(5,2) LX(6,2) LX(7,2) LX(8,1) LX(9,1)

OU

LISREL Estimates (Maximum Likelihood)

LAMBDA-X

	sq1	sq2
s1	0.84	—
	(0.07)	
	11.22	
s2	0.72	—
	(0.08)	
	8.97	
s3	0.53	—
	(0.09)	
	6.09	
s4	—	0.85
	(0.07)	
	11.74	
s5	—	0.88
	(0.07)	
	12.47	
s6	—	0.81
	(0.07)	
	10.85	
s7	—	0.91
	(0.07)	
	13.04	
s8	0.63	—
	(0.08)	
	7.59	

s9	0.79	—
	(0.08)	
	10.26	

PHI

	sq1	sq2
sq1	1.00	
sq2	0.86	1.00
	(0.04)	
	24.26	

THETA-DELTA

s1	s2	s3	s4	s5	s6
0.30	0.48	0.72	0.28	0.22	0.35
(0.05)	(0.07)	(0.09)	(0.04)	(0.04)	(0.05)
5.60	6.93	7.60	6.47	5.93	6.90

THETA-DELTA

s7	s8	s9
0.18	0.60	0.38
(0.03)	(0.08)	(0.06)
5.31	7.32	6.33

Goodness of Fit Statistics

Degrees of Freedom = 26
Minimum Fit Function Chi-Square = 39.10 (P = 0.048)
Normal Theory Weighted Least Squares Chi-Square = 38.56 (P = 0.054)
Estimated Non-Centrality Parameter (NCP) = 12.56
90 Percent Confidence Interval for NCP = (0.0 ; 33.28)

Minimum Fit Function Value = 0.31
Population Discrepancy Function Value (F0) = 0.099
90 Percent Confidence Interval for F0 = (0.0 ; 0.26)
Root Mean Square Error of Approximation (RMSEA) = 0.062
90 Percent Confidence Interval for RMSEA = (0.0 ; 0.10)
P-Value for Test of Close Fit (RMSEA < 0.05) = 0.30

(Continued)

(Continued)

Expected Cross-Validation Index (ECVI) = 0.60
90 Percent Confidence Interval for ECVI = (0.50 ; 0.77)
ECVI for Saturated Model = 0.71
ECVI for Independence Model = 6.10

Chi-Square for Independence Model with 36 Degrees of Freedom = 756.24
Independence AIC = 774.24
Model AIC = 76.56
Saturated AIC = 90.00
Independence CAIC = 808.91
Model CAIC = 149.74
Saturated CAIC = 263.34

Normed Fit Index (NFI) = 0.95
Non-Normed Fit Index (NNFI) = 0.97
Parsimony Normed Fit Index (PNFI) = 0.68
Comparative Fit Index (CFI) = 0.98
Incremental Fit Index (IFI) = 0.98
Relative Fit Index (RFI) = 0.93

Critical N (CN) = 149.23

Root Mean Square Residual (RMR) = 0.043
Standardized RMR = 0.043
Goodness of Fit Index (GFI) = 0.94
Adjusted Goodness of Fit Index (AGFI) = 0.89
Parsimony Goodness of Fit Index (PGFI) = 0.54

Summary Statistics for Fitted Residuals

Smallest Fitted Residual = −0.13
Median Fitted Residual = 0.00
Largest Fitted Residual = 0.08

Stemleaf Plot

−12|0
−10|
−8|9
−6|75
−4|725
−2|9753
−0|63876421000000000
0|6936

2|2246
4|457711
6|95
8|0

Standardized Residuals

	s1	s2	s3	s4	s5	s6
s1	—					
s2	−0.33	—				
s3	1.11	−0.08	—			
s4	0.75	−2.00	0.33	—		
s5	−0.86	0.63	−1.18	0.43	—	
s6	1.02	1.12	0.86	−2.06	0.53	—
s7	−0.32	−1.14	−0.31	1.09	−0.18	−0.08
s8	1.81	1.91	0.83	−1.50	−3.28	−0.82
s9	−1.91	−0.22	−1.45	2.06	1.69	2.01

Standardized Residuals

	s7	s8	s9
s7	—		
s8	−2.66	—	
s9	1.71	−0.46	—

Summary Statistics for Standardized Residuals

Smallest Standardized Residual = −3.28
Median Standardized Residual = 0.00
Largest Standardized Residual = 2.06

Stemleaf Plot

− 3|3
− 2|710
− 1|95421
− 0|9853333221100000000
0|3456889
1|01117789
2|01

Largest Negative Standardized Residuals
Residual for s8 and s5 −3.28
Residual for s8 and s7 −2.66

EXHIBIT SOURCE: Adapted from *Computer Speech and Language, 19*(1), Viswanathan, M., & Viswanathan, M., Measuring speech quality for text-to-speech systems: Development and assessment of a modified mean opinion score (MOS) scale, pp. 55–83, Copyright 2005. Reprinted with permission from Elsevier.

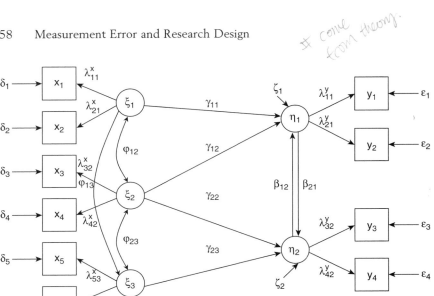

Figure 1.15   Combined Measurement Component and Structural Component of the Covariance Structure Model

SOURCE: Long, J. S., *Covariance structure models: An introduction to LISREL*, p. 18, copyright © 1983. Reprinted by permission of Sage Publications, Inc.

NOTES: The measurement model for independent variables consists of the following:
ξ = latent variable
x = observed variable
δ = unique factor or error
λ = loading of x on ξ
$x_1 = \lambda_{11}^x \xi_1 + \delta_1$.
The measurement model for dependent variables consists of the following:
η = latent variable
y = the observed variable
ε = unique factor or error
λ = loading of y on η
$y_1 = \lambda_{11}^y \eta_1 + \varepsilon_1$.
The structural model relating independent to dependent latent variables consists of the following:
η related to ξ by γ, with error represented by ζ
$\eta_1 = \gamma_{11}\xi_1 + \gamma_{12}\xi_1 + \beta_{12}\eta_2 + \zeta_1$
The xs are independent observed variables related to the dependent variables by the slope coefficients β_1 and β_2.

As illustrated in Figures 1.15 and 1.16, and as explained in the adjoining notations and equations, the structural model relates latent variables to each other, whereas the measurement model relates to the operationalizations of

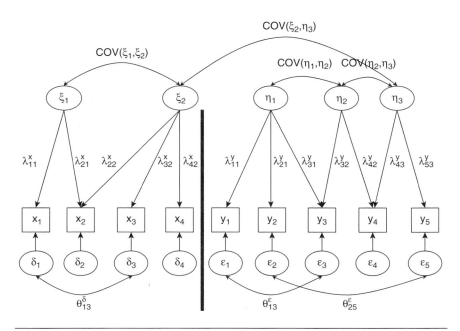

Figure 1.16   The Measurement Component of the Covariance Structure Model

SOURCE: Long, J. S., *Covariance structure models: An introduction to LISREL*, p. 18, copyright © 1983. Reprinted by permission of Sage Publications, Inc.

latent variables through observed variables. In specifying the measurement model, items could be aggregated into parcels or subsets. Method factors could be specified. For instance, if specific methods are used to collect data on specific items, they could be incorporated into the model as separate factors in addition to the latent variables. For example, in Figure 1.14, ξ_3 could be considered as a method factor for items x_2 and x_7. Thus, the effect of specific methods is explicitly incorporated. Correlated errors between items also can be specified, as shown in Figure 1.16 between x_1 and x_3 or between y_1 and y_3. Considerable caution and strong rationale are necessary to specify method factors and correlated error terms. Otherwise, this approach essentially can be misused to fit the model to the data.

A key issue in structural equation modeling is identification, or whether model parameters can be uniquely determined from the data (Bollen, 1989; Kaplan, 2000). Another issue relates to procedures used to estimate the model, such as maximum likelihood—used in the example on speech quality in Exhibit 1.5—and generalized least squares (Kaplan, 2000). A considerable amount of work has focused on the nature of statistical tests and overall fit indexes, and their vulnerability to factors such as sample size. The chi-square statistic reflects the level of mismatch between the sample and fitted covariance matrices (Hu & Bentler, 1998); hence, a nonsignificant chi-square is desirable. However, this statistic is influenced by a number of factors, including sample size. On the other hand, fit indexes quantify the degree of fit. They have been classified in several ways, such as absolute (i.e., directly assessing goodness of a model) versus incremental (assessing goodness of a model in comparison with a baseline model, such as a model in confirmatory factor analysis where each item is a distinct factor). Specific fit indexes, such as the goodness-of-fit index, the adjusted goodness-of-fit index, the normed fit index (ranging from 0 to 1), and the non-normed fit index, are each vulnerable to various factors, such as sample size (e.g., Bollen, 1986; Mulaik et al., 1989). Fit indexes have been compared on criteria such as small sample bias and sensitivity to model misspecification (Hu & Bentler, 1998). The standardized root mean square residual and the root mean square error of approximation are other indexes used to gauge fit. Considerable literature has compared various indexes of fit. As an exemplar of such literature, Hu and Bentler (1998) recommend the root mean square residual along with one of several indexes, including the comparative fit index (Hu & Bentler, 1998). The comparative fit index currently is the most recommended index (Bagozzi & Edwards, 1998). Important here is the usage of several indexes, including those currently recommended in the literature and generally produced in programs such as LISREL 8.5, as well as consideration and presentation of full information on the results, ranging from chi-square to multiple fit indexes to variance extracted and standardized root mean square residuals. Computations for some fit indexes are shown in Appendix 1.1. What specific value constitutes acceptable fit is another area with a wealth of literature. Some guidelines are provided in Chapter 5.

In comparing SEM versus the traditional approach to measurement, the traditional approach is a necessary step to developing measures and assessing reliability, dimensionality, and validity. In using SEM, a key issue is that many different models may fit the data. Therefore, SEM could be used for confirmatory factor analysis after some initial work has been completed on a measure such as the PNI scale. Preliminary empirical and conceptual work would serve to purify measures before using SEM. SEM can also be used for assessing different types of validity, as discussed subsequently. If confirmatory factor analysis is used in an exploratory fashion, the findings have to be confirmed with new data. If this procedure is used to test alternative models, then the chosen model should be tested with new data. Such testing is extremely important, because many different models can lead to good fit. Furthermore, a model could be modified in many ways to achieve fit (for example, in a simple unidimensional model,

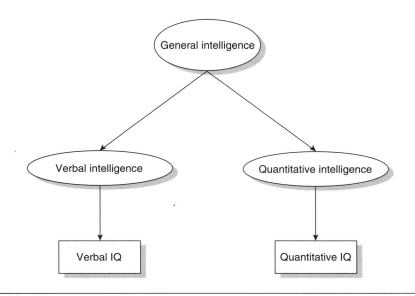

Figure 1.17   Hierarchical Factor Structure

correlated errors could be used to achieve fit). If two items of the same construct or of different constructs are influenced by an identifiable factor (say, the same measure at different points in time), then using a model with correlated error may be useful. Noteworthy here is that there are many ways to improve fit, and plausible reasoning should precede modeling. Furthermore, SEM ideally should not be used during the early stages of measure development for item purification.

It should be noted that hierarchical factor analyses can also be performed using structural equation modeling, wherein a set of factors loads onto higher level factors, such as, say, quantitative and verbal intelligence loading onto general intelligence. Thus, second-order factor analysis would involve an intermediate level of factors that loads onto higher order factors (Figure 1.17).

Validity

Whether a measure captures the intended construct, or whether the core tapped by a measure is the intended core, is the purview of validity. Assessing validity is like searching for an object at the bottom of the ocean with a searchlight, not knowing what the object looks like! Such searches may employ certain predetermined criteria (i.e., target areas on which to focus that are akin to representative domain, and content validity in terms of what the object might look like and indicators to look for in the ocean). When multiple searchlights and search crews are used and converge on the same location (i.e., multiple measures), then one type of evidence of validity is provided. When an unseen object has to be located, different types of evidence are needed to locate it.

The distinction between reliability and validity, and how one can actually be unrelated to the other, is brought out by the following stark example modified from Nunnally (1978). Consider an exercise where a stone of a certain weight is thrown as far as possible over 20 trials with sufficient rest between trials and under conditions with no wind and comfortable weather. Is this a reliable measure of intelligence? Yes, if the same measure a week later yields the same average throwing distance. In the social sciences, the criterion for consistency is often the relative standing of a set of people at test versus retest as reflected in a correlation, the requirement of the exact throwing distance between test and retest being stringent for the nature of the phenomenon being studied. Note that multiple trials and rest between trials may minimize variations because of arm weariness and may average out errors. Whether throwing stones captures intelligence is the purview of validity. This is an extreme scenario because a reliable measure is typically likely to have some degree of validity as a result of procedures employed to capture the content of a construct. However, the scenario is instructive in illustrating that a reliable measure is nothing more than a replicable measure. Hence, in colloquial language, a reliable friend who is late but consistently late by the same amount of time would still be considered reliable in the measurement world.

Several types of validity need to be considered (Churchill, 1979; Cronbach & Meehl, 1955; Nunnally, 1978). Very brief descriptions are provided below, demonstrated in Exhibit 1.6, and listed in Figure 1.18.

1. Content validity (subjective judgment of content, following proper procedures to delineate content domain, using a representative set of items, assessing if items make sense)

2. Face validity (Does the measure look like it is measuring what it is supposed to measure?)

3. Known-groups validity (Does the measure distinguish between groups that are *known* to differ on the construct, such as differences in scores on measures between people with or without specific medical conditions?)

4. Predictive validity (Does the measure predict what it is supposed to predict, such as an external criterion, say GRE or university entrance exam and grades in college?)

5. Convergent validity (Does the measure correlate or converge with another measure of the *same* construct?)

6. Discriminant validity (Is the measure of a construct not correlated with measures of constructs to which it is not expected to be related?)

7. Nomological validity (Does the measure of a construct relate to measures of other constructs with which it is theoretically expected to be correlated; that is, considering a nomological or theoretical network of constructs, does the measure behave in theoretically expected ways?)

8. Construct validity (Does a measure measure what it aims to measure; does a measure or operationalization correspond to the underlying construct it is aiming to measure?)

Exhibit 1.6   Validity Analysis of the PNI Scale

Correlations Between PNI Scale and Other Scales

	PNI	MEN	MVL	MTH	ATF	ATC
MEN	0.67					
MVL	0.56	0.41				
MTH	0.74	0.93	0.73			
ATF	0.57	0.42	0.46	0.50		
ATC	0.51	0.65	0.41	0.66	0.49	
ATS	0.61	0.64	0.49	0.69	0.79	0.92

NOTES: All correlations were significant at the 0.01 level. MEN = Enjoyment of mathematics scale; MVL = Value of mathematics scale; MTH = Total attitude toward mathematics scale; ATF = Attitude toward statistics field scale; ATC = Attitude toward statistics course scale; ATS = Total attitude toward statistics scale. All scales scored such that higher scores indicate more positive attitudes toward statistics, mathematics, and so on.

	PNI
AMB	−0.24**
NFC	0.30**
SOC	0.03

NOTE: Scales scored such that higher scores indicate more tolerance for ambiguity and higher need for cognition.

**$p < .01$.

Scale Descriptions

Attitude Toward Mathematics Scale (MATH). This scale is divided into (a) an Enjoyment of Mathematics scale (MATHEN)—"a liking for mathematical problems and a liking for mathematical terms, symbols, and routine computations"

(Continued)

(Continued)

(Aiken, 1974, p. 67); sample item: "Mathematics is enjoyable and stimulating to me" (Aiken, 1974, p. 68); and (b) a Value of Mathematics scale (MATHVAL), which relates to "recognizing the importance and relevance of mathematics to individuals and to society" (Aiken, 1974, p. 67); sample item: "Mathematics is not important for the advance of civilization and society" (Aiken, 1974, p. 68).

Intolerance for Ambiguity Scale (AMB). This scale defines "a tendency to perceive or interpret information marked by vague, incomplete, fragmented, multiple, probable, unstructured, uncertain, inconsistent, contrary, contradictory, or unclear meanings as actual or potential sources of psychological discomfort or threat" (Norton, 1975, p. 608). A sample item is "I do not believe that in the final analysis there is a distinct difference between right and wrong" (Norton, 1975, p. 616).

Attitude Toward Statistics Scale (STAT). This scale is a measure of attitudes held by college students toward an introductory course in statistics (Wise, 1985). This scale is divided into Attitude Toward Course (STCOURS) and Attitude Toward the Field (STFIELD) subscales.

Need for Cognition (NFC). This scale defines "the tendency of an individual to engage in and enjoy thinking" (Cacioppo & Petty, 1982, p. 116).

Results

The relationship between the PNI scale and the Social Desirability scale (Crowne & Marlowe, 1964) was assessed to examine whether responses to items indicating a higher (or lower) preference for numerical information may be partially explained by a motive to appear socially desirable, and to provide evidence for the discriminant validity of the PNI scale. A possible explanation for such responses may be based on a perception that it is more socially desirable to indicate greater preference for numerical information. This may be particularly likely given the composition of the sample, which consisted of undergraduate students at a midwestern U.S. university. Having taken quantitative courses, students may be likely to indicate a greater preference for numerical information as a means of appearing socially desirable. PNI had no significant correlations with the 33-item Social Desirability scale ($r = 0.03$). Therefore, it appears that social desirability is not a significant factor in explaining responses to items on the PNI scale, with the result providing evidence for the discriminant validity of the PNI scale.

The relationship between PNI and Need for Cognition—the "tendency of an individual to engage in and enjoy thinking" (Cacioppo & Petty, 1982, p. 116)—was assessed to provide evidence of the nomological validity of the PNI scale. Because the PNI scale is argued to tap individuals' preference for engaging in thinking involving numerical information (as captured by aspects such as enjoyment and liking), a positive relationship was expected between PNI and Need for Cognition. Individuals who have a tendency to enjoy thinking may be more likely to enjoy thinking based on a particular type of information (i.e., numerical information) than individuals who do not enjoy thinking. PNI had a positive correlation with Need for Cognition ($r = 0.30$, $p < .01$). The significant correlation provides evidence for the claim that the PNI scale taps proclivity toward thinking based on one type of information (i.e., numerical information). However, the size of the correlation suggests that a tendency to enjoy thinking per se is not strongly related to a tendency to enjoy thinking based on information in a numerical form, perhaps because numerical information is just one of several types of information that could be used in thinking. This is a form of evidence for nomological validity in tapping enjoyment of thinking based on one type of information.

Given the numerical content in statistics and mathematics, positive correlations between preference for numerical information and attitudes toward statistics and mathematics were expected in order to provide evidence of the nomological validity of the PNI scale. Positive correlations were obtained between the PNI scale and the Enjoyment of Mathematics scale ($r = 0.67$, $p < .01$); the PNI scale and the Value of Mathematics scale ($r = 0.56$, $p < .01$); and the PNI scale and the total Attitude Toward Mathematics scale ($r = 0.74$, $p < .01$). Positive correlations were also obtained between the PNI scale and the attitude toward statistics course scale ($r = .57$, $p < .01$); the PNI scale and the attitude to statistics field scale ($r = 0.51$, $p < .01$); and the PNI scale and the total statistics scale ($r = 0.61$, $p < .01$). The results suggest that PNI has moderate to strong relationships with the various subscales relating to mathematics and statistics, thereby providing evidence for the nomological validity of the PNI scale due to the overlap between these scales in terms of numerical content. The PNI scale had comparable or higher correlations with the subscales of attitude toward mathematics (statistics), such as the Enjoyment of Mathematics and Value of Mathematics scales, than the correlations between these subscales, possibly because PNI overlaps with both subscales in terms of numerical content, whereas the subscales overlap in terms of mathematical (statistical) content.

EXHIBIT SOURCE: Adapted from Viswanathan (1993).

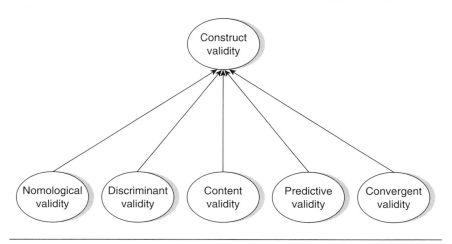

Figure 1.18   Types of Validity

Content validity relates to whether a measure is representative of a domain and whether appropriate procedures have been employed for the development of items. Content validity comes into play if a measure is construed to represent just one or a few aspects of the domain. Assessments of content validity focus on whether aspects of the domain of a construct have been excluded and aspects of the domain of a distinctly different construct have been included. Content validity is a subjective assessment of the representativeness of a measure and the procedures used to develop the domain. Whereas most other validity assessments are mainly empirical in nature, content validity is not and is also a central indicator of the representativeness of a measure. For the PNI scale, content validity evidence resides on documentation of procedures for domain delineation and item generation (Exhibit 1.1). Face validity relates to whether a measure looks like it is measuring what it is supposed to measure, a very preliminary judgment about validity.

Several other types of validity depend on empirical evidence. Convergent validity tests assess the degree to which two measures of a construct converge (i.e., are highly correlated or strongly related). Convergent validity between two measures is somewhat akin to internal consistency between items of a measure. The logic of convergent validity is that a measure of a construct should converge with another validated measure of the same construct, assuming such a measure is available. However, convergence alone is not definitive evidence of validity because both measures could be invalid. No two measures in practice are likely to be exactly identical and lead to perfect convergence. In fact, such similar measures may not serve to test convergent validity if they are really trivially different from each other. The aim here is to attempt different approaches to measuring the same construct, which generally may translate to less-than-perfect correlation among alternative measures. Two different ways of measuring the same thing may not, in practice, be identical. Just as items get at different aspects of a domain, different ways or methods of measuring something may get at different aspects of a construct. Different approaches also differ methodologically, contributing to the less-than-perfect correlation to be expected between two measures of the same construct. In fact, as knowledge in an area progresses, researchers may well conclude that what were originally considered two measures of the same construct are really measures of different constructs. But this is one way in which knowledge in an area progresses, different ways of attempting to measure constructs being central in advancing such knowledge. Convergence between measures of the same construct is a matter of degree for a variety of reasons. Note that convergent validity is not involved when two measures of constructs are shown to be related. Rather, it is useful to restrict this type of validity to the relationship between two measures of the *same* construct. Relationships between measures of related constructs are captured under nomological validity.

Nomological validity demonstrates that a measure is related to a construct to which it is theoretically expected to be related. Discriminant validity assesses the degree to which a measure is not related to constructs to which it is not supposed to be related. Hence, it is the empirical counterpart of the notion that domain delineation spell out what a construct is not. Significant relationships with constructs to which a measure is expected to be related provide evidence of nomological validity, whereas nonsignificant relationships with constructs to which a measure is expected to be unrelated provide evidence of discriminant validity. However, such a statement is polarized in that evidence of small relationships could also provide evidence of either type of validity (e.g., the relationship between PNI and need for precision) (see Exhibit 1.6). For example, if the expected theoretical relationship is small and such a pattern is found, then it could provide evidence of either nomological or discriminant validity.

Discriminant validity and nomological validity are two sides of the same coin. A small relationship between a measure and another measure could provide evidence of both and could well be considered nomological validity; that is, are measures of constructs behaving in theoretically expected ways in nonrelationships or in small relationships? A simple version of discriminant validity is to show that a measure of a construct is unrelated to a measure of a construct to which it is not supposed to be related. For example, a measure of intelligence could be shown to have discriminant validity by showing a nonrelationship with stone throwing, a measure of arm strength. A measure of preference for numerical information could be shown to be unrelated to a measure of extroversion. Clearly, a completely unrelated measure could be selected from an infinite set to demonstrate discriminant validity. Often, measures are shown to be unrelated to individual differences in social desirability in order to demonstrate that the measure in question is not eliciting responses based on respondents' needs to appear socially desirable. Such assessments play an important role in showing that response tendencies unrelated to content drive scores on measures.

However, showing that a measure is unrelated to measures of other constructs may be a weak form of evidence of discriminant validity. After all, a construct would likely be unrelated to numerous constructs from completely unrelated domains. The need for a reasonable test arises only when there is some possibility of a relationship and a specific psychometric purpose in assessing the relationship, such as showing that a measure is not influenced by social desirability. For the PNI scale (Exhibit 1.6), its relationship with social desirability is assessed to show that responses are not being influenced by social desirability—a plausible alternative for students rating preference for numerical information. In a similar vein, showing that a measure is unrelated to a few measures from a large pool of potentially unrelated measures in itself does not provide sufficient evidence about the discriminant validity of the measure. Perhaps stronger evidence can be provided by showing that a measure has a small relationship with a measure of a construct to which it is likely to be related; that is, these related measures are indeed tapping into different constructs. For the PNI scale (Exhibit 1.6), its relationship with need for cognition is assessed to show a significant but small relationship. A subtler form of discriminant validity is to show a differential relationship between two related measures and a third measure. Examples of each of these types of evidence are presented below for the PNI scale (Exhibit 1.6). Here, the PNI scale and a measure of a construct to which it is strongly related are shown to have a differential relationship with a third measure. Thereby, the PNI scale is shown to be distinct from a measure of a construct to which it is strongly related.

Predictive validity is related to whether a measure can predict an outcome, and it has relevance in practical settings. In descriptive research, predictive validity is often subsumed under nomological validity. Known-groups validity is a form of predictive validity wherein a measure is shown to distinguish between known groups in terms of scores (e.g., differences in scores on measures between people with or without specific medical conditions in clinical settings, or differences in PNI scores for undergraduate majors in mathematics vs. art).

Construct validity is an umbrella term that asks the basic question, Does a measure measure the construct it aims to measure? There is no empirical coefficient for construct validity, just increasing amounts of evidence for it. Therefore, there is no correlation coefficient for construct validity, only degrees of evidence for it using all the types of validity listed above. Construct validity is the most important and most difficult form of validity to establish. It is akin to establishing causality between variables in substantive research, only causality is between a construct and its measure.

Although Exhibit 1.6 presents correlations between measures, it should be noted that structural equation modeling can be used to assess different types of validity while accounting for measurement error, such as unreliability in measures. Relationships between a focal measure and measures of other constructs in nomological validity tests can be assessed while accounting for measurement error. Discriminant validity can be shown by differential relationships between a target measure of a construct and a measure of a related construct and a third variable (Judd, Jessor, & Donovan, 1986). Discriminant validity could also be demonstrated by specifying a one- versus two-factor model of measures of two different constructs and showing that the two-factor model has superior fit.

An example of the entire measure development process for a somewhat different construct is presented in Exhibit 1.7. This construct is, in some ways, more complex than PNI and is used to illustrate a different scenario.

Exhibit 1.7   Developing a Scale of Consumer Literacy: A Different Type of Scale

---

Whereas the scales used as examples earlier relate to attitudes, other scales, such as intelligence tests, may be ability-related. Some scales may be on the margin between ability and attitude, such as the consumer literacy scale for people with low levels of literacy.

First Phase: Literature Review and Exploratory Interviews

In the first phase, exploratory research is undertaken to (a) examine parallel measures of ability and skill through a literature review; (b) assess adult education tests and textbooks for examples in consumer contexts; (c) examine assessment tools in literacy, adult education, and, more broadly, education, such as the National Adult Literacy Survey (1993); and (d) interview educators in adult education. The aim of this phase is to develop comprehensive grounding before developing the measure and conceptualizing the construct.

Second Phase: Conceptualization and Domain Delineation

In the second phase, the domain of consumer literacy is carefully delineated. In conceptually defining a construct, it should be sufficiently different from other existing constructs and should make a sizable contribution in terms of explanatory power. This step involves explicating what the construct is and what it is not. This is also a step where the proposed dimensionality of the construct is described explicitly. Keeping in focus the need to have a measure at the low end of the literacy continuum, this delineation of domain needs to list the basic skills necessary to complete fundamental tasks as consumers. A matrix of basic reading, writing, and mathematical skills versus consumer tasks should be created to provide a complete delineation. This listing of skills and associated consumer tasks needs to be examined by several individuals with different types of expertise, such as consumer researchers, adult education teachers, education researchers, and students at adult education centers who have progressed through to completion of the GED and further education. A team of experts can be formed consisting of teachers/directors at adult education centers, researchers in consumer behavior, and researchers in educational measurement. Experts can be provided with conceptual definitions of various dimensions of consumer literacy and associated listings of skills and consumer tasks and asked to evaluate the definitions and the domain delineation for completeness and accuracy. Such careful delineation of the domain is very important in any measure development process, all the more so for a construct as complex as consumer literacy.

(Continued)

(Continued)

Third Phase: Measure Construction and Content Validity Assessment

In the third phase, the measure should be constructed through item generation. In this phase, a large pool of items (i.e., consumer tasks) is developed to identify specific aspects of the domain explicated in the previous phase. A large pool of items is important, as are appropriate procedures to develop individual items. Redundancy is a virtue at this stage in the process, with the goal being to cover important aspects of the domain (DeVellis, 1991). Researchers have documented a host of issues that need to be addressed in developing items (DeVellis, 1991; Haynes et al., 1995). Several such procedures should be employed, such as asking experts to generate items on the basis of definitions of specific dimensions of consumer literacy, and asking experts to evaluate items in light of conceptual definitions. Thus, item generation draws on the team of experts mentioned in Phase 2. Through these means, the ever-pertinent issue of understanding of items by low-literate individuals is also addressed. Thus, items and usage conditions are assessed together and modified. The procedures discussed so far relate to the content validity of a measure, or whether a measure adequately captures the content of a construct. There are no empirical measures of content validity, only assessments based on whether (a) a representative set of items was developed and (b) appropriate procedures were employed in developing items (Nunnally, 1978). Hence, assessment of content validity rests on the explication of the domain and its representation in the item pool.

Fourth Phase: Reliability and Validity Assessment

In the fourth phase, empirical studies should be conducted to assess the reliability, dimensionality, and validity of the consumer literacy measure. Convenience samples can be drawn for all studies from students at adult education centers. This method also allows for access to the records of participants on important and relevant tests. The consumer literacy measure is broad in scope and ideally applies to low-literate individuals in general. In this regard, students at adult education centers should be distinguished from other functionally low-literate consumers in their motivation to become functionally literate. Nevertheless, the choice of students at adult education centers greatly facilitates efficient access and recruitment of a group that is very difficult to sample and provides a sound starting point. Convenience sampling is suited for these studies rather than probabilistic sampling because the aim is not to establish population estimates, but rather to use correlational analysis to examine relationships between items and measures. Several pilot tests should be conducted in which students at adult education centers complete the measure. Through observation and explicit feedback from students and teachers, the measure can be modified as needed. Such pilot testing is expected to be carried out in many stages, each using a small set of respondents, with the measure being adjusted between stages. Improvements in the measure during pilot testing, both in changing individual items and in addressing administration procedures, are likely to be considerable and to go a long way toward minimizing sources of measurement error in the final measure. Four to five larger scale studies are required in this phase, each employing sample sizes of 100–150. The first two to three large-scale studies should aim to assess and purify the scale through assessment of the reliability of individual items, and through initial assessment of validity and dimensionaity. Subsequent studies with a purified measure are more confirmatory and assess dimensionality as well as test validity in a detailed manner.

After item generation, measures typically are assessed for internal consistency reliability, and items are deleted or modified. Internal consistency frequently is the first empirical test employed and assesses whether the items in a set are consistent with each other or belong together. Such internal consistency assessment is pertinent in evaluating items within each dimension of consumer literacy for consistency in response.

An important form of reliability in this context is test-retest reliability, where the measure is completed twice by the same individuals with an interval of, typically, a few weeks. In a sense, test-retest reliability represents a one-to-one correspondence with the concept of reliability, which is centered on replicability or consistency. Test-retest reliability offers direct evidence of such consistency over time.

Exploratory factor analysis should be employed for preliminary evaluation of the dimensionality of the measure by assessing the degree to which individual items are correlated with respective dimensions or factors. However, confirmatory factor analysis is required for conclusive evidence (Gerbing & Anderson, 1988). Confirmatory factor analysis imposes a more restrictive model, where items have prespecified relationships with certain factors or dimensions.

Item-response theory (Hambleton, Swaminathan, & Rogers, 1991) offers another scaling technique that is particularly relevant here, because sets of items may require similar levels of skill. Therefore, responses to such sets of items may be similar. Item-response theory can specify the relationship between a respondent's level and the probability of a specific response. This approach can be used to assess measurement accuracy at different levels of ability and also to construct measures that have comparable accuracy across different levels of ability. The use of item-response theory for the National Adult Literacy Survey (1993) provides guidance in this regard.

Tests of different types of validity take measure development to the realm of cross-construct relationships. Whereas reliability establishes consistency and the lack of random error, validity pertains to whether a measure measures what it purports to measure (i.e., the lack of random and systematic error). Several types of validity need to be considered, and very brief descriptions are provided below along with examples of possible tests.

Content validity relates to a subjective judgment of content, based on adherence to proper procedures to delineate content domain and on generation of a representative set of items. For example, content validity could be assessed and enhanced by a team of experts reviewing the conceptual definition, domain delineation, and item generation. *Convergent validity* relates to whether the measure correlates or converges with another measure of the same construct. This type of validity is not directly applicable here because no other measure of consumer literacy is available.

(Continued)

(Continued)

However, a proxy measure can be created from current functional literacy measures using tasks oriented toward consumer economics. Other types of validity include *known-groups validity*, where a measure is shown to distinguish between known groups, such as individuals with or without an illness in clinical settings. In this context, this form of validity can be evaluated by assessing differences in the consumer literacy measure for students with 0 to 4th- versus 5th- to 8th- versus 9th- to 12th-grade reading levels. *Predictive validity* is related to whether a measure can predict a criterial outcome. In this context, one way in which predictive validity can be assessed is by relating the measure to performance in specific consumer tasks. *Nomological validity* demonstrates that a measure is related to a construct to which it is theoretically expected to be related. Examination of the relationship between consumer literacy and traditional functional literacy tests is an example of a nomological validity test. *Discriminant validity* assesses whether the measure of a construct correlates weakly or not at all with measures of constructs to which it is expected to relate weakly or not at all, respectively. Small or moderate correlations between a measure of consumer literacy and basic measures of reading literacy would provide a form of evidence of discriminant validity.

The aim of all of the measurement procedures described above is to provide evidence of *construct validity*, an umbrella term that asks the basic question, "Does a measure measure the construct it aims to measure?" There is no empirical coefficient for construct validity, just increasing amounts of evidence for it.

In all phases of measure assessment, both individual items and administration procedures need to be adjusted carefully. This is critical for the proposed measure; both the items of a measure and the conditions of their use have to be carefully assessed to minimize measurement error.

It should be noted that validity tests rest on several assumptions (Figure 1.19). To validate a measure of a construct by relating it to another measure of a different construct (say, in a test of nomological validity), it is important to use a reliable and valid measure of this different construct. It is also important to have a sufficient support for the hypothesized relationship between two constructs. Thus, only one of the three branches in Figure 1.19 is being tested and results can be interpreted clearly.

Looking at the broad picture of the relationship between reliability and validity, reliability is a necessary but not sufficient condition for validity. Although reliability and validity are both a matter of degree, generally speaking, a valid measure is reliable, but a reliable measure is not necessarily valid. Reliability is about random error, and if random error has not been reduced, the issue of validity does not arise.[12] If a measure is reliable, it

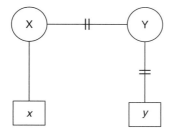

Figure 1.19   Assumptions of Validity Tests

Assumptions

- Construct X is related to Construct Y
- y is a reliable and valid measure of Y

$\therefore$ r_{xy} can be used to assess r_{xX}

$$r_{xy} = r_{xX} \cdot r_{XY} \cdot r_{Yy}$$

means that a large proportion of the total variance is due to common sources. Then, it is pertinent to discuss validity. Even if a measure looks face valid, if it is not reliable, it is not valid. Reliability and validity have been viewed as being the ends of a continuum where reliability relates to agreement between the same or similar methods, whereas validity relates to agreement between different methods (Campbell & Fiske, 1959). This view is consistent with the difference between reliability and convergent validity discussed here.

The multitrait-multimethod approach systematically examines the effect of using identical versus different methods (Campbell & Fiske, 1959). It can be illustrated using the PNI construct, essentially adapting similar matrices presented in past research (Campbell & Fiske, 1959) (see Figure 1.20). Consider three different ways of measuring preference for numerical information: (a) a self-report scale as shown earlier (self-report), (b) a rating by observers based on a half-hour of observation of behavior in a controlled setting on the degree to which individuals spend time with numerically oriented tasks (observation), and (c) a diary that individuals complete of numerically oriented tasks in which they engaged every day for a few weeks (diary method). Consider also two other traits that are measured through these three methods: Need for precision (NFP) (Viswanathan, 1997) and social desirability (SOC). A hypothetical pattern of correlations is shown in Figure 1.20 and represents data from the same individuals on these different methods and traits.

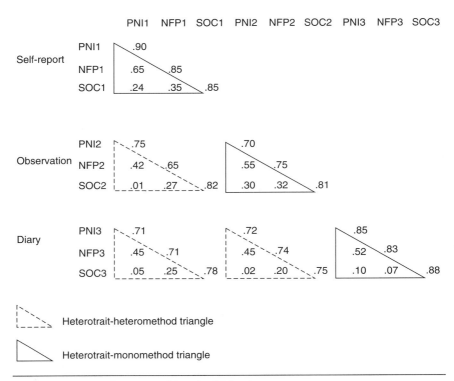

Figure 1.20   Multitrait-Multimethod Matrix

The reliability <u>diagonal</u> refers to the reliability of the measures and is essentially the correlation of a measure with itself. This is consistent with indicators of reliability, such as coefficient alpha, being the proportion of variance attributable to common sources and test-retest reliability being the test-retest correlation. Reliability is the relationship of a measure with itself. The validity diagonal (that is, heteromethod-monotrait) lists correlations between measures of the same construct using different methods. This is convergent validity, the relationship between two different measures of the same construct. The heterotrait-monomethod triangle shows the relationship between measures when using the same method. These correlations may have been inflated by the use of the same method, say, capturing individuals' tendencies to respond in certain ways to certain methods, such as in using the positive end of self-report scales. This is an example of a type of systematic error—consistent differences across individuals over and above the construct being measured—that may inflate or deflate correlations. Whereas random error reduces observed correlations, systematic error may inflate or deflate observed correlations. A simplified example of systematic error was illustrated with the weighing machine example. Subsequent chapters will introduce a nuanced discussion of systematic error. To examine the effect of method, these correlations have to be compared to the heterotrait-heteromethod triangle. The effect of using the same method can be gauged by comparing correlations between measures using different methods versus the same method. For example, the correlation between PNI and NFP is considerably lower when using observation for NFP and self-report for PNI (0.42) than when using self-report for both (0.65). Therefore, the differences in correlations using the same versus different methods provide an estimate of the effect of a common method. In contrast, the diary method does not have as much of a common method effect as self-report (0.52 vs. 0.45). Social desirability has a correlation of 0.24 and 0.35 with PNI and NFP, respectively, using self-report. However, for PNI, the corresponding correlations in the heteromethod-heterotrait triangle are considerably lower (0.01 and 0.05) but remain small but sizable for NFP (0.27 and 0.25). This pattern points to problems in the self-report NFP scale in terms of being associated with social desirability, an undesirable characteristic in this context. On the other hand, the diary method of assessing NFP does not have this problem.

The multitrait-multimethod approach outlined above suffers from several problems (Bagozzi & Yi, 1991). One problem is the absence of clear standards for ascertaining when any particular criterion is met, because only rules of thumb are available. Another problem is the inability to assess separate amounts of trait, method, and random error in the data, all confounded by examining only the raw correlations. Several assumptions are made, such as no correlations between trait and method factors, all traits being equally influenced by method factors, and method factors being uncorrelated (Bagozzi & Yi, 1991). The use of structural equation modeling for multitrait-multimethod matrices has several advantages, such as providing measures of the overall degree of fit and providing information about whether and how well convergent and discriminant validity are achieved (Bagozzi & Yi, 1991). Figure 1.21 illustrates such an approach where method factors are incorporated into the model. Other approaches to modeling the relationships include using correlated error terms between items that share the same method.

General Issues in Measurement

One issue about constructs is noteworthy: The strength and relevance of constructs may vary across people. The notion of a metatrait has been used

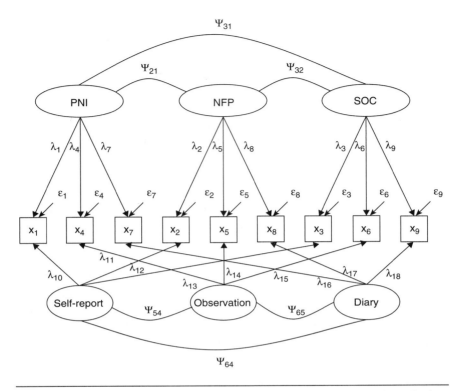

Figure 1.21   Using Structural Equation Modeling for Multitrait-Multimethod
Data

to refer to possessing or not possessing a trait (Britt, 1993). Moreover, many
questions used in a research design are really just that and do not purport to
assess an underlying abstract construct. For instance, they may assess specific
behaviors, such as spending on entertainment. Nevertheless, examination of
the intended thing being measured using the measure development process
described can be very beneficial. Such examination can lead to insights, precise wording of the question to enable consistent interpretation, and a broadened examination of multiple issues about this phenomenon through several
questions. For example, with entertainment spending, pertinent questions
relate to what entertainment is and what is included or excluded.

A few general points are noteworthy with regard to psychometrics. First,
relatively large sample sizes are essential for various psychometric procedures (Guadagnoli & Velicer, 1988; Nunnally, 1978). Small samples lead to
large sampling errors and add new forms of uncertainty into psychometric

estimates of reliability and validity. Coefficient alpha has a confidence interval associated with it as well that is based on sampling error (Appendix 1.1). Second, lack of sufficient variation inhibits the ability of an item to covary or correlate with other items and with the total measure. Covariations, reflected statistically in correlations, are the underpinning of psychometric analyses, and lack of sufficient variation inhibits the ability of an item to covary with other items. Third, although reliability and validity are the key concepts in measurement, dimensionality is discussed separately earlier. However, it is subsumed within validity, the aim being to understand what a measure is capturing both conceptually and empirically. Fourth, and more generally, measure validation is an ongoing process whereby measures are refined; items are added, modified, or deleted; dimensions are expanded; and constructs are redefined. Therefore, no single study is definitive in terms of measure validation. Fifth, empirical testing of measures rests on relative ordering, correlations being largely determined by relative standing between variables (Nunnally, 1978). Relationships examined in substantive studies in the social sciences are correlational in nature as well, reflecting the nature of the phenomenon and the precision with which relationships can be specified. Sixth, an attenuation formula to allow for unreliability in studying the relationship between two variables is available in the literature and presented in Appendix 1.1. However, there is no substitute for well-designed, reliable, valid measures to begin with. More generally, data analysis may not be able to account for problems in research design. Finally, generalizability studies may be a useful alternative by formalizing the effects of occasions and items (Cronbach, Rajaratnam, & Gleser, 1963; Rentz, 1987). Generalizability studies assess measurement error across facets or conditions of measurement, such as items, methods, and occasions. This approach relates to generalizing from observations to a universe of generalization consisting of the conditions of measurement of facets. Effects of facets and interactions between them are analyzed in this approach. The generalizability approach blurs the distinction between reliability and validity in that methods could be a facet of generalization (Rentz, 1987). However, this approach may be complex to design and implement (Peter, 1979).

Summary

Accurate measurement is central to scientific research. There are two basic types of measurement error in all of scientific research—random error and systematic error. Measures relatively free of random error are reliable, and measures relatively free of random and systematic error are reliable and valid.[13] The measure development process consists of a series of steps to develop reliable and valid measures. It starts out by carefully understanding what is being measured, through definition of the construct and delineation of its domain. Rather than proceed directly from an abstract construct to its concrete measurement, the distance between the conceptual and the operational has to be traversed carefully and iteratively. Internal consistency reliability, test-retest reliability, dimensionality, and validity tests are performed on measures, with items being added, modified, or deleted along the way.

Measure development should ideally combine empirical assessment with conceptual examination. A purely empirical approach may neglect the content of items, whereas a purely conceptual approach neglects empirical reality and how respondents are actually interpreting an item. A purely conceptual approach that neglects empirical results rests on the notion that the measure or individual items are reliable and valid no matter what the outcomes say. A purely empirical approach rests on the assumption that, somehow, item content and domain representation are irrelevant once data are collected. For instance, an item that has moderate item-to-total correlation may still be worth retaining if it is the only item that captures a certain aspect of the construct's domain. Even an item with low item-to-total correlation may be worth editing if its content is uniquely capturing some aspect of a construct's domain. Similarly, conceptual reasoning for an item cannot overrule poor empirical outcomes, which are essentially suggesting problems in the item's interpretation.

Low reliability and low validity have consequences. Random error may reduce correlations between a measure and other variables, whereas systematic error may increase or reduce correlations between two variables. If there is a key theme in all of this, it is that a construct and its measure are not the same, and imperfect measurement of any construct has to be taken explicitly into account.

A metaphor that can be used to understand measurement is to consider the universe and the location of specific planets or stars, which are like abstract concepts. Although we are unable to see them, they have to be located through paths from Earth to them, akin to a path from a measure to the underlying concept. Reliability refers to whether the paths (measures) can be reproduced across time. Convergent validity refers to whether two different paths (measures) converge on the same planet (construct). Discriminant validity refers to whether the path (measure) to one planet (construct) is different from a path (measure) leading to a different planet (construct). Nomological validity refers to whether the path (measure) relates to other known paths (measures) to different planets (constructs) in expected ways in light of where the target planet (construct) is expected to be. Construct validity refers to whether the path (measure) indeed leads to the intended planet (construct).

The book has so far provided a brief overview of traditional measure development procedures. The rest of the book will provide more in-depth understanding of measurement error leading to important insights for measure development and methodological design. Thus, the rest of the material will break new ground in understanding measurement error and methodological design.

Notes

1. Nunnally (1978) is cited throughout the book wherein both the Nunnally (1978) book and the later edition by Nunnally and Bernstein (1994) can be cited.

2. The term *measure* is sometimes used interchangeably with the term *scale* in this book.

3. Many words used in science, of course, refer to things other than constructs, such as umbrella terms referring to topic areas, stimuli, or artifacts, such as a not-for-profit organization. Any stimulus object could be viewed in terms of numerous underlying constructs, with the specific object having specific levels of magnitude on these constructs. A not-for-profit organization, for instance, needs to be differentiated from other organizations by isolating the key dimensions of distinction. A construct can be viewed as having levels that are either along a quantitative continuum or are qualitatively distinct.

4. Whether a true value really exists is a relevant issue. When dealing with psychological phenomena, responses are often crystallized where questions are posed. The notion of a true value that exists when all the factors of a response situation are controlled for is somewhat like the notion of infinity, a useful concept. What usually matters in the study of relationships in the social sciences is the accurate relative ordering of individuals or stimuli.

5. Consistency is a central element of scientific research. A key characteristic of science is replicability.

6. Can measurement error be categorized in some other way? Perhaps error can be classified further in terms of having constant versus variable effects. Subsequent discussion will address this issue.

7. Researchers have suggested alternative approaches to the measure development process. For example, the C-OARS-E procedure (Rossiter, 2002) emphasizes content validity. The steps in this procedure—reflected in the acronym—are Construct definition (where the construct is defined initially in relation to object, attribute, and rater entity, e.g., IBM's [object] service quality [attribute] as perceived by IBM's managers [raters]), Object classification (where raters are interviewed to classify object as concrete or abstract and items are developed accordingly), Attribute classification (where raters are interviewed to classify attributes similarly as objects), Rater identification (where the rater is identified), Scale formation (where the scale is formed from object and attribute items, response categories are chosen, and items are pretested), and Enumeration.

8. As the number of items in a measure increases, it could be argued that there is a greater likelihood of picking items to cover different aspects of a domain, akin to randomly picking states in the United States and covering the geographic area. In practice, though, the opposite may happen sometimes, where items are picked from one or a few subdomains. Moreover, the issue of representing different aspects of the domain is not one of reliability but one of validity. In fact, representing a broad domain may actually lower reliability while enhancing validity.

9. For oblique rotations, a factor pattern matrix and a factor structure matrix are reported in factor analysis. The former, which is easier to interpret and usually reported, shows the unique loadings of items on factors, whereas the latter shows correlations between items and factors that include correlations between factors (Hair et al., 1998).

10. Another issue in factor analysis is the use of factor scores, which are estimates of the values of common factors. Problems with factor scoring procedures suggest that careful evaluation of factor scores is needed before using them (Grice, 2001).

11. This type of factor analysis is referred to as R factor analysis and is distinguished from Q factor analysis, where individuals load on factors and correlations are computed across stimuli (Hair et al., 1998; McKeown & Thomas, 1988). For example, in a Q sort method, 53 respondents ranked 60 statements on morality by ordering them from −5 to +5 (i.e., most unlike to most like respondents' views) (McKeown & Thomas, 1988). The rankings were then correlated and factor analyzed. Groups of individuals loaded on specific factors. The Q factor analysis approach is not used often because of problems with computation (Hair et al., 1998).

12. One way in which reliability and validity have been illustrated is through bullet holes in a shooting target, wherein the bull's-eye is analogous with the construct that a measure aims to measure. A set of bullet holes close together in proximity suggests consistency and reliability, whereas a set of scattered bullet holes suggests unreliability. A set of bullet holes close together around the bull's-eye suggests reliability and validity.

13. These statements describe reliability and validity in a mathematical sense in terms of the types of error. It is possible for a measure to be perfectly reliable and valid in capturing an unintended construct. Therefore, validity relates conceptually to whether a measure measures the construct it purports to measure. Measurement of a different construct reliably and validly would not, of course, meet this requirement. For instance, the stone-throwing exercise may be a reliable measure of intelligence, and perhaps a valid measure of arm strength, but it is not a valid measure of intelligence because it lacks content validity. Therefore, the mathematical description of reliability and validity in terms of error, in some sense, works when it is assumed that the intended construct is captured along with error. In other words, the observed score is the sum of the true score and error. But in extreme scenarios, lacking the true score term to begin with because of measurement of the unintended construct, the mathematical expression does not fully reflect the concept of validity. Observed scores on an unintended construct may be viewed as reflecting scores on the intended construct. For instance, in the case of the stone-throwing exercise, consistency may be achieved internally; however, the pattern of responses would be unrelated to true scores on intelligence. Noteworthy is that the issue of reliability is internal to a measure.

Appendix 1.1

Selected Metrics and Illustrations in Measurement

Random and Systematic Errors

$X_o = X_t + X_r + X_s$
X_o = observed score
X_t = true score
X_r = random error
X_s = systematic error

SOURCE: Adapted from Churchill, 1979.

Illustration of Internal Consistency

Sample Item Responses for the PNI Scale After Reverse Scoring Items

				Items				
Respondents	N1	N2	N3	N4	N5	N6	N7	Total
1	1	2	2	1	2	2		31
2	3	3	4	2	3	3		58
3	4	4	5	3	3	3		83
99	5	6	6	4	4	5		102
100	7	7	6	5	6	7		122

NOTE: Responses are reverse scored so that higher values denote higher preference for numerical information.

Covariance:

$$\sigma_{xy} = \frac{\sum_{i=1}^{n}[(x_i - \bar{x}) \cdot (y_i - \bar{y})]}{n - 1}$$

Correlation$_{xy}$:

$$\frac{\text{Covariance}_{xy}}{\sqrt{\sigma_x^2 \cdot \sigma_y^2}}$$

σ_x^2 = x true score variance
σ_y^2 = y true score variance

Item-to-total correlation = Cov (N1, Total)/Sq rt [Var(N1)Var(Tot)]

$$Cov = Covariance$$
$$Var = Variance$$
$$Sq\ rt = Square\ root$$

Computation of coefficient alpha (DeVellis, 1991; Nunnally & Bernstein, 1994, p. 232)

$$Coefficient\ alpha = k\bar{r}/[1 + (k - 1)\bar{r}]$$
$$k = number\ of\ items\ in\ a\ measure$$
$$r = average\ interitem\ correlation$$

The expression of alpha presented above is based on a variance-covariance matrix of all the items in a measure. Alpha is the proportion of variance due to common sources. The elements in a covariance matrix can be separated into unique variances represented by diagonal elements and covariances between items represented by off-diagonal elements. A three-item example is shown below.

$$\begin{bmatrix} \sigma_{11} & \sigma_{12} & \sigma_{13} \\ \sigma_{21} & \sigma_{22} & \sigma_{23} \\ \sigma_{31} & \sigma_{32} & \sigma_{33} \end{bmatrix}$$

Alpha = [$k/(k - 1)$][1 – (Sum of unique elements/Sum of covariance elements)]
$k/(k - 1)$ is a correction term applied to restrict the range of alpha from 0 to 1.
For example, coefficient alpha = $k\bar{r}/[1 + (k - 1)\bar{r}]$
For a 3-item scale:
If $r = 0$, then alpha = 0; If $r = 1$, then alpha = $3 \cdot 1/[1 + (3 - 1)1] = 1$.

Attenuation Formula for Reliability

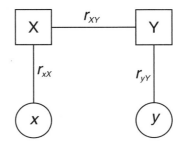

x is a measure of construct X
y is a measure of construct Y
r_{xy} = observed correlation between x and y
r_{XY} = true correlation between X and Y
r_{xX} = correlation between measure x and construct X
r_{yY} = correlation between measure y and construct Y

$$r_{xy} = r_{xX} \cdot r_{XY} \cdot r_{Yy}$$

r_{xX}^2 = reliability of x; r_{yY}^2 = reliability of y
(i.e., the proportion of variance attributed to the true score)

$$\therefore r_{xy} = \sqrt{\text{Rel}_x} \cdot r_{XY} \cdot \sqrt{\text{Rel}_y}$$

Rel_x = Reliability of measure x; Rel_y = Reliability of measure y
If r_{XY} = .5, Rel_x = .5, and Rel_y = .5,
Then = $r_{xy} = \sqrt{.5} \cdot .5 \cdot \sqrt{.5}$ = .25

SOURCE: Nunnally and Bernstein (1994), p. 241.

Kuder-Richardson Formula 20 for Reliability of Dichotomous Item Scale

$$r_{xx} = \frac{N}{N-1} \left(\frac{S^2 - \sum pq}{S^2} \right)$$

N = number of items
S^2 = variance of the total score
p = proportion passing each item; $q = 1 - p$

SOURCE: Nunnally and Bernstein (1994), p. 235.

Standard Error of Measurement (SEM) for Reliability

$$SEM = \sigma_x \cdot \sqrt{1 - r_{xx}}$$

σ_x = Standard deviation of the distribution of total scores on the test
r_{xx} = reliability of the test

SOURCE: Nunnally (1978), p. 239.

Illustration of Test-Retest Reliability

Respondents	N1	N2	N3	Total	RN1	RN2	RN3	RTotal
				Items				
1	1	2	2	31	2	2		29
2	3	3	4	58	3	3		59
3	4	4	5	83	3	3		77
99	5	6	6	102	4	5		98
100	7	7	6	122	6	7		127

NOTES: Responses on items N1, N2, and so on are at test, and RN1, RN2, and so on are at retest. Items are reverse scored so that higher values denote higher preference for numerical information. Total and RTotal are total scores at test and retest, respectively.

A Simplified Illustration of Exploratory Factor Analysis

The following are equations and computations showing the relationships between two uncorrelated factors and four items.

F = factor
x = item
l = loading or correlation between an item and a factor
e = error term

Numbers refer to different factors or items.

$$x_1 = l_{11}F_1 + l_{12}F_2 + e_1$$
$$x_2 = l_{21}F_1 + l_{22}F_2 + e_2$$
$$x_3 = l_{31}F_1 + l_{32}F_2 + e_3$$
$$x_4 = l_{41}F_1 + l_{42}F_2 + e_4$$

In matrix form:

$$\begin{bmatrix} x_1 \\ x_2 \\ x_3 \\ x_4 \end{bmatrix} = \begin{bmatrix} l_{11} & l_{12} \\ l_{21} & l_{22} \\ l_{31} & l_{32} \\ l_{41} & l_{42} \end{bmatrix} \times \begin{bmatrix} F_1 \\ F_2 \end{bmatrix} + \begin{bmatrix} e_1 \\ e_2 \\ e_3 \\ e_4 \end{bmatrix}$$

Communality of $x_1 = l_{11}^2 + l_{12}^2$.
More generally, communality of $x_i = \Sigma_{j=1}^{n} l_{ij}^2$, where i is the ith item and j is the jth factor with n factors.
Variance explained by F_1 in eigenvalues $= l_{11}^2 + l_{21}^2 + l_{31}^2 + l_{41}^2$.

More generally, variance explained by F_j in eigenvalues, $F_j = \Sigma_{i=1}^{m} l_{ij}^2$, where i is the ith item and j is the jth factor with m items.

A Simplified Illustration of Confirmatory Factor Analysis

In confirmatory factor analysis, rather than every item being allowed to be related to every factor (as shown in the equations earlier), specific models are tested. Consider a model where the first two of four items are hypothesized to load on the first factor and the last two items are hypothesized to load on the second factor.

$$x_1 = l_{11}F_1 + 0F_2 + e_1$$
$$x_2 = l_{21}F_1 + 0F_2 + e_2$$
$$x_3 = 0F_1 + l_{32}F_2 + e_3$$
$$x_4 = 0F_1 + l_{42}F_2 + e_4$$

In matrix form:

$$
\begin{bmatrix} x_1 \\ x_2 \\ x_3 \\ x_4 \end{bmatrix}
=
\begin{bmatrix} l_{11} & 0 \\ l_{21} & 0 \\ 0 & l_{32} \\ 0 & l_{42} \end{bmatrix}
\times
\begin{bmatrix} F_1 \\ F_2 \end{bmatrix}
+
\begin{bmatrix} e_1 \\ e_2 \\ e_3 \\ e_4 \end{bmatrix}
$$

Any correlation between items from different factors—say, x_1 and x_3—occurs only because of a relationship between F_1 and F_2. Confirmatory factor analysis assesses the degree to which the proposed model is consistent with the data in terms of relationships between items belonging to the same factor (say, x_1 and x_2) and the relationship between items belonging to different factors (say, x_1 and x_3). For instance, if an item actually measures two factors, then its relationship with an item from the second factor will be high, leading to a poor fit for the overall model. Confirmatory factor analysis assesses internal consistency across items from the same factors and external consistency across items from different factors.

Internal and External Consistency in Confirmatory Factor Analysis

The product rule for internal consistency for correlation between two indicators i and j of construct ξ, where t is the true score, is

$$\rho_{ij} = \rho_{i\xi}\rho_{j\xi}.$$

The product rule for external consistency for correlation between two indicators i and p, p being an indicator of another construct ξ^*, is

$$\rho_{ip} = \rho_{i\xi}\rho_{\xi\xi^*}\rho_{p\xi^*}.$$

SOURCE: Gerbing and Anderson (1988).

Expressions in Structural Equation Modeling

Reliability of item (Bagozzi, 1991)

$$\rho_{x_i} = \frac{\lambda_{x_i}^2}{\lambda_{x_i}^2 + \text{var}(\delta_i)}$$

Reliability of measure with p items (Bagozzi, 1991)

$$\rho_c = \frac{\left(\sum_{i=1}^{p} \lambda_{x_i}\right)^2}{\left(\sum_{i=1}^{p} \lambda_{x_i}\right)^2 + \sum_{i=1}^{p} \text{var}(\delta_i)}$$

Average variance extracted for measure with p items (Fornell & Larcker, 1981)

$$\rho_{vc} = \frac{\sum_{i=i}^{p} \lambda_{x_i}^2}{\sum_{i=1}^{p} \lambda_{x_i}^2 + \sum_{i=1}^{p} \text{var}(\delta_i)}$$

ξ = latent variable
x = observed variable
δ = error
λ = loading of x on ξ
var = variance

Alternative Overall Fit Indexes

Normed fit index (Bentler & Bonnett, 1980)

$$\frac{T_b^2 - T_n^2}{T_b^2}$$

T_b^2 = chi-square for baseline model
T_n^2 = chi-square for hypothesized model

Incremental fit index (Bollen, 1989)

$$\frac{T_b^2 - T_n^2}{T_b^2 - df_n}$$

df_b = degrees of freedom for baseline model
df_n = degrees of freedom for hypothesized model

Comparative fit index (Bentler, 1990)

$$\frac{(T_b^2 - df_b) - (T_n^2 - df_n)}{T_b^2 - df_b}$$

Tucker-Lewis index (Tucker & Lewis, 1973)

$$\frac{T_b^2/df_b - T_n^2/df_n}{T_b^2/df_b - 1}$$

Appendix 1.2

Sample Scales (Response Categories Adapted to 7-Point Scales for Convenience)

Consumer independent judgment-making (Manning, Bearden, & Madden, 1995[1])

	Strongly Disagree					Strongly Agree	
Prior to purchasing a new brand, I prefer to consult a friend that has experience with the new brand.	1	2	3	4	5	6	7
When it comes to deciding whether to purchase a new service, I do not rely on experienced friends or family members for advice.	1	2	3	4	5	6	7
I seldom ask a friend about his or her experiences with a new product before I buy the new product.	1	2	3	4	5	6	7
I decide to buy new products and services without relying on the opinions of friends who have already tried them.	1	2	3	4	5	6	7
When I am interested in purchasing a new service, I do not rely on my friends or close acquaintances that have already used the new service to give me information as to whether I should try it.	1	2	3	4	5	6	7
I do not rely on experienced friends for information about new products prior to making up my mind about whether or not to purchase.	1	2	3	4	5	6	7

Consumer novelty (Manning et al., 1995[1])

	Strongly Disagree					Strongly Agree	
I often seek out information about new products and brands.	1	2	3	4	5	6	7
I like to go to places where I will be exposed to information about new products and brands.	1	2	3	4	5	6	7
I like magazines that introduce new brands.	1	2	3	4	5	6	7
I frequently look for new products and services.	1	2	3	4	5	6	7
I seek out situations in which I will be exposed to new and different sources of product information.	1	2	3	4	5	6	7

I am continually seeking new product experiences.	1	2	3	4	5	6	7
When I go shopping, I find myself spending very little time checking out new products and brands.	1	2	3	4	5	6	7
I take advantage of the first available opportunity to find out about new and different products.	1	2	3	4	5	6	7

Material values—Defining success (Richins & Dawson, 1992[2])

	Strongly Disagree					Strongly Agree	
I admire people who own expensive homes, cars, and clothes.	1	2	3	4	5	6	7
Some of the most important achievements in life include acquiring material possessions.	1	2	3	4	5	6	7
I don't place much emphasis on the amount of material objects people own as a sign of success.	1	2	3	4	5	6	7
The things I own say a lot about how well I'm doing in life.	1	2	3	4	5	6	7
I like to own things that impress people.	1	2	3	4	5	6	7
I don't pay much attention to the material objects other people own.	1	2	3	4	5	6	7

Material values—Acquisition centrality (Richins & Dawson, 1992[2])

	Strongly Disagree					Strongly Agree	
I usually buy only the things I need.	1	2	3	4	5	6	7
I try to keep my life simple, as far as possessions are concerned.	1	2	3	4	5	6	7
The things I own aren't all that important to me.	1	2	3	4	5	6	7
I enjoy spending money on things that aren't practical.	1	2	3	4	5	6	7
Buying things gives me a lot of pleasure.	1	2	3	4	5	6	7
I like a lot of luxury in my life.	1	2	3	4	5	6	7
I put less emphasis on material things than most people I know.	1	2	3	4	5	6	7

Material values—Pursuit of happiness (Richins & Dawson, 1992[2])

	Strongly Disagree					Strongly Agree
I have all the things I really need to enjoy life.	1	2	3	4	5	6	7
My life would be better if I owned certain things I don't have.	1	2	3	4	5	6	7
I wouldn't be any happier if I owned nicer things.	1	2	3	4	5	6	7
I'd be happier if I could afford to buy more things.	1	2	3	4	5	6	7
It sometimes bothers me quite a bit that I can't afford to buy all the things I'd like.	1	2	3	4	5	6	7

Value consciousness (Lichtenstein, Ridgway, & Netemeyer, 1993[3])

	Strongly Disagree					Strongly Agree
I am very concerned about low prices, but I am equally concerned about product quality.	1	2	3	4	5	6	7
When grocery shopping, I compare the prices of different brands to be sure I get the best value for the money.	1	2	3	4	5	6	7
When purchasing a product, I always try to maximize the quality I get for the money I spend.	1	2	3	4	5	6	7
When I buy products, I like to be sure that I am getting my money's worth.	1	2	3	4	5	6	7
I generally shop around for lower prices on products, but they still must meet certain quality requirements before I will buy them.	1	2	3	4	5	6	7
When I shop, I usually compare the "price per ounce" information for brands I normally buy.	1	2	3	4	5	6	7
I always check prices at the grocery store to be sure I get the best value for the money I spend.	1	2	3	4	5	6	7

Price consciousness (Lichtenstein et al., 1993[3])

	Strongly Disagree					Strongly Agree
I am not willing to go to extra effort to find lower prices.	1	2	3	4	5	6	7

I will grocery shop at more than one store to take advantage of low prices.	1	2	3	4	5	6	7
The money saved by finding lower prices is usually not worth the time and effort.	1	2	3	4	5	6	7
I would never shop at more than one store to find low prices.	1	2	3	4	5	6	7
The time it takes to find low prices is usually not worth the effort.	1	2	3	4	5	6	7

Coupon proneness (Lichtenstein et al., 1993[3])

	Strongly Disagree					Strongly Agree	
Redeeming coupons makes me feel good.	1	2	3	4	5	6	7
I enjoy clipping coupons out of the newspaper.	1	2	3	4	5	6	7
When I use coupons, I feel that I am getting a good deal.	1	2	3	4	5	6	7
I enjoy using coupons regardless of the amount I save by doing so.	1	2	3	4	5	6	7
Beyond the money I save, redeeming coupons gives me a sense of joy.	1	2	3	4	5	6	7

Sale proneness (Lichtenstein et al., 1993[3])

	Strongly Disagree					Strongly Agree	
If a product is on sale, that can be a reason for me to buy it.	1	2	3	4	5	6	7
When I buy a brand that's on sale, I feel that I am getting a good deal.	1	2	3	4	5	6	7
I have favorite brands, but most of the time I buy the brand that's on sale.	1	2	3	4	5	6	7
I am more likely to buy brands that are on sale.	1	2	3	4	5	6	7
Compared to most people, I am more likely to buy brands that are on special.	1	2	3	4	5	6	7

Consumer ethnocentrism (Shimp & Sharma, 1987[4])

	Strongly Disagree					Strongly Agree	
American people should always buy American-made products instead of imports.	1	2	3	4	5	6	7

Only those products that are unavailable in the U.S. should be imported.	1	2	3	4	5	6	7
Buy American-made products. Keep America working.	1	2	3	4	5	6	7
American products, first, last, and foremost.	1	2	3	4	5	6	7
Purchasing foreign-made products is un-American.	1	2	3	4	5	6	7
It is not right to purchase foreign products.	1	2	3	4	5	6	7
A real American should always buy American-made products.	1	2	3	4	5	6	7
We should purchase products manufactured in America instead of letting other countries get rich off us.	1	2	3	4	5	6	7
It is always best to purchase American products.	1	2	3	4	5	6	7
There should be very little trading or purchasing of goods from other countries unless out of necessity.	1	2	3	4	5	6	7
Americans should not buy foreign products, because this hurts American business and causes unemployment.	1	2	3	4	5	6	7
Curbs should be put on all imports.	1	2	3	4	5	6	7
It may cost me in the long run but I prefer to support American products.	1	2	3	4	5	6	7
Foreigners should not be allowed to put their products in our markets.	1	2	3	4	5	6	7
Foreign products should be taxed heavily to reduce their entry into the U.S.	1	2	3	4	5	6	7
We should buy from foreign countries only those products that we cannot obtain within our own country.	1	2	3	4	5	6	7
American consumers who purchase products made in other countries are responsible for putting their fellow Americans out of work.	1	2	3	4	5	6	7

Need for cognition (Perri & Wolfgang, 1988[5])

	Strongly Disagree						Strongly Agree
I would prefer complex to simple problems.	1	2	3	4	5	6	7
I like to have the responsibility of handling a situation that requires a lot of thinking.	1	2	3	4	5	6	7

Thinking is not my idea of fun.	1	2	3	4	5	6	7
I would rather do something that requires little thought than something that is sure to challenge my thinking abilities.	1	2	3	4	5	6	7
I try to anticipate and avoid situations where there is likely chance I will have to think in depth about something.	1	2	3	4	5	6	7
I find satisfaction in deliberating hard and for long hours.	1	2	3	4	5	6	7
I only think as hard as I have to.	1	2	3	4	5	6	7
I prefer to think about small, daily projects to long-term ones.	1	2	3	4	5	6	7
I like tasks that require little thought once I've learned them.	1	2	3	4	5	6	7
The idea of relying on thought to make my way to the top appeals to me.	1	2	3	4	5	6	7
I really enjoy a task that involves coming up with new solutions to problems.	1	2	3	4	5	6	7
Learning new ways to think doesn't excite me very much.	1	2	3	4	5	6	7
I prefer my life to be filled with puzzles that I must solve.	1	2	3	4	5	6	7
The notion of thinking abstractly is appealing to me.	1	2	3	4	5	6	7
I would prefer a task that is intellectual, difficult, and important to one that is somewhat important but does not require much thought.	1	2	3	4	5	6	7
I feel relief rather than satisfaction after completing a task that required a lot of mental effort.	1	2	3	4	5	6	7
It's enough for me that something gets the job done; I don't care how or why it works.	1	2	3	4	5	6	7
I usually end up deliberating about issues even when they do not affect me personally.	1	2	3	4	5	6	7

Consumer susceptibility to interpersonal influence (Bearden, Netemeyer, & Teel, 1989[6])

	Strongly Disagree					*Strongly Agree*	
I often consult other people to help choose the best alternative available from a product class.	1	2	3	4	5	6	7

If I want to be like someone, I often try to buy the same brands that they buy.	1	2	3	4	5	6	7
It is important that others like the products and brands I buy.	1	2	3	4	5	6	7
To make sure I buy the right product or brand, I often observe what others are buying and using.	1	2	3	4	5	6	7
I rarely purchase the latest fashion styles until I am sure my friends approve of them.	1	2	3	4	5	6	7
I often identify with other people by purchasing the same products and brands they purchase.	1	2	3	4	5	6	7
If I have little experience with a product, I often ask my friends about the product.	1	2	3	4	5	6	7
When buying products, I generally purchase those brands that I think others will approve of.	1	2	3	4	5	6	7
I like to know what brands and products make good impressions on others.	1	2	3	4	5	6	7
I frequently gather information from friends or family about a product before I buy.	1	2	3	4	5	6	7
If other people can see me using a product, I often purchase the brand they expect me to buy.	1	2	3	4	5	6	7
I achieve a sense of belonging by purchasing the same products and brands that others purchase.	1	2	3	4	5	6	7

Notes

1. From Manning, K. C., Bearden, W. O., & Madden, T. J., Consumer innovativeness and the adoption process, in *Journal of Consumer Psychology*, 4(4), copyright © 1995, pp. 329–345. Reprinted by permission.

2. From Richins, M. L., & Dawson, S., Materialism as a consumer value: Measure development and validation, in *Journal of Consumer Research*, 19, pp. 303–316, copyright © 1992. Reprinted by permission of the American Marketing Association.

3. From Lichtenstein, D. R., Ridgway, N. M., & Netemeyer, R. G., Price perceptions and consumer shopping behavior: A field study, in *Journal of Marketing Research*, 30, pp. 234–245, copyright © 1993. Reprinted by permission of the American Marketing Association.

4. From Shimp, T. A., & Sharma, S., Consumer ethnocentrism: Construction and validation of the CETSCALE, in *Journal of Marketing Research*, 24,

pp. 280–289, copyright © 1987. Reprinted by permission of the American Marketing Association.

5. From Perri, M., & Wolfgang, A. P., A modified measure of need for cognition, in *Psychological Reports*, *62*, pp. 955–957, copyright © 1988. Reprinted by permission.

6. From Bearden, W. O., Netemeyer, R. G., & Teel, J. E., Measurement of consumer susceptibility to interpersonal influence, in *Journal of Consumer Research*, *15*, pp. 473–481, copyright © 1989. Reprinted by permission.

2

What Is Measurement Error?

Overview

What is measurement error? Chapter 2 will attempt to answer this question. Scientific observations have been conceptualized as being the sum of true scores and error, with the latter being categorized into random and systematic error (e.g., Churchill, 1979). The two central concepts in scientific measurement are reliability and validity. Reliable measures are relatively free of random error. Valid measures are relatively free of both random and systematic error (Churchill, 1979; Nunnally, 1978). This chapter provides an in-depth discussion of random and systematic errors in measurement.[1] Different types of measurement error will be described with concrete examples. Measurement error will be divided more finely into types of random and systematic error. Random error is categorized into generic random error, which affects a large proportion of respondents, and idiosyncratic random error, which affects a small proportion of respondents and is likely to be accounted for in large samples. Systematic error is categorized into additive systematic error, which inflates or deflates responses in a constant way across individuals, and correlational systematic error, which refers to consistent differences across individuals over and above the construct being measured. Illustrations show how these errors are manifest in responses. An exercise is presented in Appendix 2.1 that illustrates the relationship between errors in measurement, response patterns, and sources of error. This exercise can be completed again after Chapter 3 to enhance understanding.

Random Error

Random error is any type of error that is inconsistent or does not repeat in the same magnitude or direction except by chance. Using the weighing machine example, random error occurs when repeated readings for a person whose weight has not changed are all over the place. Gulliksen (1950) defines random error in a statistical sense in terms of the mean error, the correlation between the error and the true score, and correlation between errors being zero. Nunnally (1978) uses the example of a chemist who, because of blurred vision, reads a thermometer incorrectly and consequently records the temperature to be slightly higher or lower, over many readings, leading to a distribution of errors. Bagozzi (1984) describes random error as the result of several forces (such as variations in data collection) that tend to cancel out in the long run. Ghiselli (1964) describes unsystematic variation as occurring when no trend is discernible from differences in responses across occasions. In essence, a way to visualize random error conceptually is to examine whether inconsistent responses are provided across time (or items) when the phenomenon in question has not changed (such as an enduring trait). For instance, Item 12 of the PNI scale in Chapter 1 lacks consistency with other items. The very notion of consistency implies consistency across some unit, such as time or items.

Some causes of random error include complex wording or language, questions requiring estimation, vagueness in questions or response categories (Churchill, 1979; Nunnally, 1978), the nature of administration through distracting factors and inconsistent administration procedures (cf. Churchill, 1979), and personal factors such as mood. Random error may be due to some aspect of the item, such as ambiguous wording, that causes respondents to provide a response with some variation (e.g., "Numbers are redundant for most situations" may be an item where what represents "most situations" may vary considerably). Such random error may attenuate correlations between an item and other items or measures. Considering consistency across time for illustrative purposes, the presence of such factors as ambiguity can lead to responses that are not consistent over time. Respondents may be unable to provide consistent responses for a variety of reasons, such as not knowing the answer because it requires estimation ("How much beer did you drink last year?"), unclear wording, ambiguity in wording ("Do you exercise regularly?"), or double-barreled questions ("Do you like the price and quality of this product?"). Respondents may provide an answer that is inconsistent, such as taking a wild guess. The test of inconsistency across time is whether a different (i.e., inconsistent) response would have been obtained if the question had been posed again. The assumption in retesting is that respondents do not recall their previous answer (hence, a sufficient time interval is needed). This is akin to the weighing machine not having any memory of previous weighings. Moreover, the phenomenon is assumed to be unchanged. Thus, the notion of inconsistency across time is premised on some sort of retesting, even if actual retesting does not occur. A thought experiment has to be conducted: Will the question lead to consistent responses across time when the phenomenon has not changed?

Systematic Error

Systematic error is any error that has a consistent effect. Systematic error results from consistent but inaccurate responses. Gulliksen (1950) refers to systematic error as constant error, using the example of a tape measure that has stretched over time, leading to constant underestimation. Using the weighing machine example from Chapter 1, readings that are consistently off in one direction reflect systematic error, although additional nuances are discussed subsequently. Causes of systematic error could be leading or biased questions, or aspects of the measurement process that typically cause respondents to be unwilling to provide an accurate response (e.g., "Do you support the president's stance on . . . ?"). Being unwilling to provide an accurate response, respondents may provide a response that is inaccurate, yet consistent. For example, with a leading question, respondents may consistently provide a response that is more acceptable. With a question requiring estimation of the amount of beer consumed, respondents may systematically underestimate the true value if they want to downplay their amount of drinking.

The literature on questionnaire design has often distinguished between respondents being unable versus unwilling to provide a response. Unwillingness to provide an accurate answer typically arises with threatening questions, such as those on sensitive topics requiring private information. Inability to provide an accurate answer arises because of factors such as difficult or ambiguous questions. Factors such as leading questions may lead respondents to provide inaccurate but consistent responses. Random error is usually caused by a respondent's inability to answer questions accurately. However, it should be noted that random error might also be due to respondents being unwilling to provide a response and therefore filling in a random response. For example, if a question on income is viewed by respondents as being intrusive, they may deliberately provide a wildly inaccurate answer. Similarly, respondents may also provide consistent responses when they are unable to answer accurately, such as through using the middle alternative. Moreover, the distinction between inability and unwillingness is itself often blurred as a function of the underlying psychological mechanisms involved in response generation. Nevertheless, a useful rule of thumb is that inability may lead to random error, and unwillingness may lead to systematic error.

Types of Random and Systematic Error

Although generic definitions of random and systematic error were provided above, finer distinctions need to be made within these types of errors for a complete understanding of measurement error. Illustrations are provided through sample responses in Exhibit 2.1 and mathematical notations in Exhibit 2.2.

Exhibit 2.1   Illustrations of Types of Measurement Error Through Scale Responses

The following represents a very simplified representation of scale responses that reflect certain types of errors. Because only a specific type of error is represented in each set of responses and the number of respondents is low, actual correlations are inflated and unstable, and inferences drawn from them can be misleading. Likely changes in correlations rather than actual changes for the data set below are discussed.

Time 1

	T	I	G1	G2	G3	A1	A2	C1	C2	C3	C4	C5
I1	10	10	9	5	10	10	10	7	10	8	2	6
I2	9	9	9	2	9	10	10	7	10	7	6	5
I3	8	8	10	3	8	10	10	6	10	6	9	5
I4	7	5	9	7	7	9	10	6	9	8	6	6
I5	6	6	5	10	6	8	10	6	9	9	4	5
I6	5	5	3	8	5	7	10	5	2	1	10	6
I7	4	4	6	4	4	6	9	5	2	6	5	6
I8	3	3	5	6	3	5	8	5	1	5	10	5
I9	2	2	1	1	2	4	7	4	1	5	9	6
I10	1	1	2	7	1	3	6	4	1	4	3	5

Time 2

	T	I	G1	G2	G3	A1	A2	C1	C2	C3	C4	C5
I1	10	10	10	1	10	10	10	7	10	8	2	6
I2	9	9	10	5	10	10	10	7	10	7	6	5
I3	8	8	6	8	10	10	10	6	10	6	9	5
I4	7	7	9	5	10	9	10	6	9	8	6	6
I5	6	8	6	3	9	8	10	6	9	9	4	5
I6	5	5	4	10	8	7	10	5	2	1	10	6
I7	4	4	6	4	7	6	9	5	2	6	5	6
I8	3	3	2	9	6	5	8	5	1	5	10	5
I9	2	2	1	8	5	4	7	4	1	5	9	6
I10	1	1	3	2	4	3	6	4	1	4	3	5

NOTE: I1 to I10 = Respondents.

(Continued)

T = Item that captures true score without error.

I = Item with idiosyncratic random error for respondent I4 at Time 1 and I5 at Time 2; correlation with T and with itself across time is not significantly affected with large sample sizes; high internal consistency and high stability.

G1 = Item with generic random error illustrated by adding +2 through −2 randomly at test and at retest; item captures true score with some random error; correlation with T and with itself across time is decreased; decreased internal consistency and stability (decreased correlations are when compared to the correlation between T and the true score, i.e., 1).

G2 = Item with generic random error illustrated by generating a set of random numbers; item has correlation close to zero with true score; very low internal consistency and stability.

G3 = Item with random error across administrations illustrated by responses at Time 2 that reflect an interaction between setting and item, such as upward additive effect, at second administration; decreased stability.

A1 = Item with additive systematic error generated by adding 2 to true scores; correlation with T is slightly decreased; high internal consistency and high stability.

A2 = Item with additive systematic error generated by adding 3 to true scores; correlation with T is decreased; decreased internal consistency and high stability.

C1 = Item with within-measure correlational systematic error due to a common method such as extreme response anchors leading to use of middle response categories; decreased internal consistency and high stability.

C2 = Item with within-measure correlational systematic error due to a common method such as moderate response anchors leading to use of extreme response categories; inflated/decreased internal consistency and high stability.

C3 = Item with within-measure correlational systematic error due to a different trait/method that is positively related to true score; decreased internal consistency and high stability.

C4 = Item with within-measure correlational systematic error due to a different trait/method that is unrelated to true score; low internal consistency and high stability.

C5 = Item with correlated systematic error, use of the middle alternatives due to inability or unwillingness to respond to items, high negative chance correlation between true score and method factor leading to very low correlation of item with true score; low internal consistency.

Idiosyncratic Versus Generic Random Errors

A distinction can be made between idiosyncratic random error, which affects a small proportion of individuals in an administration—such as those that result from mood or language difficulties—and generic random error, which has a broad-based effect across a sizable proportion of respondents in an administration, such as those that result from item-wording effects (Figure 2.1; Exhibit 2.1, columns I, G1, and G2). Using the example of a weighing machine, if reading errors in a study of weight are restricted to a small proportion of individuals—say, errors due to reading the weight from different angles—then large sample sizes will likely minimize such error. In Exhibit 2.1 (column I), idiosyncratic random error occurs when a single respondent provides a response that is unrelated to other responses. Such

Exhibit 2.2   Mathematical Representation of Measurement Error

---

$x_{o1} = x_{t1} + d_{as1} + d_{cs1} + d_{r1}$

$x_{o2} = x_{t2} + d_{as2} + d_{cs2} + d_{r2}$

x_{o1} = observed score on Item 1

x_{o2} = observed score on Item 2

x_{t1} = true score on Item 1

x_{t2} = true score on Item 2

d_{as1} = additive systematic error in Item 1

d_{as2} = additive systematic error in Item 2

d_{cs1} = correlational systematic error in Item 1

d_{cs2} = correlational systematic error in Item 2

d_{r1} = random error in Item 1 (if proportion of observed scores with random error is low; d_{r1} is idiosyncratic random error)

d_{r2} = random error in Item 2 (if proportion of observed scores with random error is low; d_{r2} is idiosyncratic random error)

$Cov(d_{r1}, x) = 0$; $Cov(d_{r2}, x) = 0$; where x = other variables (e.g., x_1, x_2, d_{as1}, d_{as2}, d_{cs1}, d_{cs2}); $E(d_{r1}) = 0$; $E(d_{r2}) = 0$

d_{as1} = constant; d_{as2} = constant; $Cov(d_{as1}, x) = 0$; $Cov(d_{as2}, x) = 0$

$r_{xo1,xo2} = Cov(x_1 + d_{as1} + d_{cs1} + d_{r1})(x_2 + d_{as2} + d_{cs2} + d_{r2})/$

$$[(Var(x_1) + Var(d_{as1}) + Var(d_{cs1}) + Var(d_{r1})*$$

$$(Var(x_2) + Var(d_{as2}) + Var(d_{cs2}) + Var(d_{r2})]$$

$$= Cov(x_1, x_2) + Cov(x_1, d_{cs2}) + Cov(x_2, d_{cs1}) + Cov(d_{cs1}, d_{cs2})/$$

$$[(Var(x_1) + Var(d_{as1}) + Var(d_{cs1}) + Var(d_{r1})*$$

$$(Var(x_2) + Var(d_{as2}) + Var(d_{cs2}) + Var(d_{r2})]$$

NOTE: x_{t1} and x_{t2} are items at test, and x_t is a measure at test. x_{r1} and x_{r2} are items at retest, and x_r is a measure at retest.

error may occur because of a number of factors, such as language difficulties, the individual in question being in an extreme mood, or an error in the mechanics of completing the response. The key here is that such error is restricted to a small proportion of the entire sample and hence is <u>not likely to affect overall statistics</u>. Such a distinction is useful in understanding the relationship between certain sources of random error commonly discussed in the literature, such as mood, and likely outcomes in terms of error. For

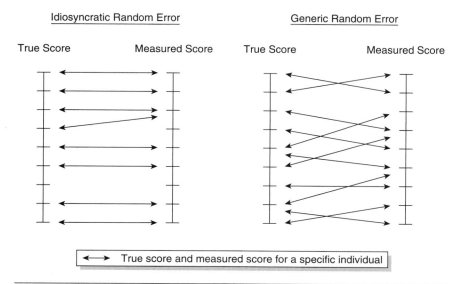

Figure 2.1   Type of Measurement Error

instance, mood is often suggested as a source of random error, when it may well be a source that leads to idiosyncratic random error that can be minimized through the use of sufficiently large sample sizes. If sources of random error, such as mood state, are assumed to conform to a normal distribution, then outliers that cause random error are likely to be idiosyncratic in nature. Some factors that can cause idiosyncratic random error are presented in Chapter 3.[2]

Generic random error is reflected in the responses of a sizable proportion of respondents. Typically, such generic random error is likely to be caused by factors with pervasive effects, such as item wording (e.g., ambiguous wording) or the nature of the setting (e.g., a noisy setting). The distinction between idiosyncratic random error and generic error may be blurred as a function of the proportion of respondents who are affected by a factor or error source, such as mood. For example, differences in language ability may be idiosyncratic, whereas item wording problems may be more broad-based and may affect a sizable proportion of respondents, thereby leading to generic random error. Nevertheless, the distinction between idiosyncratic and generic random error is very useful in conceptual examination of the likely outcomes of specific sources of error and enables the researcher to identify and categorize the likely nature of error. Factors such as mood are often suggested as sources of random error along with other factors, such as ambiguous wording. Here, a useful distinction can be made between sources that are likely to lead to idiosyncratic random error versus those likely to lead to generic random error.

Random error in measures attenuates observed relationships (Nunnally, 1978).[3] When a measure with random error and unreliability is related to a measure of a different construct in substantive research, the observed relationship is likely to be smaller than the true relationship. Whereas the effect of idiosyncratic random error can be minimized through larger sample sizes, generic random error in the measurement of a construct attenuates relationships. The effects of errors on relationships hold on average and relate to expected values rather than individual outcomes. In a statistical sense, idiosyncratic random error is a form of sampling error that can be minimized with larger samples. In this regard, Nunnally (1978) has pointed out the importance of large samples in measurement because measurement indicators, such as coefficient alpha, themselves have a degree of precision or a confidence interval associated with them as a function of sample size, as discussed in Chapter 1.[4]

Random Error Within Versus Across Administrations

As the various descriptions of the concept of random error suggest, a fundamental characteristic of random error is that it is expected to average out over many readings to a mean of zero. Such averaging could be across different units, across time or administrations, or across items within a single administration. Hence, an important distinction is between random error within an administration—reflected in inconsistent responses within a single administration—and random error across administrations or occasions—reflected in inconsistent responses across administrations (Figure 2.1; Exhibit 2.1, column G3 across Times 1 and 2). For instance, random error in items in an administration may average out across multiple items, assuming a large set of items. Similarly, random error could average out across a large set of administrations. In practice, however, large sets of administrations are not feasible, which is another reason for minimizing random error during measure development.

A response to an item may be sensitive to factors across administrations, such as interactions with settings and mood. As mentioned earlier, it is useful to distinguish between idiosyncratic random error and generic random error that affects the entire administration. If responses to an item have idiosyncratic random error in both administrations, such error is addressed through large samples (Exhibit 2.1, column I across Times 1 and 2). Factors such as mood have been mentioned in the literature as potential sources of random error (Churchill, 1979). An item requiring aggregation across events or behaviors (e.g., "Generally speaking, retail outlets do not cheat") may lead to different responses for people in a negative mood. If such a pattern of responses is restricted to a small proportion of individuals (i.e., is idiosyncratic), such a possibility can be minimized through large samples and the assumption of a normal distribution of mood in the first and second administrations. On the other hand, an interaction between an item and a variable, such as setting or interviewer effect, that varies across administrations and affects a sizable proportion of respondents will likely lead to random error across administrations. For example, if an item is prone to interviewer effects and there is inconsistency across administration in the degree to which interviewers lead the respondents, or in interviewer appearance and associated perceptions of socially desirable answers, this could cause generic random error across administrations. If other aspects of administrations are inconsistent, such as the use of distracting settings in one administration, all of the items or the items that are susceptible to distracting factors (e.g., more difficult items) may be affected. In this regard, Ghiselli (1964) distinguishes between varying unsystematic factors that vary across individuals on a single occasion (e.g., comfort of seating, lighting, hearing based on distance from instructor, transient individual factors such as fatigue) and constant unsystematic factors that affect all individuals in a similar way but vary across occasions (e.g., poor lighting throughout an administration). Varying unsystematic factors can cause idiosyncratic and generic random error within an administration as well as across administrations, whereas constant unsystematic factors can cause generic random error across administrations.[5]

Figure 2.2 summarizes the types of error in a single administration and their influence on generic random error across administrations and stability. Idiosyncratic random error does not affect stability assuming sufficient sample sizes. Generic random error within administrations can lead to generic random error across administrations, as indicated by the negative directionality of the relationship between such error and the stability of an item.

Additive Versus Correlational Systematic Error

As discussed in Chapter 1, a way of visualizing systematic error is in terms of a thermometer or a weighing machine that consistently deviates from the true value in a specific direction by a constant sum, say, as a result of an error in calibrating the zero point on the device (Figure 2.3; Exhibit 2.1, columns A1 and A2). Such error is a type of systematic error called additive systematic error. As shown in Exhibit 2.1, additive systematic error inflates or deflates responses by a constant magnitude and may result in reduced correlations with other items. It should be noted that additive systematic

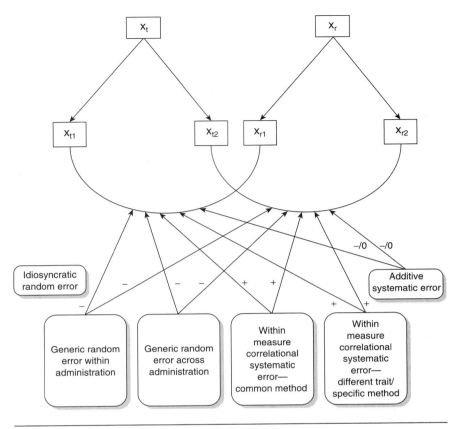

Figure 2.2   Random Error Across Administrations

NOTE: X_{t1} and X_{t2} are items at test, and X_t is a measure at test. X_{r1} and X_{r2} are items at retest, and X_r is a measure at retest.

error can be constant across responses and therefore have no effect on relationships, or it can be partial in the sense that the additive effect deflates or inflates responses to one end of the scale and restricts variance (Figure 2.3). This issue is discussed in more depth subsequently in this chapter. Such additive error could be caused by several factors, such as leading questions, interviewer bias, unbalanced response categories, consistently lenient or stringent ratings due to wording or other factors, or a tendency to agree or disagree. Factors that cause responses to be consistently off in one direction across respondents lead to additive systematic error.[6] An item in the PNI scale such as "Learning and remembering numerical information about various issues is a waste of time," that is somewhat extremely worded in terms of "waste

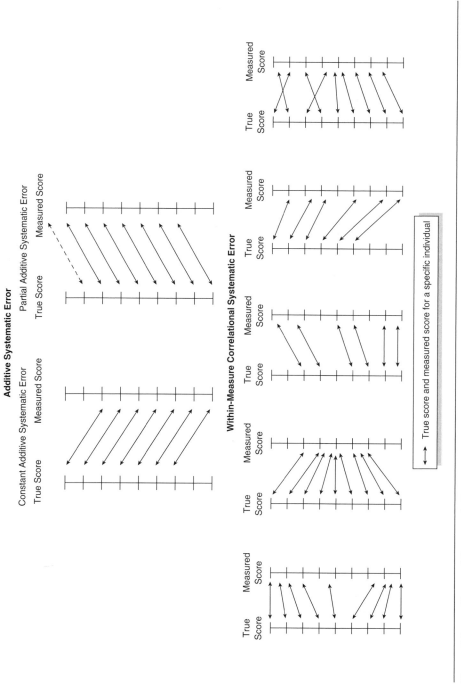

Figure 2.3   Types of Systematic Error

of time," can lead to additive systematic error. However, such additive systematic error (i.e., consistent error that deviates by a constant magnitude from the true score) is not as problematic in academic research when compared to survey research. Academic research emphasizes accurate estimates of relationships between variables rather than accurate estimates of absolute values (Groves, 1991). Additive errors matter only to the extent that they reduce scale variance and consequently deflate correlations. In this regard, Nunnally (1978) highlights the importance of relative standing in typical statistical analyses used in the social sciences, which are correlational in nature. Correlations are largely influenced by relative standing of values on variables (Nunnally, 1978). To the extent that relative standing along variables is preserved, correlations are not significantly affected.

A more problematic form of systematic error is correlational systematic error, which consistently deflates or inflates the relationship between two or more variables (Figures 2.3 and 2.4; Exhibit 2.1, columns C1 to C4). Correlational error occurs when individual responses vary consistently to different degrees over and above true differences in the construct being measured; that is, it is a result of different individuals responding in consistently different ways over and above true differences in the construct. Using the weighing machine example, if readings are off in a certain direction and also in proportion to somebody's weight, then that is an example of correlational error (e.g., if the weighing machine shows an additional 5 pounds for a 100-pound person and an additional 10 pounds for a 200-pound person).

In Exhibit 2.1, correlational systematic error is illustrated in responses reflecting consistent individual differences over and above true differences in the construct being measured. C1 is an item with correlational systematic error due to a common method, such as extreme response anchors (e.g., hate-love), leading to the use of middle response categories. Correlational systematic error occurs if different individuals interpret and use response categories in consistent but different ways. For example, C1 is an item with correlational systematic error due to a common method, such as extreme response anchors, leading to the use of middle response categories, whereas C2 is an item with correlational systematic error due to a common method, such as moderate response anchors (e.g., like-dislike), leading to the use of extreme response categories. Correlational systematic errors can be caused by the use of response scales of a similar format across items, including what are referred to in the literature as method factors. For example, a certain set of response categories is employed (say, *very good* to *very bad*) and respondents interpret the categories in certain ways (*very good* means more or less positive for different respondents). In this scenario, the covariance across items will be due, at least partially, to the method factor, or the use of

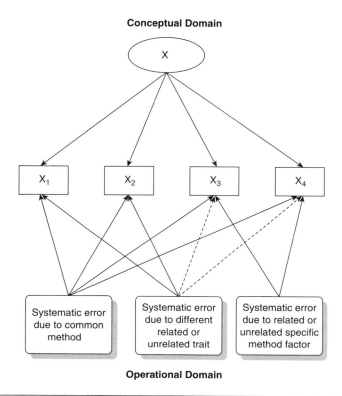

Figure 2.4   Within Measure Correlational Systematic Error

NOTES: X = Construct; x_1 to x_4 = items of a measure of construct X; common method refers to aspects of the method that are common across all items; specific method refers to aspects of the method that influence a subset of items; trait may affect a subset of items or all items and this is shown above with a combination of dashed and solid lines

identical response formats (see Andrews, 1984). Similarly, correlational systematic error may arise as a result of other aspects of the research method, such as variation in the interpretation of the instructions and the questions (Andrews, 1984).[7] Such error may arise out of items tapping into different traits. For instance, items of the consumer ethnocentrism scale (Appendix 1.2), such as "Buy American-made products. Keep America working" and "American products, first, last, and foremost," may tap into individual differences in social desirability.

Additive systematic error in an administration can have either no effect or a negative effect on stability and test-retest correlations if it is high enough to significantly inhibit variation on an item[8] (Figure 2.2). Additive systematic error is likely to have no effect or to attenuate relationships due to decreased variance. It should be noted that any constant additive error, by definition, cannot affect correlations. The point here, however, is that if there is an additive effect and finite end points to a scale, then responses are all biased upward (or downward) toward the end of the scale, thus reducing its variance and its ability to covary. In a strict sense, if additive systematic error is restricted to pure additive effects that are unaffected by the ends of a scale (e.g., an additive effect of +1 on a 7-point scale where all values are 6 or below), then additive systematic error would have no effect on correlations. As noted later, the form of error where an additive effect decreases variance due to finite scale ends could also be discussed as being a different type of systematic error. Here, it is referred to as partial additive systematic error and is subsumed under additive systematic error. Correlational systematic error can strengthen or weaken observed relationships (Nunnally, 1978). Consistent differences across individuals over and above the construct being measured may be positively correlated, negatively correlated, or not correlated with the construct.

Within-Measure Correlational Systematic Error

Correlational systematic error can be distinguished within measures versus across measures. The latter refers to correlational systematic error that occurs between measures of different constructs. Within-measure correlational systematic error occurs between different items of a measure. It can be the result of responses to items being influenced by the use of a common method or by different trait or specific method factors that may or may not be related to the trait being measured (Figures 2.3 and 2.4; Exhibit 2.1, columns C1 to C4). For instance, all the positively worded items in the PNI scale may be influenced by individual differences in tendencies to agree. Some items in the consumer ethnocentrism scale (Appendix 1.2) may be influenced by social desirability in responses. Within-measure correlational systematic error due to a common method factor is used to refer to aspects of the method that are common across all items, such as response categories (Figures 2.3 and 2.4). This is similar to the use of the term *common method factor* in a multitrait, multimethod context (Campbell & Fiske, 1959). Within-measure correlational systematic error due to a common method factor may arise from the use of the same response format, similar stems, or the completion of items in close proximity, and it can typically lead to inflated relationships between items of a measure. Within-measure correlational systematic error can also occur as a result of items measuring different traits or method factors than intended. For instance, such error can occur due to the measurement of a different but closely related trait, or the influence of specific method factors that affect a few items, such as social desirability in wording (Figures 2.3 and 2.4). Some method factors may affect a few items, such as shared context or social desirability effects. For instance, some items in the value consciousness scale may share the context of a grocery store (Appendix 1.2). Some items may also tap into different traits due to their substantive content. Such traits or method factors may be positively or negatively related or unrelated to the focal construct, leading to different directional effects for such systematic error.[9] If the trait being measured by an item is positively related to the focal construct, but a method or a different trait captured by the same item is negatively related to the focal construct (essentially, the sum of two systematic errors), then the item will be identified as having random error (i.e., the item would not be correlated with other items that actually capture the focal construct).[10] The distinction between a common method factor affecting all items and specific method factors affecting a subset of items may be blurred as a function of the number of items that are affected by specific method factors. Nevertheless, this distinction is useful to examine the nature of measurement error in a measure.[11] Within-measure correlational systematic error can have a positive influence on stability, such as the consistent measurement of a different but stable method factor or construct (Figure 2.2).

An example of within-measure correlational systematic error is halo error in the completion of items within a measure—a tendency to provide similar responses across items that are thought to be related (see Chapter 3). Researchers have demonstrated how responses to earlier items of a measure can affect responses to later items, with the latter becoming more polarized and more consistent with adjacent responses (Feldman & Lynch, 1988; Knowles, 1988; Simmons, Bickart, & Lynch, 1993). Knowles and Byers (1996) demonstrate the increased reliability of later items through the clarifying role played by earlier items. Such error can be as a result of a within-measure halo effect in that a general impression based on earlier items influences responses to later items. Therefore, responses to later items are consistent with responses to earlier items. Responses to the first item in the PNI scale, "I enjoy work that requires the use of numbers," may affect responses to subsequent items.

Across-Measure Systematic Error

Whereas within-measure correlational systematic error occurs between items of a measure, across-measure correlational systematic error occurs across measures of different constructs. Essentially, across-measure correlational systematic error occurs if measures of different constructs are influenced by a trait or a method factor, or by different but related traits or method factors, thus inflating or deflating true correlations between them (Figures 2.5 and 2.6). A common method factor that affects both measures is a source

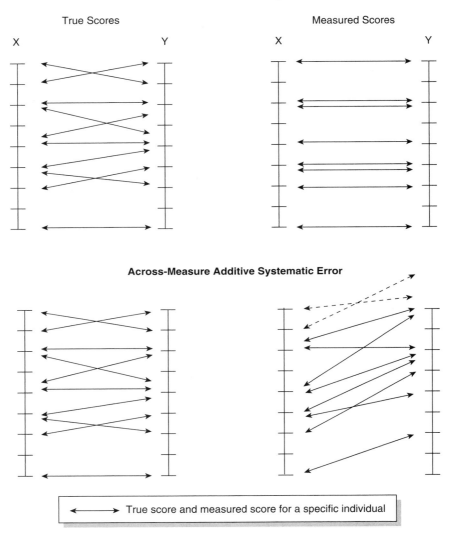

Figure 2.5   Across-Measure Systematic Error

of across-measure correlational systematic error. For example, the use of the same paper-and-pencil method (that taps, say, a response style of using certain parts of the scale) is likely to inflate correlations. Likewise, if subsequent measures are influenced by earlier ones, then the scales completed first introduce systematic error in later measures. For example, hypothesis guessing may

Conceptual Domain

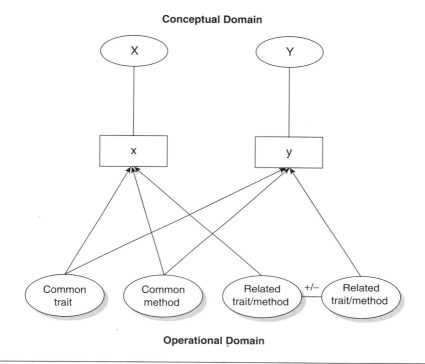

Operational Domain

Figure 2.6   Across-Measure Correlational Systematic Error

NOTE: X and Y are constructs and x and y are measures of these constructs.

result from responses to the first measure influencing responses to the second measure. If data are collected on the value consciousness scale followed by the price consciousness scale (Appendix 1.2), responses to the first measure may influence responses to the second measure. In data collection involving two constructs, error in a measure that is completed second in sequence by respondents may be correlated with the true score as well as with error in the first measure. For instance, consider a study where both perceived quality and perceived value of a product are measured, perceived value capturing benefits weighed against costs, or what a consumer receives weighed against what has to be given in return, such as price paid. Responses to one may influence responses to the other. The reverse is not possible in research designs where sequencing of measures is controlled, but it may occur when sequencing is not controlled, such as in mail surveys. Use of common instructions or even the same page for different measures can also cause correlational systematic error (Lennox & Dennis, 1994). Across-measure correlational systematic error also occurs when a subset of items from measures, rather than entire measures, is influenced by a different trait or method factor. For instance, a subset of items in the value consciousness scale and the price consciousness scale (Appendix 1.2) may share the context of a grocery store.

It should be noted that across-measure systematic error could also lead to an additive effect that does not affect correlations (Figure 2.5). Completion of one measure may lead to inflated responses on a subsequent measure (i.e., across-measure constant additive systematic error). When finite endpoints play a role, such inflation could decrease correlations (i.e., across-measure partial additive systematic error). For example, completion of the coupon proneness scale may prime sales events and lead to inflated ratings on the sale proneness scale (Appendix 1.2). Or, inflated ratings may be obtained on the consumer ethnocentrism scale if it follows a patriotism scale (Appendix 1.2). Whereas the correlational type can inflate or deflate correlations, the additive type can either deflate or not affect correlations. Therefore, the broader term, *across-measure systematic error*, is used here. Narrower terms that specify the correlational or additive nature of error are used to describe the specific types of across-measure systematic error.[12]

In summary, a host of errors identified in the literature fall under the rubric of systematic errors of an additive or a correlational nature. Systematic errors can be distinguished within measures versus across measures. Within-measure correlational error can occur because of a common method and also because of different traits or specific method factors.

Illustrations of Measurement Error Through Response Patterns

Measurement error is illustrated in Exhibit 2.1 through response patterns. In column 1, responses to an item consist of a set of random numbers. Although the item may have been designed to measure a construct, responses to the item are purely random and therefore completely unrelated to the construct being measured. Such random responses can be caused by a variety of factors, such as complex wording, lengthy wording, or question difficulty. They also can be caused by respondents being unable to provide a response, thereby providing a random response. Because the response is purely random, it will be uncorrelated with other variables. As illustrated in Figure 2.7, purely random responses provide a stark demonstration of the effects of random error on two measures that are perfectly correlated. Random error attenuates relationships with variables. Hence, if Y is a variable whose measure is completely random in nature and X is a variable that is measured without error, random error in Y leads to an insignificant correlation with X. Items that are completely influenced

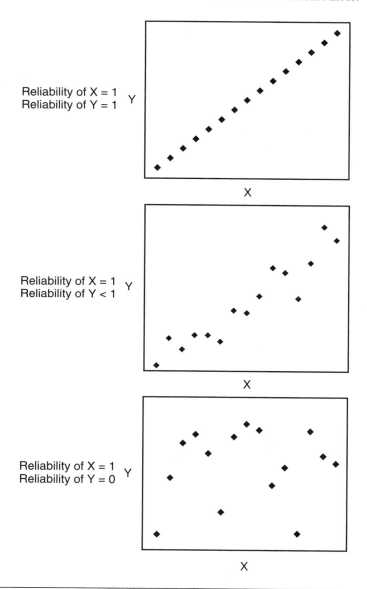

Figure 2.7   Effect of Random Error on Relationship Between Measures

by random error can be identified because of their insignificant correlation with other items measuring the same construct. However, this is provided that multiple items are used to measure a construct, emphasizing the dangers of using a single-item measure. If single-item measures are used, low correlations with other variables may be due to unreliability and may not be detectable.

Item responses may also be partially influenced by random error. In Exhibit 2.1, such responses are generated by randomly adding a number from −2 to +2 (column G1). Such partial random error may be due to some aspect of the item, such as ambiguous wording, that causes respondents to provide a response with some variation (e.g., "Numbers are redundant for most situations" may be an item where what represents "most situations" may vary considerably). Such random error may attenuate correlations between an item and other items/measures. Several factors may lead to random error, such as a lack of clarity in wording, items requiring estimation, confusing/ambiguous category labeling, and a high number of response categories. Some aspects of administration, such as a distracting setting, variations in administration, and fatigue because of lengthy procedures, may also cause random error.

Random error may also occur in the responses of a small proportion of individuals, that is, idiosyncratic random error (Exhibit 2.1, column I). An individual in a distracted state of mind may provide random responses. Transient individual mood states may affect the responses of a small proportion of individuals. Usually, such transient states are likely to lead to random error in responses for a small proportion of individuals. However, some aspect of the administration or setting may affect the transient states of a large proportion of respondents (e.g., a noisy setting or bad weather). Some factors that may lead to idiosyncratic random error include language difficulties experienced by a small proportion of respondents, which may lead to random responses. Similarly, variation in administration factors may lead to idiosyncratic random error, as may mechanical/motor vacillations in completing responses.

Exhibit 2.1, columns A1 and A2, demonstrate additive systematic error and the effect of a factor that inflates or deflates all responses. Such a factor may not affect correlations or may deflate correlations by reducing the variance. If the additive effect is minimal, item responses may capture most of the variance, and, hence, correlations with other items/measures may not be affected. However, sizable additive effects may reduce variance—when responses are inflated or deflated toward either end of a scale—thus reducing variation. In measure development, such instances can be identified through item means. For example, such error can be caused by leading questions, questions that require estimation and are likely to be over- or underestimated (e.g., "How much alcohol did you consume last week?"), or items that are stated in the extreme ("Have you ever . . . ?"). These questions may cause respondents to consistently inflate or deflate their responses.

In columns C1 to C5, several types of correlational errors are presented. If response categories lead respondents to provide more extreme responses, this leads to consistent differences across respondents over and above differences in the construct being measured. Hence, correlational error occurs when there are consistent, individual differences over and above the construct being measured. At the other extreme, if response categories lead respondents to use the middle of a scale, correlational error is negatively related to the construct being measured.

Random and systematic error can jointly manifest in responses to items such as the amount of beer consumption last year, where there may be a tendency to underestimate (or overestimate) and a random component. This pattern, a combination of columns G1 and A1, is essentially a combination of random and additive systematic error. Similarly, a combination of columns G1 and C1 (i.e., random error and correlational systematic error) could occur. Such combinations may be more realistic representations of actual response patterns than any single error.

Patterns of Responses in Measurement Error

What are the possible patterns in data responses beyond idiosyncratic and generic random error? A consistent additive effect constant across individuals is one pattern. A consistent dispersive effect is another, say, one that moves responses toward extremes on opposite sides of the scale (Figure 2.3). This effect may be constant across individuals; it could move responses toward the extreme end of the scale to which they are closer by one unit, yet it is not an additive effect but a correlational effect in that there are consistent differences across individuals (i.e., ones on the high end vs. the low end) over and above the construct being measured. Any dispersive effect is correlational because differences across individuals over and above the construct being measured are reflected. A consistent effect that varies across individuals is another. If an additive effect occurs in response patterns that varies consistently across individuals (i.e., more additive for some, less for others), then the effect is not just additive but correlational as well (i.e., these two elements can be separated). If a tendency to use the extremes of scales varies across individuals, it is like an additive effect for each individual but represents consistent differences across individuals over and above the construct being measured.

Additive patterns at one end of a scale (say, a +2 for all respondents) may manifest as correlational patterns, because the ends of the scale prevent the full additive component from being reflected in responses. For instance, consider a question that leads respondents toward the positive end of a scale through an addition of two scale points. If three respondents' true ratings are 5, 6, and 7 out of 7, then this is akin to correlational systematic error that is due to the finite end points of the scale. It represents consistent differences over and above the construct being measured of +2, +1, and 0, respectively. Here, this kind of error is subsumed under additive systematic error and referred to as partial additive systematic error, as distinct from constant additive systematic error (Figure 2.3). Such error could just as easily have been referred to as partial correlational systematic error, but the arbitrary choice of partial additive systematic error works well with the content in this book.

This discussion brings out the continuous nature of the distinction between additive and correlational systematic error. As long as there are constant additions across individuals that are not affected by finite end points, the effect is additive. If additive effects vary across individuals, then they could be partitioned into additive systematic error and correlational systematic error. For instance, a question may be leading across all respondents by a unit of +1, but responses may additionally reflect consistent differences across individuals over and above this effect (say, 0, +1, or +2 for different individuals depending on their tendencies toward providing a socially desirable response). Dispersive effects consistent across individuals are correlational, that is, they lead to consistent differences in the construct being measured and an additional dispersive effect. For instance, if the use of mild end anchors (like-dislike) leads some respondents to choose one extreme and others to choose the other extreme, this is correlational systematic error. In reality, all of these effects are combined into a response pattern.

Although the extreme scenarios of additive systematic error or correlational systematic error (i.e., individual differences on a variable over and above the construct in question) are relatively easy to distinguish, subtler forms of errors arise. With finite scale extremes, there is a temptation to label additive systematic error as correlational systematic error, especially because errors are outcomes, not sources. However, it is useful to conceptually distinguish additive systematic error further into constant additive systematic error and partial additive systematic error, the latter occurring because of finite end points. Thus, the umbrella of additive systematic error is used here to describe these two types of error. Due to finite scale extremes, partial additive systematic error may lead to reduced variance and, hence, lower correlations, never enhancing them. Additive systematic error either does not affect correlations or reduces them, whereas correlational systematic error may inflate or deflate or not affect correlations. Other sources lead to nonadditive error, such as constant dispersions, which, because of finite scale extremes, may affect correlations. Correlational systematic error was defined earlier as consistent differences across individuals over and above the construct being measured. Such error disperses or converges responses, or it differentially deflates or inflates responses across individuals over and above differences along the construct being measured. It is useful to distinguish such error from additive error that may be constant or nonconstant (partial additive), the latter case arising because of finite end points of the scale.

A variety of response errors can be reflected in scale responses—biased upward, downward, to the middle, to the extremes, all over the place, and so on. If error is random, then responses have a random spread to them. If responses are purely random, the entire response is determined by random error. The responses would have only chance correlations with other variables and a correlation likely to be close to 0 on average with large sample sizes. If responses are partially random, then there is a consistent component overlaid with some random variation. If there is no random component, then the only possible error is consistent in nature.

Consistent error can inflate or deflate in an additive form, compress or decompress in a correlational form (e.g., like an elastic band), or be some combination of the above. Inflation and deflation may have the indirect effect of compression because scales have finite end points. Hence, if true scores are marks on a portion of a partially extended elastic band, error that forces responses toward the middle versus the extremes can be represented by an unextended versus a fully extended elastic band.

On the other hand, constant additive bias would be represented by movement of the entire band in one direction. With finite end points, movement in one direction may also cause compression. Random error is represented by random movements of the band in either direction. When there is partial random error, this is the case. With complete random error, the elastic band is twisted to lose ordinality. Errors that affect a small proportion of individuals would be categorized under idiosyncratic random error. For example, distraction due to a noisy setting that affects few respondents may lead to such random error. An inadvertent wrong check-off is similar. In summary, a variety of sources can lead to outcomes (i.e., errors). An understanding of sources that are germane in a situation and errors they may cause is most useful in conducting research.

Summary

Measurement error can be categorized as random and systematic error. Each of these types of errors can be further categorized into subtypes: idiosyncratic and generic random error, additive (constant and partial) systematic error, within-measure correlational systematic error, and across-measure systematic error. These types of error are reflected in response patterns that are assessed by psychometric procedures. Every distinct type of error does not have a unique correspondence with a distinct type of response pattern. For instance, response patterns for partial additive systematic error cannot be distinguished from some types of correlational systematic error.

Chapter 3 shows that a variety of sources of error lead to specific types of error. Using the category of errors presented here, likely sources of error can then be related to each type of error. Through an understanding of the relationships between various sources of error and different types of error, the development of items, measures, and methods can be improved. Chapter 4 shows that psychometric procedures used to analyze response patterns confound different types of error.

Notes

1. Both random and systematic error are defined here in terms of the net outcomes. Outcomes should be distinguished from sources that are typically associated with random and systematic error. This is an important distinction because a variety of factors can cause respondents to provide responses that have random error. For example, unclear words in an item may lead to respondents being unable to provide a response and, therefore, a random response. However, the same factor may also lead to systematic error if respondents adopt a strategy of using the middle alternative when they are unable to provide a response. Sources typically associated with random error, such as ambiguous wording, may lead to random error or sometimes systematic (i.e., consistent) error as well, as in the case of ambiguous wording leading to use of the middle alternative. Hence, separating the sources of errors from the errors is important. Ghiselli (1964) makes a similar distinction between unsystematic and systematic errors and unsystematic and systematic factors causing error.

2. In a statistical sense, idiosyncratic random error is a form of sampling error that can be minimized with larger samples. In this regard, Nunnally (1978) has pointed out the importance of large samples in measurement because measurement indicators such as coefficient alpha themselves have a degree of precision associated with them as a function of sample size.

3. Random error can inflate observed relationships in multivariate analysis (Bollen, 1989).

4. More generally, empirical outcomes reflecting conceptual categories of measurement error discussed here can be translated into the language of statistics, although strict parallels are not possible. For example, idiosyncratic versus generic error in psychometric language does not fully parallel sampling versus measurement error in statistical language, which is based on whether or not parameter estimates are biased. Measurement error in statistics includes several types of errors in addition to generic random error, such as additive and correlational systematic error, that can also bias parameter estimates. Moreover, omitted variables and misspecification biases can also cause systematic error in a statistical sense.

5. Factors internal to a measure, such as item wording, versus factors external to it, such as administration, do not correspond with random error within versus across administrations. In a single administration, factors such as interviewing and distracting setting can cause random error within the administration. Similarly, item wording may cause random error across administrations. Vaguely worded items may be subject to different interpretations by the same individual across time.

6. *Additive* systematic error is used here as the preferred term to indicate a constant additive effect similar to its usage in a variety of research, including experimental research, and contrasted with *correlational systematic error, which is not a constant additive effect. Other possible terms that could be used here include constant versus nonconstant systematic error*. Although additive and correlational errors are distinguished here, nonlinear errors, such as multiplicative errors, may also occur (Bagozzi & Yi, 1991; Campbell & O'Connell, 1967; please see Bagozzi, 1993, and Bagozzi & Yi, 1992, for examples and discussion). One such example is listed in Chapter 3.

7. It should be noted that systematic error encompasses more than just the use of the same method and relates to all aspects of the research method that may influence responses. For example, two measures completed in close proximity may lead to hypothesis guessing even if different methods are used in a single administration, such as a paper-and-pencil method and actual behavior. In this regard, method variance has been used to refer to variance due to the method rather than the construct being measured, and it varies in level of abstraction from item wording and scale types to halo effects and social desirability (Bagozzi & Yi, 1991; Fiske, 1982). Systematic error has also been categorized as being form-related (e.g., leniency error arising out of the response format) and respondent-related (e.g., the halo effect arising out of respondents' perceptions) (Bardo, Yeager, & Klingsporn, 1982). Campbell and Fiske (1959) distinguish between shared method variance and basic trait similarity in their classic work on multitrait-multimethod matrices. The key point to note here is that everything that is done by way of collecting the data—including the setting, the method of administration, and the type of questionnaire—is a part of the method and can lead to systematic error. Whether a method employs paper and pencil versus some other procedure is just one aspect of the entire research method.

Several sources of systematic error have been identified in the literature. *Response set* is an umbrella term defined as the criteria by which respondents assess item content (Rorer, 1965). Response set issues have been widely researched in the falsification of responses to personality tests (Edwards, 1957; Meehl & Hathaway, 1946). Nunnally (1978) differentiates between response styles (i.e., consistent individual differences due to measurement problems) and response biases (i.e., differences in average responses due to measurement problems). Systematic error sources include leniency (i.e., consistently positive ratings) and stringency (i.e., consistently negative ratings). Social desirability bias refers to presentation in a favorable light (Edwards, 1957; Fisher, 1993; Furnham, 1986) and can lead to systematic error. The experimental literature has identified factors such as hypothesis guessing, which could lead to systematic error (Cook & Campbell, 1979). One specific form of systematic error is halo error, which relates to the use of a global impression to complete ratings on various distinct dimensions (Lance, LaPointe, & Stewart, 1994). A common form of systematic error arises when agreement toward an item indicates presence of a trait, with responses thereby capturing a tendency to acquiesce instead of, or over and above, the construct in question (Lennox & Dennis, 1994).

8. In theory, even with minimal variation, test-retest correlation can be computed and should be unaffected by additive systematic error. This line of reasoning examines the effect of additive systematic error strictly in isolation. In this strict sense, when additive systematic error fully inhibits variation (say, inflates all values to a 7 on a 7-point scale), test-retest correlations cannot be computed; however, when there is even minimal variation, test-retest correlation should be unaffected.

In practice, however, additive systematic error is likely to occur in combination with other types of error. Therefore, additive systematic error is likely to negatively impact test-retest correlation when it significantly inhibits variation.

9. It should be noted that whether a factor is a different trait or method is dependent on the nature of the focal construct; for example, social desirability could be a trait or a method factor (Crowne & Marlowe, 1964).

10. Systematic error includes responses that are consistently in the middle of the scale because of, say, difficult wording (Exhibit 2.1, column 5). This error is correlational or proportionate in the sense that there is not a constant addition to the true score across individuals, but that the actual addition or subtraction from the true score varies, with the net effect being the choice of the middle alternative. It is useful to distinguish such proportionate systematic error that is, in essence, a convenient inference drawn from a response pattern that is unaffected by the true score or any other trait, from other types of correlational systematic error that are the result of a trait and/or method. This pattern represents a consistent effect that is caused by sources that typically lead to random error; hence, it is useful to distinguish between errors and their *sources* as discussed earlier and explained in Chapter 3.

11. Within-measure correlational systematic error may also be inferred when researchers model a construct as being unidimensional when it is, in fact, multidimensional.

12. In categorizing errors in this book, the term *correlational* is used to distinguish from additive in the sense of consistent differential effects across individuals versus constant effects across individuals. Therefore, these differential effects across individuals covary with differences because of the construct in question. Dictionary meanings of the term *correlational* include the description of a simultaneous change in value of two variables. Here, correlational error is used to refer to such a simultaneous change in value across individuals on the construct in question and on the differential effects across individuals over and above the construct in question.

Across-measure correlational systematic error is used in terms of consistent differential effects across individuals over and above the construct being measured for a measure on which data are collected along with another measure in the context of a method. Therefore, the term *across measure* is used to suggest that measures of different constructs are influenced by a trait or a method factor, or by different but related traits or method factors, thus inflating or deflating true correlations between them. In this regard, responses to a subsequent measure may be affected by completion of a preceding measure and, more generally, by the use of a common method. Such an effect could also be additive—completion of one measure may lead to inflated ratings on a subsequent measure. Therefore, the broader term *across-measure systematic error* is used here. Narrower terms that specify the correlational or additive nature of error are used to describe the specific types of across-measure systematic error.

SEM ↓ Account of measurement error.

Regression ↓ measurement itself is construct. (No measure error)

What Is Measurement Error? 123

Appendix 2.1

Exercise on Individual Responses and Error

This hypothetical exercise is useful in illustrating errors and their sources.

Random Error

Consider a set of individual responses to a 10-item measure of a unidimensional construct—say, PNI—where N1 to N10 refer to items, and I1 to I10 refer to individuals (where responses from 1 to 10 happen to be their true scores, respectively). The assumption here is that each item has identical true scores; each item is a mirror reflection of others in terms of distribution of true scores.

	N1	N2	N3	N4	N5	N6	N7	N8	N9	N10	Total
I1	10	10	10	10	10	10	10	10	10	10	100
I2	9	9	9	9	9	9	9	9	9	9	90
I3	8	8	8	8	8	8	8	8	8	8	80
I4	7	7	7	7	7	7	7	7	7	7	70
I5	6	6	6	6	6	6	6	6	6	6	60
I6	5	5	5	5	5	5	5	5	5	5	50
I7	4	4	4	4	4	4	4	4	4	4	40
I8	3	3	3	3	3	3	3	3	3	3	30
I9	2	2	2	2	2	2	2	2	2	2	20
I10	1	1	1	1	1	1	1	1	1	1	10

Now, this looks like a perfect measure, but of course, it is most unrealistic to find in practice.

To understand the role of random error in reliability, consider all items being driven by PNI except Item 10, which is completely determined by random errors. The set of numbers in N10 is replaced by a set of random numbers. Naturally, the item-to-total correlation of this item is likely to be close to zero on average. Random error typically results in reduced correlations. Also, the total score now does not reflect the true score.

	N1	N2	N3	N4	N5	N6	N7	N8	N9	N10	Total
I1	10	10	10	10	10	10	10	10	10	7	97
I2	9	9	9	9	9	9	9	9	9	2	83
I3	8	8	8	8	8	8	8	8	8	4	76
I4	7	7	7	7	7	7	7	7	7	5	68
I5	6	6	6	6	6	6	6	6	6	9	63
I6	5	5	5	5	5	5	5	5	5	3	48
I7	4	4	4	4	4	4	4	4	4	1	37
I8	3	3	3	3	3	3	3	3	3	10	37
I9	2	2	2	2	2	2	2	2	2	8	26
I10	1	1	1	1	1	1	1	1	1	6	15

Question: What are some sources that could cause such random error?

This is perhaps an unrealistic picture, because although some item responses may be completely determined by random error, most item responses are typically caused by both the construct and random error. This can be simulated by adding a random component to a true component as shown for N9, by adding a number from –2 to +2 to the true response.

	N1	N2	N3	N4	N5	N6	N7	N8	N9	N10	Total
I1	10	10	10	10	10	10	10	10	8	7	95
I2	9	9	9	9	9	9	9	9	10	2	84
I3	8	8	8	8	8	8	8	8	6	4	74
I4	7	7	7	7	7	7	7	7	5	5	66
I5	6	6	6	6	6	6	6	6	6	9	63
I6	5	5	5	5	5	5	5	5	5	3	48
I7	4	4	4	4	4	4	4	4	2	1	35
I8	3	3	3	3	3	3	3	3	1	10	35
I9	2	2	2	2	2	2	2	2	4	8	28
I10	1	1	1	1	1	1	1	1	2	6	16

The scores for individuals are now approximate when compared to true scores.

Question: This exercise can be attempted with random error for each item. What does this do to the total score?

Question: What are some sources that could cause such random error?

Question: In light of earlier answers, what does random error mean? How can it be minimized?

Before moving on, consider for a moment the notion of test-retest reliability. If measuring individuals across time, similar tables for items for two administrations could be created. Now consider Items 8, 9, and 10 across two administrations, assuming for a moment that Item 8 is perfect, Item 9 has some random error, and Item 10 is completely determined by random error.

	Time Period 1				Time Period 2			
	N8	N9	N10	Total	N8	N9	N10	Total
I1	10	8	7	25	10	9	2	21
I2	9	10	2	21	9	7	3	19
I3	8	6	4	18	8	7	8	23
I4	7	5	5	17	7	6	9	22
I5	6	6	9	21	6	5	5	16
I6	5	5	3	13	5	5	1	11
I7	4	2	1	7	4	2	4	10
I8	3	1	10	14	3	1	7	11
I9	2	4	8	14	2	2	6	10
I10	1	2	6	9	1	3	10	14

Note how the relative ordering of total scores is now different from the ordering for the true scores in both administrations. This is because there are fewer items, and the impure items have a bigger impact.

In the second administration, a new set of random components has been added to N9, and a new set of random numbers has been generated for N10—that's what random means. With large samples, one would expect the correlation between the two tests of Item 10 to be close to 0 on average. The correlation between the two tests of N9 is an empirical issue. If it is low, then this item lacks stability.

Now consider a variation in responses to Item 9.

	N8	N9	N10	Total	N8	N9	N10	Total
I1	10	8	7	25	10	8	2	20
I2	9	10	2	21	9	10	3	22
I3	8	6	4	18	8	6	8	22
I4	7	5	5	17	7	5	9	21
I5	6	6	9	21	6	6	5	17
I6	5	5	3	13	5	5	1	11
I7	4	2	1	7	4	2	4	10
I8	3	1	10	14	3	1	7	11
I9	2	4	8	14	2	4	6	12
I10	1	2	6	9	1	2	10	13

Question: Although Item 9 has a random component, this random component is constant across administrations, leading to high stability for this item. How could that be possible? What is causing randomness at each administration? How is this different from what is causing randomness across administrations in the earlier case?

Next, consider how a multi-item scale with random error in each item really adds up to form a measure that is reliable. Now consider the same set of items. In reality, each item may differentiate on the underlying construct in different ways. These are like different questions in an exam, some being easy and some being difficult. As a result, some questions discriminate among the better performers, and some discriminate among the poorer performers. Similarly, items could elicit responses that differentiate among different levels of the underlying construct. Here is a set of responses.

	N1	N2	N3	N4	N5	N6	N7	N8	N9	N10	Total
I1	10	9	8	7	10	10	10	10	10	5	89
I2	9	9	8	7	10	10	9	9	10	4	85
I3	8	8	8	7	10	10	8	8	10	3	80
I4	7	7	7	7	7	10	7	7	7	2	68
I5	6	6	6	6	6	10	6	6	7	1	60
I6	5	5	5	5	5	1	5	5	4	1	41
I7	4	4	4	4	4	1	5	4	4	1	35
I8	3	3	3	3	1	1	5	4	4	1	28
I9	2	2	2	2	1	1	5	4	1	1	21
I10	1	1	1	1	1	1	5	4	1	1	17

Question: Inspect each item and consider why it is eliciting the kind of responses shown. Consider items of the PNI scale or some other scale and develop reasons and sample items that would cause each set of responses.

Question: What are the correlations between items likely to be? How do they add up to form a reliable scale (notice how the total scores preserve the original ordering)? Consider the definition of coefficient alpha and examine how small correlations between items add up to form a highly reliable scale. What, then, is the effect of the number of items in a scale?

Examine the effect of random error in correlations across variables. Say that there are two constructs, captured by measures named P and Q, each having a four-item scale with responses from 1 to 4. P is a perfectly reliable and valid measure leading to the true scores shown on the next page. Now if Q is a completely random measure obtained here by generating a set of random numbers, the correlation is likely to be close to 0 on average. If it is measured by a perfectly reliable and valid measure, the correlation will be the true correlation. If it is measured by a measure with some random error (obtained here by adding a random number from −4 to +4 to the true score), then the correlation will be expected to be less than the true correlation.

	P	Q (rel = 1)	Q (rel = 0)	Q (0 < rel < 1)
I1	16	15	10	13
I2	15	16	8	16
I3	14	13	12	11
I4	13	14	11	16
I5	12	11	9	13
I6	11	12	6	11
I7	10	9	7	9
I8	9	10	5	7
I9	8	7	9	5
I10	7	8	14	10
I11	6	5	16	9
I12	5	6	15	5
I13	4	4	4	7

Inspect the correlation matrix below for intercorrelations among all measures.

	P	Q (rel = 1)	Q (rel = 0)	Q (0 < rel < 1)
P	1.00			
Q (rel = 1)	.97	1.00		
Q (rel = 0)	−.13	−.15	1.00	
Q (0 < rel < 1)	.80	.83	0.00	1.00

Question: In light of these correlations, what does random error do?

Question: Plot P versus Q when both are measured with perfect reliability. Now repeat the plot when Q has some random error, and when Q is completely random. What is the effect of random error?

The same logic in relating two variables applies to relating two items of a construct.

Question: Enumerate several sources of random error in a single administration and across administrations. Now examine the effect of each using the learning points in this exercise as a basis.

Systematic Error

Consider a four-item measure P of a construct with responses from 1 to 4 for each item. The true scores are listed as follows.

	N1	N2	N3	N4	Total
I1	4	4	4	4	16
I2	4	4	4	3	15
I3	4	4	3	3	14
I4	4	3	3	3	13
I5	3	3	3	3	12
I6	3	3	3	2	11
I7	3	3	2	2	10
I8	3	2	2	2	9
I9	2	2	2	2	8
I10	2	2	2	1	7
I11	2	2	1	1	6
I12	2	1	1	1	5
I13	1	1	1	1	4

Consider a method factor that leads individuals to use the extremes of the scale for each item. The individual responses are shown below along with the true scores and the true scores of another construct measured by Q. They were generated by converting a number to the nearest extreme point.

	N1	N2	N3	N4	Total	P (True Score)	Q (True Score)
I1	4	4	4	4	16	16	15
I2	4	4	4	4	16	15	16
I3	4	4	4	4	16	14	13
I4	4	4	4	4	16	13	14
I5	4	4	4	4	16	12	11
I6	4	4	4	4	16	11	12
I7	1	1	1	1	4	10	9
I8	1	1	1	1	4	9	10
I9	1	1	1	1	4	8	7
I10	1	1	1	1	4	7	8
I11	1	1	1	1	4	6	5
I12	1	1	1	1	4	5	6
I13	1	1	1	1	4	4	4

The correlation between P and Q falls to 0.87 from 0.97 (not a big deal!), but this exercise is using high correlations just to make intuitive sense.

Question: What sources could cause such individual responses?

Consider a method factor that leads individuals to use the middle of the scale for each item. The individual responses are shown on the next page, along with the true scores and the true scores of Q. They were generated by converting a number to the nearest middle point (either 2 or 3).

	N1	N2	N3	N4	Total	P (True Score)	Q (True Score)
I1	3	3	3	3	12	16	15
I2	3	3	3	3	12	15	16
I3	3	3	3	3	12	14	13
I4	3	3	3	3	12	13	14
I5	3	3	3	3	12	12	11
I6	3	3	3	3	12	11	12
I7	2	2	2	2	8	10	9
I8	2	2	2	2	8	9	10
I9	2	2	2	2	8	8	7
I10	2	2	2	2	8	7	8
I11	2	2	2	2	8	6	5
I12	2	2	2	2	8	5	6
I13	2	2	2	2	8	4	4

The correlation between P and Q falls to 0.87 from 0.97.

Question: What sources could cause such individual responses?

Consider a method factor that leads individuals to inflate their responses by one unit. The individual responses are shown below, along with the true scores and the true scores of Q.

	N1	N2	N3	N4	Total	P (True Score)	Q (True Score)
I1	4	4	4	4	16	16	15
I2	4	4	4	4	16	15	16
I3	4	4	4	4	16	14	13
I4	4	4	4	4	16	13	14
I5	4	4	4	4	16	12	11
I6	4	4	4	4	16	11	12
I7	4	4	3	3	14	10	9
I8	3	3	3	3	12	9	10
I9	3	3	3	3	12	8	7
I10	3	3	3	2	11	7	8
I11	3	3	2	2	10	6	5
I12	3	2	2	2	9	5	6
I13	2	2	2	2	8	4	4

The correlation between P and Q drops slightly to 0.92 from 0.97.

Question: What sources could cause such individual responses?

Consider a method factor that leads individuals to inflate their responses by two units. The individual responses are shown as follows, along with the true scores and the true scores of Q.

	N1	N2	N3	N4	Total	P (True Score)	Q (True Score)
I1	4	4	4	4	16	16	15
I2	4	4	4	4	16	15	16
I3	4	4	4	4	16	14	13
I4	4	4	4	4	16	13	14
I5	4	4	4	4	16	12	11
I6	4	4	4	4	16	11	12
I7	4	4	4	4	16	10	9
I8	4	4	4	4	16	9	10
I9	4	4	4	4	16	8	7
I10	4	4	4	3	15	7	8
I11	4	4	3	3	14	6	5
I12	4	3	3	3	13	5	6
I13	3	3	3	3	12	4	4

The correlation between P and Q falls to 0.75 from 0.97.

Question: What sources could cause such individual responses?

Consider a method factor that leads individuals to inflate their responses by 3 units.

Question: If a method factor leads to inflation for all items (i.e., it is additive), why should there be any effect?

Now, some of the scenarios above are repeated while adding random error. A number from −4 to +4 is added to each measure.

	P (True Score)	Q (True Score)	P (Random Error)	Q (Random Error)
I1	16	15	14	13
I2	15	16	16	16
I3	14	13	15	11
I4	13	14	11	16
I5	12	11	10	13
I6	11	12	13	11
I7	10	9	9	9
I8	9	10	8	7
I9	8	7	4	5
I10	7	8	8	10
I11	6	5	8	9
I12	5	6	6	5
I13	4	4	7	7

Question: Inspect and explain the following correlation matrix.

	P	Q (True Score)	P (Random Error)	Q (Random Error)
P	1.00			
Q (True Score)	.97	1.00		
P (Random Error)	.85	.86	1.00	
Q (Random Error)	.80	.83	.81	1.00

Now consider a method factor, which leads to the inflation of each score by four units because of the inflation of each item by one unit.

	P (true)	Q (true)	P (random)	Q (random)	P (both)	Q (both)
I1	16	15	14	13	16	16
I2	15	16	16	16	16	16
I3	14	13	15	11	16	15
I4	13	14	11	16	15	16
I5	12	11	10	13	14	16
I6	11	12	13	11	16	15
I7	10	9	9	9	13	13
I8	9	10	8	7	12	11
I9	8	7	4	5	8	9
I10	7	8	8	10	12	14
I11	6	5	8	9	12	13
I12	5	6	6	5	10	9
I13	4	4	7	7	11	11

Inspect the correlations below.

	P (true)	Q (true)	P (random)	Q (random)	P (both)	Q (both)
P (true)	1.00					
Q (true)	.97	1.00				
P (random)	.85	.87	1.00			
Q (random)	.80	.83	.81	1.00		
P (both)	.83	.85	.96	.85	1.00	
Q (both)	.79	.78	.84	.94	.91	1.00

Question: What has happened to the correlation? Why? How are random error and systematic error different in their impact on correlations?

Now consider a method factor, which leads to the decrease in high scores by 4 and increase in low scores by 4 (i.e., due to a tendency of each item to force scores to the center by one unit).

	P (true)	Q (true)	P (random)	Q (random)	P (both)	Q (both)
I1	16	15	14	13	10	9
I2	15	16	16	16	12	12
I3	14	13	15	11	11	7
I4	13	14	11	16	7	12
I5	12	11	10	13	6	9
I6	11	12	13	11	9	7
I7	10	9	9	9	13	13
I8	9	10	8	7	12	11
I9	8	7	4	5	8	9
I10	7	8	8	10	12	10
I11	6	5	8	9	12	13
I12	5	6	6	5	10	9
I13	4	4	7	7	11	11

Inspect the correlations below.

	P (true)	Q (true)	P (random)	Q (random)	P (both)	Q (both)
P (true)	1.00					
Q (true)	.97	1.00				
P (random)	.85	.87	1.00			
Q (random)	.80	.83	.81	1.00		
P (both)	−.22	−.20	.06	−.24	1.00	
Q (both)	−.20	−.19	−.20	.11	.41	1.00

Question: What is the effect of the combination of random and method factors?

Now consider measures R and S of two different constructs.

	R (True Score)	S (True Score)	R	S
I1	16	10	16	14
I2	15	12	15	15
I3	14	7	14	14
I4	13	13	13	13
I5	12	11	12	11

(Continued)

I6	11	10	11	12
I7	10	9	10	9
I8	9	10	9	8
I9	8	9	8	7
I10	7	13	7	5
I11	6	9	6	6
I12	5	11	5	4
I13	4	10	4	3

The correlation between true scores is .01, but the correlation between observed scores is .98!

Question: What sources could cause such responses?

Question: How are random and systematic errors different in the way they influence correlations?

Now consider measures T and U of two different constructs.

	T (True Score)	U (True Score)	T	U
I1	16	14	16	16
I2	15	15	15	16
I3	14	14	14	16
I4	13	12	13	16
I5	12	14	12	16
I6	11	10	11	16
I7	10	10	10	16
I8	9	11	9	16
I9	8	9	8	15
I10	7	11	7	16
I11	6	7	6	13
I12	5	5	5	11
I13	4	7	4	13

The correlation between true scores is .91, but the correlation between observed scores is .74.

Question: What sources could cause such responses?

Question: Say there are two variables that have a correlation of 0.50. What are three sources that could lead to the observed correlations between these variables being greater than 0.50? Less than 0.50?

Question: Enumerate several sources of random error in a single administration and across administrations. Now examine the effect of each, using the exercise as a basis.

Consider what causes random and systematic error. Based on the list of effects identified, can a particular cause lead to no error in one situation and to random error in another? Can a cause lead to systematic error in one situation and no error in another? Can a cause lead to systematic error in one situation and random error in another? What, then, is meant by random error and by systematic error?

Summary

Starting with randomness at a single administration (i.e., different individuals responding differently to an item such that the pattern across individuals is random rather than systematic), sources such as item wording (ambiguity, difficulty, double negatives), different people filling out the measure in different settings, fatigue, and interviewer effects cause error. This is called random error in that the pattern of responses across individuals is random for this item in comparison to other items; hence, there will be low item-to-total correlation. An item may be completely described by randomness versus being partially influenced by randomness. The key here is how randomness is determined—that is, by the outcome of the empirical procedure (i.e., coefficient alpha). Randomness at each administration versus randomness across administrations would be assessed by internal consistency and test-retest reliability, respectively. The exercise illustrated a pattern of item responses that show how responses to items have different distributions similar to difficult and easy questions in an exam. Each item captures the construct in different ways such that when they are added, the result is a reliable scale that averages across all of these items. Random error also is illustrated in its effect of reducing correlations.

Systematic error could reduce or increase correlations between variables. Some factors that could cause systematic error include completion of one scale being influenced by completion of another scale because of hypothesis guessing, and the use of extremes versus the middle of a scale. Again, how systematic error is determined depends on the empirical procedures used. Usually, what is causing random and systematic error is not known with certainty. Therefore, the issue becomes an empirical one. For example, individuals might tend to use the middle of a scale, resulting in systematic error for an item. But the way it might be assessed is through low item-to-total correlation, leading to item deletion. Similarly, if there is an additive effect in response to an item that leads to little variation in the item, then that would lead to low item-to-total correlation. Random and systematic errors are defined here in terms of outcomes, although it is useful to know what causes these errors to enable their reduction in measurement procedures.

3

What Causes Measurement Error?

Overview

What causes measurement error? An understanding of different sources that can cause errors is important in trying to minimize errors to begin with. Whereas Chapter 2 discussed several types of errors, Chapter 3 discusses several sources that result in these errors. This chapter cross-lists *sources* of errors mentioned in the literature and likely *outcomes* in terms of different types of measurement error. Although this listing is the result of a detailed examination of error sources discussed in the social sciences literature, it is intended to be illustrative and not exhaustive. An understanding of the relationship between sources of error and the specific nature of measurement error they are likely to cause can be used to minimize error before the fact by designing appropriate items and measures.

Sources of Measurement Error

A variety of sources can cause measurement error, including response styles, specifically acquiescence, disacquiescence, extreme response, response range, midpoint responding, and noncontingent responding (Baumgartner & Steenkamp, 2001; Podsakoff, MacKenzie, Lee, & Podsakoff, 2003). Acquiescence bias occurs when individuals differ in their tendency to agree with item statements. Such bias adds individual variation over and above variation in the construct being measured (Table 3.1). Agreement bias is a tendency to agree with statements, irrespective of the content of the item. Also referred to as acquiescence response style (Martin, 1964), it can be caused by several factors (Baumgartner & Steenkamp, 2001): stimulus-seeking extroverts (Couch & Keniston, 1960; Messick, 1991); lower status or cognitive ability of respondents (Knowles & Nathan, 1997; Messick, 1991; Schuman & Presser, 1981); ambiguous, vague, or neutral items (Messick, 1967; Paulhus, 1991; Ray, 1983); or distraction, time pressure, or other such factors (McGee, 1967). If higher levels of agreement occur because of pervasive factors such as wording, then this pattern leads to additive systematic error. If individuals vary consistently in their tendency to agree over and above the construct being measured, then this pattern leads to within-measure correlational systematic error. Disacquiescence response style, also referred to as disagreement bias or nay-saying, is the opposite of acquiescence response style and could be caused by stimulus-avoiding introverts (Couch & Keniston, 1960). Net acquiescence response style (Baumgartner & Steenkamp, 2001) is the sum of these two response styles and is also referred to as direction bias. In studies of response style effects (Baumgartner & Steenkamp, 2001; Martin, 1964), such response styles are assessed by the degree of agreement (or disagreement) with heterogeneous items from multiple scales without much in common, or from the extent of agreement with positively and negatively worded items from one scale before reverse scoring.

Location bias occurs when individuals differ in the manner in which they use response scale categories (e.g., a tendency to scale upward or use extremes). Leniency is the tendency of a respondent to rate too high or too low. Severity (or stringency) is the opposite of leniency. Midpoint responding, a tendency to use the middle scale point irrespective of content (Baumgartner & Steenkamp, 2001), may be caused by evasiveness, indecision, or indifference (Messick, 1968; Schuman & Presser, 1981). This response style has been measured by the proportion of use of midpoints (Chen, Lee, & Stevenson, 1995; Stening & Everett, 1984). Midpoint responding leads to use of middle alternatives and is likely to cause within-measure correlational systematic error. In other words, although not affecting means, this type of error can lead to consistent differences over and above the construct in question. If any such error affects a small proportion of individuals, it may be identified as idiosyncratic random error. However, if a factor such as the use of extreme wording in the end anchors has a more pervasive effect, then the result is within-measure correlational systematic error.

(Text continues on page 141)

Table 3.1 Incomplete Taxonomy of Error Sources and Errors

Sources of Error	Category of Measurement Error						Description
	Random Error			Systematic Error			
	Idiosyncratic	Generic		Additive	Within Measure Correlational	Across* Measure	
		Within Administration	Across Administration				
Idiosyncratic individual-related							
Language difficulties	X						
Transient personal factors							Churchill (1979)
Mood		X					
Fatigue		X					
Memory/attention vacillations		X					Bagozzi (1984); Ghiselli (1964)
Mechanical/motor vacillations		X					Check in wrong box (Bagozzi, 1984; Churchill, 1979)
Noncontingent responding		X					Marsh (1987); Watkins and Cheung (1995)
Other idiosyncratic responses		X					All sources of error below that affect few respondents
Generic individual-related							
Individual differences in social desirability					X	X	Crowne and Marlowe (1964)
Charitability bias					X	X	Couch and Keniston (1960)
Faking good/faking bad					X	X	Meehl and Hathaway (1946)
(Dis)Acquiescence bias					X	X	Nunnally (1978); Lennox and Dennis (1994); Martin (1964); Ray (1983); Couch and Keniston (1960)

(Continued)

Table 3.1 (Continued)

Sources of Error	Category of Measurement Error					Description
	Random Error		Additive	Systematic Error		
	Idiosyncratic	Generic		Within Measure Correlational	Across* Measure	
	Within Administration	Across Administration				
Rater dispersion bias				X	X	Use of more extreme scores leading to higher standard deviation (Braucht, 1972; Greenleaf, 1992b; Wyer, 1969)
Extreme response style				X	X	
Standard deviation or response range				X	X	Tendency to use a wide or narrow range of responses (Greenleaf, 1992a; Hui & Triandis, 1985; Wyer, 1969)
Midpoint responding				X	X	Tendency to use the midpoint irrespective of content (Messick, 1968; Schuman & Presser, 1981)
Item content-related						
Lack of clarity of measures	X	X				Ambiguous wording, incomplete wording, poorly defined terms (Churchill, 1979; Fowler, 1993)
Estimation	X	X	X			
Leading questions			X			
Direction of wording effects				X	X	Cronbach (1946)
Common stem/similar wording				X	X	Lennox and Dennis (1994)
(Dis)Acquiescence bias			X	X	X	Nunnally (1978); Lennox and Dennis (1994); Martin (1964); Ray (1983); Couch and Keniston (1960)

Table: Category of Measurement Error

Sources of Error	Random Error — Idiosyncratic: Within Administration	Random Error — Generic: Across Administration	Generic: Additive	Systematic Error: Within Measure Correlational	Systematic Error: Across* Measure	Description
Midpoint responding				X	X	Tendency to use the midpoint irrespective of content (Messick, 1968; Schuman & Presser, 1981)
Response format-related						
Rater location bias				X	X	
Rater dispersion bias				X	X	
Extreme response style				X	X	Use of more extreme scores (Braucht, 1972; Greenleaf, 1992b; Wyer, 1969)
Standard deviation or response range				X	X	Tendency to use a wide or narrow range of responses (Greenleaf, 1992a; Hui & Triandis, 1985; Wyer, 1969)
(Dis)Acquiescence or yea-/nay-saying			X	X	X	Tendency to agree or disagree with items (Greenleaf, 1992a; Hui & Triandis, 1985; Wyer, 1969)
Leniency/stringency			X	X	X	Consistently too positive/negative (Alliger & Williams, 1992)
Central tendency				X	X	Avoiding extreme scores (Guilford, 1954)
Unbalanced category labeling			X			
Confusing/ambiguous category labeling	X	X				
Number of response categories	X	X				Cox (1980)

(Continued)

Table 3.1 (Continued)

Sources of Error	Category of Measurement Error						Description
	Random Error			Systematic Error			
	Idiosyncratic	Generic — Within Administration	Generic — Across Administration	Additive	Within Measure Correlational	Across Measure*	
Administration related							
Learning/training		X			X	X	Ghiselli (1964)
Fatigue		X	X		X	X	Ghiselli (1964)
Distracting setting			X				
Interviewer biases				X		X	Interviewers who probe differently (Churchill, 1979)
Variations in administration			X				
Logical error in rating					X	X	Similar responses to items presupposed to be logically related (Bardo et al., 1982; Newcomb, 1931)
Proximity error					X	X	Similar responses to items close together (Stockford & Bissell, 1949)
Common instructions across measures						X	Lennox and Dennis (1994)
Halo					X	X	Similar responses to items related to general construct (Bardo et al., 1982; Thorndike, 1920)
Social desirability				X	X	X	Crowne and Marlowe (1964)
Experimenter expectancy				X	X	X	Cook and Campbell (1979)
Hypothesis guessing					X	X	Cook and Campbell (1979)
Differential augmentation/ attenuation						X	Similar methods increase (and dissimilar methods decrease) observed relationship between traits as the true relationship between traits increases (Bagozzi & Yi, 1991; Campbell & O'Connell, 1967)

*Across-measure additive and correlational systematic error are combined into a single category here.

Extreme response style refers to choosing extreme responses irrespective of content (Greenleaf, 1992b). It could be caused by several factors (Baumgartner & Steenkamp, 2001): an intolerance for ambiguity or dogmatism (Hamilton, 1968); anxiety (Hamilton, 1968); respondents lacking appropriate cognitive schemas (Shulman, 1973); or stimuli that are meaningful, important, or involving to respondents (O'Donovan, 1965). It has been measured by the extent of use of extreme categories (positive or negative) (Bachman & O'Malley, 1984). Response range is the tendency to use response categories in a narrow or wide range (Greenleaf, 1992a; Hui & Triandis, 1985; Wyer, 1969) and may be caused by factors similar to those that cause extreme response style (Baumgartner & Steenkamp, 2001). It has been measured by the standard deviation in an individual's responses across items (Greenleaf, 1992a; Hui & Triandis, 1985; Wyer, 1969). Noncontingent responding is the tendency to be careless, random, or nonpurposeful in responding (Baumgartner & Steenkamp, 2001; Marsh, 1987; Watkins & Cheung, 1995) and may occur because of lack of motivation. It has been measured by summing the absolute differences between pairs of items that are highly correlated and have similar means across respondents, and that are worded in the same direction (Bachman & O'Malley, 1984; Baumgartner & Steenkamp, 2001; Watkins & Cheung, 1995).

Halo effect also causes within-measure correlational systematic error and is a tendency to provide similar responses across items that are thought to be related. Again, such error, if restricted to a small proportion of individuals, is similar to idiosyncratic random error. Proximity error relates to similar responses to items in proximity and can also result in within-measure correlational systematic error. Nay-saying and yea-saying can also lead to error. If wording leads respondents to agree (disagree) to a greater degree, this could lead to additive systematic error. However, if yea- and nay-saying vary consistently across individuals (i.e., lead to individual differences in yea- and nay-saying), then the resulting error is within-measure correlational systematic error. In other words, individuals differ on yea-saying and nay-saying tendencies, and their responses reflect these tendencies over and above the construct being measured. Social desirability, a tendency to present oneself in a favorable light, can similarly lead to additive or correlational systematic error. Standard deviation error—a tendency to use a wide or narrow range of responses—can increase or reduce spread. If individuals vary consistently in standard deviation, this pattern leads to within-measure correlational systematic error (i.e., consistent differences across individuals over and above the construct being measured). If a constant, pervasive effect leads to greater or lesser spread, this pattern is also an example of within-measure correlational systematic error.

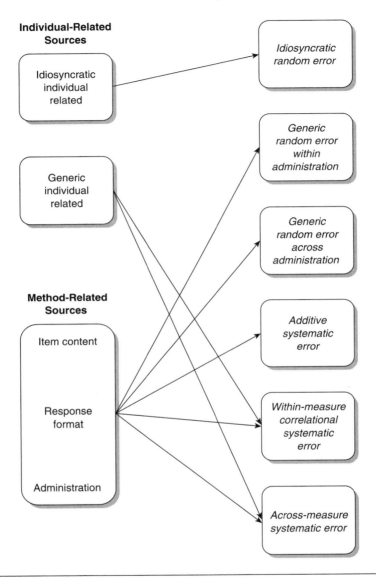

Figure 3.1   Summary of Error-Sources and Errors

In sum, within-measure correlational systematic error can be caused by consistent individual differences over and above the construct being measured. It results from underlying individual differences that lead to varying responses across individuals or pervasive wording or other factors that lead to constant dispersions across individuals, but reflect differences over and above the construct in question. It should be noted that additive systematic error is also constant across individuals but in one direction. Hence, it does not affect differences except when it reduces variance due to finite scale ends (i.e., partial additive systematic error).

Taxonomy of Error Sources

A taxonomy of sources of measurement error is developed here as a way to organize different sources (Table 3.1 and Figure 3.1). Past research lacks a taxonomy of a wide variety of error sources. The incomplete taxonomy lists several sources of errors mentioned in the literature and is intended to be illustrative and not exhaustive.

Past research has categorized sources of errors in several ways. Bardo et al. (1982) differentiate between respondent-related errors that are content-specific and form-related errors that are due to respondents' use of response formats. Method variance has been described as varying in level of abstraction from item wording and scale types to halo effects and social desirability (Bagozzi & Yi, 1991; Fiske, 1982). Ghiselli, Campbell, and Zedeck (1981) distinguish between situation-centered and person-centered sources of errors across administrations. However, past research is characterized by the lack of a taxonomy of a wide variety of error sources.

Several points are noteworthy about the taxonomy developed here. First, sources of error are differentiated from errors, an important and necessary distinction. Sources usually associated with random error can sometimes lead to systematic error and vice versa. Random and systematic measurement errors are outcomes of error sources. Second, no single category completely captures a source of error; hence, this taxonomy is necessarily an approximate one. At a broad level, all sources of errors arise out of the data collection event, which has been referred to as the union between a trait and a method (Campbell & Fiske, 1959).[1] A method is used here to refer to all the things that are done to collect the data, including the setting, administration procedures, and the measure itself. More specifically, sources of error may arise because of certain respondent characteristics, certain characteristics of the method, or interactions between these two categories.

The following categorization separates *individual-related* sources of errors (idiosyncratic and generic) from *method-related* sources of errors, with the latter being separated into item content, response format, and administration issues. Hence, there are certain characteristics (enduring and transient) that individuals bring into a data collection event, and there are certain characteristics of the data collection event. Each of these sets of characteristics can dominate in affecting responses. In addition, these sets of characteristics can interact to affect responses as well. The present classification focuses on categorization into single categories with the assumption that there is a likely dominant effect. Clearly, interactions between each of these components could lead to more complex categorization of error sources, and few such examples are provided. Despite the difficulty involved in clear categorization, such a taxonomy enables understanding of error sources and possible errors that can arise as consequences. Likely outcomes of error sources in terms of errors are identified here, fully recognizing that error sources could lead to errors other than the ones identified here.

Idiosyncratic Individual-Related Factors

Idiosyncratic individual-related factors are those that can affect a small proportion of individuals and include transient factors such as mood or language difficulties or distractions (Table 3.1). These sources of errors are usually idiosyncratic to individuals and are likely to lead to idiosyncratic random errors. They arise out of the state that the individual is in, such as an extreme mood, or are due to some idiosyncratic factors, such as mechanical variations. An individual's state could interact with some aspect of item wording or response format to lead to error. In other words, idiosyncratic individual factors could interact with aspects of the method to lead to error, but the outcome is idiosyncratic random error because it affects only a small proportion of individuals. Also, whether an error source is idiosyncratic or generic depends on how pervasive the error is. This distinction can be blurred as a function of the proportion of respondents affected. Moreover, if any of the other sources listed below affect a small proportion of individuals, they are indistinguishable from idiosyncratic individual-related factors.

Generic Individual-Related Factors

This category refers to individual differences along certain dimensions, such as social desirability, that are more pervasive than idiosyncratic factors (Table 3.1). Such factors, by their very nature, lead to correlational systematic error through the relationship between such individual differences and differences along a trait. They arise because of variations in the way individuals provide responses that are affected to different degrees for different individuals, over and above true differences in the construct being measured.

Hence, individual differences in impression management, charitability, or "faking good" may lead to correlational systematic error. It should be noted that whether individual-related factors are generic or idiosyncratic depends on how pervasive the factors are in influencing responses. Any generic factor could also be idiosyncratic in nature (e.g., faking good) if it affects only a small proportion of individuals, again highlighting the difficulty of separating out different sources of error.

Item Content-Related Factors

These factors relate to item wording effects, such as ambiguity and complexity, that may lead to pervasive errors (Table 3.1). A poorly defined word or term could lead to random error (e.g., "How much did you spend on recreational activities?"). Items to which respondents are unable to respond may lead to random error. Leading questions may lead to additive systematic error. Questions requiring estimation (e.g., "How many cans of Coke did you drink last year?") may lead to random error (because of guessing) or additive systematic error (because of underestimation or overestimation, say, because an inflated rate is computed based on purchase rather than usage by multiplying the cans purchased per week by the number of weeks in a year). Ambiguity could lead to use of the middle option and, hence, correlational systematic error that is coincidentally negatively related to the trait being measured. Again, it should be noted that if item-related factors affect a small proportion of individuals, they are indistinguishable from idiosyncratic individual-related factors.

Response Format-Related Factors

Response format-related factors have been included among what have been referred to in the literature as method factors (i.e., factors in the method employed that may cause responses). These response format-related factors include variations in the use of extremes or different parts of a scale (Table 3.1). They could lead to correlational systematic error either within or across measures, as well as additive systematic error and random error. Central tendency can cause correlational systematic error in that it is coincidentally negatively related to the trait being measured. Yea- and nay-saying tendencies may lead to additive systematic error. Unbalanced response categories (i.e., a set of response categories that does not have corresponding positive and negative levels, such as *excellent, very good, good, fair,* and *poor*) may lead respondents in one direction and cause additive systematic error. For instance, if most of the response categories in a scale are positive, they may cause responses to move toward the positive end of the scale. The close relationship between response format-related factors and generic individual-related factors is noteworthy. When enduring individual differences lead to responses being affected to different degrees, then the error source is categorized as generic individual-related and the outcome is correlational systematic error. When characteristics of the response format dominate and lead to dispersion or inflation/deflation (i.e., in one direction, or central tendency), then the error source is categorized under response format-related factors. Arguably, several of the error sources listed under this category could fit as interactions between generic individual-related factors and response format-related factors or under generic individual-related factors (e.g., a tendency toward yea-saying could be a generic individual difference or an interaction between individual- and response format-related factors, or it could be elicited by the response format). As discussed, sources such as acquiescence response style could be caused by individual differences (extroversion or cognitive ability), item content (ambiguity), or administration factors (time pressure). Potential interactions between individual differences and response format could lead to more complex forms of error. Again, it should be noted that if response format-related factors affect a small proportion of individuals, they are indistinguishable from idiosyncratic individual-related factors.

Administration-Related Factors

Administration-related factors include the setting, procedures (e.g., sequencing or administering items/measures contiguously), and interviewer/experimenter-related factors (e.g., leading on the part of the interviewer or experimenter). Interviewer biasing can lead to additive systematic error; it can also lead to correlational systematic error, for instance, because different respondents are differentially and consistently affected. Distracting settings and variations in administration are similar to ambiguous wording in terms of leading to generic random error. Similarly, logical error in rating (similar responses to items thought to be logically related) and halo effects can lead to correlational error within and across measures. Halo and proximity error sources are classified under administration-related factors because they arise out of items being administered together. Procedures can also elicit social desirability of an additive or correlational form, or even yea-saying tendencies and other sources listed under response format.

Interactive effects between traits and methods are also listed under administrative factors. Differential augmentation (Bagozzi & Yi, 1991; Campbell & O'Connell, 1967, 1982) occurs when "the higher the basic relationship between two traits, the more the relationship is increased when the same method is shared" (Campbell & O'Connell, 1982, p. 95). For instance, raters may have theories about how a pair of traits (say, value consciousness and price consciousness) is related. In such a situation, the stronger the true association between the traits, the more likely it is noticed and inflated (Bagozzi & Yi, 1991). Differential attenuation (Bagozzi & Yi, 1991; Campbell & O'Connell, 1967, 1982) occurs when "not sharing the same method dilutes or attenuates the true relationship, so that it appears to be less than it should be" (Campbell & O'Connell, 1982, p. 95). For instance, when collecting data on multiple occasions, the correlation between two related traits is attenuated for longer than for shorter intervals, whereas with two unrelated traits, no attenuation is possible (Bagozzi & Yi, 1991; Campbell & O'Connell, 1967, 1982).

The same sources could be categorized under item content-related factors, response format-related factors, generic individual-related factors, or administration factors. For instance, socially desirable responses may be caused by item content- or administration-related factors such as interviewer bias, or a generic individual difference. The resulting error could be additive systematic error, say, interviewer bias or item content, moving responses in one direction. The resulting error could be correlational systematic error, say, item content, interviewer bias, or response format (e.g., end anchors such as *like-hate,* the latter being extreme and perhaps socially undesirable) differentially affecting individuals who differ on tendency toward social desirability. Therefore, consistent differences over and above the construct being measured result. For correlational systematic error to occur, a source has to have a consistent, differential influence across individuals. Again, several of these sources could fit under generic individual differences or under interactions described below.

Sample Interactions

Generic individual-related factors, such as ability or tendency toward impression management, could interact with administration-related factors, such as interviewer bias or item content-related factors, or response format-related factors, such as task-related ability (e.g., computer skills and language processing ability), central tendency, or leniency. Individual differences could be accentuated by response formats. Similarly, item content can interact with generic individual-related factors (such as individual differences in social desirability and item wording to elicit social desirability). Item content can interact with response format through the tone of the item (e.g., extreme wording) and the use of extremes versus the center of a scale. Similarly, administration-related factors can interact with other categories of factors (e.g., interviewer bias and generic individual differences in impression management, response format, or item wording). Administration-related factors, item content-related factors, and response format-related factors can also interact with idiosyncratic individual factors to lead to idiosyncratic random error.

Summary

Many sources can cause each of the types of measurement error described in Chapter 2. By understanding what causes error, these sources can be minimized in the design of items and measures. These sources can be roughly categorized into individual-related sources of errors (idiosyncratic and generic) and method-related sources of errors, the latter being separated into item content, response format, and administration issues. Hence, there are certain characteristics (enduring and transient) that individuals bring into a data collection event, and there are certain characteristics of the data collection event. In turn, the sources in each category can cause the different types of measurement error described in Chapter 2. Although the taxonomy simplifies reality by categorizing sources into single categories, many sources can be categorized as interactions among these categories.

Note

1. The term *method* has been used in different ways covering narrow to broad issues. Method is used here in its broadest sense, to refer to everything that is done to collect the data, including the setting, the administration procedures, and the measure itself. All of the things that are done to collect data can cause error, and all of them are included here in the notion of a method. The term *method* has been used sometimes in the literature to refer to two different ways of collecting data, such as a paper-and-pencil method versus an observation, or a Likert approach versus a behavioral inventory. These are narrower uses of the term because other issues beyond the use of one format versus the other are involved in a method and could cause error.

4

Can Empirical
Procedures Pinpoint
Types of Measurement Error?

Overview

Many empirical procedures are used in measure development and validation. Can these procedures accurately pinpoint the type of measurement error that occurs? This chapter shows that these procedures confound different types of error. Chapter 1 covered the psychometric procedures employed to evaluate scales. These procedures aim to identify measurement error. Chapters 2 and 3 provided a discussion of types of errors and potential sources of error, respectively. In Chapter 4, commonly used psychometric procedures are evaluated in terms of the types of errors they reflect. Chapter 4 shows that psychometric procedures used to analyze response patterns confound different types of error.

Empirical procedures commonly employed during measure development—specifically, internal consistency, test-retest reliability, factor analyses, and validity tests—are examined here in terms of how these procedures operationalize random and systematic errors. These procedures are shown to capture a wider set of errors than intended. For instance, a low correlation between an item and the total score could be caused by several errors other than random error, and an understanding of such issues is important in measure development and validation.

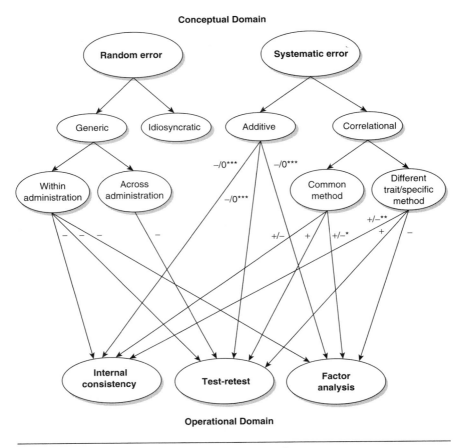

Figure 4.1   Random and Systematic Errors Within Measures

* '+' for unidimensional measures; '–' for multidimensional measures
** '+/–' for related/unrelated traits/methods, respectively
*** '0' for constant additive and '–' for partial additive error

Throughout the discussion, reference is made to Figure 4.1, which summarizes the distinctions drawn between the concepts of measurement error and their relationships to empirical outcomes for internal consistency, test-retest reliability, and factor analysis procedures.

Internal Consistency Reliability Procedures

Internal consistency procedures are heavily employed during measure development, specifically through identifying items with low correlations with the total score on a scale during measure development and assessing coefficient alpha (Churchill, 1979; Cronbach, 1951; Peterson, 1994). Several types of errors may influence reliability as operationalized through internal consistency beyond just random error.

Random Error

In terms of randomness at a single administration (i.e., different individuals responding differently to an item such that the pattern across individuals is random rather than systematic), factors such as item wording (ambiguity, difficulty, double negatives), measure completion in different settings, fatigue, and interviewer effects may contribute to unreliability (Fowler, 1993; see also Chapter 3). Such error is referred to as random error in that the pattern of responses across individuals is random for an item in comparison to other items, resulting in low item-to-total correlation. Specifically, when correlations between an item and other items of the same measure are deflated, the outcome is categorized as random error. If random error is idiosyncratic to a small proportion of individuals because of factors such as mood, then such error is not likely to be identified or reflected in significantly lower item-to-total correlation in a single administration employing large samples. This suggests the use of sufficient sample sizes in all stages of measure development, including preliminary stages, to minimize the undue influence of idiosyncratic random error (Exhibit 2.1).[1] Hence, idiosyncratic random error is not likely to affect empirical outcomes in internal consistency procedures, whereas generic random error may reduce item-to-total correlations and coefficient alpha (Figure 4.1; Exhibit 2.1, columns I, G1, and G2).

Additive Systematic Error

An item may have systematic error that is consistent and additive in nature, and consequently either does not affect correlations or deflates them. For instance, a leading question or an extremely worded question, "Using numbers is a waste of time," may bias responses in one direction. However, if such error deflates correlations, it is likely to be categorized as random error because it is identified by the pattern of results from the empirical procedure (i.e., item-to-total correlations in internal consistency) (Figure 4.1; Exhibit 2.1, columns A1 and A2). It should be noted that additive systematic error would deflate correlations because of finite end points of a scale. As mentioned, such partial additive systematic error is discussed under the umbrella of additive systematic error throughout the book and distinguished from constant additive systematic error.

Within-Measure Correlational Systematic Error

Within-measure correlational systematic error occurs between different items of a measure and can be due to responses to items being influenced by the use of a common method factor or by different trait or method factors that may or may not be related to the trait being measured (Figure 4.1; Exhibit 2.1, columns C1 to C5). An item designed to measure a construct may be tapping into a different construct, say, individual differences in social desirability (e.g., "Numbers are essential to the normal functioning of society"). Although this error is systematic, whether it is identified is subject to several possibilities. First, if the item-to-total correlation is high because the trait being captured is closely related to the trait being measured, the item will be identified as adequate. If the correlation is low or negative, then the item will be identified as having random error (Figure 4.1). The same holds true for a common method factor that affects all items (e.g., all items valenced toward agreement such that higher agreement suggests higher scores on the trait being measured) or for a specific method factor that affects a few items, such as wording that elicits social desirability. If the trait being measured has a positive effect, but a common method factor or a specific method factor has a negative effect, then the item will be identified as having random error (essentially, the sum of two systematic errors).

The within-measure halo effect and other such effects due to the use of a common method, or due to different traits/specific method factors, may be empirically indistinguishable from trivial redundancies between items. Minor variations of items (such as "I enjoy jobs that require the use of numbers" and "I enjoy tasks that require the use of numbers") would lead to high internal consistency, as would a within-measure halo effect. Whereas redundancy, whether trivial or useful, is recommended at the item generation stage, and useful redundancy is recommended in the final versions of a scale (DeVellis, 1991), trivial redundancy in the final scale may lead to a narrow operationalization that does not fully capture the domain of a construct (Epstein, 1983). Hence, the scale may have high internal consistency, yet low content validity. Correlational systematic error may also occur among groups of items within a measure as a result of factors such as shared context or wording, increasing internal consistency but affecting the unidimensionality of the measure. Similarly, within-measure correlational systematic error may undermine distinctions between dimensions of a measure, as discussed under factor analysis.

Summary

A number of random and systematic (additive and correlational) errors can lead to identification of an item as causing random error in internal consistency procedures (Figure 4.1). In the final analysis, random error is operationalized as any error that reduces correlations within a measure. It could be caused by additive systematic error that reduces variance; by within-measure correlational systematic error, such as an item tapping a negatively related, unrelated, or a moderately related trait or a method factor; or by generic random error at a single administration, all resulting in reduced item-to-total correlations.[2] In moving from the conceptual to the operational, additive systematic error and within-measure correlational systematic error would then be identified as random error or not identified at all. Moreover, because both random and systematic errors can potentially generate the same outcome (i.e., deflate correlations), the empirical procedures employed dictate how errors are categorized.

Test-Retest Reliability Procedures

Random error across administrations is typically identified by low correlations between items or entire scales across administrations using test-retest correlations (Nunnally, 1978). Several assumptions of this procedure are noteworthy, such as the phenomenon in question being unchanged across administrations, with no carry-over effects from the first administration. Several types of errors can influence test-retest correlations, leading to important implications for measure development.

Random Error Within Administrations

Any form of random error within a single administration due to item wording factors such as ambiguous wording or inconsistent procedures that are identified by low item-to-total correlations may lead to low test-retest correlations across administrations as well (Figures 4.1 and 4.2; Exhibit 2.1, columns G1 and G2 across Times 1 and 2). If random error is idiosyncratic to a small proportion of individuals because of factors such as mood, then such error may not be identified or reflected in significantly lower item-to-total correlation in a single administration employing large samples and, therefore, may not affect test-retest correlations (Exhibit 2.1, column I across Times 1 and 2).

Additive Systematic Error

Additive systematic error in a single administration may either deflate or not affect correlations (Figures 4.1 and 4.2). For example, an extremely

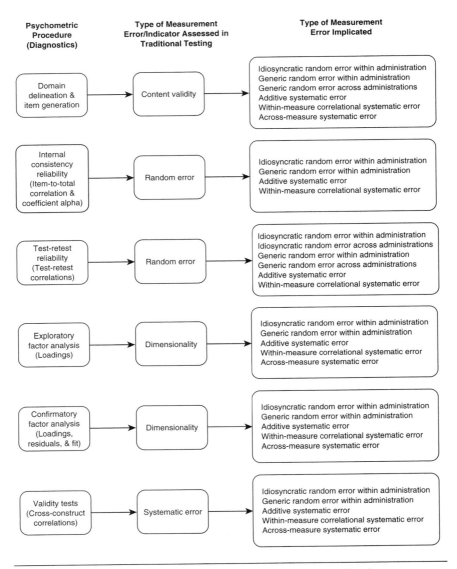

Figure 4.2   Understanding Measurement Error in Measure Development
Procedures

worded item such as "Numbers are a waste of time" may lead to inflation of
all responses, but correlations are likely to be unaffected unless this inflation is
high enough to significantly inhibit variation on this item across respondents

(i.e., partial additive systematic error due to finite end points to the scale). Several factors may lead to additive systematic error, that is, a consistent (systematic) effect across administrations. Because such error is consistent across administrations, it may affect test-retest correlations only if inflation or deflation significantly inhibits variation; otherwise, it will have no effect (Exhibit 2.1, column G3 across Times 1 and 2). If an additive effect, such as interviewer biasing, occurs during one administration but not the other, it is an inconsistent effect across administrations and therefore not systematic in nature, an issue discussed under random error across administrations.

Within-Measure Correlational Systematic Error

An item that captures a related trait or a method factor, such as individual differences in yea-saying, can lead to within-measure correlational systematic error due to a different trait/specific method factor resulting in moderate or even high test-retest correlation (Figures 4.1 and 4.2). For instance, consider Item 12 of the PNI scale, "I enjoy thinking based on qualitative information." If this item is capturing preference for qualitative information, perhaps a related trait, it may have high test-retest correlation. Similarly, within-measure correlational systematic error due to a common method factor is likely to be positively related to test-retest correlations (Exhibit 2.1, columns C1 to C5 across Times 1 and 2). An item could have high test-retest correlation yet low to moderate internal consistency if it is tapping a different construct or method factor, and such a pattern may provide diagnostic information for item evaluation (e.g., Item 8 of the PNI scale, "Numbers are not necessary for most situations," wherein the socially desirable answer, particularly among student samples, may be to disagree, and the item taps into individual differences in social desirability). For instance, if the item captures individual differences in social desirability or in yea-saying tendency reliably, it may have high test-retest correlation but low internal consistency.

If test-retest is viewed as a strict replication of all controllable facets of testing and items are administered together, the within-measure halo effect is likely to influence the pattern of responses. In other words, test-retest reliability assesses the degree of relationship between an item at test and retest in the context of other items. This issue has implications for how a measure is used in future applications, discussed in Chapter 5. How a measure is validated, such as in the sequencing of items, also has implications for how the measure is used in future applications. If the validation takes advantage of a particular sequencing of items, then such a sequencing would have to be maintained in future applications.

Random Error Across Administrations

An item may have low to moderate test-retest correlation, even with high internal consistency, because of different sources of random error that operate in a single administration versus across administrations (Figures 4.1 and 4.2). A response to an item may be sensitive to factors across administrations, such as interactions with settings or mood. For instance, an item with a single negative or a double negative may be more susceptible to misreading in a distracting setting (e.g., "Numbers are not useful in most situations"). If such a pattern of responses is restricted to a small proportion of individuals (i.e., it is idiosyncratic), such a possibility can be accounted for through large samples. On the other hand, an interaction between an item and a variable, such as the setting or the interviewer, that varies across administrations and affects a sizable proportion of respondents will likely lead to low test-retest reliability.[3] It is sometimes likely to be identified in test-retest procedures but not internal consistency procedures because effects may be uniform across items in a single administration, yet lead to low or moderate test-retest correlations (Exhibit 2.1, column G3 across Times 1 and 2).

Summary

This analysis suggests that random errors within administrations have similar effects on test-retest reliability as on internal consistency reliability (Figure 4.1). Additive systematic errors are likely to have no effect on test-retest correlations and may deflate correlations only when variation on an item is significantly inhibited. Correlational systematic errors due to an item tapping a related or unrelated method or trait may actually lead to high test-retest correlation, yet moderate or low internal consistency. In terms of random error across administrations, idiosyncratic random error, such as mood differences for a small proportion of individuals across administrations, is not problematic as long as large samples are used. Random error across administrations is caused by sources such as interactions between items and administrations.

Interactions between administrations and items might be a source of differences between test-retest reliability and internal consistency.[4] A pattern of high test-retest correlation with moderate item-to-total correlation may suggest correlational systematic error, whereas a pattern of low to moderate test-retest correlation and high item-to-total correlation may suggest lower stability due to the nature of random error across administrations (i.e., interactions between items and administrations). When items in a measure are completed in sequence, internal consistency and test-retest reliability assessments may be subject to the within-measure halo effect. Items tapping constructs in the context of other items but exhibiting low to moderate stability could be identified through test-retest correlations. Items can have moderate or low test-retest correlation while having moderate or even high item-to-total correlations. Items tapping related or unrelated traits or methods could be identified through moderate item-to-total correlations and factor analyses.

Factor Analysis Procedures

Factor analysis procedures are employed during measure development to assess item loadings on factors and dimensionality of measures. Several types of errors may influence factor analysis procedures (Figure 4.2). Whereas the effect of idiosyncratic random error can be minimized through sufficient sample sizes, generic random error in items will decrease loadings with factors, and additive systematic error may have no effect (i.e., the constant additive type) or may decrease loadings (i.e., the partial additive type). For example, Item 12 in the PNI scale in Chapter 1 identified through item-to-total correlations as having generic random error (Exhibit 1.2) has decreased, actually negative loading with the first factor (Exhibit 1.4). Item 18 (Exhibit 1.2) has relatively lower loading on the first factor possibly due to additive systematic error (Item mean = 5.24/7) (Exhibit 1.4). These errors have similar effects on loadings as on item-to-total correlations. Within-measure correlational systematic error resulting from an item tapping into a common method or a different trait or specific method factor (say, social desirability) may be identified through factor analysis as a distinct factor. For instance, Items 11 and 19 ("Quantitative information is vital for accurate decisions" and "I like to go over numbers in my mind," respectively, in Exhibit 1.4) of the PNI scale have sizable loadings with the second factor, and Items 17 and 18 have sizable loadings with the third factor ("Numbers are redundant for most situations" and "Learning and remembering numerical information about various issues is a waste of time," respectively). Items 17 and 18 relate to the degree to which numbers are redundant or a waste of time and share this context. If an item captures a trait or method in addition to the trait being measured, then this item may be identified as adequate because of a high loading on the first factor.

Within-measure correlational systematic error due to a closely related trait or method factor is likely to be positively related to factor loadings and the identification of single dominant dimensions (Figure 4.2). However, such within-measure correlational systematic error may blur differences across multiple dimensions of a measure (Figures 4.1 and 4.2). For instance, placing items from the defining success and acquisition centrality dimensions of the material values scale in proximity may blur distinctions between these dimensions (Appendix 1.2). Placing items of a multidimensional scale in close proximity may result in high degrees of within-measure correlational systematic error in confirmatory factor analysis procedures, as indicated by overall fit indexes, loadings, and residuals. For scales that purport to be unidimensional with a sizable number of items, shared wording and context between subsets of items may also adversely affect the results of confirmatory factor analysis and undermine unidimensionality. In summary, a number of different types of error are reflected in factor analyses.

Validity Tests

Validity tests move measure assessment to the realm of cross-construct relationships. Consequently, several issues discussed above translate from the item to the measure level in terms of the unit of analysis. Issues relating to the methodological design of validity tests overlap with methodological design for substantive tests of hypotheses as well, as discussed subsequently. In tests of validity, a correlation between two measures may be the result of a substantive relationship and/or due to several types of random and systematic errors. Among these types of errors, random error in measures attenuates relationships (Nunnally, 1978). Whereas the effect of idiosyncratic random error can be minimized through large sample sizes, generic random error in the measurement of one or more constructs in an administration attenuates relationships. Additive systematic error is likely to have no effect or to attenuate relationships because of decreased variance. Systematic error across measures can strengthen or weaken observed relationships. A structural equation modeling-based approach to validity testing can estimate relationships between measures that take into account and correct for types of measurement error, such as generic random error in individual measures, as discussed in Chapter 1.

Across-measure systematic error, both correlational and additive, affects validity tests.[5] Some types of validity, such as nomological validity, rest on sizable correlations between focal measures being assessed and measures of constructs that are expected to be theoretically related. However, if a focal measure of price consciousness is placed contiguous to and immediately following a measure of value consciousness (Appendix 1.2) in a test of nomological validity, several sources of error could inflate the observed relationship between these two measures. For example, a halo effect in completing the value consciousness measure or hypothesis guessing could affect responses to the price consciousness measure and inflate observed relationships. Because across-measure correlational systematic error can inflate observed relationships in such designs, strong evidence of nomological validity cannot be inferred from sizable correlations. On the other hand, discriminant validity tests rest on showing small correlations between focal measures and measures of constructs that are expected to be theoretically unrelated or weakly related. If a focal measure of product quality is placed contiguous to a measure of familiarity in a discriminant validity test, strong evidence of such validity can be inferred from nonsignificant correlations. This is because across-measure correlational systematic error would have inflated observed correlations, and yet small or nonsignificant correlations are found.

A guiding principle in evaluating the design of validity tests relates to the direction in which across-measure systematic error is likely to influence the relationship between two variables. If across-measure systematic error due to research design is likely to inflate correlations, a nonsignificant correlation provides strong evidence of discriminant validity. On the other hand, a sizable correlation between two variables provides strong evidence of nomological or convergent validity when across-measure systematic error due to research design is likely to deflate correlations or is not likely to inflate them.

Summary

In this chapter, commonly used psychometric procedures were evaluated in terms of the types of errors they reflect. Empirical procedures commonly employed during measure development—specifically, internal consistency, test-retest reliability, factor analyses, and validity tests—were shown to capture a wider set of errors than intended. A low correlation between an item and the total score could be caused by several errors other than random error. An understanding of the variety of errors that can cause specific empirical outcomes is important in measure development and validation, as elaborated in Chapter 5.

Notes

1. A detailed discussion of recommended sample sizes that represent large samples for various procedures is beyond the scope of this book. Detailed discussions

of statistical considerations are available in past research (Guadagnoli & Velicer, 1988; Nunnally, 1978). Moreover, sample size criteria may have to be met not just to minimize the likelihood of idiosyncratic random error, but to meet other statistical requirements, such as those for confirmatory factor analysis. For the purposes of explication of idiosyncratic random error, sufficient sample sizes in measurement development procedures are assumed.

2. Alliger and Williams (1992) make a similar argument in exploring the relationship between internal consistency and rater response tendencies.

3. Schmidt and Hunter (1996) describe a source of transient error that could enhance internal consistency on a given occasion while decreasing stability across administration. They use the example of the mood state of different individuals affecting responses and point out that coefficient alpha includes variance due to transient error as true variance. In this book, this type of error is captured under within-measure correlational systematic error (Chapter 3). It occurs to the extent that individuals vary in differing degrees in their responses to items of a measure over and above true variation. For instance, if idiosyncratic mood states lead to more consistent responses across items, these are sources of within-measure correlational systematic error. If this factor affects a small proportion of individuals, then it is categorized under idiosyncratic random error. If it is more pervasive and affects a sizable proportion of individuals, it may cause random error across administrations.

4. In comparing test-retest to internal consistency reliability, the different theoretical foundations underlying these two forms of reliability and the consequent differences in empirical outcomes should be noted (Parameswaran, Greenberg, Bellenger, & Robertson, 1979). Test-retest reliability has its roots in the theory of true and error factors wherein an observed score consists of a true score and an error score, and an important assumption is that the trait being measured endures over time. Internal consistency reliability has its roots in the domain sampling model with the assumption that the average interim correlation is the same for all items in a domain. Cronbach (1951) carefully distinguished between equivalence and stability. The focus here is on identifying and analyzing error sources and errors that may affect one form of reliability versus another with a view to drawing pragmatic implications for the use of each of these approaches. Hence, the starting point here is a conceptual understanding of types of measurement error and the interplay between error sources, errors, and scale responses rather than the different theoretical foundations underlying forms of reliability.

5. It should be noted that across-measure systematic error includes both the correlational and the additive types. If completion of one measure leads to inflated responses on a subsequent measure of a different construct, it may not affect observed relationships (i.e., constant additive systematic error), or it may deflate observed relationships (i.e., partial additive systematic error). Therefore, the broader term *across-measure systematic error* is used here. Narrower terms that specify the correlational or additive nature of error are used to describe the specific types of across-measure systematic error.

5

How Can Measurement Error Be Identified and Corrected For in Measure Development?

Overview

This chapter uses the discussion in previous chapters to develop guidelines to identify and correct for error in developing and using measures. Using distinctions between types of measurement error in Chapter 2, Chapter 4 showed that traditional psychometric procedures reflect a wider set of errors than intended. In Chapter 5, a three-step process is presented for identifying and correcting for measurement error at each stage of measure development: (a) assessing diagnostics from traditional psychometric procedures, design characteristics of psychometric tests, and conditions of future usage; (b) identifying specific types of error using these diagnostics; and (c) correcting for error. Following a discussion of the three-step process, the chapter is organized by specific diagnostics.

Researchers who design or use measures typically conduct global assessments of measure quality but often do not attempt to identify specific types of measurement error. Researchers who develop scales should report systematic assessment of the specific types of measurement error. When researchers use scales in new settings, examination of measurement error is often insufficient even when psychometric properties are marginal. Reexaminations of previously validated scales should incorporate systematic assessments of measurement error. Guidelines are developed here to identify specific types of measurement error and suggest appropriate ways of correcting for each type of error. The guiding premise here, as in the rest of the book, is that identifying the nature of the measurement error involved enables its correction.

As discussed in Chapter 4, heavily or exclusively used traditional psychometric procedures, such as internal consistency and test-retest reliability, confound random and systematic errors. Nevertheless, these procedures are discussed here because they are important in the preliminary development of measures in order to develop robust items that then can be employed in confirmatory factor analysis and structural equation modeling. Moreover, a large proportion of the recent articles that use empirical measures report coefficient alpha based on internal consistency, either exclusively or supplemented with exploratory factor analysis or test-retest reliability. Coefficient alpha is the most widely used indicator of reliability (Peterson, 1994). Ideally, later stages of measure development should employ structural equation modeling that incorporates internal consistency and test-retest reliability.

Although this chapter focuses on empirical procedures employed in reliability and dimensionality assessment, the procedures used to develop a set of items to begin with are critical in minimizing different types of measurement error. The starting point for measure development is the definition of the construct to be measured and delineation of its domain. Careful procedures to generate and edit items tapping into the domain of a construct are crucial for the content validity of a measure. The issues that arise in modifying a measure during the early stages of measure assessment are the same issues that can be minimized during item generation and editing, as suggested by the iterative procedures of measure development (Churchill, 1979) and the nature of recommendations developed below.

Guidelines for Identifying and Correcting For Error in Measure Development

A stepwise process is presented for identifying and correcting for measurement error when developing measures. Although this process is discussed here in a context where items have been developed and are being assessed, the recommendations presented here are useful in developing items to begin with. The first step in measure assessment after data have been collected involves assessing psychometric diagnostics. Diagnostics extend beyond traditional empirical indicators from psychometric procedures discussed in earlier chapters and include consideration of the design of psychometric tests, and conditions of future usage. The second step involves identifying specific types of measurement error on the basis of these diagnostics. The nuanced presentation of types of errors presented in earlier chapters is very relevant here. Recognizing the specific type of measurement error in the process of developing measures leads to corresponding recommendations to minimize them. Therefore, the third step involves recommendations for correcting for specific types of error. Understanding the specific type of error involved in a situation and the likely sources enables correcting for such error.

Step 1: Computing and Evaluating Relevant Diagnostics

A variety of psychometric diagnostics are traditionally used in measure development and need to be computed and evaluated in this step (Tables 5.1 to 5.3; Figure 5.1). Table 5.1 is organized around psychometric procedures, whereas Table 5.2 is an abridged version organized around diagnostics. In addition to the traditional empirical indicators, item means and standard deviations should be explicitly considered in light of the earlier discussion about additive systematic error. Extreme item means, due to sources such as extreme wording or moderate end anchors, can reflect additive systematic error and inhibit the ability of an item to covary.

Diagnostics used in this step should extend beyond empirical results of psychometric tests to include consideration of the design of psychometric tests and future applications of the measure. What is validated is not so much a measure as its use in specific ways. The interplay between test design, empirical outcomes, and future applications is central to the development of measures. Measures are assessed and validated through an iterative process of designing psychometric tests and interpreting empirical outcomes. Psychometric tests involve design choices, such as sample size and the sequencing of items, that bear on understanding possible sources of measurement error. Empirical outcomes of tests provide additional understanding of measurement error. A validated measure is then used in a variety of applications. However, what is validated is really the use of a measure under certain conditions (Finn & Kayande, 1997). Therefore, future applications of a measure must be anticipated during development in order to validate it.

In this step, computed diagnostics need to be evaluated in terms of their magnitude. Rough guidelines are provided for psychometric diagnostics from past research where available (Table 5.3). However, these guidelines are approximate and need to be adapted to the specific research context. Many treatments of rules of thumb in the literature emphasize this important point. For example, as Peterson (1994) notes, the literature has little by way of recommended reliability levels. Moreover, when such recommendations are presented, they lack appropriate justification beyond experience.

(Text continues on page 178)

Table 5.1   Guidelines for Identifying and Correcting For Error in Measure Development

Internal Consistency	Procedures	Diagnostics	Possible Type of Measurement Error	Recommendations
Design	Assess sample size	Small sample size[a]	Idiosyncratic random error within administration	Increase sample size
Empirical outcome	Assess item-to-total correlations and item means in the context of coefficient alpha	Low/moderate item-to-total correlations and nonextreme item means[b]	Generic random error within administration	Delete item or assess content and reword if item captures unique aspect of domain
		Low/moderate item-to-total correlations and extreme item means	Additive systematic error	Tone item or delete; assess sample composition; assess labeling and number of response categories if means for all items are high
		Moderate/high item-to-total correlations and extreme item means	Additive systematic error	Assess content and tone item; assess sample composition; test using appropriate samples; assess labeling and number of response categories if means for all items are high
		Moderate/high item-to-total correlations	Within-measure correlational systematic error	Reduce trivial redundancy; assess domain representation by items; delete/reword/add items; assess item for method factors or different constructs and delete or reword; assess dimensionality through factor analysis
	Assess item-to-total correlations across studies	Item-to-total correlations sizably different across studies	Idiosyncratic random error	Increase sample size
Future applications	List future applications	Likely future usage under different conditions, such as item ordering, use of fillers, sample composition, or short forms	Within-measure correlational systematic error	Match measure testing to subsequent usage conditions—use multiple internal consistency procedures in different settings and across different populations; use empirical tests of item characteristics through sequencing, fillers, short forms and so on; specify usage conditions

Test-Retest Reliability	Procedures	Diagnostics	Possible Type of Measurement Error	Recommendations
Design	Assess sample size	Small sample size	Idiosyncratic random error within administration; Idiosyncratic random error across administrations	Increase sample size
Empirical outcome	Assess item-level test-retest correlations and item means across administrations within context of measure-level test-retest correlation	Low/moderate item-level test-retest correlation and item means significantly different across administrations	Generic random error across administrations due to additive error within administration	Assess administration procedures; reassess test-retest reliability using strict replication; use multiple internal consistency procedures in subsequent analyses; delete or reword item
		Low/moderate item-level test-retest correlation and item means not significantly different across administrations[c]	Generic random error across administrations due to different sources	Assess administration procedures; reassess test-retest reliability using strict replication; use multiple internal consistency procedures in subsequent analyses; delete or reword item
			Generic random error across administrations due to low stability of individual items	Use generalizability studies in subsequent analysis; delete or reword item
		Moderate/high item-level test-retest correlation	Within-measure correlational systematic error due to common method	Study item characteristics through sequencing in subsequent analysis or reword
			Within-measure correlational systematic error due to a common method or a different construct/method	Assess content for dimensionality for different constructs or method factors; assess dimensionality in subsequent analyses
	Assess item-level test-retest correlations across studies	Item-level test-retest correlations sizably different across studies	Idiosyncratic random error	Increase sample size
Future applications	List future applications	Likely future usage under different conditions, such as item ordering, use of fillers, sample composition, time intervals in longitudinal designs, or short forms	Within-measure correlational systematic error	Test to match usage conditions—use multiple internal consistency procedures in different settings; use empirical test-retest of item characteristics through sequencing, fillers, short forms, and so on; specify usage conditions (e.g., time interval in longitudinal designs)

(Continued)

Table 5.1 (Continued)

Exploratory Factor Analysis	Procedures	Diagnostics	Possible Type of Measurement Error	Recommendations
Design	Assess sample size	Small sample size	Idiosyncratic random error within administration	Increase sample size
Empirical outcome	Assess factor loadings of items on primary and secondary factors and item means in the context of variance explained by each factor	Low/moderate factor loading on primary factor and extreme item means	Additive systematic error	Tone item or delete; assess sample composition; assess labeling and number of response categories, if means for all items are high
		Low/moderate factor loading on primary factor and moderate/high factor loading on secondary factor	Within-measure correlational systematic error due to a different construct/method or common method[d]	Delete or reword item; reassess conceptual model
		Low/moderate factor loading on primary factor and low/moderate loading on secondary factor	Within-measure correlational systematic error due to a different construct/method[e]	Assess content for dimensionality and reword or delete
		Moderate/high loading on primary factor and moderate/high loading on secondary factor	Within-measure correlational systematic error due to a different construct/method or common method	Assess content and delete or reword; assess dimensionality through CFA; reassess conceptual model
		Factor loadings across multiple dimensions blurred for all items	Within-measure correlational systematic error due to a common method	Assess content and reword; assess sequencing; assess dimensionality; reassess conceptual model
		Factor loadings across multiple dimensions blurred for some items	Within-measure correlational systematic error due to a different construct/method	Assess content and reword or delete; assess dimensionality in subsequent analysis; reassess conceptual model
	Assess loadings across studies	Factor loadings sizably different across studies	Idiosyncratic random error within administration	Increase sample size
Future applications	List future applications	Likely future usage under different conditions, e.g., item-ordering, use of fillers, sample composition, or short forms	Within-measure correlational systematic error	Test to match usage conditions—factor analysis procedures in different settings across different populations; factor analysis empirical tests of item characteristics through sequencing, fillers, short-forms, and so on; specify usage conditions

Confirmatory Factor Analysis	Procedures	Diagnostics	Possible Type of Measurement Error	Recommendations
Design	Assess sample size	Small sample size	Idiosyncratic random error within administration	Increase sample size
Empirical outcome	Assess residuals within dimensions	Residuals within dimensions among all items	Within-measure correlational systematic error due to a common method	Use prior analyses to specify method factor; assess sequencing and use of fillers and retest; delete item or reword; reassess conceptual model
		Residuals within dimensions among subset of items	Within-measure correlational systematic error due to a different construct/method	Use prior analyses to specify correlated errors or method factors; delete item or reword; reassess conceptual model
	Assess residuals across dimensions	Residuals across dimensions among all items	Within-measure correlational systematic error due to a common method	Use prior analyses to specify method factor; assess sequencing and use of fillers and retest; delete item or reword; reassess conceptual model
		Residuals across dimensions among subset of items	Within-measure correlational systematic error due to a different construct/method	Use prior analyses to specify correlated errors or method factors; delete item or reword; reassess conceptual model
	Assess residuals across measures	Residuals across measures	Across-measure systematic error	Use prior analyses to specify correlated errors or method factors; assess sequencing and use of fillers; delete item or reword
Future applications	List future applications	Likely future usage under different conditions, such as item ordering, use of fillers, sample composition, or short forms	Within-measure correlational systematic error	Test to match usage conditions—CFA procedures in different settings across different populations; CFA empirical tests of item characteristics through sequencing, fillers, short forms, and so on; specify usage conditions

(Continued)

Table 5.1 (Continued)

Validity Tests	Procedures	Diagnostics	Possible Type of Measurement Error	Recommendations
Design	Assess grouping or separation of central variables	Grouping of central variables in tests of convergent and nomological validity (contiguous administration, such as same page or in sequence; common method, including same response format; common instructions; labeling measures)	Across-measure systematic error	Separate central variables—separation across time within an administration, use of fillers; separation through different methods; separate instructions; different response formats; dual administration; dual or multiple informants or independent sources for different variables; labeling measures / Specify correlated errors or method factors in SEM
		Separation of central variables in test of discriminant validity (separation across time within an administration; separation through different methods; separate instructions; different response formats; dual administration; dual or multiple informants or independent sources for different variables; labeling measures; using filler tasks of different nature)	Across-measure systematic error	Group central variables—contiguous administration (e.g., same page or in sequence); common method (including same response format); common instructions; labeling measures / Specify correlated errors or method factors in SEM / Differential relationship between measures of two related constructs and a third construct
Empirical outcome	Assess sample size	Small sample size	Idiosyncratic random error within administration	Increase sample size
	Assess reliability of individual measures	Low/moderate reliability	Generic random error	Use reliable measures of constructs; use SEM-based approach to account for unreliability
	Assess correlations	High correlations for tests of convergent and nomological validity and central variables grouped	Across-measure systematic error[f]	Separate central variables / Specify correlated errors or method factors in SEM

Validity Tests	Procedures	Diagnostics	Possible Type of Measurement Error	Recommendations
		Low correlations for tests of discriminant validity and central variables separated	Across-measure systematic error	Employ multitrait, multimethod (MTMM) approach; apply confirmatory factor analysis to MTMM data
				Group central variables
				Specify correlated errors or method factors in SEM
				Employ multitrait, multimethod (MTMM) approach; apply confirmatory factor analysis to MTMM data
Future applications	List future applications	Likely future usage under different conditions, such as item ordering, use of fillers, sample composition, or short forms	Across-measure systematic error	Test to match usage conditions—validity tests of randomized order of items from different measures; validity tests using filler items; validity tests across populations; specify usage conditions

NOTE: Significance refers to statistical significance in all tables unless otherwise stated.

a. Several rules of thumb are available on sample size, such as using five times the number of items. For a thorough discussion of sample sizes required for various psychometric procedures, please refer to Nunnally (1978) and Guadagnoli and Velicer (1988).

b. What constitutes low, moderate, or high item-to-total correlations can only be interpreted in context. For example, measures of broad constructs may have low item-to-total correlations, because each item is tapping into some aspect of a diverse domain; hence, an item-to-total correlation of 0.20 may be considered appropriate. On the other hand, for a more homogeneous domain, an item-to-total correlation of 0.25 may be low. The relative magnitude of an item-to-total correlation compared to other item-to-total correlations is very useful in this regard. Similarly, what constitutes an extreme mean really can be judged only in the context of the construct in question, the sample being employed, and the samples to be employed in future applications. Any mean that restricts variation, and thus the ability of an item to correlate, is clearly too extreme at the development stage. However, means may be extreme (say, more than 5 on a 7-point scale) while still capturing variation and having satisfactory item-to-total correlations. Whether such means are too high would depend on the sample in question and the expected strength of the construct in other populations where the scale would be used. For example, high item means with student samples suggest item toning, if the strength of the construct in other populations is likely to be much higher. Standard deviations across item means can be employed to judge the extremity of a specific item mean.

c. Such a pattern may also reflect generic random error within administration, addressed in internal consistency procedures. Examination of internal consistency and test-retest reliability of individual items in conjunction provides further insight into measurement error. Some items may have high internal consistency as well as stability. Other items may have moderate internal consistency and low stability. The reverse may also occur, that is, high stability and moderate internal consistency. Such a pattern is potentially indicative of items tapping a different construct and, hence, not as strongly related to other items in a measure, or alternately, capturing some aspect of the construct that is not captured by other items. Test-retest reliability in conjunction with internal consistency can be employed to distinguish between several types of measurement error. By assessing relative magnitudes of item-to-total correlations versus test-retest correlations, several insights can be drawn, as discussed in Chapter 6.

d. Whether within-measure correlational systematic error is due to a common method or to a different construct/method can be determined by assessing whether the pattern of correlations is across all items or a subset of items of a dimension, respectively.

e. Such a pattern may also reflect generic random error, addressed in internal consistency procedures.

f. As discussed, a variety of errors in the measurement of individual constructs can influence outcomes of validity tests.

Table 5.2 Abridged Guidelines for Identifying and Correcting For Error in Developing Measures

Step 1: Assess Psychometric Diagnostics			Step 2: Identify Types of Error	Step 3: Correct for Specific Types of Error
Diagnostics	Rules of Thumb	Procedure		
Small sample size	< 100–200 < 5–10 × number of items	All psychometric procedures	Idiosyncratic random error within administration	Increase sample size
Indicators significantly different across studies			Idiosyncratic random error across administration	Increase sample size
Low item-to-total correlations	< 0.30	Internal consistency	Generic random error within administration	Assess content and delete or reword item; reword if item captures unique aspect of domain
Low item-level test-retest correlation	Nonsignificant	Test-retest reliability	Generic random error within administration	Assess content and delete or reword item; assess administration procedures; reassess test-retest reliability using strict replication; use multiple internal consistency procedures to assess differences in administration in future use
Item means different across administration	Significant		Generic random error across administration	
Extreme means (low standard deviations)		All psychometric procedures	Additive systematic error	Assess content and delete or tone item in light of sample composition; test using appropriate samples; assess labeling and number of response categories, if means for all items are high
High item-to-total correlation	> 0.30	Internal consistency	Within-measure correlational systematic error	Assess item for method factors or different constructs and delete or reword; reduce trivial redundancy; assess domain representation by items; assess dimensionality through factor analysis
High item-level test-retest correlation	Significant	Test-retest reliability	Within-measure correlational systematic error	Assess content for dimensionality and for different constructs or method factors; assess dimensionality through factor analysis; study item characteristics through sequencing

Step 1: Assess Psychometric Diagnostics			Step 2: Identify Types of Error	Step 3: Correct for Specific Types of Error
Diagnostics	Rules of Thumb	Procedure		
High loadings on secondary factors Loadings blurred for some/all items across multiple dimensions	> 0.30–0.50	Exploratory and confirmatory factor analysis	Within-measure correlational systematic error	Assess item for method factors or different constructs and delete or reword; assess sequencing and use of fillers between individual items or sets of items representing dimensions; assess dimensionality through confirmatory factor analysis; reassess conceptual model
Standardized residuals within or across dimensions for some/all items	> 2–2.58	Confirmatory factor analysis	Within-measure correlational systematic error	Assess item for method factors or different constructs and delete or reword; assess sequencing and use of fillers between individual items or sets of items representing dimensions; use prior analyses to specify method factor; reassess conceptual model
Likely future usage under different conditions		All psychometric procedures	Within-measure correlational systematic error	Match measure testing to conditions of future use (e.g., different settings and populations, different forms of a measure, such as sequencing, fillers, short forms, labeling); specify usage conditions
Standardized residuals across measures for some/all items	> 2–2.58	Confirmatory factor analysis	Across-measure systematic error	Delete item or reword; assess sequencing and use of fillers; specify correlated errors or method factors
Grouping (separation) of central variables		Nomological/ convergent (discriminant) validity	Across-measure systematic error	Separate (group) central variables; design strong tests of discriminant validity tests through differential relationships between two measures and a third, and through plausible method factors; specify correlated errors or method factors in structural equation modeling
High (low) correlations		Nomological/ convergent (discriminant) validity	Across-measure systematic error	Separate (group) central variables; infer strong/weak evidence of validity on the basis of separation or grouping or nature of discriminant validity tests; specify correlated errors or method factors in structural equation modeling

NOTE: This is a shortened set of guidelines that contains many of the key elements from Table 5.1.

Table 5.3 Assessing Psychometric Diagnostics

Step 1: Assess Psychometric Diagnostics

Diagnostics	Rules of Thumb	Procedure	Illustrative Cite	Comment
Small sample size	< 100	Internal consistency	Mendoza, Stafford, and Stauffer (2000)	Mendoza et al. (2000) show that confidence intervals for reliability and validity are accurate when the size of a random sample is greater than 100. A variety of rules of thumb for factor analysis include sample sizes no less than 100 and sample sizes five or 10 times the number of variables (Iacobucci, 1994). However, this issue is more complicated and depends on a variety of factors, such as the magnitude of communalities (MacCallum et al., 1999). Some analyses have suggested sample sizes greater than 100 (Anderson & Gerbing, 1984; Boomsma, 1982), greater than 150 (Guadagnoli & Velicer, 1988), and greater than 200 (Comrey, 1978). Researchers are reluctant to suggest rules of thumb regarding sample sizes for structural equation modeling (MacCallum & Austin, 2000).
Indicators significantly different across studies	< 100	Test-retest correlation	Mendoza et al. (2000)	
	< 100; < 5–10 times the number of items	Exploratory factor analysis	Iacobucci (1994)	
	< 100–200	Confirmatory factor analysis	Boomsma (1982); Anderson and Gerbing (1984); Comrey (1978)	
	< 100	Validity correlations	Mendoza et al. (2000)	
Low item-to-total correlations	< 0.30	Internal consistency	Briggs and Cheek (1988); Nunnally (1978) and others summarized in Peterson (1994)	The literature lacks prescriptions on minimum item-to-total correlation; 0.30 is suggested, similar to the recommendation for factor loadings below (Hair et al., 1998). However, what constitutes low, moderate, or high item-to-total correlations can be interpreted only in context. For example, measures of broad constructs may have low item-to-total correlations, because each item is tapping into some aspect of a diverse domain, hence an item-to-total correlation of 0.20 may be considered appropriate. On the other hand, for a more homogeneous domain, an item-to-total correlation of 0.25 may be low. The relative magnitude of an item-to-total correlation compared to other item-to-total correlations is very useful in this regard.
Low inter-item correlation	< 0.20			
Coefficient alpha	< 0.70–0.80			Recommended reliability levels are often in the vicinity of 0.70 for preliminary research, 0.8 for basic research, and 0.95 for applied research (Peterson, 1994).

Step 1: Assess Psychometric Diagnostics

Diagnostics	Rules of Thumb	Procedure	Illustrative Cite	Comment
Low item-level test-retest correlation	Nonsignificant	Test-retest reliability		The literature lacks rules of thumb for test-retest correlations; hence, statistical significance is suggested as a starting point. Statistical significance should be interpreted in light of sample sizes with the magnitude of the correlation being a central consideration.
Item means different across administrations	Significant			
Extreme means (Low standard deviations)		All psychometric procedures		What constitutes an extreme mean can really be judged only in the context of the construct in question, the sample being employed, and the samples to be employed in future applications. Any mean that restricts variation, and thus the ability of an item to correlate, is clearly too extreme at the development stage. However, means may be moderately high or low (say, more than 5 or less than 3 on a 7-point scale) while still capturing variation and having satisfactory item-to-total correlations. Whether such means are too high or too low would depend on the sample in question and the expected strength of the construct in other populations where the scale would be used. For example, high item means with student samples suggest item toning if the strength of the construct in other populations is likely to be much higher. Standard deviations across item means can be employed to judge the extremity of a specific item mean.

(Continued)

Table 5.3 (Continued)

Step 1: Assess Psychometric Diagnostics

Diagnostics	Rules of Thumb	Procedure	Illustrative Cite	Comment
High loadings on secondary factors; loadings blurred for some/all items across multiple dimensions	>0.30–0.50	Exploratory and confirmatory factor analysis	Hair et al. (1998)	Hair et al. (1998) suggest factor loadings greater than 0.30 as meeting the minimal level, greater than .40 as being important, and greater than .50 as being practically significant. In assessing statistical significance while interpreting loadings, the sample size has to be taken into account. Similarly, several criteria, such as scree tests and eigenvalues, are suggested for identifying the number of factors.
Standardized residuals within or across dimensions for some/all items	>2–2.58	Confirmatory factor analysis	Bagozzi and Yi (1988); Hair et al. (1998)	Bagozzi and Yi (1988) suggest that standardized residuals greater than 2 are considered high. LISREL VII and later programs suggest standardized residuals > 2.58 (Hair et al., 1998). Bentler and Bonnett (1980) suggested that fit indexes should be 0.90 or above. However, others have proposed more conservative rules of thumb close to 0.95 (Hu & Bentler, 1998).
Overall fit index	<0.90		Bentler and Bonnett (1980)	
Standardized root-mean-square residuals	>0.05–0.08		Hu and Bentler (1998)	
Variance extracted	<50%		Fornell and Larcker (1981)	
High (low) correlations		Nomological/convergent (discriminant) validity		Some statistical textbooks have categorized high, medium, and low correlations (e.g., > 0.50 is high). However, rules of thumb here are again very much subject to the research context.

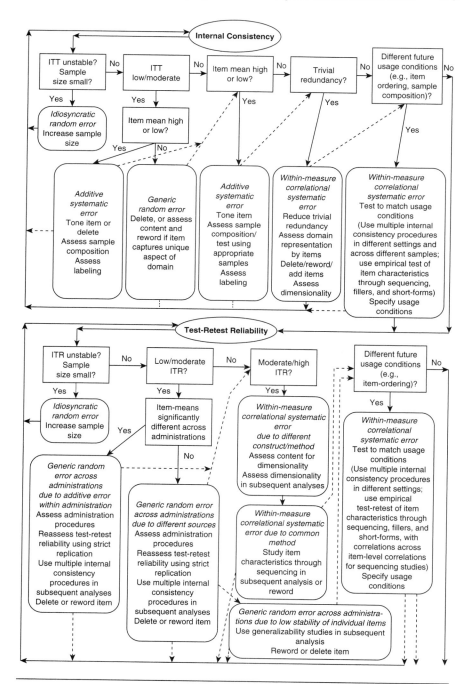

Figure 5.1   Analytical Framework for Measure Development and Validation

(Continued)

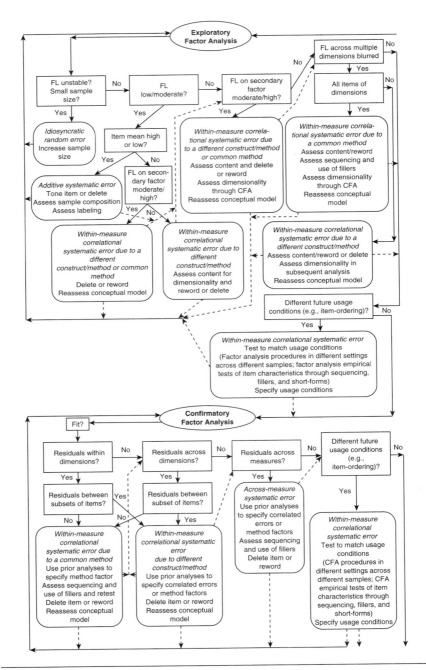

Figure 5.1 (Continued)

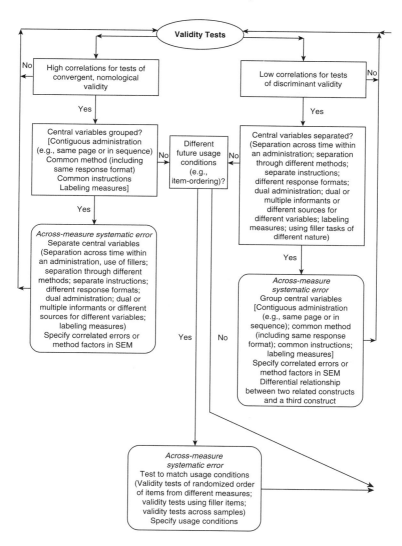

NOTES: ITT = item-to-total correlation; ITR = item-level test-retest correlation; FL = Factor loading; solid lines represent single paths; dashed lines represent multiple paths depending on judgment at previous step; dashed lines that advance an item or a measure to the next step apply when statistics for item/measure is acceptable and the item/measure has been considered acceptable after assessment on issues in previous step (for example, considering an item with low/moderate ITT and with item means that are not extreme, if the item is considered acceptable for issues listed under generic random error, and if the item has satisfactory ITT, i.e., moderate ITT, it can advance to the next step; assessment of magnitudes of ITT or ITR of FL are not exact but approximate and judgments have to be made as to what is in the low to moderate range and what is in the moderate to high range based on a variety of factors in a specific situation; see Table 5.3).

Recommended reliability levels also depend on the purpose and stage of research (Peterson, 1994), again emphasizing the importance of context. The issue of rules of thumb is just as complex for sample sizes for different psychometric procedures.[1]

Step 2: Identifying Types of Error From Psychometric Diagnostics

The second step in the proposed process is to identify the specific type of measurement error based on psychometric diagnostics. The types of error associated with specific psychometric diagnostics are summarized in Table 5.1, based on earlier discussion. As discussed in Chapter 4, psychometric diagnostics from traditional procedures reflect a wider set of errors than intended (Figure 4.1). Additionally, design characteristics of psychometric tests (i.e., the use of small sample sizes) can cause idiosyncratic random error (Tables 5.1 and 5.2; Figure 5.1). Generic future usage conditions, such as sample composition, item sequencing, the use of short forms, and the use of fillers can also lead to measurement error. Within-measure correlational systematic error is a key consideration in assessing a measure for the conditions of future use. For example, the halo effect occurs within a measure when responses to later items are based on a general impression created by earlier items. Such error is not problematic if the measure is the unit of analysis and items in the measure are to be arranged in the same sequence in future applications. It may be problematic, however, if individual items are used in a shorter form or in a random order, or interspersed with items measuring other constructs or fillers.[2]

Step 3: Correcting for Specific Types of Errors in Measure Development

Knowing the exact nature of measurement error involved enables solutions for its correction. Recommendations are made at five different levels: item (e.g., changes in wording of items), measure (i.e., the aggregate set of items that comprises the measure, such as changes to response scales, changes in sequencing of items, short forms, use of filler items from other measures between items), administration (i.e., aspects of a method at a more aggregate level than a single measure, such as sequencing of measures of multiple constructs, procedures, settings, and samples); data analysis (e.g., specifying method factors), and construct (i.e., reassessing the construct conceptually and rethinking its dimensionality). A summary of recommendations is presented in Figure 5.2. The guidelines are summarized by type of error in Tables 5.1 and 5.2.

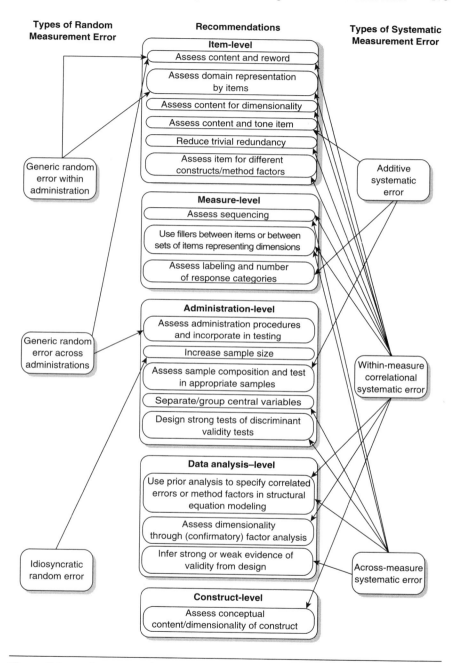

Figure 5.2   Summary of Recommendations for Correcting Measurement Error

Generic Issues in Designing Psychometric Tests

The use of small sample sizes in psychometric procedures employed during measure development may lead to idiosyncratic random error. This points out the need to use large samples without which meaningful conclusions are difficult, if not impossible (Tables 5.1 and 5.2; Figures 5.1 and 5.2). The practice of using small samples in preliminary stages of measure development can lead to the selection of inappropriate items for subsequent stages. This guideline reinforces the importance of recognizing that measurement is a large-sample theory, and that measurement indicators such as reliability have precision estimates as well (Nunnally, 1978). Item-to-total correlations, item-level test-retest correlations, factor loadings, or correlations in validity tests that vary sizably from study to study suggest the need to increase sample sizes to avoid idiosyncratic random error.

Item-to-Total Correlations (Internal Consistency Procedures)

Low Item-to-Total Correlations: Generic Random Error Within an Administration

Low item-to-total correlations point toward generic random error within an administration. Such a pattern suggests deleting an item in traditional internal consistency procedures. If an item captures the appropriate content of a focal construct, rewording can resolve problems that contribute to error (e.g., ambiguous or complex wording). Additionally, the item should be assessed for content and reworded if it captures a unique aspect of the domain that is not captured by other items (Tables 5.1 and 5.2; Figures 5.1 and 5.2). Thus, the content validity of the scale is enhanced by using a representative set of items.

High Item-to-Total Correlations: Within-Measure Correlational Systematic Error

High item-to-total correlations are the ideal outcome for items in internal consistency procedures. However, such correlations may be due to within-measure correlation systematic error caused by a common method. Identical response categories, and wording that elicits response sets, are some sources of such error (e.g., common word stems for items of a scale of sentiment toward advertising, such as "Most advertising . . . ," or all items worded so that agreement indicates negative sentiment). This type of error may lead to high internal consistency, but it may also undermine the dimensionality and content validity of a measure. Within-measure correlational systematic error due to a different, but related, construct or method may also cause similar results. Such error may be caused by factors such as shared context or wording among a subset of items. For example, a subset of a measure of value consciousness may share a specific context, such as grocery shopping (e.g., "When grocery shopping, I compare the prices of different brands to be sure I get the best value for the money" and "I always check prices at the grocery store to be sure I get the best value for the money I spend"; see Appendix 1.2). This type of error increases internal consistency but undermines unidimensionality or distinctions between items representing different dimensions of a measure.

Therefore, items must be examined for common method factors, different constructs, or specific method factors. They must also be examined for representation of the entire domain of the construct rather than some narrow aspect of it. High internal consistency among a set of items may result from trivial redundancy (e.g., very similar items with minor differences in syntax). Redundancy, whether trivial or useful, is recommended when generating items, and useful redundancy is recommended in the final versions of a measure (DeVellis, 1991). Trivial redundancy may lead to a final measure that does not fully capture the domain of a construct (Epstein, 1983), but rather narrowly operationalizes the underlying construct. Within-measure correlational systematic error cannot be detected empirically through internal consistency procedures. Therefore, items should be carefully examined for content. The dimensionality of items should also be assessed empirically through factor analysis, particularly confirmatory factor analysis (Bagozzi, 1980, 1983; Gerbing & Anderson, 1988).

Item Means

Extreme Item Means (All Psychometric Procedures): Additive Systematic Error

Item means should be examined to supplement diagnostic information. Item means that are extreme suggest additive systematic error for a specific sample. Sources of such error include extremely worded items (e.g., "I hate products . . ." or "I always shop . . ." or "American products, first, last, and foremost," the latter item being an example from the consumer ethnocentrism scale in Appendix 1.2) or mildly worded end anchors (e.g., *agree-disagree* or *good-bad*) that can cause mean responses to be extreme. Items with which nearly everyone (or no one) may agree can cause such error, such as, "I sometimes use numerical information to make decisions." When extreme means and low standard deviations occur with low item-to-total correlations or low factor loadings, additive systematic error may be inhibiting the ability of an item to covary (e.g., "Learning and remembering numerical information about various issues is a waste of time"; Mean = 5.24; Exhibit 1.2). Although the item may be deleted, the occurrence of such a pattern may warrant assessing the content of an item and moderating its wording, that is, toning it. This recommendation is particularly relevant if the item captures a unique aspect of the focal domain (Tables 5.1 and 5.2; Figures 5.1 and 5.2). If all items have extreme means, it might suggest using more extreme end anchors or a larger number of response categories at the measure level.

Relatively high or low item means can also occur with moderate or high item-to-total correlations or factor loadings when means are not extreme enough to restrict covariation. In traditional internal consistency and factor analysis, such items are often considered acceptable. However, such items should also be examined for item content and moderated in wording or valence (i.e., toned) if necessary. Such toning should be done in light of the sample composition. This issue is all the more relevant when a relatively homogeneous sample, such as a student sample, is used to develop a measure and is expected to differ in item means from a different population in which the measure will be used. For example, say, scores on the consumer ethnocentrism scale (Appendix 1.2) are expected to be higher in nonstudent, adult populations than in student populations. Even with satisfactory item-to-total correlations, high item means for a consumer ethnocentrism measure with student samples suggest the need for item toning if the strength of the construct in other relevant populations is likely to be much higher. On the other hand, low item means in nonstudent, adult populations suggest problems with lower means with student samples. Through explicit consideration of additive systematic error, items can be modified during the development of measures to capture variation in different populations in which they are likely to be used.

Different Item Means (Test-Retest Reliability): Generic Random Error Across Administrations

Traditional test-retest reliability analyses should also be supplemented with item means for diagnostic purposes. Means for specific items may be significantly different across administrations because of random error across administrations. A pattern of different item means may occur because of item-level issues, such as wording (e.g., items lacking specific context, such as "I use numbers in most situations"), suggesting deleting or rewording an item. At the administration level, interviewer bias in one administration or differences in method of administration between test and retest (e.g., personal vs. online surveys) may cause such a pattern. This suggests that the researcher should examine administration procedures and reassess test-retest reliability as a strict replication. Alternatively, multiple internal consistency procedures in various settings anticipated in future applications are appropriate if differences across administrations reflect likely future uses of the measure.

Test-Retest Correlations (Test-Retest Reliability)

Low Item-Level Test-Retest Correlations: Generic Random Error Across Administrations

Traditional analyses of overall measure-level test-retest correlation should be supplemented with item-level test-retest correlations for diagnostic purposes. Such item-level correlations reflect the stability of individual items. Low item-level test-retest correlations can be caused by generic random error across administrations. Such error may occur because of poor stability of individual items. For example, items that have a general rather than a specific context, such as "I find advertising believable," may be interpreted differently across time. Here, because the problem is at the item level, individual items should be examined for content and either deleted or reworded (Tables 5.1 and 5.2; Figures 5.1 and 5.2). Such error may also be caused by differences in procedures or settings across administrations (e.g., using personal vs. online surveys, at test vs. retest, respectively). At the administration level, such error suggests assessing administration procedures for differences. Test-retest reliability should be reassessed after reducing such differences between test and retest (i.e., using strict replication). Lacking strict replication, test-retest reliability is not appropriate because results, such as low test-retest correlations, are open to multiple interpretations. If differences across administrations reflect conditions under which the measure will be used (e.g., personal vs. mail surveys), multiple internal consistency procedures should be conducted rather than test-retest reliability procedures. Thus, measures would be assessed under conditions of their future use.[3] Generalizability studies may be a useful alternative by formalizing the effects of occasions and items (Cronbach et al., 1963).

Low Item-Level Test-Retest Correlations: Within-Measure Correlational Systematic Error

Within-measure correlational systematic error due to a common method, such as a halo effect, may also be reflected in low item-level test-retest correlation. As discussed, item responses may be consistent within an administration because of a within-measure halo effect, and yet lack stability. Such a pattern may occur with items lacking specific context that are open to interpretation across time, but may lead to consistent responses within an administration among the items. For example, a set of items lacking specific context, such as "I find advertising useful" and "Advertising is believable," may elicit consistent responses within an administration. However, individual items may not elicit consistent responses across time because of the general wording. Individuals may use different points of reference across administrations for items such as "Numbers are redundant for most situations." The situations they think about in responding to this item may vary across administrations.[4] Items should be reworded if the problem lies at the item level. The problem may also lie at the measure level. In such a scenario, measure-level studies of sequencing (i.e., ordering items in different ways), or the use of fillers (i.e., interspersing items from other measures), are recommended. These alternatives evaluate items after isolating them from the context of other items. The within-measure halo effect is beneficial in achieving internal consistency but should not be at the expense of stability.

High Item-Level Test-Retest Correlations: Within-Measure Correlational Systematic Error

Items with high test-retest correlations are considered acceptable in traditional test-retest reliability analysis. However, as noted, high test-retest correlations can result from consistent responses across administrations to items that reliably measure a different construct or method. For example, if an item that aims to measure value consciousness actually measures price consciousness or individual differences in social desirability, it may reliably capture this different construct or method factor across time (Appendix 1.2). Item 12 in the original PNI scale may have had high test-retest correlation if it reliably measured preference for qualitative information. Although measuring a different construct or method factor, such an item would be acceptable on the basis of item-level test-retest correlation. Within-measure correlational systematic error caused by a common method, a different construct, or a specific method factor needs to be addressed in this scenario. The content of items with high test-retest correlations should be carefully assessed for dimensionality and for different constructs or method factors. This possibility also emphasizes the need to assess the dimensionality of items through exploratory and confirmatory factor analysis (Gerbing & Anderson, 1988).

Factor Loadings (Exploratory Factor Analysis)

High Loadings on Secondary Factors: Within-Measure Correlational Systematic Error

High loadings on secondary factors can indicate the possibility of within-measure correlational systematic error. Such error can be caused by a different construct or method factor affecting a subset of items or a common method affecting all items. For example, high loadings on secondary factors can be caused by responses that reflect individual differences in tendency toward agreement, particularly when all items are valenced in the same direction (e.g., items in a consumer ethnocentrism scale worded so that higher agreement denotes higher consumer ethnocentrism; see Appendix 1.2). High loadings on secondary factors can also be caused by a subset of items sharing a certain context or tapping into a different construct. For example, a subset of items in a consumer ethnocentrism scale may share a specific context, such as imports, or may measure country attitudes, a different construct (e.g., "American people should always buy American-made products instead of imports" and "Only those products that are unavailable in the United States should be imported"; see Appendix 1.2). When high loadings on secondary factors are coupled with low loadings on the primary factor, items should be deleted or reworded.[5] At the construct level, researchers should reexamine the underlying construct as well as the delineation of its domain. Specifically, the hypothesized dimensionality of the measure should be carefully reassessed. For example, a unidimensional structure may have been hypothesized when, in fact, a multidimensional structure is more appropriate. This could lead to low loadings on the primary factor. Thus, when dimensionality is specified incorrectly, it can be interpreted as within-measure correlational systematic error.

High loadings on secondary factors may be coupled with high loadings on the primary factor. Item-level issues, such as shared wording, or items tapping into method factors or different constructs should be examined and items reworded (e.g., Item 11 of the PNI scale has a high loading on a secondary factor as well: "Quantitative information is vital for accurate decisions"). Constructs must also be reexamined conceptually. Additionally, at the measure level, alternatives, such as sequencing items differently or using filler items from other measures, should be assessed. These alternatives are means of separating items presented contiguously. However, such approaches may be effective in reducing error when a common method or a specific method factor influences items, but not when the content of items represents a different construct. Presenting items contiguously may exacerbate such sources of error as shared wording. However, using a different sequence or using fillers cannot solve problems caused by items tapping into different constructs. Dimensionality should also be assessed subsequently through confirmatory factor analysis.[6]

Loadings Across Dimensions: Within-Measure Correlational Systematic Error

Items with high loadings on multiple dimensions suggest within-measure correlational systematic error. Such error due to a common method occurs when all items of a specific dimension have high loadings on multiple dimensions. This type of error can be caused by the use of identical response categories or similar word stems in items or contiguous placement. Such error can also be caused by a different construct or specific method factor affecting a subset of items (e.g., items "I like to own things that impress people" and "The things I own aren't all that important to me" of the defining success and acquisition centrality dimensions, respectively, of the materialism scale sharing a certain context, such as ownership). Similar recommendations at the item, measure, and construct levels apply, as described above when loadings on primary and secondary factors are high. Additionally, items should be worded to capture single dimensions. Fillers could also be used between sets of items representing individual dimensions. Dimensionality should also be assessed subsequently through confirmatory factor analysis.

Residuals (Confirmatory Factor Analysis)

Residuals for individual items can supplement indexes of overall fit and loadings in confirmatory factor analysis. As discussed, residuals between items denote the degree to which observed relationships deviate from hypothesized relationships. A positive residual between two items suggests that the observed relationship between two items is more positive than hypothesized, and vice versa.

Residuals Within Dimensions:
Within-Measure Correlational Systematic Error

Similar recommendations at the item, measure, and construct levels apply in the case of residuals within dimensions, such as those for high secondary loadings in exploratory factor analysis (Tables 5.1 and 5.2; Figures 5.1 and 5.2), with the following qualifications. At the item level, although the rewording of items is a possibility, the need to do so would be minimized by following the proposed guidelines in preceding psychometric tests to develop robust items. Additionally, at the data analysis level, insights gained from preceding analyses can be employed to specify a method factor. However, such specification should be used with the utmost caution (Bagozzi, 1984).

Residuals Across Dimensions:
Within-Measure Correlational Systematic Error

Similar recommendations at item, measure, and construct levels apply for residuals across dimensions as those for loadings across dimensions in exploratory factor analysis. Similar qualifications relating to item and data analysis levels apply, as discussed for residuals within dimensions above.

Residuals Across Measures:
Across-Measure Systematic Error

Residuals across measures suggest across-measure systematic error. At the item level, items need to be examined for content and, if necessary, deleted or reworded. At the measure and administration levels, respectively, the use of fillers between items of measures or between sets of items representing different measures can be assessed. Although such an approach can address method factors, it will not be effective if the content of items reflects a different construct than intended. At the data analysis level, preceding analyses can be used to specify correlated errors or method factors. However, as discussed subsequently, such approaches need to be used with caution and appropriate rationale.

Cross-Construct Correlations (Validity Tests)

As discussed, a variety of errors relevant to the measurement of individual constructs can influence validity tests (Figure 5.1). This emphasizes the need to employ reliable measures of focal constructs and reliable and valid measures of other constructs. A structural equation modeling-based approach can account for several types of measurement error, such as due to unreliability in individual measures. Method factors and correlated errors can be incorporated into a structural equation model with appropriate rationale. Discriminant and convergent validity can also be incorporated into a structural equation modeling approach.

Additionally, across-measure systematic error, correlational and additive, affects validity tests. Some types of validity, such as nomological validity, rest on sizable correlations between focal measures and measures of constructs that are expected to be theoretically related. However, if a focal measure of perceived product quality is placed contiguous to and immediately following a measure of perceived product value in a test of nomological validity, several sources of error could inflate the observed relationship between these two measures. For example, a halo effect in completing the perceived value measure or hypothesis guessing could affect responses to the perceived quality measure and inflate observed relationships. Because across-measure correlational systematic error can inflate observed relationships in such designs, strong evidence of nomological validity cannot be inferred from sizable correlations. On the other hand, discriminant validity tests rest on showing small correlations between focal measures and measures of constructs that are expected to be theoretically unrelated or weakly related. If a focal measure of perceived product quality is placed contiguous to a measure of product familiarity in a discriminant validity test, strong evidence of such validity can be inferred from nonsignificant correlations. This is because across-measure correlational systematic error would have inflated observed correlations, yet small or nonsignificant correlations are found.

A guiding principle in evaluating the design of validity tests relates to the direction in which across-measure systematic error is likely to influence the relationship between two variables. If across-measure systematic error due to research design is likely to inflate correlations, a nonsignificant correlation provides strong evidence of discriminant validity. On the other hand, a sizable correlation between two variables provides strong evidence of nomological or convergent validity when across-measure systematic error due to research design is likely to deflate correlations or is not likely to inflate them.

Design of Validity Tests: Across-Measure Systematic Error

Strong tests of nomological validity or convergent validity can be designed by separating the central variables in question (Tables 5.1 and 5.2; Figures 5.1 and 5.2). Separation can be achieved through several approaches at the administration level, such as separating by time or by the nature of the tasks involved. Consequently, across-measure systematic error between central variables is decreased by reducing the likelihood of sources of error such as halo effects and hypothesis guessing. These sources are more likely to occur with contiguous placement. Central variables can be separated in the sequence in which they are completed by using fillers between measures (i.e., unrelated items or measures). Items from measures of various constructs completed by participants could also be interspersed instead of using fillers.[7] For example, in validating a focal measure of power, items from this measure could be interspersed with items from other measures used for testing validity, such as opportunism and influence. A requirement here is that these measures have identical response categories. Otherwise, fillers should be used between measures rather than between items. Interspersion also comes with trade-offs in the potential for confusing respondents, thereby leading to unreliability. Hence, interspersion may be most appropriate when the total number of items for the entire method is not large. Alternatively, separation can also be achieved through using dual administrations, although this approach raises the costs involved. Different approaches can be used to collect data on different constructs and to achieve separation (e.g., behavioral inventories vs. Likert scales, open-ended tasks vs. closed-ended scales, or self-reports vs. secondary data). Multiple measures of the same construct employing different approaches (say, self-reports vs. secondary data) can also be used. Central variables can be separated by using multiple informants to obtain data on different constructs, as is often the case with dyadic approaches, or by using independent sources (say, self-reports vs. secondary data). Separation can also be achieved by avoiding common instructions or response formats, or avoiding close proximity between measures (e.g., presentation on the same page) (Lennox & Dennis, 1994).[8]

Strong tests of discriminant validity can be designed by grouping central variables. Grouping involves presenting central variables in proximity (through time, method, etc.), wherein across-measure correlational systematic error is likely to inflate correlations. Grouping can be achieved through approaches, such as contiguous administration, common instructions, common methods, and the labeling of measures. Labeling may group items psychologically within a measure from the respondent's perspective. By clearly suggesting the constructs being measured, as well as the relationships between constructs, labeling can lead to hypothesis guessing and the tendency to look for a relationship. Such across-measure correlational systematic error is likely to inflate correlations. Thus, labeling can provide strong tests of discriminant validity when different measures are presented contiguously. However, by clearly distinguishing one measure from another, labeling can also lead to psychological separation among variables and serve as a strong test of nomological validity. Labeling can have multiple effects and must be examined empirically. The likely nature of systematic error with grouping can be examined at different levels of abstraction, from item wording and scale types to halo effects and social desirability (Bagozzi & Yi, 1991). In terms of more concrete method factors, grouping, such as through a common method, is likely to inflate systematic error. At a more abstract level, psychological grouping that clearly suggests the constructs being measured (e.g., through grouping items of a measure and labeling), as well as the relationships between constructs (through contiguous presentation of different measures), can lead to hypothesis guessing and the tendency to look for a relationship.[9]

A number of caveats should be noted with the approaches discussed above, such as labeling. The full effects of different types of labels for a measure need to be understood during measure validation. For instance, the effects of labeling need to be understood prior to validity tests, such as discriminant validity tests. Different types of labeling can lead to varied performance on validity tests. Using very different or ambiguous labels for measures of different constructs can lead to empirical support in discriminant validity tests. On the other hand, using similar labels can lead to support in nomological validity tests. The key in using this approach is to fully understand the effect of these administration factors and provide conceptual arguments along with empirical evidence wherever possible.

Whereas the approaches discussed above relate primarily to the use of a single method, the multitrait-multimethod (MTMM) approach (Campbell & Fiske, 1959) enables accounting for across-measure systematic error in tests of convergent and discriminant validity. Using this approach, evidence for convergent validity is provided through sizable correlations between two different methods of measuring the same construct. Across-measure systematic error due to the use of a single method is accounted for by using different methods. Campbell and Fiske (1959) suggest several criteria for discriminant validity, including (a) higher correlations between different methods of assessing the same construct than between different methods of assessing different constructs, and (b) higher correlations between different methods of assessing the same construct than between the same method of assessing different constructs (Bagozzi, 1993). More recently, Bagozzi (1991) applied confirmatory factor analysis to the MTMM context (Figure 1.21), thereby addressing several problems with the traditional MTMM approach (Tables 5.1 and 5.2; Figures 5.1 and 5.2). Multiple methods and constructs can be used to establish the construct validity of a measure and minimize the impact of across-measure systematic error.

An understanding of across-measure systematic error also enables the design of strong discriminant validity tests. A relatively weak form of evidence for discriminant validity may be provided by showing nonsignificant relationships with theoretical constructs, there likely being many constructs unrelated to the focal construct. For instance, relatively weak evidence is provided by a nonsignificant relationship between a focal measure of value consciousness and a measure of, say, extroversion. Value consciousness is presumably unrelated or weakly related to many other theoretical constructs. However, nonsignificant relationships with plausible methodological sources of across-measure systematic error, such as social desirability, can provide relatively strong evidence of discriminant validity. A weak relationship of value consciousness with a plausible method factor, such as individual differences in social desirability in responses, provides relatively strong evidence of discriminant validity. Differential patterns of relationships between two related constructs and a third construct can provide strong evidence of discriminant validity (Judd et al., 1986). For example, strong evidence of discriminant validity is provided if a focal measure of value consciousness is shown to be related to a measure of quality consciousness, and yet these two measures have a differential pattern of relationship with a measure of a third construct, say, coupon proneness. Such tests account for across-measure systematic error caused by a common construct or method influencing measures of different, but related, constructs. It should be noted that discriminant validity can also be assessed for each item of a measure.

Interpreting Outcomes of Validity Tests: Across-Measure Systematic Error

For empirical results, this analysis suggests that correlations employed in validity tests should be interpreted in the context of the design. The interpretation of empirical results mirrors design issues discussed with regard to the separating or grouping of central variables. Thus, strong or weak evidence for convergent, nomological, or discriminant validity may be inferred from the separating or grouping of central variables. Similarly, strong or weak evidence for discriminant validity may be inferred from tests that show differential patterns of relationship between two related measures and a third, or that show nonsignificant relationships with measures of theoretical constructs or method factors.

Specification of Structural Equation Models: Across-Measure Systematic Error

For both types of validity tests, at the data analysis level, correlated errors or method factors should be appropriately specified in structural equation models. Systematic error can be represented partially by correlated errors and more completely by separate method factors (Bagozzi, 1984). Bagozzi (1984) advises caution in using these approaches and recommends using them only as a last resort. Correlated errors can be used when there are identifiable sources of systematic error (e.g., measurement of the same variable at different points in time, or the use of common procedures to collect data) and when correlated errors are small (Bagozzi, 1984; Fornell, 1983; Gerbing & Anderson, 1984). Similarly, a method factor may be appropriate to specify when a rationale exists for introducing it, provided its effect is small (Bagozzi, 1984; Fornell, 1983). As discussed, confirmatory factor analysis can be applied to multitrait, multimethod data to explicitly model methods and constructs (Bagozzi, 1991).

Conditions of Future Use of Measures

Measure development should anticipate future applications and perform appropriate tests. Although it may be difficult or impossible to anticipate all future uses, some generic factors, such as sample composition, item sequencing, the use of short forms, and the use of fillers, should be anticipated and tested. Procedures for developing measures should match their future use (Tables 5.1 and 5.2; Figures 5.1 and 5.2). As a central part of measure development, researchers should clearly specify conditions of use based on validation work. Presently, such specification is implicit at best, and researchers who develop or use measures discuss the issue minimally or not at all.

As discussed, within-measure correlational systematic error is a key consideration in assessing a measure for conditions of future use. For example, halo error within a measure when responses to later items are based on a general impression created by earlier items might not be problematic if the measure is the unit of analysis and items in the measure are to be arranged in the same sequence in future applications. It may be problematic, however, if individual items are used in a shorter form or a random order, or they are interspersed with items measuring other constructs or fillers.

All psychometric procedures should match future use by conducting tests for different forms of a measure (different sequencing, short forms, use of fillers, labeling, etc.) in different settings and in different populations. Such testing for internal consistency also serves to assess previously satisfactory items for the need for toning across populations. Measures should be assessed for capturing the variations in populations in which they are likely to be applied. Once they have been validated across different populations, measures can be used in substantive studies, and even in subpopulations with extreme means and small variation. For exploratory and confirmatory factor analysis, interspersing items with fillers or ordering items differently could alleviate problems relating to loadings of items on multiple dimensions. However, these approaches warrant testing under conditions that mimic future uses and explicitly specifying the uses of a measure. Validity tests that reflect future applications serve to delineate uses of measures by mimicking their usage in substantive studies. Because validity tests are similar to research designs used to test substantive hypotheses, they, in effect, also serve as pilot tests for future applications.

Discussion

The proposed stepwise process of identifying and correcting for error can be employed at each stage of measure development. Although this stepwise process can be used for isolated psychometric procedures, such as internal consistency reliability, the nature and variety of measurement errors discussed earlier warrant systematic assessment through the use of different psychometric diagnostics as well as consideration of the design characteristics of psychometric tests and assessment of future usage conditions of measures. As discussed, some heavily used psychometric diagnostics, such as item-to-total correlations (internal consistency) and test-retest correlations (test-retest reliability), confound different types of errors, strongly suggesting that they be used in the preliminary stages of measure development. They should be followed subsequently by more recent approaches using structural equation modeling, incorporating internal consistency and test-retest reliability, and confirmatory factor analysis.

Summary

This chapter presented a detailed approach for identifying and correcting for error. A three-step process was presented for identifying and correcting for measurement error at each stage of measure development: (a) assessing diagnostics from traditional psychometric procedures, design characteristics of psychometric tests, and conditions of future usage; (b) identifying specific types of error using these diagnostics; and (c) correcting for error. This process was derived from discussions in earlier chapters about the sources of error, the types of measurement error, and the confounding of different types of error in empirical outcomes. Recommendations were made at five different levels: item (e.g., changes in wording of items); measure (i.e., the aggregate set of items that comprise the measure, such as changes to response scales, changes in sequencing of items, short forms, use of filler items from other measures between items); administration (i.e., aspects of a method at a more aggregate level than a single measure, such as sequencing of measures of multiple constructs, procedures, settings, and samples); data analysis (e.g., specifying method factors); and construct (i.e., reassessing the construct conceptually, such as rethinking its dimensionality). The recommendations developed here apply in piecemeal fashion as well, not just in terms of strictly adhering to the process suggested here. Moreover, although the process applies to assessment after preliminary development of a measure, the recommendations can be used before the fact in preventing error to begin with through appropriate design of items.

Notes

1. For example, what constitutes low, moderate, or high item-to-total correlations for internal consistency reliability can be interpreted only in context. Essentially, absolute and relative assessments of magnitudes of empirical indicators have to be interpreted in light of factors such as the nature of the construct and the sample composition. Similarly, sample size criteria may have to be met not just to minimize the likelihood of idiosyncratic random error but also to meet other statistical requirements, such as those for confirmatory factor analysis. The precision of estimates, such as reliability, needs to be incorporated into sample size considerations. A detailed discussion of rules of thumb, such as recommended sample sizes for specific procedures, is beyond the scope of this book but is available in past research (Guadagnoli & Velicer, 1988; Nunnally, 1978).

2. Future usage conditions, including sample compositions, involve within-measure correlational systematic error in that they relate to differences in responses over and above the construct being measured. Such error occurs because of ordering, or interspersion, as a result of sources such as the within-measure halo effect. For example, a measure that does not capture variation in true scores in a specific population has within-measure correlational systematic error due to the measure capturing differences over and above the construct. If high means are found in a population requiring item toning, the issue is one of additive systematic error. However, if future usage conditions are now anticipated by testing in new populations, then within-measure correlational systematic error is implicated. Thus, additive systematic error relates to setting a convenient baseline for the scale, whereas within-measure correlational systematic error relates to differences over and above the construct in question as the measure is tested in new populations.

3. Relevant in situations where there are changes in true scores across administrations is methodological design to achieve control and careful specification of different errors in a structural equation modeling-based approach.

4. In a sense, the more general an item, the more susceptible it is to multiple interpretations. However, items have to vary in how general they are, depending on the construct being measured. Specific items have their own problems because of confounding the construct being measured with a specific context. This trade-off is inherent in measuring abstract constructs with relatively concrete items. The key is to enhance consistent interpretation through careful wording and empirical testing.

5. Primary and secondary factors are used here to refer to factors that a set of items purports to measure and extraneous factors, respectively. For a unidimensional scale, the primary factor is likely to be the first factor extracted, although such assumptions need conceptual and empirical support.

6. Although it is assumed that individual items should load on single factors, measures could employ individual items that load on multiple factors. However, such an approach is problematic for a variety of reasons.

7. Interspersed sequencing of items separates variables through the ungrouping of items from a single measure. Hence, this approach works even though different measures are presented contiguously at the item level. In this sense, it is the opposite of labeling, discussed subsequently, which serves to group items from a single measure. Interspersion is not without disadvantages, such as in reducing internal consistency.

8. When a specific order of a pair of measures may lead to error in responses to the second measure completed, counterbalancing the order across distinct sets of respondents may serve to average out the effects of order. However, counterbalancing is problematic if order effects are inconsistent (i.e., the effect of completing Measure A on Measure B is very different from the effect of completing Measure B on Measure A). It may be preferable to consider a specific ordering that minimizes error, as well as design characteristics, such as separation, that minimize order effects to begin with.

9. The outcome of psychological grouping is not always clear. Some respondents may guess nonrelationships, "good" respondents may try to confirm hypotheses, and negative respondents may try to disconfirm hypotheses (Cook & Campbell, 1979; Sawyer, 1975; Shimp, Hyatt, & Snyder, 1991).

6

How Can Error Be Identified Through Innovative Design and Analyses?

Overview

The earlier chapters provided a nuanced presentation of measurement error. Implications from understanding measurement error at a conceptual level include innovative design and analyses that can be used to identify measurement error in both measure development and research design. In this chapter, empirical illustrations are suggested that can provide additional insight into the nature of measurement error during measure development: using internal consistency and test-retest reliability in conjunction, using correlations across item-level correlations, and assessing effects of item ordering. These empirical illustrations are derived from earlier discussions of measurement error.

Using Internal Consistency and Test-Retest Reliability in Conjunction

As suggested by the previous discussion, item-to-total correlations and test-retest correlations each provide insight into measurement error. Examination of internal consistency and test-retest reliability of individual items in conjunction provides further insight into measurement error. Some items may have high internal consistency as well as stability. Other items may have moderate internal consistency and low stability. The reverse may also occur (i.e., high stability and moderate internal consistency). Such a pattern is potentially indicative of items tapping a different construct and, hence, not being related as strongly to other items in a measure, or alternatively, capturing some aspect of the construct that is not captured by other items. Test-retest reliability in conjunction with internal consistency can be employed to distinguish between several types of measurement error. By assessing relative magnitudes of item-to-total correlations versus test-retest correlations, several insights can be drawn.

Internal consistency and test-retest reliability can be used in conjunction to assess measurement error. In Table 6.1 and Figure 6.1, some general conclusions from an earlier discussion are presented. In Table 6.2, instructive examples involving items are presented. Item-to-total correlations and test-retest correlations are presented for 1-week and 12-week test-retest data. Some items may have high internal consistency as well as stability (e.g., "I enjoy work that requires the use of numbers"), whereas others have varying internal consistency and low stability. An item such as "Numbers are not necessary for most situations" may be moderately internally consistent because of the within-measure halo effect. But this item may lack stability because responses require aggregation across a range of situations and, consequently, are affected by factors such as memory accessibility to different episodes at different points in time. In some instances, the reverse may occur (i.e., high stability and moderate internal consistency, such as the item "I enjoy tasks that require me to be exact"). Such a pattern may be indicative of an item tapping a different trait and hence not being strongly related to other items in a measure. Alternatively, the item may be capturing some aspect of the trait that is not captured by other items. Confirmatory factor analysis can be employed to examine these possibilities.

Using Correlations Across Item-Level Correlations

The approach described above entails examination of individual item-to-total and test-retest correlations and can be employed for scales with a small number of items. If the number of items in a measure is high enough, correlations across item-level correlations can also be computed to supplement individual item-level correlations. The relationship between test-retest correlation and item-to-total correlation at test and at retest provides a means of examining test-retest and internal consistency results in conjunction. Item-level correlations for each item can be used as data points to compute correlations across items. Considering a matrix of three columns

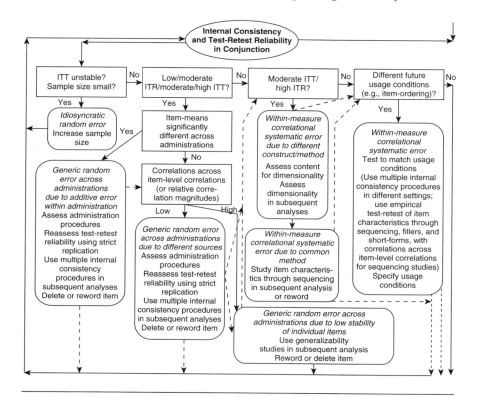

Figure 6.1   Using Internal Consistency and Test-Retest Reliability in Conjunction

NOTES: ITT = item-to-total correlation; ITR = item-level test-retest correlation; solid lines represent single paths; dashed lines represent multiple paths depending on judgment at previous step; dashed lines that advance an item are considered acceptable after assessment in previous step (for example, considering an item with low/moderate ITR/high ITT and with item means that are not extreme that is assessed under generic random error across administrations due to low stability, if the item is considered acceptable for issues listed under this type of error, and if the item has satisfactory ITR, i.e., moderate ITR, it can advance to the next step; assessment of magnitudes of ITR are not exact but approximate and judgments have to be made as to what is in the low-to-moderate range and what is in the moderate-to-high range based on a variety of factors in a specific situation; see Table 5.3)

representing item-to-total correlations at test, item-to-total correlations at retest, and item-level test-retest correlations, where each row contains these correlations for a specific item, correlations can be computed across items between item-to-total correlations and test-retest correlations. Such correlations across item-level correlations represent the relative standing of items in terms of their item-to-total correlations versus their test-retest correlations. A high correlation across correlations suggests that items high on

Table 6.1   Using Internal Consistency and Test-Retest Reliability in Conjunction

	Item-Level Test-Retest Correlation		
	High	Medium	Low
High		Item tapping common source(s), moderate stability. Consider rewording.	Within-measure halo effect but poor stability. Reword or delete item.
Medium	Item tapping aspect of domain or related trait/method. Assess content and dimensionality.	Item tapping aspect of domain or related trait/method, moderately stable. Assess content and dimensionality.	Within-measure halo effect but poor stability. Reword or delete item.
Low	Unrelated trait/method. Delete item.	Unrelated trait/method. Delete item.	Delete item.

(Row label on the left side, rotated: Item-to-Total Correlation)

item-to-total correlations are also high on test-retest correlations. If the same sources of random error affect internal consistency and test-retest reliability, then correlations across items between item-to-total correlations and test-retest correlations should be large and positive. However, a high correlation is only a necessary and not a sufficient condition for suggesting that similar sources of random error contribute to internal consistency and test-retest reliability. Similarly, low correlations across items for item-to-total correlations at test versus retest suggest that the sources of random error vary across administrations. Such a pattern emphasizes the need to use multiple administrations of internal consistency procedures to assess scales during development.

Examples of high and low correlation conditions for several scales are presented in Table 6.3.[1] For the PNI scale, the correlation across items between item-to-total correlations and test-retest correlations was high for 1-week and 12-week intervals, suggesting that similar sources of random error may be acting across administrations. The high correlation suggests that items high on item-to-total correlation are also high on test-retest

Table 6.2   Sample Item-Level Correlations

Construct Item	Item-to-Total Correlation At Test/Retest		Test-Retest Correlation At Test/Retest	
	1 Week	12 Weeks	1 Week	12 Weeks
Preference for numerical information[a]				
Numbers are not necessary for most situations.	.41/.24	.30/.34	.28	−.01
I enjoy work that requires the use of numbers.	.80/.68	.84/.71	.87	.69
Understanding numbers is as important in daily life as reading or writing.	.44/.24	.52/.52	.60	.39
Need for precision[b]				
I enjoy tasks that require me to be exact.	.42/.26	.60/.35	.58	.60
Vague descriptions leave me with the need for more information.	.41/.29	.39/.14	.34	.35
I like to use the precise information that is available to make decisions.	.51/.44	.64/.50	.47	.24

a. Viswanathan (1993).
b. Viswanathan (1997).

correlation and vice versa. A high correlation was also found across items for item-to-total correlations at test versus retest, suggesting again that similar sources of random error may be acting across administrations. An attenuation is found for the longer interval, as would be expected. The Need for Precision scale, in comparison, has low correlations across items between item-to-total correlations and test-retest (0.52 and −.06 for the 1-week interval and −.21 and −.01 for the 12-week interval). The same is the case for correlations across items between item-to-total correlations at test and retest, suggesting different sources of random error within versus across

Table 6.3   Correlations Across Item-Level Correlations

Preference for Numerical Information Scale—20 items—1-week interval

	ITT Test[a]	ITT Retest
ITT retest	.82	
Test-retest	.74	.81

Preference for Numerical Information Scale—20 items—12-week interval

	ITT Test	ITT Retest
ITT retest	.71	
Test-retest	.75	.64

Need for precision—13 items—1-week interval

	ITT Test	ITT Retest
ITT retest	.19	
Test-retest	.52	−.06

Need for precision—13 items—12-week interval

	ITT Test	ITT Retest
ITT retest	.36	
Test-retest	−.21	−.01

a. ITT = Item-to-total correlation; correlations were computed across items using item-to-total correlations and item-level test-retest correlations as data points.

administrations. Lower correlations suggest that the sources of random error vary across administrations and emphasize the need to use multiple administrations of internal consistency procedures to assess scales during development. Such an approach, in combination with item-level statistics and content analysis, can help isolate items during measure development.

Empirical Assessment of Item-Sequencing Effects

Previous chapters bring out the importance of assessing measures using conditions similar to their subsequent usage in methodological designs. Recommendations developed earlier suggest approaches such as sequencing of items to reduce within-measure correlational systematic error, while also suggesting the need to test measures under different usage conditions.

To demonstrate the use of empirical approaches to assess measure characteristics such as sequencing, a study was conducted. The objective was to illustrate the importance of assessing measures using conditions similar to their subsequent usage in methodological designs by examining the effect of one pervasive factor, sequencing of items. Undergraduate students at a midwestern U.S. university completed the same set of scales twice with a 5-week interval between test and retest. During the test phase, scale items for each of five scales (preference for numerical information, need for precision, enjoyment of mathematics, tolerance for ambiguity, and innovativeness) were presented in consecutive order (i.e., all items of a specific measure were presented together). In the retest phase, one set of respondents completed the items in the scales in identical sequence ($n = 127$), whereas another set completed items from the five scales in interspersed sequence ($n = 61$)—that is, items from different measures were interspersed with each other randomly.

Summary data for the five scales are presented in Table 6.4. The comparable level of test-retest correlations, item-to-total correlations, and coefficient alphas are striking across all scales, suggesting that the scales perform comparably when items are presented in consecutive sequence versus in interspersed sequence with items from other scales. At this level of analysis, the items in the scale appear to perform comparably with random sequencing as well. However, correlations across item-level correlations provide further insight.

Correlations across items for item-level correlations and test-retest correlations are presented in Table 6.5 for the consecutive versus interspersed sequencing conditions. As discussed earlier, low correlations suggest different sources of error within versus across administrations. Moreover, differences in magnitudes of correlations across the sequencing conditions suggest order effects. For the PNI scale and the tolerance for ambiguity scale, there are considerable differences in the sizes of correlations for the consecutive versus interspersed sequencing. The interspersed sequence of item presentation appears to lead to different sources of randomness affecting scale response when compared to a consecutive sequence of items. Therefore, although the earlier analysis from Table 6.4 suggested that the items were performing at a comparable level for both types of sequencing, Table 6.5 suggests that different sources of random error may be in effect. On the other hand, differences based on sequencing of items are not as high for the enjoyment of mathematics scale, the need for precision scale, or the innovativeness scale. For the innovativeness scale, the correlation across items between test-retest correlations and item-to-total correlations is low for both consecutive as well as interspersed sequencing of items, suggesting different

Table 6.4   Summary Statistics for Consecutive Versus Interspersed Item Sequencing for Dataset 1

Construct Item	Order of Items at Retest	
	Consecutive	Interspersed
Test-retest correlation across scales[a]		
Preference for numerical information	.77	.89
Need for precision	.79	.85
Tolerance for ambiguity[b]	.67	.63
Innovativeness[c]	.72	.78
Enjoyment of mathematics[d]	.86	.88
Average item-level test-retest correlation[e]		
Preference for numerical information	.50	.54
Need for precision	.49	.49
Tolerance for ambiguity	.47	.48
Innovativeness	.50	.50
Enjoyment of mathematics	.64	.52
Item-to-total correlation (test/retest)		
Preference for numerical information	.34/.36	.32/.38
Need for precision	.25/.29	.33/.19
Tolerance for ambiguity	.20/.14	.11/.14
Innovativeness	.30/.33	.32/.38
Enjoyment of mathematics	.40/.37	.44/.44
Coefficient alpha (test/retest)		
Preference for numerical information	.91/.92	.90/.92
Need for precision	.81/.84	.86/.75
Tolerance for ambiguity	.78/.69	.62/.69
Innovativeness	.81/.83	.83/.87
Enjoyment of mathematics	.89/.88	.90/.90

a. Test-retest correlation across total scores on scales.
b. Norton (1975).
c. Hurt, Joseph, and Cook (1977).
d. Aiken (1974).
e. Test-retest correlation for each item, averaged across items.

sources of randomness within versus across administrations for both conditions. This empirical approach, in combination with item-level analysis and examination, could be used to purify measures and use them in different sequencing conditions.

To further demonstrate these empirical approaches, another study was conducted to examine the effect of sequencing of items. Undergraduate

Table 6.5   Correlations Across Item-Level Correlations for Consecutive Versus Interspersed Item-Sequencing for Dataset 1

	ITT Test[a]	ITT Retest
Preference for numerical information		
Items in consecutive order at retest		
ITT retest	.94	
Test-retest	.84	.85
Items in interspersed order at retest		
ITT retest	.59	
Test-retest	.16	.33
Need for precision		
Items in consecutive order at retest		
ITT retest	.65	
Test-retest	.59	.63
Items in interspersed order at retest		
ITT retest	.58	
Test-retest	.40	.43
Tolerance for ambiguity		
Items in consecutive order at retest		
ITT retest	.79	
Test-retest	.26	.50
Items in interspersed order at retest		
ITT retest	.28	
Test-retest	−.17	−.47
Innovativeness		
Items in consecutive order at retest		
ITT retest	.88	
Test-retest	.25	.29
Items in interspersed order at retest		
ITT retest	.78	
Test-retest	.31	.24
Enjoyment of mathematics		
Items in consecutive order at retest		
ITT retest	.97	
Test-retest	.84	.90
Items in interspersed order at retest		
ITT retest	.70	
Test-retest	.67	.83

a. ITT = Item-to-total correlation; correlations were computed across items using item-to-total correlations and test-retest correlations as data points.

students at a midwestern U.S. university completed the same set of measures twice with a 6-week interval between test and retest. During the test phase, items for each of six measures were presented in consecutive order (i.e., all items of a specific measure were presented together). In the retest phase, one set of respondents completed the items in the measures in identical sequence ($n = 101$), whereas another set completed items from the six measures in interspersed sequence ($n = 103$)—that is, items from different measures were interspersed with each other randomly. Unidimensional and multidimensional measures were selected (Appendix 1.2; consumer innovativeness, materialism, susceptibility to interpersonal influence, consumer ethnocentrism, price perceptions, and need for cognition). Validation studies employing student samples were reported for all measures selected, with the exception of two dimensions of price perception, thus supporting the sample composition employed in the present study. Seven-point Likert response scales were employed for all measures to enable interspersion. Whereas four of the measures had been validated previously using 7-point Likert scales, two had been validated with somewhat different response scales (materialism, 5-point Likert; need for cognition, 9-point fully described Likert). Departures from prior validation studies in terms of response scales or sample composition are noteworthy in interpreting the results (Tables 6.6 and 6.7).

Summary data for the six measures are presented in Table 6.6. The comparable level of test-retest correlations, item-to-total correlations, and coefficient alphas are striking for several measures. At this level of analysis, these measures appear to perform comparably with interspersed sequencing as well. Noteworthy exceptions include lower stability with interspersion for need for cognition, and three dimensions of materialism. Such a pattern suggests that the within-measure halo effect may play a central role in consecutive sequencing in enabling stability. On the other hand, relatively higher stability with interspersion is observed for consumer ethnocentrism, and two dimensions of price perception (coupon proneness and sale proneness), suggesting that the within-measure halo effect with consecutive sequencing may have a negative effect on stability for these measures. An examination of coefficient alphas suggests that all measures perform comparably across sequencing conditions and that interspersion does not affect internal consistency of the measures.

Examination of internal consistency and test-retest reliability of individual items in conjunction provides further insight into measurement error. A selective set of items is presented in Table 6.6 for illustrative purposes. Some items may have high internal consistency as well as stability, as shown for the consecutive sequencing condition in Table 6.6 (Items 6, 7, and 8).

Table 6.6   Summary Statistics for Consecutive Versus Interspersed Item Sequencing for Dataset 2

Construct Item	Order of Items at Retest	
	Consecutive	Interspersed
Test-retest correlation/		
Average item-level test-retest correlation[a]		
Consumer ethnocentrism	.69/.51	.80/.62
Need for cognition	.84/.50	.60/.38
Consumer innovativeness—Independent judgment making	.58/.39	.43/.34
Novelty seeking	.69/.52	.73/.48
Materialism—Defining success	.89/.64	.66/.52
Acquisition centrality	.80/.61	.74/.50
Pursuit of happiness	.75/.59	.71/.50
Price perception—Value consciousness	.75/.59	.75/.53
Price consciousness	.68/.50	.74/.54
Coupon proneness	.62/.51	.83/.64
Sale proneness	.47/.41	.66/.49
Susceptibility to interpersonal influence—Normative	.75/.54	.76/.50
Informational	.64/.51	.65/.43
Coefficient alpha (Test/retest)		
Consumer ethnocentrism	.96/.96	.96/.97
Need for cognition	.90/.90	.87/.90
Consumer innovativeness—Independent judgment making	.87/.81	.81/.84
Novelty seeking	.92/.92	.88/.88
Materialism—Defining success	.87/.88	.85/.84
Acquisition centrality	.79/.78	.74/.80
Pursuit of happiness	.81/.78	.76/.79
Price perception—Value consciousness	.85/.86	.88/.83
Price consciousness	.82/.79	.85/.80
Coupon proneness	.89/.89	.89/.90
Sale proneness	.84/.76	.78/.76
Susceptibility to interpersonal influence—Normative	.89/.91	.89/.87
Informational	.74/.75	.74/.78
Statistics for specific items (ITT test/ITT retest/ITR)		
Consumer ethnocentrism: We should buy from foreign countries only those products that we cannot obtain within our own country.	.71/.74/.28	.80/.66/.47

(Continued)

Table 6.6 (Continued)

Construct Item	Order of Items at Retest	
	Consecutive	Interspersed
Consumer ethnocentrism: Curbs should be put on all imports.	.61/.62/.37	.71/.74/.63
Need for cognition: I prefer to think about small, daily projects to long-term ones.	.34/.37/.50	.33/.45/.25
Need for cognition: I usually end up deliberating about issues even when they do not affect me personally.	.18/.37/.35	.27/.32/.34
Consumer innovativeness (Independent judgment making): When it comes to deciding whether to purchase a new service, I do not rely on experienced friends or family members for advice.	.69/.52/.26	.54/.56/.38
Consumer innovativeness (Novelty seeking): I am continually seeking new product experiences.	.82/.81/.61	.67/.83/.37
Materialism (Defining success): I don't place much emphasis on the amount of material objects people own as a sign of success.	.68/.59/.66	.69/.67/.40
Price perception (Value consciousness): When purchasing a product, I always try to maximize the quality I get for the money I spend.	.67/.72/.54	.77/.53/.29
Price perception (Coupon proneness): When I use coupons, I feel that I am getting a good deal.	.62/.67/.37	.76/.66/.59
Price perception (Sale proneness): When I buy a brand that's on sale, I feel that I am getting a good deal.	.64/.52/.23	.43/.46/.35
Susceptibility to interpersonal influence (Informational): To make sure I buy the right product or brand, I often observe what others are buying and using.	.31/.36/.36	.26/.34/.34

NOTES: ITR = item-level test-retest correlation; ITT = item-to-total correlation; consumer ethnocentrism, Shimp and Sharma (1987); need for cognition, Cacioppo, Petty, and Kao (1984); consumer innovativeness, Manning et al. (1995); materialism, Richins and Dawson (1992); price perceptions, Lichtenstein et al. (1993); susceptibility to interpersonal influence, Bearden et al. (1989).

a. Test-retest correlation across total scale/average ITR.

Table 6.7   Correlations Across Item-Level Correlations for Dataset 2

	ITT Test[a]	ITT Retest
Consumer ethnocentrism		
Items in consecutive order at retest		
ITT retest	.42	
Test-retest	.62	.42
Items in interspersed order at retest		
ITT retest	.36	
Test-retest	.22	.36
Need for cognition		
Items in consecutive order at retest		
ITT retest	.70	
Test-retest	−.04	.26
Items in interspersed order at retest		
ITT retest	.82	
Test-retest	.19	.15
Consumer innovativeness		
Items in consecutive order at retest		
ITT retest	.66	
Test-retest	.44	.71
Items in interspersed order at retest		
ITT retest	.45	
Test-retest	.22	−.02
Materialism		
Items in consecutive order at retest		
ITT retest	.81	
Test-retest	.37	.51
Items in interspersed order at retest		
ITT retest	.75	
Test-retest	.47	.05
Price perception		
Items in consecutive order at retest		
ITT retest	.81	
Test-retest	−.02	.22
Items in interspersed order at retest		
ITT retest	.76	
Test-retest	.24	.38

a. ITT = Item-to-total correlation; correlations were computed across items using item-to-total correlations and test-retest correlations as data points.

Noteworthy here is that the stability of these items is decreased with interspersion as shown in the right column of Table 6.6, perhaps because of the lack of a within-measure halo effect. Other items have moderate internal consistency and low stability, as shown for the consecutive sequencing condition in Table 6.6 (Items 1, 2, 5, 9, and 10). An item such as "When I buy a brand that's on sale, I feel that I am getting a good deal" may be moderately internally consistent because of the within-measure halo effect. But it may lack stability because responses require aggregation across a range of situations and are consequently affected by factors such as memory accessibility to different episodes at different points in time. For some of these items, interspersion leads to enhanced stability (Items 1, 2, and 9), suggesting a negative within-measure halo effect on stability. The reverse—high stability and moderate internal consistency—may also occur (Item 3: "I usually end up deliberating about issues even when they do not affect me personally"). Such a pattern may be indicative of items tapping a different construct and, hence, not being related as strongly to other items in a measure. Alternatively, an item may be capturing some aspect of the construct that is not captured by other items. Consistent with these possibilities, exploratory factor analysis suggested relatively low loadings on primary factors (average loading = .40) and higher loadings on secondary factors in some analyses. Noteworthy is the decrease in stability with interspersion. Another scenario involves low to moderate internal consistency and stability, suggesting similar possibilities. For example, for Item 11 (susceptibility to interpersonal influence scale), exploratory factor analysis suggested low loadings on its primary (informational) factor and higher loadings on the other (normative) factor (average loading after varimax rotation = .25 and .60, respectively, on informational and normative dimensions), and confirmatory factor analysis suggested several large residuals with items from the normative dimension. For Item 4 (need for cognition scale), exploratory factor analysis suggested moderately low loadings on primary factors (average loading = .31) and higher loadings on secondary factors in some analyses.

Confirmatory factor analyses (CFA) for retest data for each sequencing condition suggested relatively better fit for the interspersed when compared to consecutive sequencing for unidimensional and multidimensional scales. For some multidimensional scales, the number of large residuals for items from different dimensions was also lowered with interspersion. As discussed, interspersion may alleviate within-measure correlational systematic error because of sources such as shared wording and context among subsets of items in unidimensional and multidimensional measures, and among items from different dimensions in multidimensional measures. Relatively small sample sizes for CFA suggest caution in interpreting these results.

Correlations are presented in Table 6.7.[2] For several scales (consumer ethnocentrism, consumer innovativeness, and materialism), correlations across items between item-to-total correlations and test-retest correlations were moderate to high, suggesting that similar sources of random error may be acting across administrations. For these scales, there are considerable differences in the sizes of correlations for consecutive versus interspersed sequencing, suggesting that different sources of randomness may affect scale response across sequencing conditions. Correlations across items for item-level correlations and test-retest correlations show differences in magnitudes of correlations across the sequencing conditions, suggesting order effects. Therefore, although the earlier analysis from Table 6.6 suggested that the items were performing at a comparable level for both types of sequencing, Table 6.7 suggests that different sources of random error may be in effect. In comparison, the price perception scale has low correlations across items between item-to-total and test-retest correlations in the consecutive sequencing condition, suggesting different sources of randomness across administrations. These correlations remain low in the interspersed condition, suggesting different sources of randomness within versus across administrations for both conditions.

For all scales, moderate to high correlations were found across items for item-to-total correlations at test versus retest, suggesting that similar sources of random error may be acting across administrations in affecting internal consistency. Lower correlations suggest that the sources of random error vary across administrations and emphasize the need to use multiple administrations of internal consistency procedures. Such correlations in general, and those across items from different dimensions of a scale in particular, should be interpreted with caution and in conjunction with examination of magnitudes of individual correlations. In summary, the empirical approaches illustrated here, in combination with content analysis, can help isolate items during measure development. These approaches may be particularly useful in the early stages of measure development to edit and improve items.

Summary

Implications from understanding measurement error at a conceptual level include innovative design and analyses that can be used to identify measurement error in both measure development and research design. Insight into the nature of measurement error during measure development can be gained using internal consistency and test-retest reliability in conjunction, using correlations across item-level correlations, and assessing the effects of item ordering. These unique approaches can help reduce error in the development of items, measures, and methods, and validate usage of measures with different item orderings.

Notes

1. Correlations were also run across z values after performing transformations as per procedures for inference tests about correlations (Neter, Kutner, Nachsteim, & Wasserman, 1996) and led to similar results as expected because correlations are heavily influenced by relative standing (Nunnally, 1978). Histograms of raw correlations suggested approximate normal distributions. Because each item-level correlation is computed across respondents, and because responses across items for any respondent are not independent, the correlations across correlations do not meet the strict test of independent observations. However, such correlations are quite similar to correlations across mean values of stimuli obtained from the same set of respondents.

2. As mentioned earlier and repeated here, a detailed discussion of recommended sample sizes that represent large samples for various procedures is beyond the scope of this book. Detailed discussions of statistical considerations are available in past research (Guadagnoli & Velicer, 1988; Nunnally, 1978). For the purposes of explication of idiosyncratic random error, sufficient sample sizes in measurement development procedures are assumed.

7

How Do Measures Differ?

Overview

This chapter classifies measures into different types, covering issues that often remain implied and lack explicit treatment. Measures differ in fundamental ways that warrant discussion. The differences between measures discussed below affect how specific types of measures should be developed, validated, and used. These different types of scales are frequently confronted in day-to-day research. One such distinction relates to stimulus-centered versus respondent-centered scales. Another distinction relates to formative versus reflective indicators of constructs.

Stimulus-Centered Versus Respondent-Centered Scales

An important distinction should be made between stimulus-centered and respondent-centered scales. This section will argue that, for practical purposes, the distinction is not inherent in the scales used but is contingent on the purpose of the research and the nature of the analyses—that is, whether to evaluate hypotheses based on differences across individuals or differences across stimuli.[1]

Respondent-centered scales aim to place respondents on a continuum. Items in a measure are used to place individuals. The aim is to reliably place individuals on a continuum as measured across a sample of items. Stimulus-centered scales do the reverse; they place stimuli on a continuum as measured across a sample of respondents. Stimulus-centered scales include ratings of products or other stimuli, or ratings of employee performance by multiple raters. The aim is to obtain reliable differences among stimuli. Random error occurs when differences between stimuli are unreliable. Rater reliability has been recommended for stimulus-centered scales (Cox, 1980) and captures the degree to which stimulus ratings are consistent across respondents. Rater reliability is computed as the ratio of the variance between stimuli to the sum of variance between stimuli and residual variance (Ebel, 1951). This is in contrast to internal consistency reliability, where the aim is to assess whether ratings by respondents are consistent across items.

Stimulus-centered scales are employed when stimulus ratings aggregated across individuals are the unit of further analysis, such as correlations across stimulus ratings. The aim here is to establish reliable and valid differences among stimuli. Analyses with stimulus ratings as the relevant unit occur when studying stimulus characteristics. When hypotheses about relationships between constructs capturing differences across stimuli are studied, stimulus-centered scales are required. Consider a study of the relationship between price and perceived quality of products. Such a study could examine relationships between individuals' perceptions of price and perceived quality through computing correlations across individuals' ratings of the price and perceived quality of a product. Alternatively, stimulus-centered ratings could be employed to assess the relationship between price and perceived quality of a set of products by computing correlations across stimuli. Each approach provides a different perspective on the research question.

If the research method aims to obtain individuals' ratings of certain levels of stimuli, then treatment of such scales as respondent centered may be appropriate. Consider studies where respondents rate people on certain dimensions, such as extroversion, or products on certain dimensions, such as perceived value or perceived quality. Such studies are common in experimental as well as nonexperimental designs. The aim of such studies is to show that respondents differ in their perceptions of stimuli as a function of some factors. The goal is to assess respondents' perceptions; therefore, such scales can be considered respondent centered for practical purposes. Although respondents rate stimuli rather than provide self-reports on some individual trait, the key here is that respondents are ordered along some rating of stimuli in the analyses. For analyses using stimulus-centered scales, the goal would be to order stimuli along a dimension. Consider a study where a range of instances is rated by respondents, say, typicality ratings of instances of categories, such as fast food restaurants or vegetables. If the aim of the study is to assess the relationship between typicality and familiarity, then such scales are stimulus centered, and the analysis hinges on correlations computed across stimulus ratings after averaging across individuals or even for each individual. Contrast this with the many studies that involve correlations computed across respondents after averaging across items. Thus, whether a scale is stimulus or respondent centered depends on its usage. For example, a design could be used to show that individuals' ratings of typicality of stimuli are correlated with their self-reports of an individual trait, such as need for precision. Here, the purpose is to study relationships across individuals.

Contrary to viewing stimulus-centered scales as involving ratings of stimuli and respondent-centered scales as involving ratings of respondents, it may be more useful to categorize scales based on the purpose of the research and the nature of the analyses. Product ratings on dimensions or ratings of employees are examples of stimulus-centered scales, where the aim is to order products on a continuum. Here, rater reliability is a relevant psychometric property. Such reliability would assess the degree to which differences across stimuli are consistent across individuals. This type of reliability should be contrasted with internal consistency reliability—whether differences across individuals are consistent across items—and test-retest reliability—whether differences across individuals on the same item are consistent across time.

In broad terms, there are individual differences and differences among stimuli. However, most scales can be treated as respondent centered for practical purposes, most analyses being across respondents. Experimental designs—where either the same or different individuals respond to different stimuli in different treatment conditions (say, credibility of messages)—often require dependent variables that are respondent centered. Even though experiments involve analysis of mean differences in dependent variables, the aim is not to study the relationship between constructs measuring differences across stimulus levels, aggregated across individuals. Rather, mean differences in stimulus levels are created or manipulated, and dependent variables are measured. Manipulation levels are discrete; thus, the aim is to assess whether differences between individuals across manipulation levels overwhelm differences within. The aim is not to order stimuli reliably and validly to enable an assessment of the relationship between such orderings on different variables. The aim here is to capture responses that may vary across individuals in a treatment condition. Experimental tests relate to whether differences across treatment conditions are greater than differences within treatment conditions. Thus, central here is what is being measured and analyzed—differences across individuals.

Additive systematic error occurs with stimulus-centered scales when stimuli are consistently rated to be higher or lower than their true score. To assess the effect of such inflation or deflation, it is useful to examine how stimulus-centered scales are employed. Stimulus-centered scales may be used to rate stimuli on dimensions, such as product quality or performance ratings of individuals. With additive systematic error, due to sources such as wording or interviewer bias, all stimuli would be inflated or deflated in ratings. Stimulus-centered scales may be employed to rate multiple stimuli, and such ratings may be employed in tests of hypotheses. To the extent that additive systematic error (i.e., partial additive systematic error) reduces variance across stimuli, such error would have an effect similar to that for respondent-centered scales. With just constant additive systematic error, differences in stimulus ratings will not be affected. The unit of analysis here is a set of stimuli, just as the unit for respondent-centered scales is a set of respondents.

Within-measure correlational systematic error occurs when stimulus ratings differ consistently over and above true differences. Thus, if extreme anchors are used (e.g., *poor* to *excellent*), leading to compression in ratings toward the center, this is an example of within-measure correlational systematic error. Such error is difficult to detect because it shows up as a consistent effect. Halo effect may also occur in rating, say, products or employees on multiple items. The halo effect could lead to within-measure or across-measure correlational systematic error, depending on the items involved. With respondent-centered scales, factor analyses can be employed to assess within-measure correlational systematic error. Such factor analysis identifies method factors or related construct factors. With stimulus-centered scales, the aim is to assess whether measures assess a particular construct rather than methods or extraneous constructs. For respondent-centered scales, analyses such as factor analysis are conducted among items using correlations across respondents. For stimulus-centered scales, the variation across stimuli could be used to compute correlations. Thus, items and respondents translate to items and stimuli in stimulus-centered scales. Stimulus ratings scales can be evaluated for different types of validity. For example, suppose that scales of price, perceived quality, and perceived value—three related constructs—need to be assessed for discriminant validity. Validation procedures would involve correlations across stimuli rather than individuals, suggesting the need for a sufficient number of stimuli.

Stimulus-centered scales are often used without reports of psychometric properties. For example, average ratings of brands are reported, presumably with the assumption that dispersions average out. However, stimulus-centered ratings should provide a measure of the degree to which such ratings are consistent. Low rater reliability should raise concerns about the degree of random error in the scale. The presumption here may be that such variation represents individual differences in ratings. However, the reliability and validity of a stimulus-centered scale need to be demonstrated before it can be assumed that individual ratings are captured accurately. This issue arises often with scales that are "obviously" measuring what they aim to measure (i.e., they have face validity). Moreover, because responses are averaged across respondents, various errors are expected to average out, leading to a dependable mean rating. But this notion that errors average out is based on several assumptions. First, an assumption is that the underlying construct is being captured. However, this needs to be demonstrated, not assumed, even if the scale appears to be face valid. In measurement, appearances can be deceptive, and empirical evidence is essential. Even if a scale appears to be valid and appears to capture the intended construct, the proof is in the responses provided by respondents. There may always be unanticipated effects of item wording that lead to unintended interpretations by respondents. Second, another assumption is that the scale does not have a high degree of systematic error. Third, another assumption is that random errors are small in magnitude, and thus, the scale is reliable. Indeed, it is true that certain constructs can be clearly delineated and items developed that appear to be obviously valid. Consider overall attitude toward a product, with items about the product anchored by labels such as *good* to *bad*. To assess whether individuals are consistent in rating individual stimuli, multiple items can be employed and internal consistency evaluated. However, to assess whether a range of stimuli is rated consistently by individuals, additional evidence is needed.

The reliability of stimulus-centered scales can be assessed through test-retest correlations. Such correlations can be computed across stimuli for each individual or for mean ratings averaged across individuals and suggest consistency in ratings across administrations. The parallel to internal consistency in a single administration is rater reliability, which demonstrates consistency across individuals. Stimulus-centered scales should be validated through evidence of discriminant, convergent, and nomological validity. Such validations can be conducted through correlations across stimuli using mean ratings. Alternatively, such correlations can also be assessed for each individual and summed across individuals.

If the aim in developing a set of stimuli is to achieve consistency across individuals, then rater reliability is appropriate. For example, if a series of performance ratings is developed with the aim of standardization of stimuli, then consistency across individuals is important. However, if individuals can vary in their perceptions and individual differences are central, then test-retest correlations may be appropriate to assess whether relative ordering across individuals is maintained. In fact, the issue of rater reliability becomes moot, and the scale, although employed to rate a range of stimuli, can be assessed through test-retest reliability for stimuli across individuals. It is treated like a respondent-centered scale for practical purposes, the aim being to assess individual differences in perceptions. With multiple items rating individual stimuli, internal consistency procedures can be used as well to demonstrate reliability among multiple items that measure a specific stimulus on a certain dimension (e.g., the attitude measure in Exhibit 7.1). Otherwise, the use of multiple items remains unsupported. However, sufficient variation across individuals is required for internal consistency procedures. One approach used for the speech quality measure in Exhibit 1.5 was to obtain ratings on the multiple-item measure of speech quality from individuals on multiple stimuli covering a broad range of speech quality, enabling variation and internal consistency procedures.

Detailed examples of stimulus-centered scales are presented here in Exhibit 7.1. The speech quality scale in Chapter 1 (Exhibit 1.5) can be viewed as a stimulus-centered scale. Consider responses to a number of audio stimuli, each 9 sentences long, from respondents, where responses are collected using a 9-item scale of speech quality. If many stimuli are used, then either correlations across stimuli of mean ratings on the 9-item scale for each individual or mean stimuli ratings averaged across individuals can be used. Correlations of this nature could be used to test hypotheses of relationships between speech quality and other constructs. Along with such analyses, internal consistency of the multiple items of the speech quality scale can be assessed.

(Text continues on page 228)

Exhibit 7.1   Fuzzy Set-Based Indicators of Product Categorization: Examples of Stimulus-Centered Scales

---

A brief overview of this work (Viswanathan & Childers, 1999) is presented, followed by the details germane to the discussion of stimulus-centered scales. Relevant cites and rationale are not presented here to maintain readability and restrict the presentation to issues germane to stimulus-centered scales.

This research conceptualizes product categories as fuzzy sets in which products have degrees of membership on specific attributes (e.g., the Ford Contour vs. the Mercury Tracer on gas mileage). Overall membership of a product in a product category is computed by aggregating membership along relevant attributes. For instance, membership of the Ford Contour in the category Economy Cars is assessed for each attribute, such as for gas mileage, and then aggregated across attributes.

Two measures of category membership are developed that assess gradedness of category membership at the attribute level (i.e., on individual attributes), which are then combined to reach overall measures of gradedness for a product. These measures enable fine distinctions among products in terms of membership in categories. The details of the validation of these two measures are presented as follows. These two measures are referred to as direct and indirect measures.

Two Measures of Category Membership

This section can be read selectively without loss of continuity in subsequent sections.

Direct Measurement

The direct measurement approach to operationalizing fuzzy set measures directly assesses product to category relationships at the attribute level. To operationalize membership at the attribute level, responses could be elicited from individuals, such as "In terms of mileage, how good an example of an economy car is a Ford Contour?" on a 10-point scale ranging from a very bad to a very good example. This manner of assessing membership directly extends the notion of global typicality (Rosch & Mervis, 1975) to the attribute level.

Information across attributes could then be combined to arrive at a categorization decision. The implicit notion is that membership values are assessed relative to the category, with perfect membership being represented by the value of m = 1 for all of the attributes. Likewise, a perfect nonmember is expected to have a value of m = 0 for all attributes in the set. A measure of membership of a product in a category can be computed that is the membership value of a product on each attribute summed across all attributes. This leads to the specification of the following measure of fuzziness:

$$D_j = \left[\sum_{i=1}^{M} (m_{ij})^n / M \right]^{1/n},$$

(1)

where m_{ij} is the membership level of the ith attribute in the jth category for the product, and M is the number of attributes of that product. Here, a product with a level of D near 1 can be interpreted as possessing high membership in the fuzzy set, whereas a value of D near 0 can be interpreted as low membership in the fuzzy set.

For example, the Chevrolet Metro may be rated a 1.0 on gas mileage, whereas a Mercury Tracer may be rated a 0.7 and a Ford Contour may be rated a 0.4. Membership values can be similarly computed for other attributes of economy cars and summed to reach overall membership of a product in a category similar to linear compensatory multiattribute models of attitude (Fishbein & Ajzen, 1975; Wilkie & Pessemier, 1973).

Indirect Measurement

Membership could also be inferred indirectly by assessing the degree to which both a product and a category, individually, possess each attribute. This approach requires collecting information separately for each product as well as for the category

(Continued)

(Continued)

---

along specific attributes. For example, respondents could rate the category of economy cars on the attribute, gas mileage, using a response scale from very low to very high gas mileage, and rate products such as Chevrolet Metro on gas mileage on a similar scale. Given ratings for each product and for the category on each attribute, category membership could be determined by the overlap between the product and the category across all of the attributes. The distance between the product and the category on each attribute could be combined to arrive at a measure of category membership. Although a variety of distance measures can be used, a measure that captures distances along attributes between a category and a product is

$$I_j = \left(\sum_{i=1}^{M} |C_{ij} - P_i|^n / M \right)^{1/n} , \tag{2}$$

where P_i is the level of the ith attribute for the product, C_{ij} is the level of the *i*th attribute for the *j*th category, and M is the number of attributes of that product.

For example, if the category of economy cars is rated an 8 (i.e., $C_1 = 8$) on a 10-point scale on gas mileage and a Mercury Tracer is rated a 6 (i.e., $P_1 = 6$), then the difference (2) is an indicator of the distance between the product and the category. Similar distances across various attributes of economy cars are then summed to reach an overall indicator of distance. The smaller this distance between a product and a category, the higher the membership of the product within the category. Hence, the actual distance (i.e., difference in magnitude) between the product and the category along an attribute is used to indirectly infer membership, rather than using membership values as in the direct measure.

Both of these measures could be categorized as formative measures discussed subsequently, ratings on a predetermined set of attributes being combined in a specific way to lead to the overall score. Here, internal consistency or factor analysis of ratings on individual attributes is not appropriate because a product may be typical on one attribute but atypical on some other attribute. However, test-retest reliability and validity tests can be conducted to assess these measures.

Hypotheses for Validity Tests

To assess the psychometric properties of the two fuzzy measures of graded structure, a series of relationships was predicted based on the results of several past studies in the categorization literature. The rationale for each hypothesis is not presented in depth.

Convergent Validity

To assess convergent validity, the fuzzy set measures were compared to a past measure of global typicality (Rosch, 1973). Because typicality is the degree to which a product is a member of a category, there should be strong overlap with the more micro fuzzy attribute-based indicators of graded structure.

H1: Both the direct and indirect measures of graded structure should be correlated with global typicality.

The directionality of all hypothesized correlations here and in subsequent hypotheses is positive for the direct measure (Equation 1) and negative for the indirect measure (Equation 2).

Nomological Validity

To assess the validity of the fuzzy measures in a broader network of relationships, several additional predictions were made. Family resemblance has been defined as the extent to which an exemplar shares attributes with other exemplars in a category (Rosch & Mervis, 1975). Products that are more typical of a category are likely to share more attributes with other products in the category; hence, a positive relationship has been reported between typicality and family resemblance.

H2a: Both the direct and indirect measures of graded structure should be correlated with family resemblance.

Products encountered more often will become more salient and thus will be accessed more easily from memory perhaps through advertising, point-of-purchase displays, and distribution, as well as word-of-mouth exchanges (Loken & Ward, 1990). Therefore, products with more exposure are likely to be regarded as more typical of a category.

H2b-c: Both the direct and indirect measures of graded structure should be correlated with a product's (b) frequency of instantiation and (c) familiarity.

Relationships were also hypothesized between category membership and more evaluative indicators of a product, such as attitude, in line with past research.

H3a-c: Both the direct and indirect measures of graded structure should be correlated with (a) attitude, (b) attribute structure (aggregation of beliefs about individual attributes of a product), and (c) ideals (i.e., the extent to which a product fulfills the category ideals).

Discriminant Validity

To assess discriminant validity, a pattern of relationships is predicted based on past research that can be expected to vary across category level (Loken & Ward, 1990). Categories may exist at subordinate and superordinate levels. Subordinate categories are composed of different brands or stores (e.g., fast food restaurants consist of McDonald's, Burger King, etc.). Superordinate categories cut across subordinate categories and are linked by higher order or more abstract attributes (e.g., the general category of restaurants, with such members as steak, seafood, and fast food restaurants). In moving from subordinate to superordinate categories, alternatives become less comparable on a set of attributes (i.e., products in subordinate categories are more likely to have common attributes). Thus, in more homogeneous subordinate categories, there would be stronger correlations between measures of graded structure and other indicators than in more heterogeneous superordinate product categories.

(Continued)

(Continued)

H4a-c: Both the direct and indirect measures of graded structure should have higher correlations with (a) typicality, (b) attribute structure, and (c) attitude across subordinate categories versus superordinate categories.

Again, based on past research, the following hypothesis was developed.

H4d: Both the direct and indirect measures of graded structure should *not* have higher correlations with the ideals measure across subordinate categories than across superordinate categories.

Method

Following a pretest, the main study was conducted. Two hundred forty-five undergraduate students at a midwestern U.S. university participated in the study. Participants completed two parts of a self-administered questionnaire in classroom settings. Several sessions were conducted with groups of approximately 10 participants. The procedure took approximately an hour to complete. After subjects had completed the first part, a short beverage break was taken. Due to the length of the procedure, this break was intended to reduce fatigue. Half the participants were paid $10 for their time, whereas the other half completed the study for extra course credit.

Four sets of superordinate-subordinate categories totaling eight categories in all were used: types of restaurants-fast food restaurants, footgear-athletic shoes, types of candy-candy bars, and types of alcoholic beverages-beer. Each participant completed ratings on one subordinate and one superordinate category that were not related (the four pairings of categories were types of alcoholic beverages-candy bars, types of restaurants-athletic shoes, types of footgear-fast food restaurants, and types of candy-beer).

To reduce fatigue as well as carryover effects between measures, subjects completed a subset of the questions and the product categories. Product categories were rotated so that subjects provided responses on two categories, one subordinate and one superordinate. Each product category contained 15 products, and ratings were obtained for the two fuzzy set measures as well as other variables. Four or five attributes were used for each product category.

The self-administered questionnaire first provided instructions for completing the direct measure. Ratings of memberships were completed for 15 products in a category on a specified attribute. For instance, in the direct measure condition, the self-administered questionnaire first provided instructions for completing the direct measure. This measure consisted of ratings of each product on a specified attribute in terms of how good an example of the category the product was on the specified attribute. For example, the fast food restaurant Wendy's was rated on how good an example of the category of fast food restaurants it was on the attribute "speed of service." The response scale ranged from 1 (*very poor example*) to 10 (*very good example*). Ratings were completed for 15 products in a category on a specified attribute. Similar ratings were completed for several attributes in the same category. Next, a similar set of rating scales was completed for several attributes of a second category. Then, subjects rated products from the first category in terms of global typicality, followed by products from the second category. The measure of global typicality was taken from Rosch and Mervis (1975) and asked subjects to rate each restaurant on a scale from 0 (*extremely poor example*) to 10 (*extremely good example*). Following this, ratings were collected for the indirect measure.

Each product was rated along each attribute on a 10-point scale. Similar ratings were collected for several attributes of the same category. In the indirect measure condition, each attribute was assessed on a 10-point scale. For the category of fast food restaurants, a rating was obtained for speed of service on a scale of 1 (*very slow*) to 10 (*very fast*). Each of the fast food restaurants was then rated on these same scales. For example, Wendy's was rated on speed of service using the scale 1 (*very slow*) to 10 (*very fast*). Similar ratings were completed for several attributes in the same category. Next, a similar set of rating scales was completed for several attributes of a second category. The procedure was then repeated for another category.

Participants were then given a short beverage break, after which they completed the second part of the questionnaire. They were assigned to one of two groups, where they completed either a family resemblance task or an attribute structure task. The objective was to reduce the length of the procedure by assigning these two relatively longer tasks to different groups, with the rest of the questionnaire being identical for both groups. The family resemblance measure was adapted from Rosch and Mervis (1975) and followed their procedure, whereby subjects listed the attributes for each product of a category followed by a similar procedure for the second category. The attribute structure measure was taken from Loken and Ward (1990). Belief statements were provided on each of the 4–5 attributes for a category using likelihood scales ranging from 1 (*extremely unlikely*) to 7 (*extremely likely*). The same procedure was repeated for the second category.

Next, attitude toward each of 15 products in a category was measured with three 10-point scales end anchored by *low quality-high quality, bad-good,* and *unsatisfactory-satisfactory,* with the procedure then repeated for the second category. The last three sets of scales completed were for familiarity for 15 products for each of two categories. The scales were anchored from 1 (*not at all familiar*) to 10 (*very familiar*) (Hampton & Gardner, 1983). The two categories used were frequency of instantiation, anchored from 1 (*not at all frequently*) to 10 (*very frequently*) (Loken & Ward, 1990), and ideals (i.e., the extent to which each product fulfills the category ideals), anchored from 1 (*very low amount*) to 9 (*very high amount*). Within each set of ratings of 15 products throughout the survey, products were presented in random order to minimize any systematic order effects.

(Continued)

(Continued)

Results

The direct and indirect measures were computed as shown earlier. For the attitude measure, the three scales of *low quality-high quality*, *bad-good*, and *unsatisfactory-satisfactory* were combined (mean coefficient alpha = 0.91; range = 0.81–0.97). This is an example of using internal consistency procedures to demonstrate reliability for a multiple-item, stimulus-centered rating scale. For the family resemblance measure, identical procedures were used as in past research. For the attribute structure measure, belief ratings for a product were summed across attributes.

For each variable, mean ratings across individuals were computed for each product in each category. Hence, all analyses were across stimuli, a critical issue for stimulus-centered scales. Difference scores were then computed (difference in mean ratings between a product and the category to which it belonged). As in Loken and Ward (1990), correlations and regressions were computed across categories using difference scores (z scores led to similar results).

Hypothesis 1: Convergent Validity

Significant correlations were found between direct and indirect measures of graded structure and global typicality ($r = 0.64$ and -0.74, respectively, $p < .01$), providing support for H1 in overall analyses across all eight categories as well as separate analyses of superordinate and subordinate categories. These results are critical in providing evidence of convergent validity. Intercorrelations between the two fuzzy indicators were also significant in all analyses.

Hypotheses 2 and 3: Nomological Validity

As predicted, statistically significant correlations were found across all categories between the direct and indirect measures of gradedness, respectively, and family resemblance ($r = 0.24$, $p < .01$; and $r = -0.20$, $p < .05$), frequency of instantiation ($r = 0.59$ and -0.46; $p < .01$), and familiarity ($r = 0.53$ and -0.40; $p < .01$), providing evidence of nomological validity and support for H2a-c. The hypotheses H2a-c were also supported in separate analyses of superordinate and subordinate categories, with the exception of family resemblance for superordinate categories (Exhibit 7.1 Table). Overall, the direct measure had comparable or higher correlations than the typicality measure, with the pattern being supportive but mixed for the indirect measure.

As predicted, significant relationships were found across all categories between the direct and indirect measures of gradedness, respectively, and attitude ($r = 0.67$ and -0.60; $p < .01$), attribute structure ($r = 0.73$ and -0.45; $p < .01$), and ideals ($r = 0.75$ and -0.62; $p < .01$), providing evidence of nomological validity and support for H3a-c (Exhibit 7.1 Table). Similar relationships were also found between these three comparison variables and typicality, again replicating past research (Exhibit 7.1 Table). The hypotheses H3a-c were also supported in separate analyses of superordinate and subordinate categories. The direct measure of gradedness consistently generated higher correlations than the indirect and typicality measures (correlations with attitude, ideals, and attribute structure).

Hypothesis 4: Discriminant Validity

Comparisons of correlations across category levels suggested support for H4a that the direct measure would have a statistically higher correlation with typicality for subordinate categories versus superordinate categories ($r = 0.78$ vs. 0.53; $z = 2.46$; $p < .05$). However, this was not the case for the indirect measure ($r = -0.75$ vs. -0.72). In terms of correlations with attribute structure, a pattern supporting H4b was not found for either measure (Exhibit 7.1 Table). This effect was also not found for typicality. For attitude, the results supported H4c for both measures ($r = 0.79$ vs. 0.60 for the direct measure, $z = 2.02$, $p < .05$; $r = -0.69$ vs. -0.49 for the indirect measure, $z = 1.67$, $p < .05$). Consistent with H4d, no effect was obtained for the ideals measure.

Category-Level and Individual-Level Correlations

Separate correlations were computed for each category across means for 15 products. As was the case with the results of the Loken and Ward (1990) study, there was considerable variation in the magnitude of the correlations across product categories. However, by and large, the correlations were consistent with hypotheses H1-H3, with the direct measure demonstrating the highest correlations. A direct comparison of results for the four category pairs that were common with the Loken and Ward study suggested striking similarities, such as a strong effect of category level for alcoholic beverages-beer when compared to other category pairs (Exhibit 7.1 Table). Correlations across 15 means for each category for each individual were also consistent with hypotheses H1-H3, with the direct measure generally having the highest correlations. The category-level effect appeared to emerge for alcoholic beverages-beer but not for other category pairs.

Regression analyses were also conducted and were largely supportive of the hypotheses. These analyses focus on variations across stimuli summed across individuals, as appropriate for stimulus-centered scales. Such analyses as well as correlational analyses were also conducted for each individual across stimuli and aggregated across individuals.

(Continued)

Exhibit 7.1 Table Intercorrelations Among Category-Related Indicators

	Direct Measure	Indirect Measure	Typicality	Family Resemblance	Attribute Structure	Ideal	Familiarity	Frequency
Eight product categories (n = 120)								
Ind.^	-.71**							
Typ.	.64**	-.74**						
Fam. res.	.24**	-.20*	.28**					
Att. struc.	.73**	-.45**@	.44**@	.01				
Ideals	.75**	-.62**	.66**	.09	.64**			
Fam.	.53**	-.40**	.51**	.22*	.41**	.78**		
Freq.	.59**	-.46**	.57**	.26**	.45**	.81**	.95**	
Attitude	.67**	-.60**	.51**@	.09	.61**	.81**	.69**	.68**
Four superordinate categories (n = 60)								
Ind.	-.55**							
Typ.	.53**	-.72**						
Fam. res.	.15	-.12	.15					
Att. struc.	.83**	-.46**@	.42**@	-.09				
Ideals	.74**	-.52**	.64**	.03	.78**			
Fam.	.36**	-.11	.34**	.23	.35**	.64**		
Freq.	.47**	-.23	.48**	.25	.42**	.73**	.93**	
Attitude	.60**	-.49**	.35**@	.07	.71**	.67**	.46**	.47**

(Continued)

Exhibit 7.1 Table (Continued)

	Direct Measure	Indirect Measure	Typicality	Family Resemblance	Attribute Structure	Ideal	Familiarity	Frequency
Four subordinate categories ($n = 60$)								
Ind.	−.93**~							
Typ.	.78**~	−.75**						
Fam. res.	.36**	−.29*	.41**					
Att. struc.	.59**	−.44**	.47**	.12				
Ideals	.79**	−.70**	.69**	.15	.49**			
Fam.	.73**~	−.64**~	.65**~	.22	.47**	.89**		
Freq.	.77**~	−.68**~	.66**	.27*	.48**	.88**	.98**	
Attitude	.79**~	−.69**~	.64**~-@	.10	.54**	.91**	.85**	.84**

SOURCE: Adapted from Viswanathan, M., & Childers, T. L. (1999), Understanding how product attributes influence product categorization: Development and validation of fuzzy set based measures of gradedness in product categories, in *Journal of Marketing Research*, 36(1), 75–94. Published by the American Marketing Association. Reprinted with permission.

~ Significantly higher correlation for subordinate when compared to superordinate categories presented for the two fuzzy indicators and for typicality

@ Significantly lower correlation for typicality or the indirect measure when compared to the corresponding direct measure presented for attitude and attribute structure.

^ Ind. = Indirect measure; Typ. = Typicality; Fam. res. = Family resemblance; Att. struc. = Attribute structure; Fam. = Familiarity; Freq. = Frequency.

*p < .05; **p < .01; two-tailed tests.

When a sufficient number of stimuli are rated on the speech quality scale and other relevant measures to compute correlations across stimuli, a stimulus-centered scale is being used. Such correlations could be run after aggregating across individuals or for each individual. Moreover, rater reliability could be assessed based on ratings of stimuli by individuals. However, when the speech quality scale is used to rate one or a few stimuli, and variations across individuals are analyzed, then a respondent-centered scale is being used. Coefficient alpha can be used to assess the internal consistency of the items in the scale.

Now consider a scenario where a shorter stimulus (say, one sentence) is used, with the need to evaluate many such sentences necessitating a shorter scale. First, a shorter scale needs to be validated by showing, among other things, a high correlation with the total scale. A variety of analyses can be performed by collecting data on scale items, both across individuals and across stimuli, assuming a sufficient number of stimuli to enable stable correlations. Correlations across individuals address relative ordering among them. Correlations across stimuli means for each individual or averaged across individuals provide insight into the relative ordering of stimuli.[2]

Formative and Reflective Indicators of Constructs

Measures differ fundamentally in whether they are causal (formative) or effect (reflective) indicators of constructs (Bollen & Lennox, 1991; Diamantopoulos & Winklhofer, 2001; Edwards & Bagozzi, 2000; Jarvis, MacKenzie, & Podsakoff, 2003). Effect indicators are those where constructs cause responses on indicators or items.[3] Causal indicators cause or form the overall measure of a construct. For example, a measure of socioeconomic status is defined by a weighted combination of its components, such as income and education (Figure 7.1). The measure of a construct, by definition, is "caused" or "formed" by its indicators. On the other hand, effect indicators are caused by constructs. Hence, a basic preference for numerical information causes responses on items of the PNI scale. Formative measures, on the other hand, are predefined by the researcher. Socioeconomic status is defined by its components, such as income and education. A measure of customer satisfaction may be defined by certain attributes, such as speed of service. A measure based on formative indicators is one that is strictly defined by its components. Thus, this important distinction is the very first question to pose in measure development and runs through the entire development and validation process. The underlying structure of formative measures is accurate by definition; thus, definition has to be preceded with considerable conceptual work.

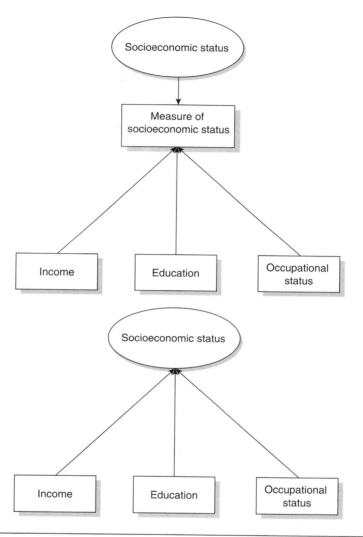

Figure 7.1   Two Illustrations of an Example of a Formative Indicator Model

The measures in Exhibit 7.1 are examples of a formative indicator model. Ratings on a predetermined set of attributes are combined in a specific way to arrive at a score on the measure of product category membership. Considering an example at the organizational level, research in the area of strategic management identifies several strategy typologies, such as prospectors and defenders. Prospectors are described as emphasizing new product development and research and development. The type of strategy a firm employs could be assessed through multiple items asking respondents to report their intentions on a range of subdomains, such as new product development or research and development. A formative approach to measuring strategy would be to define the measure as consisting of, say, rate of new product development and percentage of R&D expenses, specifying some way of combining these individual items. Thus, unlike a reflective approach, where each item is a measure, here, the components are incorporated through specific functions. Such a formative approach should be grounded in thorough conceptual arguments that specify the functional relationship between components.

The nature of the indicators is pertinent to the type of psychometric assessment (Bollen & Lennox, 1991). For example, many prescriptions in this book, such as internal consistency, are relevant only for effect indicators, where, in effect, each item is a measure of the construct. Hence, these items should be correlated to each other. However, formative indicators do not need to be correlated; they form the measure of the construct by definition. Internal consistency or factor loadings are not appropriate for formative indicators as a way of demonstrating psychometric properties. If income and education are components of a measure of socioeconomic status by definition, there is no requirement that they be positively correlated. Test-retest correlation can be applied to formative measures when the construct is expected to be unchanged across time. For example, test-retest correlation of socioeconomic status could be assessed using an interval that is short enough to assume no change. Both of the measures assessed in Exhibit 7.1 can be categorized as formative measures, ratings on a predetermined set of attributes being combined in a specific way to lead to the overall score. Here, internal consistency or factor analysis of ratings on individual attributes is not appropriate because a product may be typical on one attribute but atypical on some other attribute. However, test-retest reliability and validity tests can be conducted to assess these measures.

In comparing reflective and formative measures consider two different approaches to measuring a company's customer orientation. A reflective measure could be developed through statements that reflect an organization's intentions or descriptions of practices. Presumably, an underlying emphasis on customers leads to responses to certain statements. Alternatively, a formative measure could be developed through collecting behavioral data on aspects of customer orientation (say, percentage of customer complaints addressed, speed of service, and so on) and forming an overall indicator. Thus, aspects such as speed of service and complaints can be combined to create a formative measure, which is defined by its components. The distinction here is between aspects of a domain for a reflective indicator model and components for a formative indicator model. In formative indicator models, a measure exists only if each component is captured. By definition, the measure is a combination of certain components. For reflective indicator models, each item is a measure; however, because a sufficiently broad domain is captured, each item may capture a different but related aspect. Each item is a measure; therefore, items are strongly related to each other. The domain is sampled through items. When subdomains are sufficiently different, dimensions are formed. At this stage, items from each dimension in effect form a separate measure. Formative measures, on the other hand, may exist only when each component is measured. Dimensions in a reflective indicator model are usually identified from iterative conceptual and empirical analyses, often flowing from patterns in the data. In a sense, the relationship between a component and a measure based on a formative indicator model is deterministic, whereas the relationship between an item and the underlying construct in a reflective indicator model is probabilistic.

Reflective indicators, although employing the "each item as measure" assumption, should be representative. However, any item is replaceable, and each item is an imperfect measure of the construct. The sum of all items leads to a measure that is representative of the domain. Each item is not a necessary component that combines with other components to form the measure. The basic principle in item generation is to develop items that are directly caused by the construct. For example, responses to an item such as "I like to work with numbers" are likely to be caused by preference for numerical information.

Can a construct be measured with both formative or causal and effect indicators? Yes, if one approach combines a set of necessary parts while another assesses the construct directly. For example, product quality could be measured as the weighted sum of expert ratings, employee ratings, and consumer ratings wherein the weights are preassigned—a formative or causal indicator model. It could be measured directly as an overall attitude of consumers—an effect indicator model (e.g., using items about the quality of a product anchored *good–bad* or *poor–excellent*). Each part of a causal indicator model is necessary and not replaceable by another part, whereas each item in an effect indicator model is a measure of the underlying construct. Similarly, preference for numerical information conceivably could be measured using a formative measure—say, a weighted combination of numerical content of hobbies and numerical content of occupations. When an item is deleted in the reflective PNI scale from Chapter 1, it may reduce or eliminate coverage of some aspect of the domain of PNI. However, each item is not a necessary component of the measure that has a specific, functional relationship with the construct. Degree of category membership captured by the two measures in Exhibit 7.1 could also be measured with a reflective indicator model. Global items, such as whether a product is typical of its category (say, with labels such as *very typical–very atypical* and *poor example–good example,* the latter being similar to the global typicality measure discussed), could be used in a reflective indicator model of degree of category membership.

Some behavioral inventories may be either reflective or formative in nature. If each behavior is an indispensable component that forms the measure, such as in a scale of diversity of activities in relationships (the Relationship Closeness Inventory's diversity subscale) (Berscheid, Snyder, & Omoto, 1989), where the wide range of behavior checked off (say, doing laundry, visiting family, etc.) provides a measure of diversity, then the measure is formative (Bollen & Lennox, 1991). Diverse activities on such a scale could be combined in a predetermined way to arrive at a score of diversity. In such a scenario, the unit of analysis is the entire measure and some summary of the range of behaviors engaged in rather than each item or behavior being a measure of diversity. Alternatively, if each of a list of risky behaviors is a measure of a construct such as "proclivity to risky behaviors," with response categories based on frequency of behaviors, then the measure is reflective (e.g., frequency of engaging in behaviors such as skydiving).

Subdomains of a construct could represent dimensions. But each dimension can be measured by reflective or formative indicators. Each dimension is necessary to measure the entire construct, but the unit of relevant analysis here is whether the dimension itself is measured through a reflective or a formative measure. Moreover, the key here is the direction of the arrows; for a reflective indicator model, the arrows flow out of the dimension to individual items, and for a formative indicator model, the arrows flow out of the components to the formative measure of the dimension. In other words, the arrows are oppositely oriented for reflective versus formative indicator models.

Specific components predefine the measure of a construct in a formative indicator model, rather than emerging from iterative conceptual and empirical processes. Moreover, components define the measure of the construct in a precise manner, spelling out their functional relationship with the measure. On the other hand, dimensions are subdomains of a construct that are distinctly different; they do not combine in a predefined and specific way to form the construct. Rather, they flow from the iterative process of conceptual and empirical analyses. Moreover, the relationship between a construct and its dimensions can be viewed as being purely at a conceptual level. On the other hand, in a strict sense, the relationship between a measure based on a formative indicator model and the components of such a measure are at an operational level, although their relationship with the underlying construct is at a conceptual level. Thus, at a conceptual level, intelligence can be argued to have dimensions, such as quantitative intelligence. For a measure of socioeconomic status based on a formative indicator model, individual components are combined to operationalize the underlying concept of socioeconomic status.

Another pertinent question is whether individual dimensions are measured through reflective or formative measures. In fact, even a unidimensional measure is formed by a set of items tapping different aspects, and whether these aspects rise to the level of dimensions is a matter of degree. If dimensions are measured reflectively but measures of dimensions are later combined in some predetermined manner to provide a summary of the overall construct, then the measurement could be viewed as reflective at the level of each dimension and formative at the level of measures of dimensions combining to form the construct. It is possible for individual components of a formative indicator model to be measured reflectively, whereas the overall measure is predefined as a function of individual components. For example, in measuring customer orientation, consumer, employee, and expert ratings each may be measured through reflective measures yet combined in a predefined way as formative indicators of a measure of the underlying construct.

A key distinction in understanding formative versus reflective indicators is between the notion of causality in a real sense and in a measurement context. For formative indicators, the measure of the construct in question is a convenient summary of certain components, and actual causality flows from the components to the measure at a measurement level. The measure based on a formative indicator model is, by definition, caused by its components. The causality between components of a formative indicator model and the overall construct may be quite complex in reality. For instance, university quality may be measured by formative indicators—faculty quality and funding—each with its own complex relationship with university quality in reality. Thus, causality in a real sense and causality in terms of a construct and its measurement (i.e., responses on items of a measure) need to be distinguished.

Similarly, a latent construct may have a complex sequence of causality with the content of the items of a reflective measure. At a measurement level, though, the underlying state, trait, or level on some construct and its domain causes responses on items. Suppose that different levels of depression cause different responses to an item on sleeplessness, an aspect of the domain of depression. This does not rule out the content of the item, say, "My sleep is restless," causing the underlying construct, depression, in a real sense (Radloff, 1977, as cited in Bollen & Lennox, 1991, p. 314, who use the example of loneliness to make some of the following points). Rather, the point is that there is *causality at the measurement level* (i.e., flowing from a construct to responses to items in a measure). Thus, the definitional element is central to the formative/ reflective distinction and to the meaning of causal versus effect indicators.

Causality is used here in terms of the relationship between a construct, its measure, and the items or components of a measure, rather than in terms of the causality between the construct and the content of an item over time. Some behaviors reflected in items may cause underlying constructs and/or result from underlying constructs. Central here is the nature and direction of causality claimed by the researcher in the relationship between the conceptual and the operational *in the context of a construct and its measurement*. In other words, will higher levels of a construct lead to higher scores on the items measuring the construct? This point is not to undercut the notion discussed in Chapter 1 and later in this chapter that items should be developed to assess constructs directly rather than measure related constructs. Also, the point here is not to dilute the importance of temporal precedence, a requirement of causality, between construct and measurement (Edwards & Bagozzi, 2000). Rather, the point here is to note that the causality between the content of an item and a construct can, in reality, be complex and bidirectional. However, such complexity by itself should not rule out the use of an item as a measure of a construct. An item is generally relatively specific to a context, and the content of such specific items may have a complex relationship with the broader construct. Sometimes sleeplessness may cause depression in reality. But if depression is likely to lead to higher scores on items tapping sleeplessness, and sleeplessness is considered a direct indicator of depression reflected in the conceptual definition and domain delineation of depression, it can be used in a reflective indicator model measuring depression. However, if an item on sleeplessness is considered an indicator of a distinct construct, say, physiological health, or sleeplessness itself is considered a distinct construct that then leads to depression, then it should not be used as an indicator of depression. Items directly related to the conceptual definition of depression could be used to measure it. This discussion also highlights how theoretical and methodological sophistication go hand in hand. As constructs and conceptual relationships are clarified, measurement of individual constructs is enhanced.

Whether measures based on externally imposed definitions versus self-perceptions represent two different constructs versus the same construct is an interesting question. They could represent two different measures of the same construct, with convergence providing strong evidence of convergent validity. Alternatively, the underlying theoretical constructs could be different; this issue comes down to how a construct is conceptualized and what its level of abstraction is. For example, an organization's strategy is an abstract construct that could be approached through formative versus reflective indicators. Social class can be defined similarly. Alternatively, theoretical constructs may need to differentiate conceptually between perceptions (say, of strategy) and practices (say, manifest strategy) leading to different constructs. Such an approach may be pertinent in a study of the relationship between the two. Theoretical underpinnings and the need for specific constructs can lead to different definitions. In the final analysis, the research objective should drive how constructs are distinguished. Whether measures of perception versus practice are contrasted also depends on the state of the art or of knowledge in a research area. As research in an area progresses, what were viewed previously as two measures of the same construct may be reinterpreted as measures of related but distinct constructs.

Similarly, subjective self-assessments of product knowledge and objective tests of product knowledge may be used as alternative measures of the same construct or as measures of distinct constructs. Note that self-perceptions also can be employed in a formative indicator model, such as the example of a behavioral inventory with a set of diverse behaviors measuring diversity of behaviors or with a measure of product quality that involves some form of weighted average of ratings on individual product attributes, each attribute being a necessary component predefined as part of the construct. A measure of product quality could be a weighted combination of self-reports by consumers and ratings by experts. Rankings of universities are often implemented through a combination of ratings by faculty, recruiters, and students, along with rate of admission and entry-level scores in standardized tests. U.S. News & World Report ranks colleges through a weighted combination of academic reputation (by surveying officials at institutions), student selectivity (using factors related to admission), faculty resources, financial resources (educational expenditure per student), alumni giving (percentage of alumni donating), and graduate rate performance (difference between actual rate of graduation and expected rate in light of scores and expenditures) (Morley, Bryant, & Hatry, 2001). Here, the measure of college quality is predefined through its components. Money magazine rates best places to live using a weighted combination of such factors as weather and crime, the weights being determined by a survey that ranks importance of factors (Morley et al., 2001). Faculty evaluations could be based on a weighted average of performance in research, teaching, and service. Each component could be measured through ratings or multiple items but combined in a predetermined way to form the overall evaluation. Related issues of using natural observations as measures and the contrast between physical and psychological measurement are revisited in subsequent chapters.

Throughout the discussion above, a careful distinction is made for formative measurement in stating that the individual components cause or predefine the *measure* of a construct. This should be contrasted with the alternative of stating that the individual components cause or predefine the construct itself. The view taken here is that a construct, being an abstract concept devised for scientific study, can be measured in multiple ways, only one of which is the measure under study. Accordingly, Figure 7.1 illustrates formative measurement in two distinct ways, the first suggested here and the second often used in the literature. Several issues regarding reflective versus formative indicators are a level lower than the relationship between a measure and a construct and relate to the relationship between items or components and measures. A measure based on a formative indicator model may be created through combining components in a specific way, leading to insights about a new construct. Nevertheless, what is created is a measure of a new concept or construct, and other such measures of the construct are conceivable. In this regard, there is an asymmetry between reflective and formative indicator models; responses to items in the former model are caused by the underlying construct—hence, the appropriate illustration of the PNI construct as leading to responses on individual items in Chapter 1 and Figure 1.7. Given the item-as-measure nature of the model, the relationship between the construct and the items is shown through direct arrows. For the formative indicator model, though, the indicators combine to form the measure of the construct, not the construct itself.

In this regard, it should also be noted that each of the components of socioeconomic status, such as education, may be measured with error (Edwards & Bagozzi, 2000). The construct of socioeconomic status has a relationship with constructs underlying individual components, such as education. Socioeconomic status could be regarded, in a sense, as a higher-level construct. However, a specific measure of socioeconomic status is related to specific measures of individual components, such as education, in a predefined way, hence, the preferred illustration in Figure 7.1 of a measure level between the construct level and the components. Similarly, the direct and indirect measures of product category membership in Exhibit 7.1 are just that—distinct measures of an abstract construct.

The distinction between formative and reflective measurement relates to the causal relationship between indicators, measures, and constructs. Researchers have applied the types of evidence of causality to the relationship between a construct, its measure, and its indicators, and presented several models in addition to the formative and reflective models (Edwards & Bagozzi, 2000). For example, in the indirect reflective model, items that purport to measure a construct actually measure the effect of the construct (e.g., measuring turnover intent instead of job satisfaction with "I frequently think of quitting my job") (Edwards & Bagozzi, 2000, p. 163). The intended construct is the variable mediating the construct measured (i.e., turnover intent). Such incisive thinking of the nature of the relationship between an item and a construct is critical in measure development, as illustrated with Item 12 of the PNI scale in Chapter 1 and Figure 1.8. The point made in Chapter 1 is relevant here, to develop items that directly measure constructs, as far as possible. Similarly, of importance is the need to clearly distinguish constructs and avoid confounding the conceptual and operational levels. The conceptual level should clearly distinguish distinct constructs, and the operational level should be directly related to the corresponding conceptual level. When a measure of related construct is used as a measure of a specific construct, conceptual relationships are confounded with measurement.

Summary

This chapter examined how measures can be classified, covering issues that arise frequently yet lack appropriate treatment in the literature. Scales should be treated as stimulus centered or respondent centered, depending on their usage. Categorization into stimulus-centered versus respondent-centered scales should take the purpose of the research and the nature of the analyses into account (i.e., whether to conduct analyses across levels of stimuli or across respondents). Measures can also be categorized as being based on formative (causal) versus reflective (effect) indicator models; many of the prescriptions in earlier chapters apply to the latter. Formative indicators predefine the measure of the construct, and the issue of internal consistency does not arise, nor do some other issues germane to reflective indicators.

Notes

1. This dichotomy between stimulus-centered scales and respondent-centered scales is sometimes a simplification. For instance, the Rasch model and item response theory incorporate both item difficulty and respondents' level as mentioned in Chapter 1. Nevertheless, this distinction is of practical relevance in a number of situations in day-to-day research.

2. Several points are noteworthy. The scenario discussed here involves, first, a change in the nature of the stimuli, which necessitated a change in the measure employed. If a single-item scale is used in this study to evaluate individual sentences, a situation that should be avoided whenever possible, variations across studies may be due to real variations in perception of sentences or due to unreliability in measurement. Therefore, differences in measurement must be validated first before conducting substantive studies and interpreting data.

3. The term *indicator* is generally used in this chapter to be equivalent to an item or a subset of items parceled together—to be a component of a measure and not the entire measure. A measure is discussed as usually consisting of multiple indicators. Such usage appears appropriate for the content of this chapter. Measures resulting from formative or reflective indicators are referred to as *formative* or *reflective measures*, respectively.

8

What Are Examples of Measures and Measurement Across Various Disciplines?

Overview

This chapter provides a broad range of examples of measures and measurement in different disciplines. The aim of this chapter is to stimulate creative thinking in measure design. Brief discussions provide a sampling of the types of scales used in different disciplines. Therefore, sections of the chapter can be read in isolation. Following a discussion of types of measures and types of response formats, a variety of actual measures from a range of disciplines covering psychological, physiological, and physical measurement are presented in this chapter. Although measurement principles have been explicated earlier with self-report measures, these principles apply to a variety of different types of measures. The measures discussed here have been chosen to provide a broad perspective and present some alternatives to enable researchers to think outside the box. When the content of measures discussed here is not germane to the discussion, constructs are not defined conceptually, a sin that should not be committed in scientific research. Cross-cultural measurement is discussed in a separate section, given the unique issues that arise here.

Types of Measures

Self-reports involving degrees of agreement with statements have been widely discussed. However, measures are not restricted to such an approach. Self-reports are just one way of measuring constructs. The creativity of the researcher often may be what limits alternative ways of measuring constructs while meeting the requirement in scientific research of demonstrating psychometric characteristics. Measurement can take several forms, such as self-reports (diaries, open-ended questionnaire and scales), interviews, and observations (Pike, Loeb, & Walsh, 1995). Scales can be roughly divided into those measuring states (e.g., mood) or traits (e.g., extroversion) (Rust & Golombok, 1999). Measures can be categorized in several ways, such as being based on communication from the respondent versus observation by the researcher or rater. Communication measures can be categorized on the basis of the nature of stimuli about which responses are elicited. Ratings could be in response to observations, stimuli, visualizations by the respondents, or statements. Diaries are another self-report approach, requiring clear explanations to respondents and specific data.

Limited observations pose a variety of problems, such as the use of one or a few instances to draw conclusions about day-to-day life. Reliability in observational studies could be reported through percentage agreement between observers. However, chance may lead to sizable agreement (50% if there are two levels of observed data). The Kappa statistic takes such chance agreement into consideration. An indicator of reliability with multiple observers is percentage agreement. The problem here is that a high base rate of phenomenon can lead to high chance agreement (e.g., positive vs. negative behaviors, where most behaviors are positive) (Gardner, 1995).

One way of measuring agreement is as follows (Cohen, 1960):[1]

$$\kappa = \frac{P_o - P_c}{1 - P_c}$$

P_o = the observed proportion of agreement

P_c = the proportion predicted by chance

Proportion of agreement may be a misleading indicator of reliability. Other issues here include using previous agreements and disagreements to interpret future observations. Hence, two observers may converge on similar codings or ratings. This emphasizes the importance of independent observations. With the more traditional multiple-item scales, independence is achieved across individuals but not across items. Some degree of independence can be achieved by interspersion, or by wording items positively versus negatively in internal consistency reliability procedures and through longer intervals in test-retest reliability procedures. Within-measure correlational systematic error can be caused by sources such as halo effects.

In self-reports, open-ended questionnaires involve coding of responses by trained raters. More generally, texts are also analyzed through content analysis, in a sense similar to coding observations. In content analysis, the unit of coding has to be specified and may vary from a word to a phrase, a sentence, or a paragraph or longer (Weber, 1985). For example, paragraphs could be coded into one of several categories, such as political doctrine or welfare (Weber, 1985). Steps in content analysis include defining the recording units, defining the categories, test coding on a sample, assessing reliability and validity, and revising the coding scheme (Weber, 1985). Many issues discussed in developing self-report measures translate to content analysis. For instance, one decision relates to how broadly a category is to be defined, similar to the breadth or specificity of a construct. For coding, stability refers to consistency for the same coder across time. Reproducibility refers to intercoder reliability (i.e., consistency across different coders). In this regard, researchers have pointed out the need to assess intercoder reliability before disagreements are resolved (Krippendorff, 1980). Forms of validity, such as convergent validity and predictive validity, are germane. Additionally, semantic validity has been proposed to refer to agreement among people familiar with the language that the words placed in the same category have similar connotations (Krippendorff, 1980). Similar issues of coding arise in archival data (Elder, Pavalko, & Clipp, 1993) as in content analysis.

Measurement principles also apply to interviews (Kaplan & Saccuzzo, 2001). For instance, across-measure or within-measure correlational systematic error is an issue with halo effects in judgments, say, from early impressions. Errors can also arise in cross-cultural settings in misinterpreting behavior (e.g., interpreting avoidance of eye contact as dishonesty) (Kaplan & Saccuzzo, 2001). Another error relates to drawing inferences from a single outstanding characteristic (e.g., attractiveness) (Kaplan & Saccuzzo, 2001). Reliability, often assessed by inter-interviewer agreement, is usually higher for structured interviews. Yet such interviews may be narrowly focused in terms of content (Kaplan & Saccuzzo, 2001). In the context of an eating disorder measure, investigator-based interviews—where interviewers are trained to explain questions, probe answers, and make consistent judgments—have been distinguished from respondent-based interviews, which are essentially self-administered (Fairburn & Cooper, 1993). The former has been recommended when studying complex concepts and key terms that are not generally understood to have a particular meaning (Fairburn & Cooper, 1993). Through rigorous training and careful explication of administration procedures, reliability and validity are enhanced.

Difference scores—subtracting scores on one measure from another as a way of measuring a distinct construct (Peter, Churchill, & Brown, 1993)—are another type of measure. For example, perceived service quality could be measured by the difference between perceptions and expectations (Parasuraman, Zeithaml, & Berry, 1988). Several problems have been identified with the use of difference scores (Cronbach & Furby, 1970; Peter et al., 1993), such as the reliability of difference scores, which is influenced by the reliability of the components and the association between them, and the restriction in variance. Solutions suggested in the literature include directly asking respondents for their perceptions of differences (Peter et al., 1993), say, directly asking for a rating of the difference between perceptions and expectations in the case of service quality.

A broader issue worthy of emphasis is that the type of measure employed and the means of validation are limited only by the creativity of the researcher. As an example, an advertising agency uses several photographs of people with different expressions as response categories to measure reactions to advertisements. These photographs provide representations of a variety of emotions. Validation should include individual ratings of photographs on various dimensions to understand exactly what is being measured.

Types of Response Formats

A variety of response formats can be employed in measurement, such as agreement or disagreement with statements. Some scales use a forced-choice format where respondents typically pick one of two statements, such as the sensation-seeking scale (Zuckerman, 1979). An item on the scale is "(a) I like 'wild' uninhibited parties; (b) I prefer quiet parties with good conversation" (Zuckerman, 1979, as cited in Bearden & Netemeyer, 1999, p. 225). An item in the inner-other directedness social preference scale is "With regard to partying, I feel (a) the more the merrier (25 or more people present); (b) it is nicest to be in a small group of intimate friends (6 or 8 people at most)" (Kassarjian, 1962, as cited in Bearden & Netemeyer, 1999, p. 12). In analyzing such scales, the lack of variation in responses for each item should be noted. Typically, with a large number of items, the scale has sufficient variation. Test-retest reliability provides a means to assess consistency of the scale. At the item level, lack of variation hinders item-to-total correlations as well as item-level test-retest reliability.

With such an approach, the format itself may be a powerful means to convey levels of constructs while forcing respondents to pick one or the other. The assumption is that respondents in the middle of the continuum may pick one or the other option an approximately equal number of times. It is conceivable that such a scale may not differentiate between individuals at one extreme versus those between the middle and that extreme. For example, both sets of individuals may select the extreme option. Such a problem arises when the two options within each item are worded to be opposite extremes. However, items could be worded to provide distinction on various points on the continuum, thus substituting for direct item-level measurement of gradedness in response categories (e.g., *strongly agree* to *strongly disagree*).

The response categories for such a format are rich and thus meaningful to respondents. This is similar to a fully described response scale, such as *very important* and *somewhat important,* which convey meaningful markers but should be designed carefully to maintain equal intervals. Similarly, statements in the forced-choice option should be strictly restricted to differences in the construct in question. Otherwise, such an item is similar to a double-barreled question. This is a challenge because an item is made concrete and relevant by adding context, but this has to be accomplished without involving other constructs.

Another issue with dichotomous items is that the lack of a continuum at the item level precludes some empirical demonstrations of psychometric properties. For example, means of specific items cannot be used to assess the degree to which opposite anchors of these items cover the continuum. Given the dichotomous nature of the items, additional pretesting work is required for such scales. On the other hand, the richness of these scales may well warrant such effort. In fact, each anchor could be evaluated through Likert-type responses. Rankings and pairwise comparisons of anchors at pretesting may also be useful. Procedures to ensure content validity take on added significance with such scales. The complexity of items due to length should also be addressed. For instance, two dichotomous anchors may differ on several constructs in addition to the construct in question, a problem with the measure's validity. A set of anchors of an item of sensation seeking, such as "I like 'wild' uninhibited parties" versus "I prefer quiet parties with good conversation" (Zuckerman, 1979, as cited in Bearden & Netemeyer, 1999, p. 225), may also be different on other constructs related to, say, liking for conversations. These anchors have to be pretested by having them rated on a variety of dimensions, intended and unintended.

Consider the measure of speech quality where respondents listen to recordings of three to four sentences and rate them on multiple-item, fully labeled scales with five response categories (Exhibit 1.5 Figure). Although seven responses could be employed, relatively rich sensory stimuli may be difficult to evaluate on very fine gradation. Moreover, five response categories may allow for different rich stimuli to be psychologically managed by respondents when rating. Also, fully described response categories allow for each level to be meaningfully interpreted as shown (see Exhibit 1.5 Figure). Fully described response categories should be avoided, however, when they do not convey equidistant intervals but are ambiguous. For example, a response scale on liking labeled *not at all, a little, neutral, a lot,* and *very much* essentially blurs the differences between the extreme labels and the moderate labels (for example, *a lot* and *very much* are very similar), and is likely to cause random error. In such situations, it may be preferable to label just the ends. In contrast to items evaluating sensory stimuli, items with attitudinal statements may be more amenable to 7- or 9-point scales and numbered, end-anchored response categories. Here, respondents may be able to convert responses into gradations in terms of seven or nine levels. Therefore, response scales should be designed to fit specific situations. Ultimately, the proof is in the empirical demonstrations of psychometric properties.

A related issue here is the number of response categories to use in a scale (Cox, 1980). A key issue is to capture sufficient variation; sometimes, a 7-point scale may, in effect, be used as a 5-point scale when extreme anchors are employed (e.g., *hate it–love it* or *never–always*). Is there a downside to adding to the number of response categories, or does it not matter? After all, with a 100-point scale, those who use it like a 10-point scale can do so, whereas others may provide finer gradations. Consider ratings of liking for, say, three brands of soft drinks on a 100-point scale, completed twice with an interval of a few weeks. Are consistent responses likely? The problem here is one of inability to manage 100 response categories, leading to unreliability. Indeed, there is a downside to having too many response categories, such as the difficulty in managing many response categories or in deciding what part of the scale to use, which is likely to cause random error. Even if individuals were to use response categories consistently, the wide range may lead to consistent differences across individuals over and above the construct being measured (i.e., within-measure correlational systematic error, such as differences in deciding what constitutes high vs. low and what part of the scale to use).

In addition to balancing the need for finer gradation or discrimination with the need to take into consideration respondents' ability to manage response categories, there may be another consideration with some scales. If differences in levels of scales are used to draw inferences, then the use of a meaningful number of response categories is important as well. For example, with the speech quality scale above, the use of a number of response categories meaningful to respondents is important. But a meaningful number of response categories is also important from the perspective of drawing inferences based on differences on scales (Viswanathan, Sudman, & Johnson, 2004). Respondents may be able to reliably discriminate to a greater degree than is meaningful to them; hence, a 7-point scale that is used to capture differences that are meaningful at five levels for respondents may lead to finer, reliable discrimination (e.g., intention to purchase a product or calorie content of chewing gum on a 3- vs. a 7-point scale, where three response categories are meaningful). But the absolute differences on the scale may not translate to meaningful differences for respondents. When drawing inferences, the difference between a 6 and a 7 may not be meaningful to respondents. Therefore, although the scale may be reliable, it may not provide a basis to make valid inferences about differences. Again, reliability and validity relate to how a scale is used in terms of both how data are collected on it and how inferences are made from the data.

Some scales, such as the self-monitoring scale (Snyder, 1974), employ a true/false response format. The issues applying to a forced-choice dichotomous response apply here as well. The nature of items is also affected by the nature of the construct in question. Some constructs may well have polarized or qualitatively distinct levels; thus, measurement may involve cut-off scores. Constructs may aim to establish qualitatively different levels. With such constructs, item format could be adjusted, such as through forced-choice versus other formats. Thus, whether a construct has qualitatively distinct levels or is continuous, and whether it is bipolar or unipolar, are important considerations in designing measures. In sum, the nature of the construct influences the item format chosen. If a construct is conceptualized as being either/or, item format would be affected accordingly. For example, compulsive buying is measured by a scale (Faber & O'Guinn, 1992) where a cut-off is computed on the basis of a formula that combines responses to items. Items are statements with levels of agreement or levels of frequency (*never–very often*). Thus, the nature of the construct should be taken into consideration when designing items (i.e., statements and response categories). Consider a scale with levels of frequency as the response categories. Such scale items could be rewritten as Likert scale items, such as "I often . . ." (*agree–disagree*). However, if the construct is closely related to frequency, then frequency-based response categories (e.g., *not at all* to *very often*) may tap such a construct more directly. Actual frequencies could be used as response categories as well (e.g., *never, once a week,* and so on). Such response categories facilitate consistent interpretation across individuals. Wherever possible, it may be preferable to use actual numbers rather than vague labels. However, in some scenarios where respondents' perceptions of frequency rather than actual frequency are important to capture, using objective frequencies as response categories may not be appropriate.

In some scales, the item-level unit of analysis is not available. For example, the Rokeach Value survey (Rokeach, 1968) requires a ranking of values. Thus, rather than ratings on a continuum on each of a set of values, the level of analysis is the entire scale. The appropriate test here is test-retest reliability of the entire scale. Item-level analyses are not available, such as item-level internal consistency and item-level test-retest reliability. Ranking consistency can be checked across time. Lacking such item-level diagnostic empirical assessment, the basis for the content validity of the scale is extremely important. For example, whether the set of values captures the domain of values is a key conceptual question. It should be noted that, given the purpose of the construct, which is defined as "an enduring belief that a specific mode of conduct or end-state of existence is personally and socially preferable to alternative modes of conduct or end-states of existence" (Rokeach, 1968, p. 160), the ranking of values is an appropriate approach to measurement. A strong conceptual basis should be provided for the set of values. Again, items should be assessed individually in the degree to which they tap the intended underlying value. A construct being a concept designed for scientific purposes, the purpose is reflected in the nature of its definition and affects the measurement approach. Thus, the Rokeach values survey is related to preference for values, and a ranking is the approach employed to measure it. The List of Values (Kahle, 1983) assesses the importance of a set of values using a response scale from *very unimportant* to *very important* or from a rank ordering of values from *most important* to *least important*. Rank ordering can be assessed through test-retest reliability. Importance ratings can be assessed through traditional internal consistency, test-retest reliability, and factor analysis procedures.

Some scales can be used in a variety of contexts by allowing flexibility in wording. For example, the consumer involvement profiles scale has items such as, "When you choose _____, it's not a big deal if you make a mistake," wherein a product is inserted in the blank space. Thus, the scale can be employed for a variety of products, and its testing reflected this application (Laurent & Kapferer, 1985, as cited in Bearden & Netemeyer, 1999, p. 182). The construct has several dimensions, such as the perceived importance and risk of the product class.

To summarize, the nature of the construct influences the choice of format of items and response categories. For example, a construct relating to diversity of activities in relationships (the Relationship Closeness Inventory's diversity subscale) (Berscheid et al., 1989) would influence the choice of items. A behavioral inventory with a list of diverse activities would be somewhat more disguised than Likert-type statements about diversity of activities. Likert-type items sometimes may be indirect when compared to semantic differential items, which require direct responses on degree of diversity. A behavioral inventory has the advantage of requiring responses on specific activities, with the researcher computing a diversity score rather than requiring a direct self-report on diversity. Such an approach is consistent with the notion that when respondents are unaware of the intent, more valid data may be obtained. The nature of the construct also affects the forced-choice versus other formats. If the construct aims for relative preference or prioritization, a ranking of items leading to measure-level unit of analysis, such as the values scale, is appropriate. Alternatively, preference among types of information, such as the PNI construct, could be captured through Likert-type items.

Specific Examples of Scales From Different Disciplines

A variety of scales from different disciplines are described here. The aim is to provide a broad perspective of types of measures to facilitate thinking outside the box. The scales described here have been selected to illustrate unique elements. These examples are presented by discipline and roughly sequenced to move from psychological to physical measurement, covering ability and physiological measurement in between.

Scales of Individual Traits and Attitudes

Hemispheric orientation is measured through 7-point scales anchored with customized descriptions such as "I prefer to think in pictures (words)" (Hirschman, 1983, as cited in Bruner & Hensel, 1992, p. 263). An imagery vividness scale asks respondents to picture specific images, with responses ranging from 5 (*no image*) to 1 (*perfectly clear and vivid as normal vision*) (Marks, 1973, as cited in Bruner & Hensel, 1992, p. 823). Thus, respondents generate the stimulus here. A scale of assertiveness, with items such as "I am quick to express an opinion," has responses from *very characteristic of me, extremely descriptive* to *very uncharacteristic of me, extremely nondescriptive* (Rathus, 1973, as cited in Bruner & Hensel, 1992, p. 348). Attitudes toward a product or brand are measured through semantic differential items anchored with responses such as *good–bad* (Osgood, Suci, & Tannenbaum, 1957). A scale measuring mood at a point in time has a stem, "This moment I am feeling . . ." with response scales anchored *good–bad*, and so on (Allen & Janiszewski, 1989, as cited in Bruner & Hensel, 1992, p. 361). Because this phenomenon is not enduring, traditional test-retest reliability is not an option. Convergent validity and internal consistency take on added significance. Mood states could also be manipulated and differences on a mood scale assessed. Such an approach could also be employed to assess a form of test-retest reliability where different groups of individuals are assigned to specific mood conditions at test and then at retest. The mood manipulation would have to be assessed independently using a different validated measure of mood. A product performance evaluation scale is anchored *worst possible–best possible* on several characteristics (Korgaonkar & Moschis, 1982). Presumably, extreme standards serve as comparison points, although the actual utility of such standards is not clear because respondents may avoid using the extremes. To encourage reliable responses, the instructions could ask the respondents to provide examples of extremes (i.e., calibrate the extremes). Calibration could also be provided by the researcher in terms of examples or ideals that describe either extreme, an approach that would maintain consistency across respondents. Additionally, a sufficient number of response categories should be used to allow for avoidance of extremes. With extreme anchors, a 7-point (5-point) scale could, in effect, be used as a 5-point (3-point) scale.

Nonverbal sensitivity appears to be unstable and varies with status and social roles. People appear to be able to "turn their non-verbal sensitivity on and off at will" (DePaulo & Friedman, 1998, p. 9). The Profile of Nonverbal Sensitivity (PONS) test (Rosenthal, Hall, DiMatteo, Rogers, & Archer, 1979) and the Communication of Affect Receiving Ability Test (CARAT) (Buck, 1976) have been used to measure nonverbal sensitivity. In the former, clips of enactments of common situations in different modalities (e.g., face, body, or tone of voice) are presented with a choice of two alternatives. These enactments vary in positivity and dominance. The CARAT shows clips of facial reactions to slides, and respondents are to pick the slide that was viewed. These slides are "unpleasant, unusual, sexual, and scenic" (DePaulo & Friedman, 1998, p. 9). Nonverbal sensitivity itself breaks into distinct domains, such as assessing tone of voice versus facial expressions, that are not highly correlated.

Creativity has been measured in a variety of ways: (a) tests of divergent thinking (e.g., fluency, flexibility), (b) attitude and interest inventories, (c) personality inventories, (d) biographic inventories (e.g., items that reflect curiosity), (e) ratings by teachers, (f) judgments of products (e.g., writing a story), (g) study of eminence, and (h) self-reports of creative activities (Hocevar & Bachelor, 1989).

The Dyadic Adjust Scale (Spanier & Filsinger, 1983) relates to marital adjustment with Likert responses to items such as "religious matters" that can be completed individually by couples. Miller's Scale Battery of International Patterns and Norms (Miller, 1968, as cited in Miller, 1991,

p. 480) assesses national culture through items such as "concern for and trust of others," with detailed end and middle anchors such as *lack of concern for others* and *lack of trust*. A measure of value of an object (Deighton, Romer, & McQueen, 1989, as cited in Bruner & Hensel, 1992, p. 596) has adjectives as scale items with a response scale from *Does not describe at all* to *Describes extremely well*. Such an approach involves direct description of a target.

Scales of Emotion

Emotion is measured vocally by analyzing acoustic parameters of speech (Scherer, 1989). Emotional states have been related to indicators such as tension in vocal apparatus. Novelty, pleasantness, or other attributes of stimuli have been related to vocal changes. Noteworthy here is the development of a detailed theory of emotions and physiological responses that forms the basis for this measurement approach. Projective measures of emotion (Rorschach, 1942) are similarly based on underlying theory linking emotion and diagnostic states (e.g., obsessive) to number of responses, reaction time, and the form of response (i.e., good form vs. poor form reflecting psychopathology) (Kellerman, 1989). Form is assessed by attributes such as articulation and use of color. Emotions are also measured using adjective checklists, with adjectives such as calm and nervous. Different measures are assessed through convergent validity checks. Item-checking tendency affects checklists in that some individuals may vary in tendencies to check more versus fewer items (Lorr, 1989). In the area of identifying emotions, the idiosyncratic effects of the set of response categories are brought out (Russell, 1989). When a photograph was shown, 93% picked sad when the options were sad or happy, whereas 0% picked sad when the options were sad and upset (Russell, 1989). Such findings reinforce the importance of the set of response categories used. Another approach employs adrenaline secretion rate as a measure of stress (Russell, 1989). Unfortunately, such physiological measures cannot discriminate among several emotions characterized by the same degree of arousal.

In the measurement of constructs such as affect, the bipolar versus unipolar nature should be reflected in the measurement approach. Osgood et al. (1957) argued that affect could be measured by three bipolar dimensions: circulation (e.g., *good-bad*), activity (e.g., *fast-slow*) and potency (e.g., *strong-weak*). Several tests were conducted using single adjectives (e.g., good) looking for negative correlations between good and bad (Lorr, 1989). Such correlations were often not found, perhaps because of acquiescence or extreme response bias, which likely reduced correlations. Partialing out acquiescence led to negative correlations, suggesting bipolarity (Bentler, 1969). Redundancy of multiple factors versus the parsimony of fewer factors should also be a consideration. For instance, for the speech quality scale discussed earlier, although a unidimensional scale performs well, a two-dimensional scale may be preferred if these dimensions provide utility.

The Affective Grid (Russell, Weiss, & Mendelsohn, 1989) is a single-item measure of pleasure and arousal developed specifically for quick and repeated administration to capture frequent changes in affect. The grid consists of 9×9 cells, with the vertical and horizontal axes ranging from sleepiness to high arousal and from unpleasant to pleasant feelings, respectively. The four corners, listed clockwise starting at the lower left, are labeled depression, stress, excitement, and relaxation. Detailed instructions provide the respondents with examples of responses in different parts of the grid, thereby calibrating it for the respondent. Respondents are asked to provide a response reflecting how they currently feel, their response providing separate scores on pleasure and arousal. Because internal consistency cannot be shown with a single-item scale and test-retest reliability is not appropriate for transient states, the scale's psychometric properties were demonstrated through convergent validity with measures of pleasure and arousal and through correlations across stimuli (Russell et al., 1989). For the latter, ratings of external stimuli, such as words conveying emotion or facial expressions of emotions, were used. In one study, using two subsets of samples, means ratings on affect pleasure and arousal for each stimulus were computed. Correlations across stimuli between the two subsets of samples were shown to be high. A manipulation of affect validated independently using some other measure of affect offers additional tests of the Affective Grid. Groups of respondents could be assigned to different levels of affect at test and retest, and the Affective Grid assessed for test-retest reliability and convergent validity across these discrete groups.

The State-Trait Anxiety Inventory (Spielberger, Gorush, & Lushene, 1970) assesses state anxiety (emotional reactions to situations) and trait anxiety (a personality characteristic). The state anxiety measure has been shown to have convergent validity. As expected, it has low test-retest reliability. Moreover, it has been shown to have discriminant validity in terms of being different from the trait anxiety measure, the latter shown to be unaffected across time before and after successful surgery, whereas the former showed differences. In a sense, the use of manipulations or experimental effects to test the validity of measures is another form of assessment. If the same effect can be generated through measurement as well as through manipulation, this is a form of evidence of validity. For instance, if a manipulation of a construct leads to differences on a measure of that construct as does measurement on that construct, this is added evidence of the validity of the measure. This assumes that the manipulation of a construct was independently assessed through a different validated measure. Such a form of validity is similar to known-groups predictive validity, only the difference is across known manipulated levels rather than known groups of respondents. A valid measure of a construct should capture differences across levels of the construct (e.g., known-groups predictive validity of the PNI scale across math vs. business majors, or validity of a measure across known levels of, say, credibility or clinical conditions). Convergent and discriminant validity can be shown to be somewhat similar to manipulation and confounding checks in experimental design discussed in Chapter 10, only here the goal is to assess measures using independently validated levels of constructs.

The Test Anxiety Questionnaire, which has, for example, an item on the extent to which respondents perspire when taking a test (Mandler & Sarason, 1952), has been criticized as assessing state rather than trait anxiety (Kaplan & Saccuzzo, 2001). A later version has been validated by showing differences between high and low test-anxious individuals consistent with theoretical expectations (e.g., different reactions to instructions producing stress, different reactions to neutral feedback, different use of information, different reactions in personalized vs. task-oriented responses) (Kaplan & Saccuzzo, 2001; Sarason, 1975).

Scales for Children

Measures for children have to be creative in capturing a construct yet simple to understand and use. For example, Nguyen and John (2003) used an established materialism scale but substituted disagree/agree with NO, no, yes, and YES response categories, respectively, to facilitate comprehension. In a different measure, children were asked to make a collage about happiness, with pictures of people and pets, hobbies, sports, material things, and achievements. Children were asked to assign 20 stars to categories used for the collage task. They were instructed to use all 20 stars and to assign more stars to categories that were more important to making them happy. A different sorting task measure involved sorting of 20 index cards into four groups (YES, really important to make me happy; yes, a little important; no, not that important; NO, not important at all), wherein the cards contained descriptions of "material things" from the collage task. These measures were shown to have convergent validity through correlations with previous measures.[2]

A social competency scale aims to measure the social competence of children with mental disability (Cain, Levine, & Elzey, 1963). It has several subscales covering areas such as self-help, initiative, social skills, and communication. An interviewer administers the items to knowledgeable adults, such as parents. A sample item on dressing has five phrases from *Cannot put on any clothing* to *Completely dresses self, including shoe tying* (Cain et al., 1963, as cited in Lyerly, 1973, p. 12). Noteworthy here is the importance of having fully described response categories that represent specific levels of behavior, such as dressing (e.g., 4 = *Completely dresses self, except for shoe tying*; 2 = *Can put on most clothing, can zip, cannot button*). Thus, discrete levels of behavior are represented by discrete levels of response categories, appropriately described. These discrete levels on a scale with fully described response categories relate to meaningful differences in dressing, which in turn cover an aspect of social competence. Such a scale can be contrasted with attitudinal scales, such as preference for numerical information, which aim to capture some continuum of attitudes. The behavioral nature of the social competence scale also suggests discretization into specific behaviors. Alternatively, behavioral inventories may be composed of checklists (i.e., a discrete Yes/No to whether individuals engage in certain behaviors).

The Child Behavior Rating Scale (Cassel, 1962, as cited in Lyerly, 1973, p. 14) has items such as "often prefers to be alone," with raters (knowledgeable adults) checking off a 6-point scale labeled Yes/No at extremes. Thus, a continuum of behavior is captured. The Child Behavior Inventory (Burdock & Hardesty, 1967) has items such as "has signs of panic" (Burdock & Hardesty, 1967, as cited in Lyerly, 1973, p. 15) that capture the subdomain of "fear-worry." Responses are checked based on one or more observations of a child in a small group setting. Noteworthy here is the discrete nature of behavior. Also important are consistent administration procedures for observations that specify the duration and nature of the setting. Other behavioral scales use frequency of occurrence as a continuum. In observations, clear identification of target behavior is critical. Vague or abstract personality jargon, such as aggression, needs clarification through terms such as "strikes out at others . . ." (Taylor, 1997). Behavior should be defined in precise, observable ways. This is similar to the design of response scales to assess behaviors, such as frequency of coffee drinking, using vague labels such as *frequent, seldom,* and so on. Further refinement, such as in identifying situations when specific behaviors are not aggressive (e.g., shouting in a playground), would be preferable (Taylor, 1997). Recording procedures also need to be detailed, such as recording events in a time period and recording duration of events. Specificity enables consistent interpretation and, thus, reliability and validity.

The Vineland Social Maturity Scale has items reflecting life-age wherein examiners begin with items below a respondent's age and stop when a certain maximum level has been reached (e.g., "Tells time to quarter hour" = Life-age mean of 7.28) (Doll, 1965, as cited in Lyerly, 1973, p. 17). Thus, specific items are tied to specific points on the life-age continuum. Such scale construction requires validation at very specific levels. Calibration was carried out with children of different age groups. Thus, a continuum of scales—from end-anchored scales measuring degrees of attitude, to a few fully described discrete levels of behavior, to items ordered to capture levels of a construct—suggests different degrees of understanding between responses to items and levels of the underlying construct. For some scales, specific behaviors can be represented as discrete levels of response to items.

A measure of nutritional knowledge for children has true-false items such as "Milk contains all the vitamins you need each day" (Wiman & Newman, 1989, as cited in Bruner & Hensel, 1992, p. 373). Socioemotional measures for very young children offer another set of interesting measures (Klein-Walker, 1973). The Ammons doll-play interview (Ammons, 1950, as cited in Klein-Walker, 1973, p. 47) presents black and white dolls to children, who respond to a set of questions, such as with whom they would like to play. The relevant reliability indicator presented here is interrater reliability. A measure of racial attitudes involves stories about humans shown in pictures (Williams & Roberson, 1967). Pictures have pairs of humans of different races or gender. Children are asked to choose the person in each picture who fits positive and negative adjectives.

A Fear Faces Scale (Katz, 1982) is employed with young children. A single-item scale contains seven faces ranging from smiling to sad. Validity has been shown through relationship with observational distress. Children's scales often involve responses to questions using happy to sad faces. The Draw-Classroom test (Dowd & West, 1969) involves asking children to draw a classroom, followed by a discussion about the drawing. Responses are coded on numerous categories, interrater reliability being relevant here. The Parten social participation measure (Parten, 1932) involves observation of children during free play for specific time intervals, coded into a set of categories by trained observers.

For measurement involving children, distraction and consequent random error is a germane issue. In a sense, the phenomenon is measurable only to a certain degree of reliability. For instance, scholastic tests for children would be affected by random error. Understanding and adhering to instructions is central to minimizing random error.

Gender-Related Scales

Several scales relating to gender and sex issues (Beere, 1990) are illustrative. The Heterosocial Assessment Inventory for women (Kolko, 1985) describes situations and has several items with 9-point response scales. These situations relate to heterosocial behavior such as making conversation. Thus, this scale is stimulus-based, the stimuli being verbal descriptions of behavior. The Heterosocial Skill Observational Rating System (Kolko & Milan, 1985) consists of several verbal and nonverbal behaviors. Raters complete scales after observing a female respondent in role-plays with a male confederate. The role-plays are 4 minutes long with specific instructions that describe a situation (e.g., a party) and a goal (e.g., initiate a conversation and make a good impression). The response scale from 0 to 2 ranges from *rambling conversations* to *enhanced conversations*. Thus, in this measure, observers complete ratings based on simulated behaviors. To generate situations during measure development, women kept logs of heterosocial situations. Validation included interrater reliability. A large sample of judges completed ratings of role-plays and listed cues used in their judgments. From about 6,000 cues, 10 categories of cues were identified. The five most frequent behaviors relating to each category were also identified. Items were developed for each behavior. Thus, detailed measure development procedures were employed here.

Projective Measures

This discussion of projective tests is based on an excellent review in Kaplan and Saccuzzo (2001). Rorschach developed stimuli by folding paper after dropping ink on it (Kaplan & Saccuzzo, 2001). Ten stimuli were selected from thousands. The Rorschach test is administered individually to respondents in a relatively unstructured approach. Respondents are asked what a stimulus could be and allowed open-ended responses. Respondents may also ask clarifying questions. Examiners should avoid revealing anything about the response either verbally or nonverbally. Examiners may prompt respondents to think of a second response if only one was given earlier. These instructions serve to enhance consistency of administration and, therefore, reliability. In a second trial, cards are shown again. Responses are scored along several dimensions, such as location (where something was perceived in the inkblot), form quality (match with inkblot properties), context (e.g., human, animal), and frequency of response (e.g., rare). In terms of location, whether the entire blot, a common detail, or an unusual detail is used is noted in the scoring. Each stimulus has a location chart to enable scoring. Scoring also includes identifying a determinant (i.e., what in the inkblot—shape, color, etc.—led to a response). Ambiguity and lack of structure here is deliberate; however, a lack of clear and consistent procedures calls reliability into question.

Lack of consistency in administration and scoring causes unreliability. The amount of instructions varies across examiners, as do scoring methods. Therefore, mixed results have been obtained for reliability. Similarly, validity is an issue.

Sentence completion tests (e.g., "I am _____") (Rotter & Rafferty, 1950) are scored such that shorter sentences that are positive or humorous in nature get higher scores, and vice versa. Figure-drawing tests are scored on such attributes as size, omissions, and lack of proportion. For instance, omission of self in a family drawing could be interpreted as alienation. The reliability and validity of such measures needs to be demonstrated. Similarly, word association tests, where a set of words is presented and scoring is by comparison to norms (e.g., college students vs. schizophrenics), have problems with reliability and validity. Thematic apperception tests involve showing respondents pictures and asking them to relate a story (Murray, 1938). The aim here is to understand human needs. Numerous scoring methods exist, such as those relating to needs or outcomes. Reliability, such as test-retest reliability, and validity are problematic.

Projective tests are interesting in combining many characteristics that lead to difficulties in measurement. As discussed, inconsistencies in administrations and scoring cause unreliability. More fundamentally, these tests are not really assessing a single construct unless the construct is something immeasurably abstract, such as the human condition! Rather, results are used to infer levels of a variety of interrelated abstract concepts, such as alienation and depression. Somewhat like bouncing a ball off an uneven surface, findings are subject to myriad explanations. Reliable and valid measurement can be accomplished when individual constructs are isolated. At the least, a clear relationship between indicators and underlying constructs that is driven by theory and validated by empirical results is needed. So does this mean that such tests have little use? Quite the contrary—they provide interesting qualitative insight and working hypotheses. More specific forms of these tests with consistent guidelines for administration and scoring and narrower objectives may well be validated quantitatively, as suggested by some recent versions of these tests.

It should be noted that thematic apperception tests are based on a theory of needs (Murray, 1938), whereas Rorschach tests are atheoretical. Fundamentally, the approach of unstructured exploration of a broad range of values, needs, and motivations is inconsistent with quantitative measurement. Yet such qualitative study can result in improved quantitative measurement as well as rich, substantive insight to generate testable hypotheses. Traditional reliability and validity procedures may not be the appropriate means to assess unstructured approaches.

Medical Scales

Neurological rating scales (Herndon, 1997) provide interesting insights. The Bellevue Index of Depression (Petti, 1978, as cited in Herndon, 1997, p. 8) assesses depression in children and consists of items in domains such as sleep disturbance, with responses based on duration (*less than a month* to *2 years*) or magnitude (*not at all* to *very much*). It is separately administered to parents and children with different procedures, written versus interview, respectively. Interrater reliability is reported.

The Norris ALS (Amyotrophic Lateral Sclerosis) Scale captures change in ALS patients (Norris et al., 1974, as cited in Herndon, 1997, p. 31). Items relate to chewing, or changing leg position, with response formats such as *normal, impaired, trace,* and *no use.* Items relate to various body parts and discrete functions, with the measure administered by trained specialists. This is an example of a formative measure. Thus, test-retest reliability and interrater reliability would be applicable, not internal consistency.

Movement disorders are assessed through several scales, including diary rating (Herndon, 1997). Patients monitor motor symptoms hourly. Problems include a lack of strong relationships between self-reports and objective assessments. Diary completion has a host of problems associated with it, such as completion after the fact using retroactive memory. The Mathew Stroke Scale was designed to assess deficits due to stroke, with items relating to several functions, such as speech (anchored *normal* to *no response to pain*) (Mathew, Rivera, Meyer, Charney, & Hartmann, 1972, as cited in Herndon, 1997, p. 171). The scale has been shown to be correlated to other scales and to predict long-term outcomes; however, interrater reliability is low (Gelmers, Gorter, Weerdt, & Wiezer, 1988).

The Brief Psychiatric Rating Scale (Overall & Gorham, 1962) comprises different symptom areas, such as anxiety. Response categories are fully described 7-point scales ranging from *not present* to *extremely severe* (Overall & Gorham, 1962, p. 803). For each item, raters are provided with explanation, and ratings are based on observations or patients' self-reports. Thus, administration procedures are crucial in maintaining consistency. Other response scales in this area include *true/not true* or *absent/present.* Another response scale ranges from *nearly always* to *hardly ever,* with *occasionally, approximately half the time,* and *frequently* being the middle three points (Levine & Elzey, 1968, p. 1). Rater responses may reflect random or systematic errors. Inconsistencies in following procedures can lead to generic random error, bias can lead to additive systematic error, and within-measure correlational systematic error can creep in through inflated or deflated relationships among items because of factors such as halo effects. Should such scales be assessed with interrater reliability or internal consistency or stability? Stability or test-retest reliability is viable only when a phenomenon has not changed or when change can be modeled into the assessment. Internal consistency is not appropriate if items are combined to make up a formative measure. Thus, respondents may have some symptoms and not others; they may exhibit some behaviors and not others. Behaviors may form a construct such as social competence (Cain et al., 1963). Relevant here is the use of raters for a subset of symptoms. Generally speaking, several issues relating to administration procedures in scales used in clinical settings are germane in psychological and organizational scales.

The Hospital Stress Scale uses a graphic, single-item scale with descriptive words from *not upset* to *worst possible upset* (Bossert, 1994, as cited in Rodrogue, Geffken, & Streisand, 2000, p. 77). The question is read aloud regarding how upset a hospital visit has made a child, and descriptive words are read aloud. A child is asked to mark a response on the graphic scale (10 cm) leading to a 0 through 100 (mm) score. Spatial response of this sort requires proximity among scales (i.e., spatially arranged so that the ends of the continuum are at the same level either horizontally or vertically) to enable consistent use of scale points. In a computer-based administration, both the numbers from 0 to 100 and the spatial location could appear as a cursor that is moved along the response scale. The key point here is that match between the process underlying response formation and the format of response scales is a worthwhile goal when feasible. Validity has been shown for the Hospital Stress Scale through a correlation with trait anxiety.

Self-reports of adherence to medical regimens can be validated through biochemical measures or medication monitors (Rand, 2000). Self-reports of pain have been measured in a variety of ways: through 5-point verbal rating scales fully anchored *none* through *extremely intense,* 100-point numerical rating scales end anchored *No pain* (0) and *Pain as bad as can be* (100), and a slide rule algometer 150 mm long (Keefe, 2000, p. 320). Number production and line production have been used after a preliminary procedure where respondents produce numbers and lines to rate words describing intensity of pain (Keefe, 2000). After demonstrating high correlation, these two modes have been used to rate actual pain (Keefe, 2000).

Measures in clinical ethics provide several creative examples (Redman, 2002). The Desire for Probable Benefit Scale assesses chances of living when patients would want life-sustaining treatments (Mutran, Danis, Bratton, Sudha, & Hanson, 1997). Individual items relate to such scenarios as stoppage in heart functioning or breathing. Response categories specify chances of living, ranging from 0 to 100% in 10% increments. Internal consistency reliability and validity, through relationships with measures of constructs, such as desire to prolong life, are reported (Redman, 2002).

The Standardized Mini Mental State Exam (SMMSE) assesses orientation, memory, and other such abilities (Molloy, Alemayehu, & Roberts, 1991). Items relate to basic questions about such issues as time (e.g., year, age) and geographic location and tasks such as naming and spelling. Detailed instructions are provided on how to administer the test in terms of such issues as seating the respondent, introducing the rater, repeating directions when respondent asks for clarification, and repeating questions a specific number of times if there is no response. The rater records a score for each question. Interrater reliability is reported (Redman, 2002).

Neuropsychological Measures

Neuropsychological tests include grip strength, categorization tests, speech sounds perception tests, and finger-tapping tests. The Stroop test includes tasks where respondents name colors with stimuli being names of colors presented in different colors (e.g., the word *red* represented in a blue color) (Golden, 1978). The number of correct responses in a specific period of time is recorded. Some validity tests have been performed by classifying normal versus brain-impaired respondents on the basis of the test; however, the ability of the test to discriminate between types of brain impairment remains to be shown (Franzen, 1989).

A number of neuropsychological scales are noteworthy (Franzen, 1989). Tests of verbal functions include object naming using standardized pictures (to minimize nonstandardized procedures and stimuli and reduce random error) and the new word learning test. Tests of visual functions include tasks where abstract line drawings have to be copied and recalled, details from standard pictures have to be recalled, and identical colors have to be identified. The Luria-Nebraska Neuropsychological Battery (Christensen, 1979) is administered one-on-one by an observer with some stimuli and has several subscales, such as motor, tactile, and writing. Validation includes test-retest and interrater reliability. Standardized line drawings with norms on such factors as name agreement and image agreement are also used in experiments in cognitive psychology, again serving to enhance consistency in stimulus presentation.

Another measure used in clinical neuropsychology is the California Verbal Learning Test (Delis, Kramer, Kaplan, & Ober, 1987), which studies errors in learning tasks by assessing recall, and recognition, learning rates, and interference effects (Kaplan & Saccuzzo, 2001). Using tasks, such as repetition of a list of items, performance is analyzed across trials. The measure correlates with other measures of memory and also distinguishes between multiple factors.

The validity of neuropsychological tests has been shown through their ability to distinguish brain-impaired respondents, such as through relationships with diagnostic procedures (e.g., CT scans). The relationship between test results and recovery from surgery can also show evidence of validity using independent assessments of brain impairment or recovery from surgery.

Some neuropsychological tests provide normative data on the responses that suggest impairment (e.g., number of errors in a memory test). Such norms require extensive validation. These norms are absolute in nature, having one-to-one correspondence with distinct conditions. Other tests provide relative norms (i.e., scores greater than a standard deviation from the average suggest a distinct condition). Tests may also vary in reliability and validity based on the location of impairment.

Weight Management, Eating, and Body-Related Scales

The Perceived Somatotype Scale consists of seven line drawings of male figures representing different body builds (Tucker, 1982). Respondents indicate the drawing that resembles them and the drawing with the body build they desire for themselves. The Body Image Perception Scale (Slade & Russell, 1973) relates to self-perceptions of body size. The procedure involves physical measurement of four body parts and respondents' perceptions of body size involving a device. This device is manipulated to reflect light until the respondent thinks the size of the light matches their perception of size. Two lights are moved horizontally until the width between them reflects perception of body size. A Body Perception Index is computed as the ratio of perceived to real size for each body part. Scales relating to assessment of body image (Thompson, 1995) provide contour drawings of bodies and ask respondents to mark their current and ideal size. For such measurement, internal consistency is not applicable, but test-retest reliability can be used with additional information about weight difference to assess change in phenomena. A variety of measures are employed to assess affective ("feel"), cognitive ("think"), and behavioral ("do") aspects, including ratings while viewing in a mirror (Thompson, 1995).

A variety of measures are available to assess eating behaviors and eating styles (Schlundt, 1995), including diaries, 24-hour recalls, and microanalysis of eating behavior. A weight management diary method involves a booklet where each meal is recorded on a page (Schlundt, 1995). Respondents are given a food counter and an information booklet regarding foods and nutritional content. The Binge Scale (Hawkins & Clement, 1980) has nine items embedded in a longer questionnaire. One item asks how often a respondent binge eats, with categories ranging from *seldom* to *almost every day* (p. 221). The Bulimia Test (Smith & Thelen, 1984) has items relating to binging, use of laxatives, and other related behaviors. For example, an item asks about uncontrollable eating, with responses from *once a month or less* to *once a day or more* (Smith & Thelen, 1984, as cited in Beere, 1990, p. 498). Thus, specific objective frequencies are presented as response categories, an approach that can be used whenever possible to enable consistent interpretations when compared to the alternative of using ambiguous verbal labels (e.g., rarely, frequently). The area of eating behaviors and weight-related disorders provides a variety of scales (Allison, 1995). In the area of attitudes and beliefs about obese people, scales have items about how people who are overweight are viewed by most people and respondents (e.g., adjectives such as "lazy" as items rated on the degree to which they describe overweight people). Separate scales for respondent's attitudes versus respondent's perceptions of attitudes of most people tap distinct constructs.

A restraint scale (Herman & Polivy, 1975, p. 669) has items such as "What is your maximum weight gain within a week?" that form a weight fluctuation subscale. This subscale uses pounds as the unit of measurement. Another concern for dieting subscale has items such as "How often are you dieting?" This scale is unique in having different units of measurement for different items. Some items use a multiple-choice format and other items use a different format, such as an item on weight gain with responses in pounds. An absolute criterion variable for validating such scales is actual weight. Situational inventories include the Dieter's Inventory of Eating Temptations (Schlundt & Zimering, 1988), which presents a range of problem situations and effective solutions. An item describes eating a favorite meal where someone offers a second helping, with responses from 0 to 100% in 10% increments relating to the percentage of time the respondent would turn down a second helping. The Situation Based Dieting Self-Efficacy Scale (Stotland, Zuroff, & Roy, 1991) lists situations (e.g., at a dinner party) and elicits confidence levels in sticking to a diet on a 0 to 100-point scale. Constructs such as binge eating have specific definitions relating to excessive consumption of food in a discrete time period (Pike et al., 1995) associated with lack of control. In quantifying the amount of food consumed in a binge, a specific caloric cut-off has been argued to increase reliability (Pike et al., 1995), whereas subjective self-reports may vary widely. However, such an "objective" cut-off may be too exclusive. Thus, attempts have been made to standardize the measures as a means of achieving consistency. Subjective self-reports of binge eating may lack consistency in that a situation involving loss of control and consumption of cookies may be categorized by the respondent as being binge eating on one occasion but not on another. The parallel here is with the use of ambiguous response anchors, say, for coffee consumption, such as *very frequently*, rather than the actual number of cups. Similar inconsistencies would occur here. Similarly, in addition to a subjective feeling of loss of control, binge-eating disorder is specified when a subset from a larger list of indicators is present, such as eating until uncomfortably full (Pike et al., 1995). Thus, by being more specific, reliability is likely enhanced. A parallel here is in defining a term used in a question, such as "How much do people spend on recreational activities?" By clearly specifying what is included in recreational activities and what is not, consistent interpretation is facilitated. Such consistency leads to reliability and validity. Consistent interpretation for an individual across time and across individuals enhances reliability and validity. However, definitions should not be restrictive in terms of narrowing the domain of a construct. Multiple items should be used to cover the domain of the construct.

Similarly, the link between frequency of binge eating and bulimia nervosa involves specific criteria, including a minimum of 2 days a week of binge eating. Days rather than episodes are the relevant unit because of potential blurring of episodes within a day (Pike et al., 1995). Thus, clear definitions are specified to enhance reliability of diagnosing specific conditions. A specific threshold level is being identified through measurement in clinical applications, accentuating the need for clear specification of conditions to be met. Long-term duration of binge eating is one more such condition (Pike et al., 1995).

Occupational Interest Scales

Measures such as the Strong Vocational Interests Blank (Strong & Campbell, 1966) were developed on the basis of the insight that people who choose similar careers are likely to have similar interests. Strong aimed to match respondents on interests with people who were happy in their careers. Preliminary work involved the collection of attitudes toward an array of interests and occupations. Reliability data were satisfactory, and 20-year test-retest reliability was near 0.60. Validity was shown through prediction of job satisfaction. The Strong-Campbell Interest Inventory (Campbell, 1974) used Holland's (1975) theory of vocational choice that interests reflect personality to categorize people based on six personality factors (e.g., realistic, artistic). Thus, the measures have been influenced by a greater amount of theory. Over time, measurement catches up with theory and vice versa. The Campbell Interest and Skill Survey assesses interests in 200 topics and skills in 120 occupations (Campbell, Hyne, & Nilsen, 1992). The Kuder Occupational Interest Survey presents triads of activities, respondents selecting the most and least preferred.

Employee and Workplace Scales

Acceptance by coworkers (Dubinsky et al., 1986, as cited in Bruner & Hensel, 1992, p. 747) is a construct measured by items such as "My coworkers actively try to include me in conversations about things at work" and "I don't think my coworkers feel relaxed when they are with me." Seashore's Group Cohesiveness Index (Seashore, 1954, as cited in Miller & Salkind, 2002, p. 479) has items such as "Do you feel that you are really a part of your work group?" with responses such as *Really a part of my group* and *Don't feel I really belong.* A scale of alternate offerings (industrial sales) captures the percentage of situations from 0 to 100% for items such as "The salesperson has a wide range of alternatives to offer the customer" (John & Weitz, 1989, as cited in Bruner & Hensel, 1992, p. 762). A scale relating to participation in buying measures the proportion of time people in a buying group participate (McCabe, 1987, as cited in Bruner & Hensel, 1992, p. 1034) with responses to items (e.g., how often the respondent takes an active role in decision making) ranging from *1 = never or seldom (0–20% of the time)* to *5 = usually or always (81–100% of the time).* Noteworthy here is the specification of numerical percentages for specific labels, encouraging respondents to explicate their responses more precisely while providing comparison points using objective numbers. A job description scale requires respondents to respond with a *yes (3), could not decide (2),* or *no (1)* to adjectives (e.g., fascinating) describing areas such as work (Teas, 1983, as cited in Bruner & Hensel, 1992, p. 977). A scale of competitive strength of a business unit requires ratings relative to major competitors, with items such as quality of services (*much worse* to *much better*) (Burke, 1984, as cited in Bruner & Hensel, 1992, p. 816). Thus, the comparison is explicated, enhancing consistent interpretation and reliability as well as validity.

A School Level Environment Questionnaire (Fisher & Fraser, 1990, as cited in Lester & Bishop, 2000, p. 67) measures teachers' perceptions of school environment with items such as "most teachers like the idea of change." Thus, some items are at the unit of analysis of individuals' perceptions about other people's perceptions. Similarly, the Organizational Climate Index (Stern, 1970, as cited in Lester & Bishop, 2000, p. 75) has items such as "There is a lot of group spirit."

Subjective scales are also used to assess performance-related measures, such as workload. The Finegold Workload Scale (Finegold et al., 1986, as cited in Gawron, 2000, p. 115) has 5-point scales with items, such as "amount of total time you are busy" (end anchored *often have spare time* to *almost never have spare time*). Advantages include ease of administration and versatility. Problems include confounding of mental and physical dimensions (such as workload) and inability to repeat some aspects of performance.

The Hoppock Job Satisfaction scale is a four-item measure with fully described response anchors customized to each question (e.g., an item on how much of the time the respondent is satisfied with his or her job has responses from *never* to *all the time*) (Hoppock, 1935, as cited in Allison, 1995, p. 36). The Job Description Index (Smith, Kendall, & Hulin, 1969, as cited in Allison, 1995, p. 68) has items on dimensions such as work and supervision. An item on supervision requires *yes* or *no* responses to a set of phrases, such as "impolite," "praises good work," and "doesn't supervise enough."

Organizational Scales

The Rahim Organizational Conflict Inventory II (Rahim & Psenicka, 1984, as cited in Lester & Bishop, 2000, p. 94) has items such as "I generally avoid an argument with my _____," with words such as "boss," "subordinates," or "peers" appearing in the blank space. The Decisional Participation Scale (Alutto & Belasco, 1972, as cited in Lester & Bishop, 2000, p. 101) measures teacher participation in decisions by school systems, with items relating to whether the respondents would be involved in various domains, such as hiring faculty. The responses start out with a *yes/no* and have follow-ups such as, "If yes, in what capacity?" and "If you would be involved, with whom would you discuss this matter?" The Shared Decision-Making Survey (King & Meshanko, 1992, as cited in Lester & Bishop, 2000, p. 105) has phrases specifying situations, such as "selecting new textbooks," with responses regarding the extent to which teachers in one's school district participate in described situations ranging from *not participate* to *make the decision.*

Organizational measures often use self-reports of employees (Price, 1972). Centralization relates to degree of participation in decision making. One measure uses items such as, "I have to ask my boss before I do almost anything," with responses from *definitely false* to *definitely true* (Aiken & Hage, 1968, as cited in Price, 1972, p. 67). A measure of communication (Lawler, Porter, & Tennenbaum, 1968) asks respondents to record behavioral episodes in terms of aspects such as type of contact (e.g., memo, discussion); position of others (e.g., superiors, subordinates, outsiders); type of activity; and attitude toward episode. An issue here is to generate a detailed list of possible behaviors, such as types of contact. Other measures assess characteristics such as coordination and formalization (e.g., "There is no rules manual," with responses ranging from *definitely true* to *definitely false*) (Hage & Aiken, 1969, as cited in Price, 1972, p. 110). A measure of span of control (Healey, 1956, as cited in Price, 1972, p. 185), relating to the number of employees managed by an administrator, asks employees to list and describe functions of immediate subordinates in a hierarchical chart. It is important here to develop consistent guidelines for interpreting or coding employee descriptions and to check for consistency through some practice trials. Given the single item involved in this measure, test-retest reliability is important, as is interrater reliability and convergent validity. Span of control could also be measured through perception.

Customer loyalty has many aspects, such as customer retention (Hill & Alexander, 2000). Companies compute retention rates, or the percentage of customers from a particular year retained the next year. Anticipated future retention is assessed by questions such as, "Do you think you will be a customer of ABC in one year's time?" (p. 209), or a similar item about repurchase with responses from *definitely* to *definitely not*. Conceptual considerations should guide the choice of time period, based on the nature of the market. Recommendation is measured through an item such as, "Have you recommended ABC to anyone else?" (p. 212), with responses from *never* to *often*.

Business ratios provide measures of a variety of constructs (Gates, 1993). Sales growth is defined as the percentage difference between the current year's and previous year's sales, a straightforward computation: $100 \times$ [(Current-year sales − Past-year sales) / Past-year sales]. However, such a ratio can be supplemented with subjective measurement of sales growth in a variety of ways. For example, sales growth when compared to major competitors puts a relative emphasis on a scale from *much worse* to *much better*. A numerical comparison could also be computed. Alternatively, sales growth could be directly evaluated from *poor* to *excellent*. Such a subjective measure captures the degree to which sales growth was satisfactory in the light of a variety of factors, such as industry-wide growth. Thus, it captures satisfaction with sales growth that a straight numerical computation may not capture. This is not in any way to downplay the importance of standardized numbers. Rather, it is to supplement these numbers with different perspectives. Indeed, a question with objective measures is: What is the construct that is being objectively measured? Clearly, the numerical ratios can also be analyzed further through comparison with, say, an expected growth number to reflect a relative sense of growth. They could be compared to a norm to obtain another relative comparison. For example, if industry growth is high, then a company's growth may need to be compared to that of major competitors. Through innovative use of subjective and objective measures, a more comprehensive picture of a construct can be obtained. Indeed, objective measures provide sound footing but often capture some narrow aspect of an abstract notion. Moreover, subjectivity creeps into various choices relating to computation. For example, adjustment for inflation or dollar sales versus unit sales each have different implications. Thus, practitioners and researchers use a variety of numerical ratios to obtain a complete picture. For example, gross margin factor is gross profit/net sales, to capture costs and profits (Gates, 1993). Break-even margin is the ratio of total expenses to net sales. Return on sales is the ratio of net after-tax profit to net sales (Gates, 1993). Similar computations can be made for return on assets and other such returns. Similar ratios can be computed for debt, efficiency, and investment.

Similarly, objective and subjective measures provide indicators of the type of strategy that a firm employs (e.g., R&D investment vs. self-reports of R&D emphasis). As the state of the art progresses, however, self-reports versus actual behavior may well be treated as measures of different constructs. In essence, the distance between the conceptual and the operational varies in different research projects. Closeness between theory and measurement varies across research projects as a function of research objectives and the state of the art. Furthermore, theoretical relationships may also be inferred from indicators that are not directly related to the constructs about which inferences are made.

The fundamental point to note here is that subjective conceptualization of a concept can lead to supplemental measures as well as systematic understanding and improvement of numerical indicators. Such understanding can guide innovative use of objective indicators while fully realizing their limitations. It can lead to innovative computations using objective indicators. It can also avoid a narrow emphasis on the computable measure (cart) leading the broader construct (horse).

An important issue in organizational and interorganizational research is the need to obtain information from key informants, often due to lack of other sources of information (Bagozzi, Yi, & Phillips, 1991; Kumar, Stern, & Anderson, 1993; Phillips, 1981). However, both random and systematic error may affect information obtained from key informants. For instance, systematic error may occur due to the organizational role of the informant, say, CEOs versus lower-level executives (Kumar et al., 1993). Researchers have suggested the use of multiple informants to enhance the reliability and validity of measurement (Bagozzi et al., 1991). Two issues with the use of multiple informants relate to selection of more than one informant who can provide information and perceptual disagreement among informants (Kumar et al., 1993). Researchers have used measures of informants' competency either at a global level or at the specific level of issues (Kumar et al., 1993). Perceptual disagreement has been dealt with by (a) modeling reports from different informants as reflective indicators of a latent construct; (b) pooling responses, an approach that has been argued to require demonstration of perceptual agreement (James, 1982); and (c) developing consensus among multiple informants (Kumar et al., 1993).

Sociological Scales

Sociometry scales, relating to interpersonal relationships within a group and other related issues (Moreno, 1934), use items such as ranking five people with whom the respondent would most like to work or how the respondent feels about specific group members (like–dislike–indifferent). Test-retest correlation between scores and constancy of choice across time are reported.

Social distance relates to social acceptance between people or between social groups (Bogardus, 1959, as cited in Miller & Salkind, 2002, p. 482). Respondents rank social types on degrees of distance ranging from *acceptance to close kinship by marriage* to *would exclude from my country*. For example, a racial distance scale involves checking off a matrix of race by attributes.

Social indicators are used at state and community levels. For example, an index of social vulnerability has items such as median family incomes, percentage of families below poverty level, and rate of malaria per 100,000 population (Miller & Salkind, 2002). Hollingshead's Index of Social Position (Hollingshead, 1957, as cited in Miller & Salkind, 2002, p. 462) consists of an occupation and an education scale. An index weighs occupation a 7 and education a 4. Each scale is measured at seven levels (education: graduate through less than 7 years of school; occupation: higher executives through unskilled employees).

Siegel's National Opinion Research Center (NORC) Prestige Scores (Siegel, 1971, as cited in Miller & Salkind, 2002, p. 457) involve respondent ratings of a list of jobs on general standing with indicators such as the proportion of respondents assigning *excellent* or *good* ratings used as measures of prestige. Respondents' status and familiarity affect reliability, as do occupations at the middle of the status continuum (Miller & Salkind, 2002). Edwards's social-economic grouping of occupations (Edwards, 1934, as cited in Miller, 1991, p. 363) classifies occupations into six groups, using income and education for ranking. Reliability is shown through convergence with other occupational ranking systems. This is an example of a stimulus-centered scale.

Nam-Powers Socioeconomic Status Scores (Nam & Powers, 1965, as cited in Miller & Salkind, 2002, p. 460) for occupations used data from the 1960 census for income and education. Duncan's socioeconomic index (Reiss, Duncan, Hatt, & North, 1961, as cited in Miller & Salkind, 2002, p. 455) combined the NORC Prestige Score with socioeconomic characteristics of occupations (i.e., education and income). Reliability problems have related to converting reported occupations to occupational codes. In these scales, prestige measurement through Siegel's (NORC) scale (i.e., subjective ratings) versus the use of socioeconomic status (SES) (Reiss et al., 1961, as cited in Miller & Salkind, 2002, p. 455) to determine prestige of occupations versus the direct assessment of SES (Nam & Powers, 1965, as cited in Miller & Salkind, 2002, p. 460) should be contrasted. Test-retest reliability across 10-year intervals has been reported. The Duncan Index assigns weight to occupations via a weight on education, based on the prestige of those who are high school graduates, and a weight for income based on having an income higher than a specified amount. As discussed, these are examples of formative measures where the relationship between components of the scale are predefined; therefore, internal consistency and factor analysis are not germane. Rather, test-retest reliability is a possibility, using a time interval where socioeconomic status is not expected to change.

Measures of Macrolevel Phenomena

Measures of macrolevel phenomena can be formed from sources such as published data. For instance, types of crime can be captured in an overall measure of crime rate. Available data on crime have to be employed to develop the overall measure. For instance, the FBI reports crime statistics through its Uniform Crime Report. Here, common definitions of indicators, such as violent crimes per 1,000 population, are important (Morley et al., 2001). Central to evaluating indicators is a full understanding of how agencies collect and report data. Sometimes, discrepancies in measurement across regions may suggest deleting an indicator, excluding agencies that differ substantially in measurement, or separately reporting more than one set of data (Morley et al., 2001). For instance, in a situation where response time for high-priority calls was considered an indicator of deterrence/patrol services, considerable differences in what constituted high-priority calls for different areas prompted clarification of the indicator (Morley et al., 2001). Vague terms, such as those relating to age (e.g., *juveniles, adults*) or to time period, need precise definitions. Data may also need to be normalized, such as crimes per 1,000 population.

In using such data, terms need to be defined conceptually and compared with available data, a major problem being the misfit in conceptualization between the collector of the data and the user (Jacob, 1984). The National Crime Survey asks a sample of people about incidents when they have been victimized by crimes (Jacob, 1984). Issues with this approach include the problem of victimless crimes and crimes with multiple victims (Jacob, 1984). The FBI measure of crime, on the other hand, excludes crimes that are not reported to the police (Jacob, 1984). Changes over time can also affect published data. The Consumer Price Index, a measure of inflation, has been modified over time to include newer products and services, such as televisions in the 1950s, sometimes with delay.

Random and systematic errors may occur in using such data. Clerical errors may lead to random error. Biases in recording data can lead to systematic error. Ideological or organizational biases can affect the collection and recording of data. For instance, the rate of suicidal tendencies at a mental institution may decline because of reluctance among doctors to categorize patients as suicidal, which would involve providing costly supervision when budgetary constraints are high (Jacob, 1984).

Quality-of-Life Scales

In the areas of quality of life and subjective well-being, a number of different definitions of constructs have been employed (Alfonso, 1995). The Satisfaction With Life Scale (Diener, Emmons, Larsen, & Griffin, 1985, as cited in Allison, 1995, p. 28) has five items that get at overall judgments (e.g., "I am satisfied with my life" on a *strongly disagree–strongly agree* scale). The Extended Satisfaction With Life Scale (Alfonso, Allison, & Dunn, 1992, as cited in Allison, 1995, p. 29) is multidimensional and covers nine domains, such as social life and family life. The Quality of Life Inventory has items relating to 17 areas of life (Frisch, Cornell, Villanueva, & Retzlaff, 1992). Items have response categories from *very dissatisfied* (– 3) to *very satisfied* (+3) (e.g., How satisfied are you with LOVE in your life?). Items are weighted by importance of an area (e.g., How important is LOVE to your happiness?) with 0 (*not important*) to 2 (*extremely important*) being response categories (Frisch et al., 1992, pp. 93–94). Thus, scores on items range from –6 to +6. Another set of items relates to confidence, with responses from 0% (*not at all confident*) to 100% (*completely confident*) in 10% increments. Validation tests include negative relationships with measures of constructs, such as anxiety, and positive relationships with measures of life satisfaction. The General Health Questionnaire (Goldberg & Williams, 1988, as cited in Allison, 1995, p. 502) has items such as, "Have you recently been feeling perfectly well and in good health?" with response categories from *Better than usual* to *Much worse than usual*. Quantitative quality-of-life measures include quality-adjusted life-years (QALYs), a measure of loss of years due to diseases (e.g., a loss of 0.5 QALYs if a disease affects quality of life to this degree) (Kaplan & Saccuzzo, 2001).

Levine (1997) operationalized overall pace of life in a cross-cultural study with three measures: walking speeds (speed of people walking 60 feet alone in a downtown area), postal times (speed of postal clerks in completing a transaction), and clock accuracy (public clock accuracy). Consistent guidelines were set up for observers to be able to collect data (e.g., purchase of a stamp at a post office), along with guidelines for making corrections to the data (e.g., in instances where postal clerks provided a receipt or wrapped a stamp being purchased, adjustments to time had to be made). Several alternatives were considered as measures but not chosen, such as speed of workers at a gas station (because of cultural differences in clientele served) or speed in a specific workplace behavior, such as, say, among ticket agents (because of workers at these positions being of different nationalities). Interesting here is the search for measures comparable across cultures that reflect aspects of pace of life. Although no measures may be perfect, the use of such innovative measures gradually builds a picture of pace of life, an abstract construct.

When disparate concrete measures are studied to gain insight into a construct such as pace of life, a germane issue is whether these measures necessarily should converge if they are tapping into the same construct. Although the need for such convergence is evident when using an item as a measure model and developing multiple items to tap into a construct, "objective data" from available sources do not fall into these neat categories. Rather, items such as time taken for a transaction at the post office, or pace of walking at a downtown area, are each idiosyncratic and naturally occurring, rather than responses to a carefully designed set of items. The same is true of organization indicators such as R&D expenses or percentage of new products. In fact, each such concrete measure may provide some insight into the phenomenon yet not be considered as measuring the same thing in terms of the degree of convergence among measures. Each different measure of pace of life can, in turn, provide insight into different slices of a phenomenon. In contrast, a self-report scale of pace of life captures the domain through self-report items that are likely to covary. Measures formed from secondary data or natural observations do not fit neatly into the category of a multiple-item scale and all the related criteria. The model of a latent construct measured by covarying items maps onto traditional self-reports on multiple items. But this model is not as easily transferable to items based on data from natural occurrences.

Measures of Ability and Achievement

This discussion covers some of the nuts and bolts of measurement of ability and achievement. Excellent discussions of philosophical issues in such measurement are available elsewhere (cf. Michell, 1999). Measurement of achievement goes back at least 4,000 years to Chinese civil service exams. Tests of ability include psychomotor skills (e.g., reaction times), mechanical abilities, clerical ability (e.g., computation), and computer-related ability (Aiken, 1998). Generally, aptitude tests are better at predicting educational achievement than at predicting job performance. Even supplementing aptitude tests with interests, and personal situational variables, correlations with occupational success are not high.

When creating tests with multiple-choice items, several recommendations have been made, such as minimizing negative expressions, clearly wording items, supporting wrong items with appropriate reasoning, and grouping items from the same topic or with the same response format together (Aiken, 1998). In scoring essay answers, analytic scoring (i.e., evaluating specific components separately) has been argued to be more reliable than holistic scoring (Aiken, 1998). Training of graders, scoring all respondents on one question before moving to the next, and using multiple graders have been recommended (Aiken, 1998). Grading one question at a time can enhance consistency and, hence, reliability and validity. A number of recommendations have been suggested for writing multiple-choice test items, such as avoiding trick questions, focusing questions on specific content, keeping content independent across items, using simple vocabulary in light of respondents' level, having clear directions, avoiding negatives in the question stem, varying the locations of the correct answer, having plausible distracters, avoiding none-of-the-above or all-of-the-above alternatives, keeping choices independent, keeping the length of choices approximately equal, and avoiding clues to right answers (Haladyna, 1999). True-false formats may be influenced excessively by guessing and may be less reliable than multiple-choice formats (Haladyna, 1999). Complex multiple-choice formats (i.e., multiple correct answers) may have lower discrimination and, therefore, lower reliability (Haladyna, 1999).

Noteworthy here is the parallel with items from self-report scales. An aim is clarity to enhance reliability and minimize random error. Related to this is the effort to minimize random as well as systematic unrelated influences (e.g., language difficulties and test-taking skills). Akin to within-measure correlational systematic error due to a different construct or method factor are sources such as test-taking skills used to derive clues about the right answer or unrelated ability or inability in dealing with semantic confusion and trick questioning.[3] For instance, clueing to the right answer may occur because of absurd distracters, extreme language (e.g., never, always), and grammatical inconsistencies (Haladyna, 1999). Individuals with higher test-taking skills would perform consistently better on such items. Trick questions are similar to very ambiguous items; respondents may be unable to answer them, but the intended construct is not being tapped, some other construct is. Use of all-of-the-above alternatives may lead students toward test-taking strategies.

Criteria for writing test items include clearly defining the test's objectives, developing items that address these objectives, and using item formats that are consistent with the objectives (Osterlind, 1998). Taxonomies are used to delineate cognitive processes (e.g., analysis and synthesis) in test construction (Osterlind, 1998). Content validity in test items can be strengthened in several ways: by judges rating the degree of match between previously matched items and objectives, or by judges matching items to objectives (Osterlind, 1998). A number of procedures can be adopted to enhance content validity, starting with a careful consideration of content, such as teaching objectives in classroom testing and knowledge and skills in professional testing. Procedures include item-writer training, review of items for writing errors, content review for topics covered, editorial review, sensitivity review for bias and unfairness, and test-taker review (through posttest classroom discussion and through formal elicitation, such as thinking aloud during test completion) (Haladyna, 1999).

Differential item functioning is a means of detecting item bias. Methods include examining differences across groups while controlling for ability. Item responses are also examined in terms of fit with individuals to assess such factors as cheating, inattention, and guessing (Haladyna, 1999). Distracters can also be evaluated through an item response plot, a desirable characteristic being a decreasing function relating the choice of distracters with ability levels. Zero frequency in choosing distracters suggests implausibility, and an increasing function suggests error in scoring (i.e., in the answer key) (Haladyna, 1999).

A correction for guessing in objective tests is provided by the following formula (Rust & Golombok, 1999):

$$C = R - [W/(N - 1)]$$

where

R = Number of correct responses

W = Number of incorrect responses

N = Number of alternatives

C = Corrected score

Knowledge-based tests can be assessed through sophisticated item analysis. Two characteristics of items are noteworthy: facility or difficulty coefficient (proportion of respondents who provide the right answer)[4] and discrimination (e.g., no discrimination suggested by no relationship between item score and total score, negative and positive discrimination suggested by negative and positive relationships with total score) (Rust & Golombok, 1999). These two characteristics are used to select items. For instance, moderate facility has been argued to be a desirable characteristic. Item response theory uses the notion of an item characteristic curve, which is a plot of respondent ability and probability of correct response. Computerized testing can be used to sequence subsequent items in a test based on earlier responses to maximize the information collected (Rust & Golombok, 1999). Adaptive measurement techniques adjust task difficulty based on performance level (Weiss & Kingsbury, 1985).

Fatigue and distraction may cause unreliability among older respondents; therefore, interviewers and settings should emphasize clarity and a variety of procedures, such as practice, allowance of sufficient time for completion, and allowance for sensory deficits (Hertzog & Schear, 1989). Psychometric issues arise in measurement involving individuals with disabilities such as visual, hearing, or motor impairment. The many assumptions of tests relating to verbal communication, motor skills, or visual ability have to be reexamined with these populations. Examination of the rationale and process of development of individual items and the norms and populations of previous validation is required (Shindell, 1989). For instance, the verbal subtest of the Wechsler Adult Intelligence Scale–Revised has been shown to be appropriate for the visually impaired population, whereas the performance subtest is inappropriate and may be substituted with a tactile equivalent test (Shindell, 1989). Verbal measures are, of course, not appropriate for respondents with hearing disability (Vernon, 1989). Tests for populations with disabilities have to be designed creatively. Several tests have been designed for respondents with disabilities such as speech impairment and hearing loss. For instance, the Columbia Mental Maturity Scale requires respondents to indicate a drawing that does not belong on a set of three to five drawings on cards (Kaplan & Saccuzzo, 2001). A problem with this test and its multiple-choice format is random error, which can cause chance scores to be close to the average (Kaplan & Saccuzzo, 2001).

Manuals of tests are instructive in providing a variety of information to minimize measurement error. For instance, the Child Behavior Checklist/2–3 for assessing children's behavioral/emotional problems consists of items such as "Acts too young for age" (Achenbach, 1992, p. 4), with responses ranging from 0 (*Not true*) to 2 (*Very true* or *Often true*). Administration guidelines include reading levels of parents who may complete the scale or interviewer administration to parents. Demographic distributions on the scale are provided for variables such as socioeconomic status and ethnicity, for the total scale, for certain groupings of items to identify syndromes (e.g., withdrawn), and for individual items. The manual provides details of validation and examples of practical academic applications. The manual for the Cognitive Assessment System (CAS) (Naglieri, 1999) elaborates on the underlying PASS theory (Planning, Attentional, Sequential, and Successive processes) and sample items related to these processes. Administration covers seating arrangement (positioning of examiner and child), verbal and nonverbal directions (including gestures), time limits for items, age partitioning, ordering of subtexts, help guidelines, and procedures for language- or hearing-disabled children. Procedures for raw scoring and for conversion to ratio scores based on time taken are provided. Guidelines for interpreting scores based on a standardization sample are provided, such as categorizing scores as superior using percentiles. Some of the detailed procedures, such as the nature of settings, may well be relevant in explicating usage conditions for self-report measures. Tests of ability offer many lessons for developing self-report measures, validating their usage, and specifying usage conditions.

The robustness of some ability constructs across cultures has been shown through identical factor structures across different measures (Irvine & Carroll, 1980). Several recommendations have been presented for cross-cultural measurement: (a) representation of content, such as behaviors, across cultures; (b) use of thorough rather than literal translation; (c) adequate explanation of directions and nature of responses; (d) oral rather than written instructions, with visual aids; (e) opportunity for supervised practice; (f) provision of familiar material first to facilitate practice with responses; and (g) an enjoyable setting (Irvine, 1973; Irvine & Carroll, 1980). On the analysis side, recommendations include (a) comparing item statistics for similarity across cultures (dissimilarity strongly suggesting inappropriate measurement); (b) examining intercorrelations across cultures, including rank ordering of correlations; and (c) performing independent factor analyses and comparing results (Irvine & Carroll, 1980). Culturally loaded items may cause within-measure correlational systematic error.

Ability tests can be divided into group or individual tests. In individual tests, examiners record responses and may elicit maximum performance if procedures allow this. Greater consistency is likely in individual tests where instructions and administration are likely to be similar. Individual tests are often used in diagnosing psychological or medical problems (Kaplan & Saccuzzo, 2001).

A number of tests fall under achievement and aptitude. College entrance exams, such as the Scholastic Aptitude Test (SAT), are validated through reliability and validity tests (e.g., approximately 0.40 correlation with grades in the first year of college) (Kaplan & Saccuzzo, 2001). An issue with the SAT has been its lower predictive ability for students whose scores are in the middle range. The ACT correlates highly with the SAT. The Graduate Record Exam (GRE) has been problematic because of relatively low correlations with grades in the first year of graduate school. Accuracy improves somewhat when the GRE is combined with grades in undergraduate courses. Clearly, a number of factors affect success in college. In evaluating evidence for validity, issues such as restriction in range (e.g., grade inflation, narrow range of GRE scores) should be considered, as should the possible use of tests as a threshold indicator.

In ability tests, bias against certain groups has been discussed in detail elsewhere. Germane here is the nature of measurement error under the taxonomy employed. Responses that reflect differences over and above the construct in question cause within-measure correlational systematic error. The issue of validating measures in different usage conditions, including different samples, is of central importance here.

In addition to the issues of reliability and validity, also relevant here is the development of norms. These norms allow for comparison against an absolute standard. Moreover, norms may need adjustment over time with increases or decreases in scores. Norms also provide a way to interpret scores meaningfully. Rather than test relationships between constructs, many measures of ability are used to provide absolute values similar to opinion polls. Therefore, additive systematic error is important here. Relative ordering is not sufficient. For instance, the Brazelton Neonatal Assessment Scale (Brazelton, 1973) tests intelligence in infants up to 4 weeks of age using behavioral items and elicited responses (e.g., hand-mouth coordination, startle reactions). Problems here include the lack of norms, making meaningful comparison very difficult or impossible. Lack of predictive validity and lack of test-retest reliability are problems although inter-rater reliability is satisfactory (Kaplan & Saccuzzo, 2001).

The Gesell Development Schedules (Gesell et al., 1940) examine development in children 2½ to 6 years of age on the basis of longitudinal study. Using data on presence or absence of behavior (e.g., uttering words), a developmental quotient is computed (Kaplan & Saccuzzo, 2001). IQ is computed as the ratio of developmental quotient to chronological age. Such a scale assesses absolute levels of development at different ages based on appearance of behavior at specific ages. Unlike a measure where relative ordering is sufficient, this measure requires validation of absolute levels. Validity testing should include assessment of absolute levels of development. This is more so than for even some ability scales where performance on a test is compared to a norm. Each item in such scales has to be assessed in terms of absolute

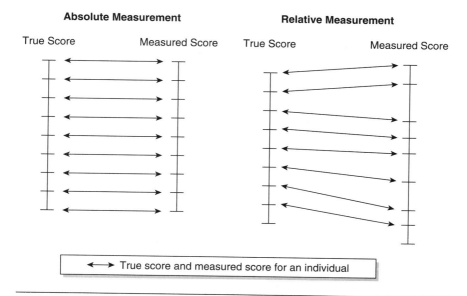

Figure 8.1   Relative Versus Absolute Measurement

levels of development at particular ages. As shown in Figure 8.1, the correspondence between the true scale and items is most detailed for absolute measurement.

Problems for Gesell Development Schedules include unsatisfactory reliability and validity and the use of an unrepresentative sample to establish norms (Kaplan & Saccuzzo, 2001). Ability measures are open to theoretical examination on several fronts. For instance, the Kaufman Assessment Battery for Children tests ability (Kaufman & Kaufman, 1983) but has been criticized as overemphasizing rote learning over learning ability, and as having a somewhat unsupported theoretical basis (Kaplan & Saccuzzo, 2001). It draws from a neuropsychological model and distinguishes between sequential-parallel processing. It includes nonverbal items administered through pantomime. The link between theory and measures needs to be established clearly in many ability tests. In visiographic tests, respondents copy designs or draw designs from memory with appropriate procedures for counting errors (Kaplan & Saccuzzo, 2001).

Validating ability measures in different samples is consistent with the prescriptions developed in Chapter 5. A theme throughout this book is the need to apply some lessons in validating complex measures in different domains to measure development in the social sciences. The development of measures of, say, developmental status is no small task. Lessons learned can be used to develop measures in other domains. The measurement of intelligence starts with the problem of defining it. Early tests of intelligence (e.g., Binet-Simon Scale) included 30 items with increasing levels of difficulty to differentiate age levels and capture the notion of a mental age. Later measures computed IQ: 100 times mental age divided by chronological age. Over time, the maximum mental age of tests and the representativeness of samples to identify norms improved. A later version had problems due to higher reliability for older respondents and for lower IQs, the lowest reliabilities being with younger people of high IQ. Therefore, an issue here is the variation in psychometric properties as a function of sample characteristics, again emphasizing usage conditions. Age groups also differed in the variance of IQs. This issue was solved by computing deviation IQs, a standard score with a mean of 100 and a standard deviation of 16. The Modern Binet scale (Thorndike, Hagen, & Sattler, 1986) is based on a more elaborate theoretical model than older scales: crystallized abilities (divided into verbal and quantitative reasoning), fluid-analytical abilities (abstract/visual reasoning), and short-term memory. Extensive psychometric assessment includes internal consistency and test-retest reliability across age groups for individual tests. Four group factors consisting of verbal reasoning (vocabulary, comprehension, absurdities, and verbal relations tests); abstract/visual reasoning (pattern analysis, copying, matrices, and paper folding and cutting tests); quantitative reasoning (quantitative, number series, and equation-building tests); and short-term memory (bead memory, memory for sentences, memory for digits, and memory for objects tests) formed the measure. Sixteen-week test-retest reliability for individual tests was low. The 15 individual tests had high loading on the general factor. Four group factors were also extracted as hypothesized. Interesting here is the hierarchical nature of deriving lower-level factors and tests from higher-level factors.

Several points are noteworthy with regard to ability tests. The importance of theory and its injection over time in strengthening measurement is noteworthy. When dealing with complex constructs, such as intelligence or developmental status, an in-depth understanding of the underlying mental and physical processes is important. It is not sufficient to define a construct and generate items. Understanding developmental ability at different ages requires detailed study. Measuring intelligence requires understanding underlying processes. Thus, detailed theoretical and empirical work has to precede sound measurement, although this is a chicken-and-egg problem. Hierarchical models are often required when dealing with very broad, abstract constructs. Thus, a general factor leads to types of abilities (e.g., crystallized) to factors (e.g., verbal and quantitative) to individual tests in intelligence measurement.

Validation across a variety of samples, such as age groups and ethnic groups, is required. Psychometric properties may vary across samples. Norms have to be developed through studies with representative samples. Although much of social science measurement hinges on relative ordering, ability testing is absolute in some ways. The absolute score on a test is compared to a norm to draw inferences. Moreover, absolute standards are developed for corresponding age groups. Thus, one-on-one correspondence within and across studies is important (Figure 8.1). In studying PNI, constant additive systemic error in one study may not matter. In studies of ability, such error may matter in, say, understanding the relationship between age and ability. This is not to suggest that additive systematic error never matters with the PNI scale. With proper norms, a study of the relationship between demographic characteristics and PNI scores would be affected adversely by additive systematic error. But many measures of constructs in the social sciences are not normed; they are used in specific studies to assess relationships. Normed measures add a degree of one-on-one correspondence to group averages on the characteristics by which groups are defined (e.g., gender and age). Although a distinction was made earlier between academic and applied research in terms of the importance of additive systematic error, this distinction is, of course, not black and white. Academic research that uses normed measures and focuses on differences vis-à-vis norms would be affected by additive systematic error. The use of unrepresentative samples in establishing norms affects inferences drawn about measurement relative to a norm. Because norms need to be carefully constructed and representative, relative inferences have to be evaluated in terms of types of errors. Individual or group measurement has to be compared to norms. Inaccurate norms can lead to various types of errors.

It should be noted that, in addition to being normed, measures of developmental status also need to be validated in terms of relating specific items to specific levels of development. The distinction here is reflected in norm- versus criterion-referenced testing. Norm-referenced testing involves comparison to norms established for groups. Medians, percentiles, and standard scores (e.g., deviation IQs) are examples of norm-referenced scoring. Tests have also been criterion referenced. Researchers have argued that a criterion is more useful than a norm in many situations, such as in testing job performance (Rust & Golombok, 1999). Criterion-referenced testing relates the score, not to scores for other people, but to the performance likely from someone with a particular score (e.g., competency in arithmetic operation, or performance at a certain age level) (Jackson, 1996).[5]

Individual Performance Measures

Human performance relates to completion of tasks by humans, ranging from card sorting to aircraft landing (Gawron, 2000). Measures are used to assess absolute error, error rate, accuracy, and reaction time in domains, such as mental arithmetic and reading. Performance measures such as reading speed (number of words read/reading time interval) (Cushman, 1986, as cited in Gawron, 2000, p. 47) are at a concrete level. However, reading speed may depend on a variety of factors, such as modality and reading angle. Thus, procedures for its administration need to be standardized and explicated. Overall reading performance has been measured as the product of reading speed and percentage of reading comprehension questions answered correctly (Cushman, 1986). Reaction time is the time taken to respond to the presentation of a stimulus. An individual difference measure can be computed through averaging across a certain number of trials.

Subjective scales are also used to assess performance-related measures such as workload. The Finegold Workload Scale (Finegold et al., 1986, as cited in Gawron, 2000, p. 115) has 5-point scales with items such as "amount of total time you are busy" (end anchored *often have spare time* to *almost never have spare time*). Advantages include ease of administration and versatility. Problems include confounding of mental and physical dimensions (such as workload) and inability to repeat some aspects of performance.

Physiological Scales

With physiological measurement, error can be introduced by factors such as physical movement. Moreover, measurement often is indirect, such as in measuring brain waves by placing electrodes on an individual's head, with the skull altering waves (Kaplan & Saccuzzo, 2001). Other problems include the impact of demographics on indicators, such as heart rate, as well as the issue of initial values (e.g., resting heart rates) (Kaplan & Saccuzzo, 2001).

The Palmar Sweat Prints (Ferreira & Winter, 1963) involve measurement of anxiety in response to stimuli or tasks. A finger is painted with ferric chloride solution and placed on a chemically treated paper. The darkness in the paper (measured with a densitometer) is proportional to the amount of sweating. Interfinger correlations and test-retest correlations provide evidence of reliability.

Physical activity relates to bodily movements that result in expenditure (Shelton & Klesges, 1995). Measurement approaches include observation, mechanical or electronic monitoring, and calorimetry. An activity monitor can be placed on parts of the body. Heart rate monitors represent another measure of physical activity. Direct calorimetry measures production of heat, where individuals are observed in special chambers. Indirect calorimetry measures oxygen consumption and carbon dioxide production through a face mask or mouthpiece. Such instruments have high levels of accuracy and are validated through convergent validity across, say, heart rate monitors and oxygen uptake. Reliability across instruments is extremely high. Relevant here is explication of the relationship between the conceptual definition of physical activity and physiological measurement (e.g., can heart rate be related to phenomena other than physical activity?).

Physical Measurement

With proper physical devices, it may appear that physical measurement can be accomplished with little error. Yet standardized procedures and standardized stimuli are needed to minimize random and systematic error. Thus, error can creep in through administration procedures (e.g., in medical measurement, say, of blood pressure). Precise physical measurement may disguise inaccuracies that are due to administration procedures. In any setting, a variety of factors may affect measures, such as word length in reading speed, or the nature of stimuli in reaction time. Such issues should be addressed carefully during measure development and are similar to the issues that arise for psychological measures in domain explication and item development.

Levine (1997) traces the history of the measurement of time. The sundial, based on the length of shadows, was an early method, with error arising out of cloudiness and other such factors. Next came measures that did not depend on sunlight, such as water clocks based on the flow of water. These were followed by mechanical clocks and then pendulums, a major breakthrough (Levine, 1997). With more accuracy came finer calibration and more precision. That time was discussed as a concrete construct along with length in Chapter 1 is really a function of the passage of time! In the days of sundials, the measurement of time may have seemed indirect.

Earthquakes were measured by a direct rating of ground movement on a 12-point scale, an approach not useful in unpopulated areas and also lacking in consistency (Plutchik, 1989). The Richter scale related the magnitude of earthquakes to variables such as the wave period. This scale was based on theory about energy and empirical data.

The wind chill index represents a formative index of how cold air feels on human skin. It combines wind speed about 5 feet above the ground (human face level) with a calculation of heat transfer, skin tissue resistance, clear night sky conditions, and a calm wind threshold of 3 miles per hour. A new index replaces another index that used wind 33 feet above the ground. The new index provides a higher temperature than the old index in most situations. Even though such an index is formed by precise observations and calculations, it requires certain assumptions, such as feet above the ground and wind at calm conditions. Needless to say, the actual effect of wind may well vary for different individuals, and the assumptions hold on average. Depending on what the "true" construct is, there may be error in these indexes, not just from observational sources but also from individual variations in heat transfer and skin tissue resistance. Noteworthy here is that physical measurement is also based on assumptions about conditions, and about factors that lead to a phenomenon, with specific measurement procedures excluding some factors and including others.[6]

There are many parallels to such measurement in the social sciences. One example is in measuring objective product quality by formative indexes that include certain dimensions and assess deviations from specifications. The choice of both dimensions and specifications involve judgments by the researcher. Such "objective" measures ultimately may have to be validated by assessing their correspondence with "subjective" measures. When components of a measure are objectively measurable, subjectivity and error can occur because of excluded components and the ways in which components are combined.

Cross-Cultural Measurement

Overview

Several issues in cross-cultural research are germane to measurement. Does a construct exist in some other culture? Is the underlying structure the same or different in terms of the number and nature of dimensions? Do the items used in one culture apply in another culture, item content often reflecting the cultural context? Are response formats usable across cultures (Heine, Lehman, Peng, & Greenholtz, 2002)? Do administration procedures need to be modified across cultures? More broadly, are cross-cultural comparisons possible? As McCrae (2001) notes, Cattell (1950) described psychological insights of culture provided by anthropologists as "oversimplified, distorted descriptions, stillborn from an infantile methodology" (p. 391). Since then, however, insights from anthropologists have been used in numerous translations of measures and, more broadly, in conducting cross-cultural research.

The area of cross-cultural research presents interesting insights. Nisbett (2003) contrasts Western and Eastern cultures in terms of analytic versus holistic thinking. A very approximate summary of this work suggests Western versus Eastern differences, respectively, in (a) separating objects from a field and focusing on objects contrasted with attention to the background (i.e., for Western versus Eastern respondents, respectively), (b) perceiving greater control over events versus less control, (c) attributing causality to objects versus the field, (d) detecting less versus more covariation across stimuli, (e) grouping objects and events based on category membership versus functional relationships, (f) using logical rules versus experience-based knowledge, (g) choosing extremes versus middle alternatives, and (h) displaying less versus more hindsight bias with surprising outcomes. Key distinctions in the literature include a fundamental attribution bias in Western cultures toward inner traits and dispositions versus situational attributions in Eastern cultures. A related bias in Western cultures is one of false uniqueness. This distinction is at the heart of a variety of individual difference measures and, more generally, a plethora of items of the "I . . ." variety. Eastern cultures may therefore be characterized by less internal consistency and test-retest reliability, presumably because of a less stable internal disposition or less attribution to internal disposition. Should items be customized to reflect more of a response to a situation rather than general disposition statements? Are respondents in Western cultures more likely to provide consistent responses, or vice versa? Controlling for language, does the strength of underlying constructs vary across cultures? Do tendencies to communicate in the context of a research design vary across cultures? Does an interpersonal orientation lead to a larger influence of factors such as social desirability? Are there cultural differences in self-categorization, as is sometimes required in self-report scales? Are there cultural differences in responses that cause different degrees of blurring across dimensions of a construct because of, say, analytic versus holistic cognition? The earlier discussion about the importance of evaluating measures under usage conditions is of central importance in cross-cultural research.

Church (2000) points out several issues in cross-cultural measurement. In a research approach where the factor structure of the Big Five personality measures are replicated across cultures, previous structure is imposed on culture (Church, 2000). In contrast, indigenous dimensions within cultures could be identified rather than imposing structure from the outside. For instance, a Big Seven construct has been suggested for a few cultures. Across cultures, similar nomological networks or relationships between constructs provide some evidence of generalizability of personality dimensions. Cultural mean differences can also be assessed to examine if expectations about differences between cultures are borne out. Several factors are confounded here, including translation, response styles, and actual differences on constructs. Interjudge agreement (e.g., correlations between self-ratings and ratings of others) is another approach that is used. The Big Five were tested across cultures by performing a combined intercultural factor analysis, where each culture was represented by a single case consisting of the mean for that culture (McCrae, 2001). Factor congruence and compatibility were based on the parallels between intercultural analysis and analysis within cultures. Therefore, each culture was essentially the equivalent of a single data point, akin to a stimulus-centered approach where each data point represents a stimulus with means averaged across respondents. Considering another example, moral reasoning is measured by the Defining Issues Test (Rest, 1979), which uses six moral dilemmas, each of which has 12 arguments to resolve. These arguments are based on a theory of stages of moral reasoning and are rated and ranked by respondents (Gielen & Markoulis, 2001). The measure has been assessed across cultures. Built-in checks in the measure include a check of consistency between ratings and rankings, and a check of endorsement of meaningless items (Gielen & Markoulis, 2001).

Several terms have been used to describe a variety of issues in cross-cultural measurement. Construct bias has been used to refer to lack of overlap of conceptual definitions across cultures (Van deVijver & Tanzer, 1997). Method bias can be due to (a) sample bias from nonequivalent samples across cultures, (b) instrument bias due to different response styles across cultures, and (c) administration bias due to communication problems (Church, 2001).

A variety of forms of equivalence across cultures needs to be considered (Helms, 1992). Linguistic equivalence may be facilitated by using a team of translators, ensuring that the team understands the theoretical underpinnings, using back translation to original language to check for equivalence, and developing measures for multiple cultures simultaneously (Duda & Hayashi, 1998). Psychometric equivalence relates to capturing the same constructs across cultures. Germane are various psychometric properties, including internal consistency and factor structure (Duda & Hayashi, 1998). Testing-condition equivalence relates to the extent to which various procedures and settings used to collect data are similarly perceived across cultures. Appropriateness of certain methods, use of response scales, and social desirability concerns are germane issues (Duda & Hayashi, 1998). Sampling equivalence in each stage of measure development is another issue. The sample is very important in cross-cultural research. Studying undergraduate students who are Westernized is far from sufficient (McCrae, 2001). Different strata of society would need to be studied across cultures. Functional equivalence relates to scores having similar meaning across cultures. Functional equivalence relates to whether a construct operates similarly across cultures (Helms, 1992). Conceptual equivalence relates to respondents interpreting items in similar ways.

Translation

A number of issues in cross-cultural research include translation. Several recommendations are made with regard to developing easy-to-translate items, such as using brief items, using active voice, and having one idea per sentence (Takooshian, Mrinal, & Mrinal, 2001). Other recommendations include avoiding metaphors and colloquialisms (which may lack equivalents), avoiding subjunctives (such as "could" or "should"), repeating nouns and not pronouns, avoiding words conveying probability, avoiding two verbs in a sentence, using words familiar to translation, and avoiding possessive forms (Takooshian et al., 2001). In focusing on preserving the content of questions during translations, reading difficulty may increase; hence, translators should be made aware of the characteristics of the target population. A team of bilinguals is recommended, with different translators working on translations, say, one translating from English to the target language and another back-translating a written comparison after some iterations (Takooshian et al., 2001). Psychometric testing can be done on bilinguals completing alternative forms as well as test-retest across a time interval using alternative forms (Takooshian et al., 2001).

Casagrande (1954) distinguished between four different types of translations: pragmatic (focusing on translating the content accurately), aesthetic-poetic, ethnographic (aiming to capture the cultural context), and linguistic (aiming to capture linguistic aspects such as grammar). Bilingual translations have problems as well; bilingual translators may overcompensate for poor-quality translations and may differ in cognitive makeup when compared to others.

Emic Versus Etic Perspectives

Emic (within one's culture) and etic (external to one's culture) approaches are very relevant in understanding measurement across cultures. The nature of measurement can be viewed in terms of a continuum of adaptation and indigenization ranging from imposed etic to emic approaches: (a) using a test as is, in the same language; (b) using literal translation; (c) adapting items; (d) conducting psychometric analysis, including norms, reliability, dimensionality, validity, differential item performance, and possible response styles; (e) developing indigenous items; (f) developing indigenous constructs; (g) using adapted response formats and administration procedures; (h) considering (f) and (g) above for indigenous subpopulations; and (i) conducting psychometric evaluation of indigenous measures (Church, 2001).

Whether a construct, its dimensionality, or its measurement applies to a new population should be viewed with a large dose of skepticism. Neither the theory underlying the construct nor the measurement approach may apply. A narrow view that minor adjustments are likely to be sufficient may, in turn, lead to vacuous insights. Rather, the construct may need to be explored conceptually (e.g., intelligence or ethical values). Otherwise, extreme within-measure correlational systematic error may result (i.e., measurement of method factors or unknown constructs or both).

Factors that may determine choice of an imported (imposed-etic) versus indigenous (emic) approach include efficiency, the nature of constructs assessed, item content in terms of extent of adaptation, ability to compare measures across cultures, and whether the research aims to study universal or culture-specific measures (Church, 2001). Whether universal or culture-specific measures are used likely influences what is found, universality or culture specificity, respectively. If items purporting to assess a set of dimensions are employed across cultures, new dimensions are not likely to emerge. On the other hand, if indigenous measurement leads to similar conclusions about dimensionality (such as with the Big Five model of personality), then strong evidence of dimensionality is suggested. Although some studies suggest that specific personality constructs generalize across cultures in terms of dimensionality, such results should be examined carefully. Some studies suggest lower internal consistency and unsatisfactory item loadings on factors across cultures (Church, 2001).

Measurement Properties Across Cultures

Some personality dimensions may retain their factor structure across cultures (Church & Katigbak, 1988). Even if this happens, some items may not perform well across cultures. Specific items have been recommended in measures within cultures (Fiske, 1971); however, such specific items may not generalize across cultures (Church & Katigbak, 1988). Specific items that capture certain behaviors in certain situations may not apply across cultures. Items are often worded concretely by providing a context, and culture, of course, influences context.

A variety of terms relating to stability have been employed in the literature, including *mean stability* (changes in means across time), *differential stability* (i.e., maintenance of relative ordering among individuals), *structural stability* (similar factor structure across time), and *temporal stability* (which has been used in a variety of ways) (Schutz, 1998). Mean differences across cultures need to be explained theoretically and methodologically (Church, 2001). Measures used need to be validated across cultures to establish measurement equivalence (Church, 2001). Differences should be replicated using multiple measures (Church, 2001). Differences on individual items need to be understood either theoretically or methodologically (Church, 2001). Structural equation modeling allows testing of a variety of models where specific constraints may be imposed, such as identical factor loadings across time or identical differential stability. For example, if a measure is repeated over five time intervals, the coefficient relating test to retest could be set to be equal to the coefficient relating retest to re-retest. Modeling can also incorporate method factors and correlated errors between individual items.

A number of studies have examined response biases across cultures (Grimm & Church, 1999). Do U.S. respondents use extreme response categories to a greater degree? Do some groups overuse extreme response categories? Do others overuse midpoints or middle categories? Do some groups respond in more socially desirable ways? Indicators of extreme response bias or high use of midpoints are developed by counting the frequency of use of certain response categories. Response biases such as acquiescence have been related to cultural characteristics of willingness to conform or willingness to have good interpersonal relationships. The use of the midpoint has been associated with reluctance to express feelings or thoughts. The results are generally quite mixed with regard to overall differences across cultures. Methodological factors have to be disentangled from constructs in cross-cultural research. A study of cultural differences (Chen et al., 1995) found that respondents from Japan and Taiwan were more likely than those from Canada and the United States to use the middle category, U.S. respondents being more likely than the others to use extreme categories. The degree to which each group endorsed individualism was positively (negatively) related to the use of extremes (the middle category).

Summary

Several issues are germane in cross-cultural measures, such as their generalizability across cultures. Whether personality constructs, such as the Big Five or facial emotions, generalize has important consequences for measurement.

Ability tests are often specific to a culture. In this regard, culture-free, culture-fair, and culture-specific tests were attempted in the course of intelligence testing (Jones, 1996). Psychopathological conditions may be specific to a culture, perceptions of normal versus abnormal behavior may vary across cultures, and symptoms may manifest differently (Takooshian et al., 2001). Therefore, a measure of depression that uses existence of certain symptoms as indictors may not be applicable across cultures (Takooshian et al., 2001).

In summary, cross-cultural measurement poses a host of challenging issues. The measurement framework developed here, with its emphasis on testing measures in specific usage conditions, is very relevant to cross-cultural measurement.

Summary

An examination of scales across different disciplines provides stimulating examples of creative design. Rather than restrict consideration to self-report measures of agreement with statements, researchers can be creative in designing scales that capture the construct of interest by considering a variety of approaches and formats from different disciplines. The level of detail provided in, say, ability measures, in terms of such issues as setting and administration procedures, may be relevant in self-report measures as well. Method of administration, scripting of verbal instructions, seating arrangements, and other such issues are also relevant to self-report measures.

At one end of what is really a continuum are purely relative scales that aim to order objects or individuals. At the other end are physical scales with a clear external standard and one-to-one correspondence (e.g., length or time). Scales with norms for age groups or other characteristics allow a way for absolute values to be interpreted and lie somewhere in between. Closer to the absolute end are scales that go further, relating certain scores to, say, specific levels of development or to distinct conditions, such as brain impairment. Here, there is more than a norm describing a demographic group and population distributions. Scores are related to absolute levels of phenomena, such as specific levels of performance or development.

Errors can creep into measures in a variety of ways (Rust & Golombok, 1999). For self-reports, sources of error include deliberate lying, presenting oneself in a positive light (additive systematic error), providing random responses (idiosyncratic or generic random error), or providing similar answers (correlational systematic error). Solutions include balancing agreement and disagreement in responses and using items to detect lying or social desirability (Rust & Golombok, 1999). For raters, sources of error include inconsistent procedures and rules for interpretation (generic random error), biased ratings (e.g., additive systematic error), and halo effects (correlational systematic error). Raters may be biased in ratings; solutions here include training using multiple raters and monitoring (Rust & Golombok, 1999). Even in physiological measurement, physical or psychological behavior can manipulate responses. Cross-cultural measurement raises a host of challenging issues relating to whether a construct exists, whether similar dimensions exist, and whether measures are valid across cultures. The emphasis on usage conditions in the framework developed in this book is all the more important for cross-cultural research.

Notes

1. A weighted Kappa allows for degrees of disagreement (Cohen, 1968). As with other methodological issues, there are several nuances in the area of interjudge reliability covered in the literature (cf. Brennan & Prediger, 1981; Perreault & Leigh, 1989; Rust & Cooil, 1994).

2. The purpose of convergent validity is not to show that two measures are identical but rather that they are highly related and can be used as measures of the same construct. Two different measures of a construct in the social sciences cannot be expected to be identical. In fact, often, the state of the art is pushed forward by having new measures that, although purporting to measure a specific construct, may do so in a slightly different way, thus moving conceptual thinking forward in an area. New measures may also result in a redefinition of a construct, the addition of dimensions to it, differentiation of a construct into multiple distinct constructs, and so on.

3. Test-taking ability is, of course, a construct distinct from ability in the content area of a test. The respondent's ability in using a method of testing is relevant here. Teaching for a test or teaching test-taking capitalizes on this.

4. Item difficulty, or the index of difficulty, sometimes has been defined in terms of proportions of specific groups of examinees who answered an item correctly and sometimes in terms of proportions who answered an item incorrectly (e.g., Ebel & Frisbie, 1986).

5. A major distinction can be made between relative and absolute measures— whether a measure achieves relative ordering or absolute levels (Figure 8.1). A similar distinction has been drawn between relative and absolute decisions made from measures (Shavelson & Webb, 1991).

6. This issue is germane when the wind chill index is 26 below zero Fahrenheit, as it is during this writing in Champaign, Illinois. For me, a person who went from tropical India to Minnesota for graduate study, this is particularly relevant because the new wind chill index has been adopted in recent years. Hence, −26°F on the new wind chill scale is −48°F on the old scale, assuming an absolute temperature of 0°F, moving it closer to my Minnesota experience!

9

What Are the Implications of Understanding Measurement Error for Research Design and Analysis?

Overview

This chapter moves the discussion from measuring one thing to measuring or manipulating multiple things in the entire research design. Although this chapter explicitly moves to the entire research design, understanding the measurement of one thing as a way to understanding the measurement or manipulation of many things and the entire design has been the theme throughout this book. The nuanced discussion of error, such as across-measure additive and correlational systematic error, and associated error sources in collecting data on measures of multiple constructs in a research design, are examples of this orientation. This orientation is also reflected in the emphasis in the framework in Chapter 5 on usage conditions and the notion that measures are validated not in isolation, but in usage. The principles described in measuring one thing are used in measuring and manipulating multiple things (i.e., in the design of an entire method).

The discussions in the first five chapters culminating in the framework and guidelines developed in Chapter 5 have implications for both the design of research and the analysis of data, such as in using existing measures in research methods, and in using structural equation modeling. Researchers typically use existing measures, previously either validated or unvalidated, in methodological design. Although the discussion in the first five chapters emphasized measure development, the same principles are involved in evaluating and using existing measures. Furthermore, measures of multiple constructs are administered together in a design. These issues are covered in this chapter. Implications also extend to the use of structural equation modeling. Implications for applied research are also discussed.

Implications for Using Measures in Research Design

Using Validated Measures

A common situation that researchers face is the need to use previously developed scales in research methods rather than developing measures for specific studies. Scales previously validated for reliability, dimensionality, and validity are often employed by researchers in methodological design. Design considerations, such as the separation or grouping of key variables, may require the modification of existing measures. Recommendations are discussed at the level of items, measures, administration, and construct.

When using existing measures, research design can be enhanced by beginning with a careful methodological review of the literature, as distinct from a substantive review. A methodological review should start with clear conceptual definitions of constructs rooted in relevant literature. The construct as defined should be delineated from related constructs by explication of relevant domains. Current definitions may need to be modified if constructs are not sufficiently distinguished or clearly defined. Constructs may not be properly defined in past research for a variety of reasons, including their "self-evident" nature. However, anything short of a clear definition warrants further attention. Available measures need to be examined carefully in a variety of ways. First, items need to be examined in light of the conceptual definition of a construct. This is not to second-guess prior work as much as it is to obtain correspondence between the conceptual and the operational. An existing measure may not capture the entire domain of a construct as defined. An important aspect of the domain may have been excluded. Measures are a work in progress needing constant improvement. However, considerable conceptual and empirical support should be provided for modifying previously validated measures. A methodological review, which parallels a substantive review of the literature, should cover various measures of a construct in terms of psychometric properties. Such a review should take into consideration the sample and usage conditions of previous psychometric work. As discussed earlier, measures are not tested in isolation but in specific usage contexts.

Items may need to be added to measures to cover certain aspects of the domain or to add a new dimension. In such situations, items could be added at the end of the measures rather than modifying existing items (Table 9.1). Thus, the original measure is preserved in terms of items and sequencing. The within-measure halo effect and other such effects present during prior validation are not disrupted. Items in a measure perform well for many reasons, not all of which are apparent or foreseeable. As discussed, measure assessment is both deductive and inductive, the latter suggesting that items may work empirically for a variety of known and unknown reasons, with the proof being in the empirical results. A specific sequencing of items could contribute to their performance. Therefore, changes in sequencing can be detrimental while also adding new variations and making it more difficult to attribute differences in results to the appropriate sources.

When adding items, new items and the entire measure should be evaluated using all psychometric procedures in order to create a basis for deleting or modifying items. Researchers should exercise caution in modifying individual items of previously validated measures. Such modification requires extensive conceptual and empirical support. Appropriate rationale, as well as empirical evidence of psychometric properties, is required for modifying either the number or labeling of response categories. Vague wording of anchors, extreme or nonextreme wording of end anchors, and a reduction or increase in the number of response categories can lead to systematic as well as random error.

At the measure level, new items should be added at the end of measures and supported by the assessment of psychometric properties at the item and measure levels. It may be necessary to add items in order to allow for a sufficient number of items representing each dimension after measure purification and item deletion. This allows the researcher to purify a measure and have an adequate number of items in the final measure (generally, a minimum of approximately four items, with broader constructs requiring a higher minimum). As discussed, researchers should exercise utmost caution in deleting existing items of previously validated measures, providing extensive conceptual and empirical support as bases. Modified measures should be assessed empirically before their use in substantive studies. The use of short forms, different sequencing, and the use of fillers require appropriate psychometric support.

At the administration level, researchers should articulate a rationale and/ or provide empirical evidence for using measures in different populations,

Table 9.1 Identifying and Correcting for Error in Using Measures in Methodological Design*

Procedures	Diagnostics	Possible Type of Measurement Error	Recommendations
Using validated measures (i.e., prior evidence of reliability, dimensionality, and validity)	Item-level modification of item	All random and systematic errors	Avoid modification of existing items; add new item(s) to end of measure; use sufficient sample size; evaluate new item(s) and entire measure using all psychometric procedures; modify existing items with utmost caution and extensive conceptual and empirical support
	Item-level modification of number or labeling of response categories	All random and systematic errors	Develop rationale and provide empirical evidence of psychometric properties
	Measure-level addition or deletion of items	All random and systematic errors	Avoid deletion of existing items; start with sufficient number of items per dimension to enable purification; add new item(s) to end of measure; use sufficient sample size; evaluate new item(s) and entire measure using all psychometric procedures; delete existing items with utmost caution and extensive conceptual and empirical support
	Measure-level use of short forms or different sequencing or use of fillers	Within-measure correlational systematic error	Evaluate measure using all psychometric procedures
	Administration-level modification of procedures/setting/samples	All random and systematic errors	Develop conceptual reasoning and/or empirical evidence of psychometric properties
	Construct-level reconceptualization of construct/dimensionality and item generation	All random and systematic errors	Conduct literature review; develop conceptual reasoning and/or empirical evidence of psychometric properties; avoid modification of existing items; add items to end of measure; start with sufficient number of items per dimension to enable purification; provide extensive conceptual and empirical support; validate prior to use in substantive studies; use sufficient sample size

Procedures	Diagnostics	Possible Type of Measurement Error	Recommendations
	Without modification	All random and systematic errors	Use sufficient sample size; report psychometric properties; purify scale and report substantive results for original and purified versions; with different dimensionality than during prior validation, report substantive results for original dimensionality and dimensionality found in usage
Using unvalidated measures	With or without modification	All random and systematic errors	Start with sufficient number of items per dimension to enable purification; assess measure using all psychometric procedures; evaluate validity through previous uses in studies; validate prior to use in substantive studies; incorporate validity tests in concurrent designs; use sufficient sample size
Designing methods	Grouping of central variables in tests of hypotheses of sizable relationships	Across-measure systematic error	Separate central variables; specify correlated errors or method factors in structural equation modeling; use pilot or concurrent tests to assess sources of error
	Separation of central variables in tests of hypotheses of small or no relationships	Across-measure systematic error	Group central variables; specify correlated errors or method factors in structural equation modeling; use pilot or concurrent tests to assess sources of error
Interpreting results	High correlations for tests of hypotheses of sizable relationships	Across-measure systematic error	Separate central variables; infer strong or weak evidence from results; specify correlated errors or method factors in structural equation modeling
	Low correlations for tests of small or no relationships	Across-measure systematic error	Group central variables; infer strong or weak evidence from results; specify correlated errors or method factors in structural equation modeling

*The starting point for all of the scenarios described in the table is a thorough methodological review.

such as student, nonstudent, or cross-cultural samples, or for making changes in procedures or method of administration.

Rethinking at the construct level and consequent changes to measures should avoid modifying existing items but should rather add items at the end of measures. Thus, the entire measure and individual items can be assessed. A sufficient number of items per dimension are needed, as discussed earlier. Such modifications also require empirical testing for all psychometric procedures. Because construct-level changes are fundamental, they require a careful review of the literature. Deleting or modifying existing items as a result of construct-level changes requires extensive conceptual and empirical support. Ideally, validation should be conducted before conducting substantive studies to avoid investing effort in research designs involving unreliable or invalid measures.

When previously validated scales are employed without modification, psychometric properties should be reported. Again, the key here is that measures have to be assessed in usage conditions, and that reliability and validity are properties of measures in specific usage conditions. Researchers have to provide evidence of reliability and validity of the measures used in a study, whether or not these measures have been validated previously. Deviations from previous findings in terms of dimensional structure may require data analyses to be adjusted accordingly. For instance, if a scale has been validated previously as being unidimensional, and two dimensions are found during usage, then substantive results ideally should be reported for each of these possibilities. Similarly, if a previously validated scale has items that need to be deleted, results should be reported for the original version as well as the modified version of the scale. Essentially, the previously validated scale has to display appropriate psychometric properties under specific usage conditions; otherwise, substantive results based on the scale are open to question. When any validation described above is conducted concurrent with or prior to hypothesis tests, sufficient sample sizes must be used in studies to enable psychometric testing and to minimize idiosyncratic random error.

Using Unvalidated Measures

Measures that have not been validated previously are often used in methodological design. Such measures may have no prior evidence of psychometric properties or may, at most, provide evidence of reliability, usually coefficient alpha, based on their use in substantive studies. Relevant here is a methodological review as discussed earlier. Validation for such measures ideally should be conducted before the measures are used in research methods to test substantive hypotheses (Table 9.1). This minimizes the likelihood of investing in unreliable or invalid measures. Such measures may need to be modified to maintain a sufficient number of items for each dimension. When validation is conducted concurrent with hypothesis tests, variables must be added to the design to incorporate validity tests. Such an approach, of course, runs the risk of placing all the eggs in one basket. Therefore, the measure itself could include additional items to allow for item deletion and measure purification. Whereas data are readily available for tests of reliability and dimensionality, the addition of a few variables can make validity tests possible. A methodological review of past use of measures also can be employed to infer evidence of validity. Sufficient sample sizes must be used to enable psychometric testing and to minimize idiosyncratic random error.

The emphasis on conceptual and empirical work is not to discourage reevaluating existing measures. Rather, measures need to be evaluated and improved constantly, and measure development is an ongoing process. However, such reevaluation has to be done carefully, with full consideration of previous work on a measure. Researchers may put together some measures for the purpose of a study without sufficient conceptual or empirical work. Hence, measures need to be examined carefully in many situations.

Designing Collection of Data on Multiple Measures

Researchers in the social sciences use surveys with organizational or individual foci and collect data on a variety of measures of constructs. Essentially, a research method consists of measurement and/or manipulation of several variables. How these variables are sequenced and administered bears on the nature of error that is likely to result. When reporting these methodological issues, the rationale that researchers provide for the sequencing of measures used in hypothesis tests is often insufficient or absent. Such a rationale should account for across-measure systematic error that is likely when data are collected on multiple measures. Discussion of such error would be appropriate both in developing the rationale for the research design before the fact, and in the interpretation of results. For example, a study of relationships between organizations may sequence a host of such measures as opportunism and power, without sufficient discussion of the rationale in terms of reducing across-measure systematic error. Or, a study may sequence a number of scales with similar response categories contiguously. Some plausible sources of error, such as hypothesis guessing, halo effects, and common method factors, require explanation in such situations. Rationale for specific design of methods and appropriate interpretation of results should be presented. Issues relating to the design of validity tests and the separation or grouping of variables directly overlap with the methodological design of substantive studies to minimize across-measure systematic error (Table 9.1). Strong tests can be designed or strong evidence can be inferred from results by assessing the separation or grouping of central variables in light of hypothesized relationships between them as discussed in Chapter 5. For example, by separating (grouping) measures of opportunism and power in a variety of ways, strong tests of hypotheses of sizable (small or nonsignificant) relationships can be created and strong evidence can be interpreted.

Additionally, pilot tests can be used to assess likely sources of error in research methods. Pilot tests are sometimes used in an experimental context to assess demand artifacts and in a survey setting to assess the wording of individual items. However, they also can be used to assess plausible sources of systematic error in correlational designs (Table 9.1). Similar tests conducted concurrently with hypothesis tests (e.g., immediately following collection of data on variables in hypothesis tests) in substantive studies rather than pilot tests can facilitate the interpretation of findings, although they are no substitute for sound methodological design. The "causal mentality" often employed in experimental research to design independent variables is just as pertinent in sequencing variables in correlational designs or in sequencing dependent variables in experimental designs to counter across-measure systematic error. As discussed, research design can be enhanced through a careful methodological review of the literature.

If existing measures of a construct are not chosen for use, then the rationale for a new measure needs to be provided. Similarly, the use of specific existing measures needs to be supported as well. If existing measures that lack psychometric testing are to be used, then studies can build in additional testing, such as validity tests. However, such designs run the risk of putting all eggs in one basket. A more efficient design can be achieved by separately testing measures before investing resources in substantive studies. A common problem in using existing measures is the need to supplement items to cover subdomains. A key recommendation here is to employ sufficient numbers of items for each dimension to allow for item deletion and a resulting scale with four items. A four-item scale may be the minimum number to demonstrate psychometric properties in most situations, although a larger minimum would apply for constructs covering complex domains. The practice of employing one or two items because of the length of questionnaires is not recommended because reliability may not be achievable or demonstrable.

Although this book strongly recommends measure assessment prior to its use in substantive testing, if such a step is not employed, the substantive study should be planned to accommodate psychometric assessment. The problem with such an approach is the confounding of methodological and substantive explanations. In addition to traditional methodological artifacts, lack of measurement reliability or validity undermines the validity of the research design.

Perhaps the most effective and efficient step in methodological design is preliminary work prior to a substantive study, be it pretesting, pilot testing, or measure development. However, this key step is often short-changed in light of pragmatic concerns such as time pressure or the lack of easy access to samples. Whereas the former requires adequate planning and the added realization of the high payoff involved, the latter is often a significant problem, particularly when respondents are not conveniently accessible for a variety of reasons (e.g., managers in organizations). Through preliminary work, in addition to a sound basis for a specific methodological study, a basis is also in place for a program of research. The payoff from a sound methodological basis can extend to several studies in a program of research. Sometimes many pilot studies are needed to calibrate stimuli and purify measures. Ideally, the measures employed in a study should have demonstrated psychometric properties that enable confidence in them, and thus in the results of a study. When there is considerable uncertainty on multiple fronts, it is difficult, perhaps impossible, to draw meaningful conclusions. For example, if the relationship between two measures of different constructs is nonsignificant, is this because (a) the two constructs in question are not related or (b) unreliable or invalid measures have been used for one or both of the constructs? In this regard, from a theoretical standpoint, measurement is often described as a large-sample theory (Nunnally, 1978), emphasizing the importance of large samples in measure development to minimize uncertainty due to sampling error.

Illustrative Scenarios on Using Measures in Research Design

Some illustrative scenarios that commonly occur in using measures are described to bring out key issues. Say a construct has been measured with a scale available in the literature. However, the construct itself has not been defined conceptually anywhere in the literature. This scenario occurs often and warrants careful examination of the domain of the construct. The available scale may capture only some aspects of the domain. Alternatively, the scale may capture a slightly different, perhaps somewhat narrower, construct. Definitions and dimensions are assumed, a sort of logic of "everyone knows what it means." There are also situations where the dimensionality of a scale has been assessed through factor analysis, yet no conceptual definition of the construct or proposed dimensions is available. Almost the first step in any research and in any presentation of research should be the definition of constructs. In other words, it is essential to understand what is being researched and what is the thing being measured. Such definition of previously undefined constructs or redefinition may lead to the addition of new items, preferably at the end of the scale.

Another common scenario occurs where a scale measuring a specific construct is available in past research and coefficient alpha is reported, but no other psychometric properties have been assessed. Can the scale be used as is? In this scenario, the psychometric evaluation of the scale is limited to internal consistency. It is well worth the effort to examine the definition and domain of the construct and assess individual scale items for representation of content. If additional items are required, they could be added to the end of the scale to maintain the sequencing of the original scale. However, items in the original scale may warrant modification because they capture a different construct or a method factor. Here, either additional items can be added or, in extreme cases, the original items can be modified. Addition of items instead of modification may lengthen measures. Essential in this scenario is the need to empirically reassess internal consistency and assess dimensionality and validity. Clearly, modifying a validated scale requires appropriate empirical support; however, mere reporting of coefficient alpha is not sufficient validation.

Another common scenario involves developing several new scales as a part of a research project to measure constructs being studied. Due to time constraints, however, data are collected for measure assessment concurrent with hypothesis testing. This scenario effectively puts all the methodological eggs in one substantive study basket. Pretesting, whether of measures or manipulations, may be very cost-effective for the effort involved. At the least, a small pilot study may identify wording problems. In the event that all eggs have to be put in one basket, it is important to carefully conceptualize constructs, delineate their domains, and edit items. A sufficient number of items to start with is essential to allow for an adequate number after purification (usually at least four at the end of the process). Broader constructs may require a larger minimum number of items.

Consider another scenario where a study uses samples that are difficult to access, say, employees of specific organizations. Several constructs are measured by single-item scales to reduce the length of the survey and increase the response rate. In this scenario, the problem lies in the inability to achieve or demonstrate psychometric properties of scales. An alternative here is to use short forms of measures. These short forms of measures could be validated in separate studies, in terms of both empirical evidence and conceptual examination to assess coverage of the domain with a representative set of items. Such an approach may lead to a trade-off between reliability and content validity (e.g., choosing items with the highest item-to-total correlations vs. items that cover the domain of the construct). Ideally, a similar sample should be used to validate the short form, but as a last resort, it could be validated in more easily available samples, provided such samples are logically reasonable alternatives (e.g., senior graduate students in business with appropriate work experience in place of managers in business research). If single items need to be employed as a last resort, they should be validated in separate studies by demonstrating a high covariation with other items of the measure, through high covariation with another measure of the construct, and through high stability (reliability across time). Such evidence, when available in previous validation work, could be used to justify the research method.

Consider another scenario where a study employs measures that are based on objective numbers (e.g., return on investment, market share). Given the availability of such numbers, these measures are considered reliable and valid. In this scenario, it is important to understand what construct is being measured. Return on investment (ROI) is an objective number, yet the aim really is to assess performance. There are many dimensions of performance; it is not self-evident that ROI alone would capture these dimensions. Thus, examination of what is being measured is useful and necessary, no matter how self-evident a measure appears. Clearly, if the construct being studied is concrete in nature, such as ROI, then the measure follows directly. But a conceptual examination of the intended construct can only help in aligning the research method with research objectives. For instance, if the research objective is to assess a firm's efficiency, then several measures beyond ROI could be used. A second issue here is the use of objective numbers. Such measures can be usefully supplemented by subjective measures, such as self-report ratings of ROI or of performance vis-à-vis major competitors or the industry. Objective numbers can themselves be standardized based on industry averages. A key issue here is that absolute numbers are interpretable when compared to some reference point. Such reference points could be used (e.g., industry averages) to standardize numbers and interpret them. Additionally, subjective direct ratings of ROI in light of various considerations can be collected. The design of such subjective ratings may enable interpretation of objective measures as well, by highlighting the limitations of objective measures and the nature of reference points against which to compare them. For example, a high ROI in terms of objective numbers, combined with a moderate or even low self-report of performance relative to the competition, points to the need for appropriate norms to interpret objective numbers for a specific time period. Similarly, self-reports also can be supplemented by measurement using objective numbers, particularly in organizational research. Such multiple approaches likely enhance clarification of constructs and their domains and provide multiple measures and a test of convergent validity.

An opposite scenario is also common, using self-report measures exclusively. Consider a situation where organizational research is conducted and measures are assessed exclusively through self-reports by employees. Here, alternative measures from independent sources should be considered. A self-report measure of a construct can be supplemented with another measure of the construct based on secondary data. Convergence between very different approaches to measuring the same construct provides strong evidence of validity. Using independent sources of data for measuring *different* constructs is also a way of reducing across-measure systematic error.

Implications for Using Structural Equation Modeling

As discussed in Chapter 1, structural equation modeling (SEM) can be used to identify and account for measurement error. The discussion of different types of error leading up to the framework and guidelines developed in Chapter 5 have implications for using SEM. Many researchers have emphasized the importance of theoretical justification for measurement models in SEM in the context of interpreting residuals, specifying item-specific factors (Anderson, 1985; Bagozzi & Yi, 1994), specifying correlated error terms and method factors (Bagozzi, 1984; Bollen, 1989; Gerbing & Anderson, 1984), and specifying reliability estimates for SEM (DeShon, 1998; Fornell, 1983). The guidelines developed here provide a measurement theory that can be used in specifying models in covariance analysis and interpreting the results. Gerbing and Anderson (1988) point out several ways of dealing with indicators: relating the indicator to a different factor, deleting it, and using correlated error terms. Each of these approaches would benefit from the proposed guidelines, which provide a basis for making these choices as well as a more robust set of items for confirmatory factor analysis to begin with. By using a test-retest approach at the item level, the proposed guidelines can also be employed to isolate item-specific factors that are not shared across items (Anderson, 1985).

Approaches to modeling measurement error in SEM include linking multiple items to a latent factor so that disattenuated relationships are computed, employing a generalizability coefficient based on extensive study of the measures, or using a reliability coefficient for a measure (DeShon, 1998). DeShon (1998) points out that a reliability coefficient used in SEM should reflect such facets as items and time period, including applications of the research, and that the use of internal consistency reliability in SEM may not be adequate. Because the guidelines proposed in this book require rigorous testing of measures in a variety of settings, they provide a set of robust items assessed under different conditions. The guidelines can also provide reliability estimates for both cross-sectional and longitudinal designs where SEM is employed (MacCallum & Austin, 2000).

In SEM, subsets of items can be combined into indicators or employed individually. Such composite indicators may be necessary (a) if there are a large number of items, (b) in order to moderate reliability of individual items, (c) if there is a lack of unidimensionality in a set of items (MacCallum & Austin, 2000), or (d) to combine dimensions for more abstract analyses. Bagozzi and Edwards (1998) point out that the careful development and assessment of individual items should precede any aggregation. They note that combinations of items may be misleading if individual items share variance across components, and that the advantages of aggregation may be at the cost of understanding the psychometric properties of a measure. Item combinations could be based on the degree to which items share meaning (Bagozzi & Heatherton, 1994), and items can be combined to form homogeneous parcels or, alternatively, domain-representative parcels (Kishton & Widaman, 1994). The proposed guidelines, with their emphasis on conceptual understanding of measurement error, can provide a basis for several decisions relating to aggregation. For instance, decisions on the number of items or specific items to use in composites can be made by identifying psychometric characteristics, such as shared variance and content.

Measurement models can be described in terms of different ways of combining items to arrive at the overall measure, such as total aggregation, partial aggregation, partial disaggregation, and total disaggregation (Bagozzi & Edwards, 1998; Bagozzi & Heatherton, 1994). In total aggregation, the construct is represented as the sum of items of its measure. An advantage of this model is its simplicity. However, its disadvantage is in not representing dimensions and therefore restricting the ability to study relationships of dimensions with other constructs. Partial aggregation and disaggregation models span the continuum between these extremes. In partial aggregation models, each dimension is a sum of its items, and the dimensions are either indicators of the underlying variable or loosely related to it. In partial disaggregation models, each dimension is a latent variable measured by composites formed by subsets of items. The total disaggregation model treats each dimension of a construct as a distinct latent variable measured by individual items. The disadvantages of this model include the amount of random error in typical items and the number of parameters that have to be estimated.

A large proportion of the recent articles in leading journals that use empirical measures report coefficient alpha based on internal consistency, either exclusively or supplemented with exploratory factor analysis or test-retest reliability. Another sizable proportion of the studies employs confirmatory factor analysis, typically using the same sample to present measurement characteristics and the results of substantive analysis. Such studies often lack sufficient preliminary development of measures and conceptual bases for confirmatory factor analysis. MacCallum and Austin (2000) review studies that employ structural equation modeling from several disciplines and note that few studies employ independent samples to evaluate modified models, which points to the lack of sufficient preliminary assessment. Heavily or exclusively used psychometric procedures, such as internal consistency and exploratory factor analysis, confound random and systematic errors. Yet these procedures are important in preliminary development of measures in order to develop robust items that then can be employed in confirmatory factor analysis and SEM. Improved understanding of measurement error in each psychometric procedure allows the guidelines proposed here for measure development to provide conceptual bases for confirmatory factor analysis and SEM.

A review of the use of SEM in some recent issues of journals in a specific discipline suggests the wide use of coefficient alpha and, to a much lesser extent, exploratory factor analysis.[1] Several studies report coefficient alphas for some measures while using data analysis techniques such as ANOVA or regression. Some studies report exploratory factor analysis in addition to coefficient alpha. Many articles employ coefficient alpha, in some instances supplemented with exploratory factor analysis. Some articles employ coefficient alpha and confirmatory factor analysis (CFA). Some articles employ SEM to assess substantive relationships.

The large percentage of studies that exclusively report internal consistency or supplement it with exploratory factor analysis would greatly benefit from employing measures developed using guidelines in Chapter 5. These guidelines are likely to lead to more robust items that can be employed in a variety of situations. Several papers report the use of coefficient alpha (and, to a lesser extent, exploratory or confirmatory factor analysis) for specific measures followed by analysis not involving SEM, such as experimental design or regression. Such papers do not use SEM for a variety of reasons and thus do not take into account measurement error in assessing substantive relationships. The analytical framework and guidelines in Chapter 5, with emphasis on the preliminary stages of measure development, would provide a more robust set of items tested for likely applications. If previously validated scales are being employed in new applications, then additional measurement data need to be reported to show the psychometric properties of the scales in new settings or samples.

Some studies report the results of CFA. In many studies, the same sample was employed to present measurement characteristics and results of substantive analysis. Other reviews of SEM applications suggest similar findings (MacCallum & Austin, 2000). One study reported deleting items following CFA, whereas another reported retaining items despite marginal performance in CFA because of its content. Again, the framework in Chapter 5 could provide a more informational basis for such decisions and perhaps a lesser need to delete items at later stages. The guidelines in Chapter 5 provide a robust set of items; a conceptual basis to evaluate the strength of evidence of discriminant and convergent validity in light of the design; a conceptual basis for modification of measures after CFA, including item deletion (presently, the same sample is often employed for exploratory and confirmatory analyses as well as for tests of hypotheses); and a conceptual basis for specifying models with method factors or correlated errors.

For studies employing SEM, the framework and guidelines in Chapter 5 would provide a basis to develop the measurement model to provide reliability estimates, to specify errors and method factors, and to form composites through combinations of items. For methodological design, the development of measures through the use of the guidelines, tested for different sequencing and other usage conditions, reduces the likelihood of across-measure systematic error. In summary, several researchers have cautioned against the improper use of SEM. Several quotes are presented below that capture the key point made here.

> The widespread, and basically correct, view that SEM corrects for measurement error may have promoted an over reliance on the method that is not justified. Using a statistical technique that accounts for measurement error does not imply that we should reduce efforts to understand measurement error and expunge it whenever possible. . . . SEM successfully corrects for measurement error, but the correction is as good as the information provided. (DeShon, 1998, p. 421)

> There is much to gain in theory testing and the assessment of construct validity from separate estimation (and respecification) of the measurement model prior to the simultaneous estimation of the measurement and structural submodels. . . . Rather than as a strict dichotomy, then, the distinction in practice between exploratory and confirmatory analysis can be thought of as that of an ordered progression. . . . Because initially specified measurement models almost invariably fail to provide acceptable fit, the necessary respecification and reestimation using the same data mean that the analysis is not exclusively confirmatory. (Anderson & Gerbing, 1988, p. 412)

Implications for Applied Research

Many of the issues discussed in this book are as important for applied research as they are for basic research. In fact, issues such as the incorporation of usage conditions are critical in applied research in enhancing generalizability of research conclusions. A few issues are emphasized below for illustrative purposes. Conceptual understanding of that "thing" being measured is as important in applied research as anywhere else. The key here, as in academic research, is to understand the abstract words being used to draw inferences from data. Consider an insurance company that wants to assess risk aversion (Churchill & Iacobucci, 2004). It is very important to first understand the domain of risk aversion and the area of risk (e.g., financial, physical) that is relevant. A set of items may well look like it captures risk aversion, yet the iterative process of traversing the conceptual to operational, with conceptual understanding as the starting point, is critical. Consider a customer feedback survey administered by a hotel. These surveys, usually available in rooms or lobbies of hotels, measure customer satisfaction. The first step in developing such measures should be to define the construct and delineate the domain (e.g., ease of registration, room service, quality of restaurant). Then, items should be developed to measure each component. In this way, diagnostic information about areas requiring improvement can be obtained. Validation during pretesting would be very useful. In terms of measurement error, random error may occur because of a variety of factors, such as respondents completing the survey in a hurry (i.e., being unable to complete). Additive systematic error may occur because of factors such as respondents inflating ratings while still in the hotel. Within-measure or across-measure correlational systematic error may occur because of halo effects across items of a measure that assess different components. The sample itself is self-selected, which leads to error in a category different from measurement error, as discussed in a subsequent chapter.

Measurement issues come into play in practice when measures or available data are equated with constructs. Hence, the Dow Jones average *is* stock market performance; the measure is used interchangeably with the construct. Other measures, such as the S&P 500, may be more accurate, and the Dow Jones Industrial Average may have systematic error based on the mix of companies included. Yet it is often used interchangeably with the underlying construct (i.e., stock market performance). Consider a company that claims the fewest complaints in the industry, implying here that the number of complaints reflects quality. This begs many questions: What do complaints measure? How are complaints measured? How are these data collected? A company that does not collect complaints would win out. How are complaints categorized? What about their seriousness? If a product is considered poor to begin with, why would consumers complain?

In practice, available data are used to draw inferences about concepts, often without much accuracy. The process of starting with a concept and designing its measurement is reversed. Rather, available data are used and interpreted in terms of abstract constructs. In some sense, data that are already available are used to fit concepts (i.e., secondary data that were not collected for a specific purpose at hand). In such scenarios, a careful assessment of what the measure actually captures and what it leaves out is very important. For instance, a count of complaints should be viewed as providing only a single narrow view into customer satisfaction.

Another issue in measurement in practice is that measurement of self-evident or obvious things such as sales may not be so obvious. Do organizational sales figures take into account discounts and allowances? Is the appropriate computation of sales used (e.g., dollar sales or unit sales)? Is the purpose of using sales to assess performance? If so, what is the domain of performance; what are its dimensions; and are there other measures to employ, such as market share? Conceptual examination of that thing to be measured cannot hurt and almost always helps.

The issue of using single-item scales is particularly relevant in applied research. The effect of the number of items on reliability has been demonstrated in Chapter 1. The use of two- or three-item scales, although reducing respondent effort, compromises the scale in terms of the degree to which items tap the intended common core. With concrete constructs, a single item may be sufficient, such as ROI, although even here, a subjective self-report of ROI relative to main competitors may be useful as supplemental information. For abstract constructs, the use of few items affects the degree to which a domain is adequately represented. Moreover, also affected is the ability to demonstrate psychometric properties such as dimensionality and internal consistency. A sufficient number of items are needed to meaningfully assess internal consistency and dimensionality. Otherwise, the assumption of a common core that is the intended common core is open to question, as is the researcher's ability to demonstrate psychometric properties. No matter how self-sufficient a single-item scale looks, even if the item taps a concrete construct, alternative ways of measuring it may be possible. As mentioned, ROI could be measured through (a) a direct number for ROI; (b) a response on a subjective scale from very low to very high; (c) a relative measure vis-à-vis competitors in the industry, such as "higher than" or "much higher than"; or (d) a scale with percentage of companies below or above, just to list a few possibilities. By including multiple items, several benefits may ensue. Multiple items allow for demonstration of psychometric properties. Multiple items allow for some sort of averaging of errors. They allow for unanticipated consequences of idiosyncratic wording. They enable coverage of different aspects of a domain. They enable a variety of covariations and relationships with other measures by increasing variation. Increased number of items translates to increased scale variance and therefore increased potential for covariance. And they may serendipitously lead to identification of distinct factors. This is not to suggest long, repetitive scales just for the purposes of boosting reliability, as indicated by the effect that the number of items has on coefficient alpha in Chapter 1. In fact, such an approach may be counterproductive; long measures and procedures can lead to fatigue and undermine reliability and validity.

Also of central importance in applied research is validating measures in specific usage conditions. Data collection in applied research may be conducted in a variety of settings. Different methods of administration may be used in applied research, such as personal surveys, online surveys, telephone surveys, and mail surveys. Measures need to be validated for specific usage conditions, such as specific methods of administration.

Summary

Issues covered in the preceding chapters have important implications for researchers who are not developing new measures but using existing measures. The taxonomies of error and error sources are central in evaluating and using existing measures with or without modification. Modification has to be undertaken with care to minimize error and build on prior validation of a measure. Implications also extend to the use of SEM. The proposed framework and guidelines can provide a robust set of items for SEM to begin with as well as sufficient preliminary work and theoretical justification for measurement models in SEM. Finally, many of the issues discussed in this book are as important for applied research as for basic research.

Note

1. A review of 3 years of journals in the area of marketing was conducted, specifically *Journal of Marketing, Journal of Marketing Research,* and *Journal of Consumer Research*. This is necessarily a superficial analysis that misses the nuances of each individual study. The aim here is not in any way to question the use of measurement procedures in these studies but to provide a rough overview of the degree of usage of various procedures. All papers involving measurement of latent traits that mentioned measurement indicators were examined. This search, of course, excluded papers based on analytical modeling or qualitative research methods. It should be noted that, in rare instances, studies reported no measurement indicators even when it may have been required. Similarly, other studies were not complete in reporting measurement information on all measures.

10

How Does Measurement Error Affect Research Design?

Overview

Chapter 10 is similar to Chapter 9 in its focus on the entire research design. As mentioned, the principles described in measuring one thing are used in measuring and manipulating multiple things (i.e., in the design of an entire method). Whereas Chapter 9 focused generically on research design and analysis, Chapter 10 focuses on specific research methods. A method comprises the choice of a type of design (e.g., a lab experiment vs. a survey), operationalization of key variables (whether measured or manipulated), samples and settings, and procedures. The method consists of everything done to collect the data. In other words, included in the method are who provides the data (sample), where they provide the data (setting), on what they provide the data (measures and manipulations), and how they provide the data (administration procedures).[1]

In this chapter, different types of designs are evaluated on the basis of the measurement framework developed earlier. Experimental designs are addressed in depth, survey designs having been addressed in several chapters earlier, with parallels between the two discussed here. Other areas covered include strength of tests of hypotheses[2] and methodological replications. The chapter concludes with a broader discussion of the application of measurement principles to the research method.

Some basics of survey design are covered in Appendix 10.1 to provide background to readers unfamiliar with this area. A simple and poorly designed study is used to illustrate experimental designs in Appendix 10.2. This example may be useful to readers with a nonexperimental background in familiarizing themselves with the terminology. This is followed by a basic discussion of the four types of validity of research designs in Appendix 10.3. The terminology introduced in these appendices is used throughout this chapter.

Types of Research Designs

The measurement framework proposed here applies to all aspects of a methodological design in addition to individual measures. The design of a method to test substantive hypotheses involves choices relating to the setting, sample, and operationalization of variables. Issues relating to the validation of measures directly translate to methodological design. Regarding terminology, correlational designs and surveys are used equivalently; the term *questionnaire* is not used to describe types of research designs because questionnaires can be used in both experiments and surveys.

Methods can be divided into correlational designs, where, at an extreme, all variables are continuous and measured, and experimental designs, where at least one independent variable is manipulated and categorical in nature. Defining characteristics of pure experiments include the *manipulation* of levels of a variable (the independent or causal variable) to study its effects on other variables (the dependent or effect variables) and random assignment of respondents to treatment versus control conditions. A continuous independent variable can also be incorporated into an experimental design. Surveys at the other extreme use a correlational approach and measure independent and dependent variables. Noteworthy in experiments is that independent variables may be manipulated in pure experiments or "naturally occurring" in quasi-experiments. The distinction can be blurred in that a correlational design could be analyzed as an experimental design by categorizing a continuous variable. Correlational designs involve measurement of all constructs, whereas pure experimental designs involve manipulation of at least one independent variable. Quasi-experiments occur, in that a categorical variable is measured or naturally occurring (e.g., smoker vs. nonsmoker, or one industry vs. another). Moreover, researchers may often examine differences in means across different levels of a measured variable. Or researchers may study a variable such as organizational size and examine data as a quasi-experiment. The point is that the distinction between experiments and surveys can be blurred, and experiments versus surveys or correlational designs can be viewed as a continuum as shown in Figure 10.1, using an experimental example from Appendix 10.2 on the effects of sales training.

Experimental Design

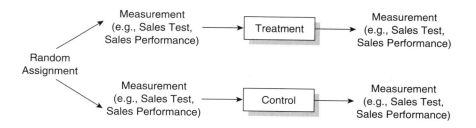

Correlational Design

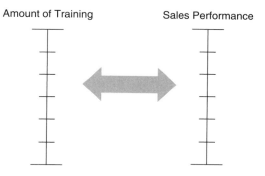

Quasi-Experimental Design

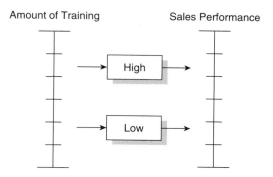

Figure 10.1   Illustration of Experimental Versus Correlational Versus
Quasi-Experimental Designs

The aim in research is usually to make causal inferences from data; therefore, the experimental approach is important in understanding survey design as well. In fact, each of these paradigms can benefit from the other. For instance, experimental designs devote considerable attention to clean inferences of causality. The issues discussed are very relevant in developing sequencing of measures in surveys to minimize across-measure correlational systematic error due to sources such as hypothesis guessing. Similarly, survey research has devoted considerable attention to question wording and related issues, as well as the measurement of a specific construct—issues that are important for the measurement of dependent variables in experiments. Different paradigms focus on different aspects of a design (i.e., implicitly prioritize different aspects of a design), sometimes allocating less attention to other aspects. For instance, the measurement of dependent variables in experiments and the sequencing of measures to make inferences of causality in survey designs are aspects that may receive relatively less attention. Essentially, prioritization of some aspects of a design may reduce the degrees of freedom on other aspects, and trade-offs may be inherent in decisions about the design. Nevertheless, lessons learned from one paradigm can be applied with benefit in the other paradigm. A causal mentality is important in designing surveys and ordering measures, as emphasized in the earlier chapters. The same issues that apply to experiments, such as threats to construct validity, apply here (e.g., hypothesis guessing). Hence, a pertinent issue is how such effects can be minimized in structuring a survey and supplementing it with data from other sources, such as from secondary data.

Measurement Error in Survey Design

A key difference between the survey tradition in applied areas and academic research is that the latter is usually not focused on accurate estimates of absolute values but rather on relationships between variables. This is reflected in the procedures for assessing reliability and validity. Ultimately, validity is really about how a measure is used. Therefore, whether a measure is used to obtain accurate absolute estimates, predict cutoffs, or study correlations, each has a bearing on the types of validity that are germane. Predictive validity is particularly important in applied settings, where variables such as future job performance are predicted from measured variables.

A key concern with survey questions is that measurement error has to be reduced before the fact, particularly when using single items in questioning about specific issues. Here, it is all the more important to edit questions before the fact, and some excellent guidelines are available (Converse & Presser, 1986; Sudman & Bradburn, 1982). Pretesting becomes critical in such situations to ensure that questions are being interpreted as intended. A variety of procedures are available, such as think-alouds (Sudman, Bradburn, & Schwarz, 1996). The process by which respondents provide a response to a survey question has been argued to have several steps, such as interpreting the question (both literally and pragmatically), generating an opinion (either retrieving a previous opinion or computing one), formatting the response, and editing the response (Sudman et al., 1996).

In this regard, as mentioned in Chapter 1, many questions are really just that and do not purport to assess an underlying abstract construct. For instance, they may assess specific behaviors, such as spending on entertainment. Nevertheless, examination of the intended thing being measured, using the measure development process described, can be very beneficial. Such examination may result in a focus on a broadened set of phenomena. It may also result in item wording that enables consistent interpretation. For example, with entertainment spending, pertinent questions relate to what entertainment is and what is included or excluded. Such examination can lead to insights about precise wording of the question, as well as a broadened examination of multiple issues about these phenomena through several questions.

In designing questions in surveys, various types of measurement error are germane. Questions that respondents are unable to answer may usually lead to random error. Lengthy surveys, ambiguous questions ("Do you spend money on recreational activities regularly?"),[3] complex questions, double-barreled questions (e.g., "Do you like the price and quality of this product?"), difficult questions, questions requiring estimates ("How much beer did you drink last year?"), vague questions ("How much did you spend on entertainment last year?"), and vague response categories ("How much coffee do you usually drink? A lot, Quite a bit, . . .") all likely cause random error. Whether respondents are able to answer a question has to be determined by the researcher before administering a survey; often, respondents may provide an answer when asked to do so. In this regard, Sudman and Bradburn (1982) draw a parallel between a survey and a conversation. A conversational norm is that the questions asked are those to which people are likely to know the answer. In a research setting, this norm may actually be accentuated in the view of the respondent; after all, the researcher ought to know what to ask and what the respondent should know. Examples of responses that express an opinion about nonexistent congressional acts or organizations, even when a *don't know* or *no opinion* option is provided, have been used in the survey literature to illustrate this point. Not knowing about an issue and unable to answer it, respondents may provide a random response. Such questions that respondents are unable to answer likely lead to random error in that inconsistent responses may be provided across time. Similarly, clear definitions of terms used in questions (e.g., what is or is not included in "entertainment" in "How much did you spend on entertainment last year?") likely reduce random error. This is because specific questions are more likely to be interpreted consistently across time and across people. A thought experiment has to be conducted to assess reliability: Will the question lead to the same response across time from a particular individual, assuming a sufficient time interval where the phenomenon has not changed and memory for the first response is not an issue? When respondents are unwilling to answer, systematic error is likely to result. Leading questions, biased wording, and questions about embarrassing behavior and private information are likely to cause systematic error. Such error may be additive (e.g., the result of a leading question eliciting inflated or deflated responses) or correlational (e.g., individual differences in social desirability leading to consistent differences across individuals over and above the construct in question). Sometimes, questions about private information may also cause random responses and random error. As discussed earlier, inability is likely to cause random error, whereas unwillingness is likely to cause systematic error. There are many exceptions, however. If a question is considered intrusive (e.g., income), respondents may provide a random response, resulting in random error. A question that respondents are unable to answer may lead to the use of the middle category, resulting in systematic error.

A variety of recommendations have been made when asking questions about behavior: (a) making the question specific (e.g., asking about behavior in a specific time period rather than about usual behavior), (b) relating the time period to the saliency of the topic, (c) using available records to improve recall, (d) using diaries when frequent behavior is being studied, and (e) using simple language that everyone would understand (Sudman & Bradburn, 1982). When asking questions that require estimates, a shorter time frame (e.g., "How much beer did you drink yesterday?" rather than "How much beer did you drink last year?") has been recommended (Sudman & Bradburn, 1982) and would likely reduce random error. The aim here is to enable respondents to answer; when respondents are unable to answer, random error may result. When asking threatening questions about behavior, recommendations include (a) using informants; (b) using response formats such as sealed envelopes or numbered cards; and (c) couching questions in nonthreatening language, including a casual approach or an "everybody" approach (e.g., in asking about specific behaviors, starting out with a sentence that suggests the behavior is common, such as, "Many people have been . . .") (Sudman & Bradburn, 1982).

With response scales, repeating the discussion from Chapter 8, a prescription for the number of response categories in a scale has been to use seven (plus or minus two) scale points (Cox, 1980). The rationale here is that too few scale points do not provide sufficient gradation. Reliability may increase with an increase in the number of response categories up to a point (Bendig, 1954). However, too many response categories may be confusing and effortful for respondents to complete, as well as cause unreliability. For example, rating liking for a product or person on a 100-point scale may cause inconsistent responses across time or across items because of the difficulty in managing 100 response categories. Using research that has shown that humans can chunk about five pieces of information, researchers have argued for five to nine response categories (Cox, 1980). It should be noted here, though, that a 5-point scale with extreme scale points (e.g., *poor–excellent*) can, in effect, be used as a 3-point scale. Other considerations here include the nature of the rating task. In the speech quality scale discussed earlier (Exhibit 1.5), fully labeled 5-point scales were used because of the complex nature of the stimuli and the need for meaningful levels of responses that were appropriately labeled. Moreover, another consideration in some situations may be to use a meaningful number of response categories, even when respondents may be able to reliably discriminate to a greater degree (Viswanathan et al., 2004). Consider, for example, consumers who think about calorie content of chewing gum in terms of three response categories (high, medium, or low). Say that rating scales are used to draw inferences about meaningful differences between brands of chewing gum. If scales with seven response categories are used, they may be more reliable in capturing variation. However, the 3-point scale may provide more valid inferences about differences on calorie content of chewing gum that actually affect behavior. Hence, what constitutes validity depends on how scales and data are used.

Researchers have also pointed out that response categories serve informative functions (Schwarz & Hippler, 1991). For example, the range of hours of TV watching that are provided (e.g., *Up to a half hour–More than 2.5 hours* versus *Up to 2.5 hours–More than 4.5 hours*) (Schwarz & Hippler, 1991) can lead to very different outcomes. Respondents may interpret the question and the likely distribution of responses from response categories. Researchers have documented the effects of ordering of response categories, such as income levels from low to high versus high to low. Similarly, when surveys of satisfaction at a business use such response categories as *excellent, very good, average,* and *below average,* it is not clear how respondents interpret the scale and what the midpoint is. Moreover, the scale is unbalanced; it does not have corresponding negative and positive labels. In this regard, both the response scale and the question should be balanced.[4] For example, "Was it a mistake?" generally should be worded "Was it right or wrong?" and "Do you like . . . ?" generally should be worded "Do you like or dislike . . . ?" Unbalanced questions or response categories could lead to additive systematic error or within-measure correlational systematic error because of such factors as individual differences in social desirability.

Labeling of all response categories can serve to make levels of a continuum meaningful to respondents (e.g., the figure on speech quality in Exhibit 1.5). However, labeling can be problematic when labels conveying equal intervals are not readily available. In such situations, it may be preferable to label just the ends of the scale. Consider the set of response categories *not at all, a little, neutral, a lot,* and *very much* to a question about liking for a product or person. In effect, the response categories convert this 5-point scale to a 3-point scale (i.e., what is the difference between *a lot* and *very much*?). Moreover, the ambiguous labeling likely causes random error because extreme and moderately extreme labels may be used interchangeably (i.e., inconsistently). The numbering of response categories may also have an effect. Response categories numbered −5 to +5 may be interpreted differently from those numbered 0 to 10. In fact, the former has been shown to lead to underuse of the lower half of a scale measuring degree of success in life (Schwarz, Knauper, Hippler, Noelle-Neumann, & Clark, 1991). The zero was associated with absence of success, whereas negative numbers were associated with failure. In a frequency scale end anchored *rarely* to *frequently,* with a numbering of 0 versus 1 for the low end, the use of zero appeared to lead to interpretation of *rarely* as *never* (Grayson, Schwarz, & Hippler, 1995).

As discussed, whenever possible, objective numbers may be preferable to ambiguous labels (e.g., frequency of coffee drinking in terms of number of cups of coffee versus labels such as *often* or *seldom*) to enable their consistent interpretation and use. Another issue with response scales is whether to provide a *don't know* option. On one hand, this can be used as a "lazy" option. On the other hand, if a sizable proportion of individuals are likely to not know enough to respond, then the lack of a *don't know* option can lead to error, such as random error. A different approach is to not provide an explicit *don't know* option and instruct respondents to leave the scale unanswered if they have no knowledge but provide a response if they have some basis to do so. Another issue with response scales is whether to number response categories. A possible advantage for numbered response categories is that equal intervals are directly conveyed rather than spatially organized. With many response categories, such as 9-point scales, numbering may lessen the effort required to provide a response when compared to spatially arranged response categories without numbering.

Order effects should also be considered in questionnaires. In deciding the sequence of questions, it is useful to have a causal mentality, as in experimental designs, to understand how subsequent questions will be influenced by responses to earlier questions, and therefore to choose the best ordering. With the sequencing of questions in a questionnaire, recommendations include the following: (a) arranging questions to increase variety and reduce response sets, (b) completing questions in a topic before moving to other topics, (c) using chronological order in collecting histories, (d) placing threatening questions at the end, and (e) generally starting with broad questions and moving to specific questions (Sudman & Bradburn, 1982). Across-measure (question) correlational systematic error is central in surveys, particularly with regard to sequencing. A funnel approach has been suggested in moving from broad to specific issues (e.g., "How are our relations with other countries?" to "How are our relations with Russia?") (Sudman & Bradburn, 1982, p. 220). If the narrower question were asked first, the answer to the narrower question would overly influence the answer to the broader question. The broader question is both logical to the respondent and less likely to influence response to the narrower question. Thus, a causal mentality is as essential in designing surveys as it is in designing experiments in academic research.

Another central issue in survey design is the method of administration, such as personal surveys, telephone surveys, online surveys, or mail surveys. Here, the importance of usage conditions emphasized in earlier chapters needs to be highlighted. The reliability and validity of individual measures need to be demonstrated for the specific method of administration to be employed. Similarly, potential errors in a research design, such as across-measure systematic error, need to be assessed for the specific usage condition, that is, the method of administration to be used. Methods of administration differ in a number of ways, such as their suitability in administering different types of questions, potential for biasing responses, and degree of control over the sequencing of questions. Factors such as yea-saying, social desirability, and use of middle versus extreme response categories may differ across different methods of administration, with implications for different types of error.

Measurement Error in Experimental Design

Overview of Experimental Design

The purpose of an experiment is to demonstrate causality. Some characteristics include an independent variable that is manipulated, random assignment, and control groups. Manipulations do not involve measurement of a latent trait but may involve creation of levels of a latent variable. A key point to note in an experiment is that anything that occurs later is influenced by anything that precedes it. This obvious yet profound notion is critical in designing the research method. Three types of evidence of causality discussed in the context of experimental designs are association or covariation, time order of cause-effect in terms of temporal precedence of cause, and elimination of other possible causal factors. A lab experiment may have all three, a field experiment the first two, and a survey the first. Data from correlational studies can be viewed as quasi-experiments when assessing differences across levels of a categorical variable (e.g., categorizing firms, industries, or people) (Figure 10.1).

Measurement is central in the process of developing reliable and valid manipulations (Perdue & Summers, 1986). Manipulations involve creating levels of an independent variable rather than measuring it (Figure 10.2). Manipulation checks involve measuring manipulations to see if levels of an independent variable have been achieved. Creating effective manipulations involves the same issues as creating good measures. It starts with the conceptual definition. In this respect, manipulations may be more difficult to create as the distance between the conceptual and the operational increases. To assess a manipulation, the convergence between a manipulation of a variable and its measurement needs to be examined through a manipulation check (Figure 10.3). For example, if the strength of an argument in an advertisement is being manipulated, different treatment levels of the ad need to be assessed through manipulation checks. Divergence between a manipulation and measures of variables that it is not supposed to manipulate needs to be assessed as well through confounding checks (Figure 10.3). For example, the manipulation of argument strength should not lead to a manipulation of, say, amount of information presented or complexity of information. Manipulation and confounding checks for assessing manipulations parallel convergent and discriminant validity in assessing measures. Ruling out all possible confounding variables when manipulating an abstract construct may not be feasible, but plausible alternatives need to be ruled out. With a two-factor design, the manipulations of the two factors need to be independent. Manipulations need to be reliable and valid. Reliable manipulations are those that have a consistent effect on respondents. Valid manipulations are those that manipulate the intended construct and do not manipulate other constructs.

Pretests (used to refer to tests of some aspect of the experiment) and pilot tests (used to refer to tests of the entire experiment) are invaluable in (a) ensuring that investment in the experiment is judicious and that an entire

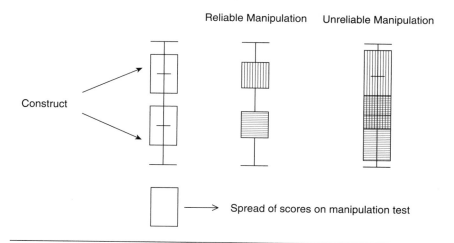

Figure 10.2   Experimental Manipulations—Generating Levels of Construct

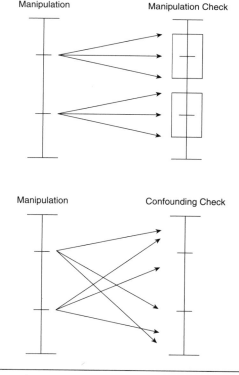

Figure 10.3   Manipulation and Confounding Checks

experiment is not completed without checking if a manipulation worked and (b) providing a basis to make design choices about all aspects of the operationalization. Open-ended approaches can be used to assess experimental procedures as well as the adequacy of various procedures, and instructions.

In experiments, levels of the independent variable should allow for sufficient variation in the dependent variables. Hence, the generated level of an independent variable should allow for sufficient variation in key dependent variables—that is, the dependent variables ideally should be in the middle of the effective range (usually but not always the middle of the actual range; for example, in a true/false recognition test where pure guessing can lead to 50% accuracy, calibration should be adjusted accordingly). This process of calibration aims to ensure sufficient variation to test hypotheses; hence, the irrelevance of experimental conditions. Clearly, different experimental conditions can lead to high or low levels of dependent variables. For example, in memory research, the number of items used as stimuli should be calibrated to enable variation in recall, recognition, or other memory tests. In researching organizations, a variety of companies need to be selected in a sample to achieve variation in dependent variables. This necessity may lead to the inclusion of organizations across industries.

In experimentation, there is a constant trade-off in designing a manipulation between making the test too strong (i.e., loading the die against) and too weak. The manipulation has to be designed to generate levels of the independent variable while not manipulating levels of confounding variables. Sufficient differences between levels of the independent variable should be generated; however, stark differences may lead to confounding variables, such as hypothesis guessing.[5] Consider a scenario where the status connoted by a product is to be manipulated to be high, medium, or low. The stimuli need to be developed to evoke status. A strong manipulation could directly state that a product is of high status or low status. Such a manipulation could be made subtler by couching the claim in other information. A strong manipulation runs the risk of hypothesis guessing. This is akin to within-measure correlational systematic error in that stimuli differ over and above the construct in question. Thus, a subtler manipulation of status may be preferred, which, in turn, runs the risk of being too weak. Pretests should ascertain whether subtler manipulations evoke status considerations. This is the constant trade-off between strong and subtle manipulations, the extremes being a direct statement of a manipulation level (or even a direct statement of the hypothesis!) versus a weak manipulation. By confounding constructs being measured, the validity of a manipulation is called into question.

The most direct form of testing is to ask respondents about a hypothesis (i.e., the relationship between two constructs). Distinct from this extreme, relatively indirect testing would involve obtaining data on individual constructs and assessing or computing association between them. Here, respondents may be aware of the relationships being tested. Alternatively, respondents may not be aware of the relationships being assessed but aware of the constructs on which data are being collected. Relatively more indirect testing occurs when respondents are not aware of the individual constructs being measured and the relationship being tested. Thus, relatively more indirect approaches may be beneficial from this perspective. Whether respondents are aware of hypotheses under study, aware of constructs and relationships under study, aware of individual constructs being studied but not of relationships, or not aware of constructs or relationships is the pertinent continuum here. Awareness of a construct being measured or of the relationship being measured could be decreased through administration procedures as well, such as interspersion of items from different measures or separation of measures discussed earlier. Administration factors, such as cover stories, separation of focal variables, and interspersion of items from different variables, would serve to disguise relationships being examined and constructs being measured.

Successful manipulations usually elicit certain levels of a construct without respondents' awareness of constructs and/or relationships between constructs or without such awareness affecting subsequent responses. Ideally, respondents should be unaware of the elicited dimension through subtle manipulations. The ideal manipulation may achieve its purpose without tipping off the respondent as to the constructs or the relationships being studied. The construct in question is manipulated and the intended effect is achieved without the respondent being aware of the measured or manipulated constructs. Alternatively, if respondents are aware of elicited dimensions, their responses should be unaffected by this awareness. Whether responses are affected by awareness of constructs being manipulated or measured needs to be determined in pretests or pilot tests. If affected, their effects have to be interpreted in light of the nature of the results and the direction of the effects. Drawing an uninformed parallel with Heisenberg's uncertainty principle that both the location and energy of an electron cannot be specified simultaneously, because location requires the use of energy that displaces the electron, the goal of a successful treatment is to elicit levels of a construct without focusing attention on it. An interesting example of the very process of measurement altering the phenomenon being measured is provided by the "stereotype threat" in ability tests. Significant differences in scores have been reported for individuals of specific ethnic backgrounds based on the cover story provided to them. Steele (1997) used a design where

African American and Caucasian students were assigned to two conditions: one where they were told their intellectual ability was being measured and another where they were told the test was unrelated to ability. They completed a test consisting of difficult verbal items from the GRE. Caucasian students scored higher than the African-American students in the former (threat) condition, but differences were not found in the latter (nonthreat) condition. These results were consistent with the prediction that was made on the grounds that informing past victims of stereotyping that their ability is being measured affects their performance. Thus, differences in scores are obtained depending on the stated purpose of the test—ability testing versus something else.

This telling example highlights the insidious nature of demand characteristics in interfering with the measurement process. It highlights the Heisenberg uncertainty principle in social science measurement. The very act of measuring a construct affects its measurement. This is the case when respondents are made aware of the "construct" being measured. Their awareness influences responses in several ways, resulting in systematic error or even random error. The example above represents a convergence of experimental and individual difference approaches. Another example (Dehaene, 1997) relates to a horse named Hans, who could "count"! In Germany in the early 1900s, Hans was "taught" to count by his trainer (Dehaene, 1997). When given a simple arithmetic problem, Hans tapped his hoof the correct number of times. Demonstrations were often conducted whereby the public posed a problem to the trainer (e.g., 5 + 3). The trainer then placed five objects and three objects, respectively, on different tables. Hans tapped his hoof eight times! He also added fractions and found divisors. Although a team of experts concluded that the feat was authentic, one psychology student probed further. Changing the method, this student presented a panel to the trainer and the horse, except that the problem was altered slightly so that the trainer saw 6 + 2, but Hans saw 6 + 3. He made errors, providing responses that were correct for the problem posed to the trainer. It appeared that Hans was sensing minor involuntary movements of the trainer's head or eyebrows when the correct number of knocks was reached. He was really sensing his trainer's reaction when the correct number of hoof taps was reached.

Experimental designs start by isolating the dimension to be manipulated when designing stimuli. Design of stimuli should aim to generate levels of the dimension in question yet ideally avoid making respondents aware of such elicitation. Pretests should aim to assess whether stimuli achieve levels of the construct being manipulated through multiple item measures. (As in item generation during measure development, it might be necessary and efficient to start out with a larger set of manipulations than required, for purposes of pretesting.) Open-ended responses to stimuli that follow such manipulations in pretests offer a means of assessing responses across treatment levels. Manipulation checks also can be embedded among other measures of potentially confounding variables as a way of gaining initial insight into discriminant validity. Such pretests could also include open-ended responses to pointed questions about the stimuli along specific dimensions. Subsequent pretests could fine-tune the stimuli with the aim of manipulating the focal construct without confounding such attempts with other variables. The notion that successful measurement and manipulation are achieved by respondents being unaware applies to hypothesis testing but is not universally the case, of course. Transparent measurement may be preferable in many situations, for, say, measuring liking for a product or person. Note, though, that the aim here is not to test hypotheses but to measure a specific variable. If the relationship between liking and purchase is to be assessed, it may be necessary to disguise the purpose of the study through separation or other means. To summarize, human beings have complex motivations and, when aware of the purpose of a study, may react differently. Each variable could be measured in an undisguised manner. However, disguising the relationship under study may be worthwhile. Such disguising could be achieved through several means discussed in earlier chapters in the context of designing tests of validity and designing studies involving data collection on multiple measures. Separating variables whose relationships are being tested is one such approach. Alternatively, one or more constructs being measured or manipulated could be disguised.

A key issue in experimental design is to prioritize the sequencing of variables to enable a manipulation of the independent variable(s) and collection of data on the central dependent variables. Independent variables and central dependent variables should be sequenced ahead of other variables to enable a clean inference of causality. If data on individual differences are collected in an experimental context, it may be preferable to sequence such measures after the central dependent variable. For instance, if data on preference for numerical information are collected as a covariate in a study examining individuals' memory for numerical versus verbal information, the manipulation of type of information and the central dependent variable (i.e., memory) should precede the PNI scale. Otherwise, completion of the PNI scale may prime numbers and attention to numerical information. This is not to preclude disguising the independent and dependent variables, such as by using fillers and distracter tasks consistently across all respondents. However, when a relevant variable precedes the independent variable or the central dependent variable, it provides an alternative explanation for differences in the dependent variable across conditions.

Measurement and Manipulation Error in Experimental Design

Measurement issues apply to the choice of appropriate samples in research designs. In sample selection, stimuli are often matched with samples to achieve certain criteria. For example, when using student samples, stimuli may be chosen about which students are knowledgeable. If the goal of a design is to "control" the variable (i.e., knowledge) at a certain level, then pretesting with the appropriate sample should lead to a narrow range or dispersion along a measure of knowledge. Thus, the design of "stimuli" is akin to generating certain levels of dimensions. Whereas some such dimensions are controlled, others are manipulated. If a heterogeneous sample rather than a student sample were employed, then a wider dispersion of knowledge would be obtained. Where the aim is to generate a specific level of knowledge, random error is introduced through dispersion along control variables.

Measurement error is germane to the design of methods through choices relating to settings, sample, and stimuli. In considering such error in an experimental context, the similarities and dissimilarities with a correlational context are noteworthy. For purposes of discussion, consider a simple experiment with one independent variable manipulated at two levels and one measured dependent variable. The issue of systematic error within measures versus across measures is blurred in an experimental context. In a correlational design, within-measure correlational systematic error could occur wherein responses reflect differences across individuals over and above the construct in question. On the other hand, across-measure systematic error occurs between measures of different constructs. In experimental designs, the manipulation is not measured but created at specific levels of the independent variable. Therefore, random error, additive systematic error, and within-measure (i.e., within-manipulation) correlational systematic error are germane only when a manipulation is being assessed in pretesting through manipulation checks (i.e., in the measurement of the levels of manipulations achieved). In an experimental context, error is reflected in the measurement of the dependent variable; therefore, errors due to the manipulation are across manipulation/measure, paralleling across-measure systematic error. If there are multiple dependent variables, across-measure systematic error occurs between these dependent variables.

A second way in which experiments are different is in the central importance of differences between groups of individuals representing treatment conditions. Individual differences within a condition are germane in adding to error variance in tests of differences. Differences across conditions are compared to differences within conditions in statistical tests.

Therefore, correlational systematic error, in the sense of differences across individuals over and above the construct in question, can influence error variance while also affecting mean differences between conditions. However, additive systematic error can affect mean differences across conditions. It is useful, in this regard, to treat conditions as the unit of analysis rather than individuals (akin to levels on a stimulus-centered scale), and to consider additive and correlational systematic error for this unit of analysis. Figure 10.4 illustrates this translation of measurement error to an experimental setting. From this perspective, variations within a condition among individuals would be categorized as random error. With these two distinctions, experimental designs are discussed below from the perspective of measurement error. A manipulation is considered first in isolation from the context of pretesting and measuring achieved manipulation levels. Then, the discussion focuses on the effects of the manipulation on dependent variables.

Random error is of concern in the design of experiments among independent variables (Figure 10.2). Random error could result from inconsistent manipulations, which deflate the relationship between independent and dependent variables. Whereas idiosyncratic random error can be accounted for through large samples, generic random error in the manipulation of independent variables in an experiment has similar effects as generic random error in correlational designs. If two levels of a certain variable need to be generated, random error is introduced because of dispersions in ratings of specific levels of dimensions. For example, consider the use of manipulation of message credibility in a distracting setting. Random error would blur the statistical difference between levels of a manipulated variable, reducing the power of the manipulation. Similarly, the use of a heterogeneous sample may cause random error in treatments.

Additive systematic error can occur in experimental manipulations (Figure 10.5). If two levels of a manipulation are inflated upward (downward) as measured by the manipulation check, this is akin to constant additive systematic error (e.g., if two levels of a credibility manipulation intended to be high vs. low are very high and medium). If such inflation is affected by finite ends of the scale, this is akin to partial additive systematic error, as indicated by ratings on manipulation checks being at the high (low) end of the scale (Figure 10.5). In addition to the manipulation, control variables and all other aspects of the design, including the sample and settings, can contribute to such error. For example, a manipulation of the strength of an argument at two levels may lead to constant additive systematic error if both levels are inflated. However, if both levels are inflated to the point of reducing the mean difference between the levels because of finite scale extremes, this is akin to partial additive systematic error. Essentially, the

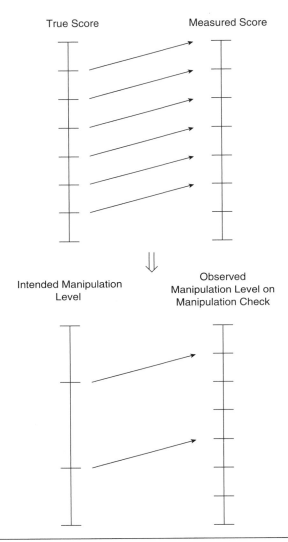

Figure 10.4   Translating Measurement Error to Experimental Settings

intended levels of the manipulation are not achieved. Rather than measure the true score of a respondent on a construct, the goal here is to create certain levels of a construct. Hence, the term *error* is used to refer to deviation from the intended level of a construct, with the measure used as a manipulation check assumed to have been validated (i.e., shown to be reliable and valid). In many scenarios, constant additive systematic error may not be noticed or even relevant because the focus is on achieving differences across

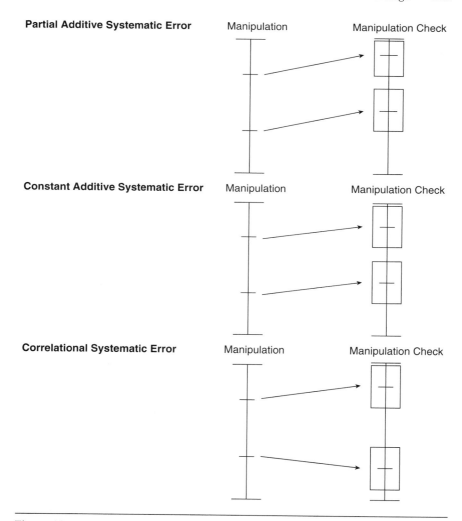

Figure 10.5   Measurement Errors in Manipulating Variables

levels of manipulation. Correlational systematic error would be reflected in differences across levels over and above the intended levels (Figure 10.5). For instance, such error would occur if the difference between two levels of a manipulation is much larger than intended. This may be particularly problematic in a within-subjects design (i.e., where the same respondents are exposed to multiple levels of a factor, as distinct from a between-subjects design, where each group of respondents is exposed to only one level of a factor). For example, when a factor in an experiment is manipulated within subjects, strong manipulations may lead to a carry-over effect. Therefore, this leads to within-manipulation correlational systematic error in terms of differences over and above the construct being manipulated.

Moreover, in any design, the actual calibration of differences may be critical; otherwise, a construct may be confounded with levels of the construct (Appendix 10.3) (Cook & Campbell, 1979). For instance, a construct manipulated at two specific levels may not lead to a significant difference on the dependent variable, yet a stronger manipulation (i.e., a larger difference between the two levels) may lead to significant differences. When manipulations generate levels of unintended constructs (say, a manipulation of product status that leads to a manipulation of product quality or price perception), this is similar to within-measure (across-treatment) correlational systematic error, except that the error is across treatment levels (i.e., generated levels of the intended construct).

With strong manipulations, multiple constructs may be unintentionally manipulated, leading to within-manipulation (across-treatment) systematic error. Weak manipulations may not capture sufficient differences in the construct of interest, whereas strong manipulations may lead to demand artifacts. Strong manipulations can lead to across-manipulation/measure systematic error by evoking confounding variables (e.g., hypothesis guessing) (see Figure 10.6). When a manipulation affects responses to dependent variables, this is akin to across-measure systematic error. However, it could be additive or correlational depending on the nature of the effect across individuals; hence, it is referred to here as across-manipulation/measure systematic error. Issues relating to separation or grouping of measures for validity tests are germane to sequencing manipulations and dependent variables.

In considering the effects of manipulations on dependent variables (i.e., across-manipulation/measure systematic error that is either correlational or additive in nature), several issues are noteworthy. Across-manipulation/ measure systematic error occurs when a manipulation leads to ceiling or floor effects in the dependent variables. Thus, stimuli should be calibrated to minimize such effects. The choice of stimuli should minimize ceiling or floor effects. Here, the design has to be calibrated subtly to avoid too weak or too strong a manipulation. Consider a control variable, such as the amount of information to be presented or the number of pieces of information to employ in a memory task. A choice should be made that enables sufficient variation on the measure of memory by achieving means near 50% through pretests. Similarly, measures of other constructs, such as attitudes, ideally should provide sufficient room for variation and be ascertained through pretests and pilot tests. Amounts that are too high or too low may lead to ceiling and floor effects, respectively, minimizing variance in dependent

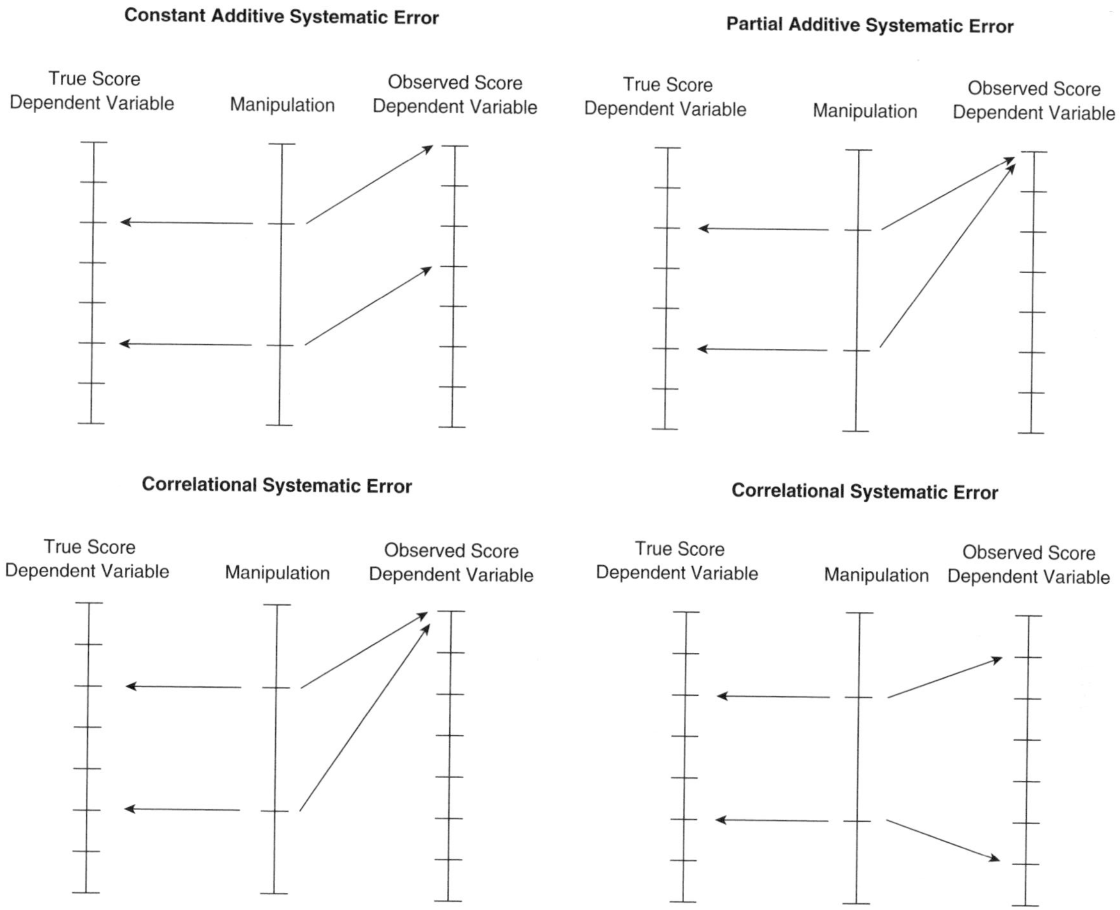

Figure 10.6   Across-Manipulation/Measure Systematic Error

variables (Figure 10.7). With constant additive systematic error, variance will not be affected. But with partial additive systematic error due to finite end points of scales, variance will be affected.

In essence, any methodological design involves certain control variables, and experiments involve manipulated variables as well. Control variables provide the context for the methodological design. For example, if an experiment requires knowledgeable respondents, knowledge may be a control variable. Similarly, if respondents are presented with information, then the amount of information is a control variable. Thus, methodological design involves many control variables. The choice of setting (e.g., classroom or lab), sample, and administration are, in effect, all control variables. The choice of a sample of respondents (such as individuals, companies, industries) should allow for sufficient variation. Experiments often involve a cover story, again aimed at establishing one or more control variables at specific levels. For example, a cover story about sources of product information, such as *Consumer Reports,* may serve to set levels of specific control variables, such as credibility of information. Correlational designs also involve control variables through the choice of settings and samples. For example, the choice of a particular industry for conducting a survey serves to set specific levels of control variables. Sufficient variance among variables is necessary to provide tests of hypotheses. Independent variables need to be designed to achieve sufficient variation in dependent variables in an experimental design. In a correlational design, variation in both independent and dependent variables is required. All of the elements of the design, such as the cover story, need to be tested to assess whether they achieve objectives, including allowing sufficient variation and controlling for specific variables.

As discussed, pilot tests involve the complete procedure used to test hypotheses with a view toward gauging the entire research method on issues such as hypothesis guessing and ceiling or floor effects. Pilot tests should also evaluate across-measure systematic error among dependent variables and across-manipulation/measure systematic error between independent and dependent variables. If there are multiple dependent variables, several sources can cause across-measure systematic error just as is the case with surveys.

The terminology of within-treatments random error, within-manipulation (across-treatment) systematic error, and across-manipulation/measure systematic error provides a means of understanding experimental design from a measurement perspective. Pretests should be used to examine such errors. Hypothesis guessing is the result of across-manipulation/measure or within-manipulation (across-treatment) systematic error, thus suggesting changes in the treatments or in some other aspect of the design, such as the use of filler tasks. Exclusive focus on treatment levels as requiring calibration

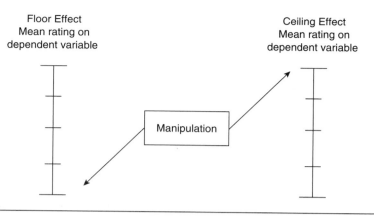

Figure 10.7   Floor and Ceiling Effects

neglects the context of the entire design. Pretests can be employed to elicit treatment levels, whereas pilot tests can assess the entire design.

Correlational designs also require a similar causal mentality wherein individual measures are assessed (instead of treatments) and across-measure systematic error is minimized. Pilot studies can be employed to assess such effects. Although pilot studies may be difficult to implement when data are difficult to obtain (e.g., data from organizations), studies that do not account for such error may not be cost-effective and may lead to the entire sample being used suboptimally. A small holdout sample could be employed to assess factors such as hypothesis guessing through open-ended, think-aloud responses; self-reports on rating scales; and open-ended responses to pointed questions. Think-aloud procedures are employed in survey research to evaluate specific questions. However, such procedures could also be employed to assess entire designs.

Research Design and Measurement Error

This section discusses broader issues in measurement error and research design that are applicable across different methods.

Strength of Tests of Hypotheses

Any research method should be evaluated in terms of its effect on the strength of a test. A weak manipulation can lead to a strong test. Student samples are often associated with <u>lack of involvement</u>. Yet such samples may provide strong tests if hypothesized results are obtained, despite low involvement and "light" attention. However, if light attention in a student sample affects the meaning that respondents assign to an experimental task, and therefore the degree to which underlying constructs are captured, it undermines the construct validity of the design. The problem occurs when hypothesized results for strong tests are not obtained—an issue that should be addressed in pretests and pilot tests while calibrating procedures to achieve manipulation effects with the sample in question. Several procedural details—such as administration in small numbers, computer-based administration, the use of short experimental sessions, provision of incentives, and adjustment of manipulations—warrant attention. The key point to note is that any sample characteristic is not, per se, a positive or a negative. In fact, a seemingly negative characteristic could well lead to strong tests. Thus, any sample characteristic—or, more broadly, methodological characteristic—has to be viewed in light of the entire design in terms of its effects.

Some researchers have argued that brevity and weakness are two characteristics of lab experiments (Ellsworth, 1977). Higher levels of a construct may be qualitatively different, thus confounding a construct with levels of a construct. Suppose that the construct in study is arousal. High levels of arousal may be qualitatively different from milder arousal that is studied in a lab experiment. Field studies with varying levels of a construct need to be conducted to assess generalizability to higher levels of a construct. A highly artificial setting can show what can happen (such as Milgram's studies where participants complied in administering electric shocks) (Mook, 1983). The critical issue here is to ensure that the study captures the essence of the theory being tested through conveying appropriate meaning to participants. As researchers have noted, the meaning that respondents assign to an experimental situation is more important to the generalizability of an experiment than surface-level similarities with reality (Berkowitz & Donnerstein, 1982). From a measurement perspective, is the construct in question being manipulated? Based on the combination of sample, stimulus, and other characteristics—essentially, everything done to collect the data—is the appropriate level of the intended construct being manipulated? All the characteristics of the method are pertinent here.

Methodological Replications

Strict replications of construct relationships are akin to test-retest reliability. A design is replicated exactly in all respects. Are the results consistent without significant changes in operationalizations? Conceptual replications use different operationalizations to test the same conceptual relationships. Such replications are similar to convergent validity. Do different operationalizations of constructs lead to similar results? This is a matter of degree and often, variations in results are explained by differences in levels of moderating variables. Scientific knowledge progresses in several ways: serendipitously, such as through variations in procedures that lead to changes in levels of moderating variables, or systematically, such as through identification of boundary conditions.

With the use of dependent variables that have not been evaluated psychometrically, such as those often employed in experimental designs, the use of conceptual replications takes on added significance. Whether a pattern of results across studies can be uniquely explained by a theory is the aim of such studies. Nevertheless, lacking psychometric assessment of the reliability and validity of operationalizations, a pattern of results is susceptible to a variety of alternative explanations. Preexperimental procedures should strive to establish evidence of the construct validity of operationalizations. Manipulations should be evaluated through manipulation and confounding checks. Dependent variables, including behavioral measures, should be supported through psychometric assessment, conceptually and empirically. When behavioral measures aim to tap into underlying abstract constructs, evidence of psychometric properties can be provided with pretesting. When behaviors are under study (e.g., recreational activities), measures should capture the range of behaviors that represents the relevant domain. Correlational studies require pilot-testing, generally associated with experimental designs, to assess method variance and across-measure systematic error.

Similarly, multiple operationalizations of specific constructs and multiple studies using different methods are recommended to establish construct validity when generalizing from the relationship between specific operationalizations of constructs to constructs. The more divergent the method, the stronger the evidence, somewhat like hearing a surprising piece of information (such as an assassination) from relatively independent sources. Multiple operationalizations enable tests of convergent validity. Multiple manipulations are similar and enable tests of replications, although the unit of analysis here is not specific constructs but relationships between constructs. Distinct from conceptual replications, strict replications provide evidence of the reliability of a result, just as test-retest reliability offers evidence of stability reliability. Are the results replicable across studies (instead of time)? The answer is provided by strict replications.

Parallels Between Measure Validation and Research Design

Measurement concepts relating to individual constructs can be applied to research methods and the relationship between constructs (Figure 10.8).

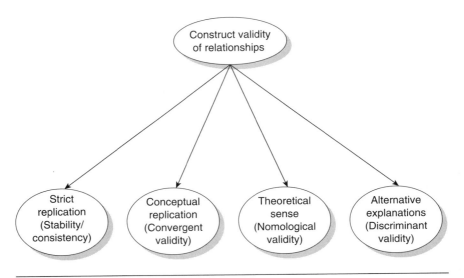

Figure 10.8   Construct Validity of Relationships

Similar to construct validity of a measure of a construct, construct validity
of a relationship is accumulated in several ways. Akin to stability are strict
replications. Internal consistency translates to the extent to which results
in the context of a single study are consistent. For example, if multiple
replications of the same manipulation were used, internal consistency
would parallel the results being replicable or consistent within the study.
Similar to convergent validity are multiple operationalizations that demonstrate the relationship—the more different the operationalizations, the
stronger the evidence. This is similar to different measures of a construct
demonstrating convergent validity—the more divergent or different the
approaches, the stronger the evidence of convergent validity. Conceptual
replications offer evidence of the convergent validity of relationships, that
is, whether different methods lead to similar findings of relationships
between constructs.

Nomological validity for individual measures, in a broad sense, places
measures of constructs in a nomological network. Similarly, relationships
between constructs in different studies can be interpreted in light of a larger
nomological network and theoretical coherence. Thus, are results of association between constructs and interrelationships with other constructs interpretable with plausible theoretical explanations? Are the results amenable to
the larger theoretical knowledge in an area? Are the results interpretable in
light of what is known?[6]

Discriminant validity is provided by the degree to which a measure is discriminating. One aspect of discriminant validity is that a measure is unrelated to other constructs to which it is supposed to be unrelated. Another sense of discriminant validity is in measures having small relationships with measures of related constructs. Moving the unit of analysis up to the level of relationships between constructs, the question of discriminant validity in the sense of nonrelationships is an interesting one. Are patterns of relationships between variables unaffected by certain alternative variables? For example, the moderating effect of a covariate, such as social desirability, should be minimal. Rather than explain the relationships between focal constructs, variables such as hypothesis guessing (i.e., alternative explanations) should be accounted for conceptually and operationally in the design of the research method. Discriminant validity at the level of construct relationships asks whether relationships between measures can be uniquely attributed to constructs, thus making threats to construct validity relevant.

Validity at the level of the research method comes in several forms: (a) whether the findings are strictly replicable either across time (akin to test-retest reliability) or across replications within an administration (akin to internal consistency), (b) whether there is convergence among multiple operationalizations of constructs (akin to convergent validity), (c) whether the operationalizations behave in theoretically expected ways in terms of relationships between constructs (akin to nomological validity), and (d) whether the operationalizations uniquely explain underlying constructs or their relationships (akin to discriminant validity). Strict and conceptual replications, theoretical consistency, and discriminability are at the center of validity. Is the result replicable across time? Across operationalizations? Is the result theoretically consistent? Is the result uniquely attributable to underlying constructs?[7]

In viewing parallels between measure validation and research design, interitem issues translate to intermeasure issues. Random error in item response translates to random error in relationships. Within-measure correlational systematic error translates to across-measure correlational systematic error. Consistency in measuring one thing across items or time translates to consistency in relationships, say, through strict replications. Convergent validity translates to conceptual replications of relationships—the more different the method, the greater the credence. Construct validity here is at the level of the relationship. Thus, at the core, what is essential is (a) consistency or replicability, (b) convergence across multiple operationalizations, (c) compatibility with existing knowledge, and (d) the ability to distinguish alternative explanations of relationships. The framework of measurement of a single construct generalizes to the entire research design. Show consistency or replicability, show convergence across different methods, place results in the context of knowledge to date, and distinguish explanations from alternative plausible explanations. That's it! It's very simple!

Summary

This chapter was similar to Chapter 9 in focus, moving the discussion from measuring one thing to measuring or manipulating multiple things in the entire research design. Understanding the measurement of one thing is central to understanding the measurement or manipulation of many things and the entire design. The principles described in measuring one thing were used in measuring and manipulating multiple things (i.e., in the design of an entire method). Different types of designs were evaluated for error on the basis of the measurement framework developed earlier. Finally, in a broader sense, measurement principles were applied to the research method and the entire research design in terms of strength of tests of hypotheses and methodological replications and in terms of the parallels between measure validation and research design.

Notes

1. For instance, one characteristic of administration procedures is duration. Lengthy procedures might cause fatigue and affect the reliability and validity of latter portions of a data collection process. Sometimes, lengthy procedures may lead to very consistent responses that are reliable but not valid, such as if respondents provide the same response to each item, and all the items are worded in the same direction such that agreement leads to higher scores on the underlying constructs. (A particularly disheartening form of such responses occurs when a single circle is drawn around a specific response category, say, 7 on a 7-point scale, to respond to all the items on a page with one stroke of the pen!) Short, interesting procedures or longer procedures with sufficient breaks and incentives are approaches to consider. Although the demands for the research may require collecting large amounts of data in an administration, the quality of the data may suffer greatly, making the entire process questionable. The length of the procedure is another issue worth pretesting.

A temptation for researchers is to collect as much data as possible in an administration. However, methods need to be designed to enable respondents to participate in a manner that captures the meaning of constructs being studied. The demands on respondents should be reasonable. Longer procedures may need more incentives and sufficient breaks to keep participants involved. In summary, interesting studies that make reasonable demands on time and effort can go a long way toward enhancing reliability and validity.

2. This footnote is intended for readers with minimal research experience. Hypotheses may vary in level of abstractness and are often somewhere between abstract concepts and concrete operationalizations in this respect. Hypotheses that are bound by the context of the proposed method may be relatively concrete, whereas those that are at a more conceptual level may be relatively abstract. The deductive process of moving from abstract theorizing to hypotheses to research method aims to achieve correspondence between theory and method. Ideally, hypotheses should be stated in succinct, testable form. Using a simple example of one independent variable and one dependent variable, hypotheses should specify different levels of a causal variable in a comparative form and the predicted direction of the effect on the dependent variable. Rationale should not be included in the statement of hypotheses. Rather, hypotheses should be stated as succinct predictions.

3. When different individuals interpret an item differently, such as when it is ambiguously worded (e.g., "I like recreational activities," wherein the term *recreational* is interpreted differently), the issue is one of reliability and validity. The need to use consistent procedures and items that are not ambiguous relates to both reliability and validity. Ambiguous words and items may be interpreted differently by the same person, causing unreliability. If the item is consistently interpreted by specific individuals, although differentially interpreted across individuals, it is likely to show high test-retest correlation but perhaps not high internal consistency.

Moreover, it is not clear when ambiguity affects just validity or both reliability and validity; it is likely to affect both. In practical terms, items are designed so that terms are understood similarly by most, if not all, respondents, while minimizing idiosyncratic interpretations. It would be impractical to design a set of items that different individuals interpreted differently but consistently. The purpose would be to achieve reliability and not validity. When items are interpreted differently but consistently by different individuals, the net effect is one of having a measure of many different things for many different people. A summary statistic on this measure essentially would be a summary of very different things that cannot be interpreted meaningfully. If an individual item in a multiple-item measure is interpreted consistently but differently across individuals, it may be identified in internal consistency reliability procedures as leading to responses that are inconsistent when compared to other items interpreted similarly across respondents.

4. A rare situation where unbalanced scales may be used is perhaps when responses are known to occur on one part of a continuum—say, using scales unbalanced in the positive direction when respondents are all known to hold a positive attitude on some issue.

5. Although hypothesis guessing is used throughout this chapter, several conditions have to be fulfilled before it affects responses: demand cues that suggest a hypothesis have to be encoded, the hypothesis has to be discerned accurately, and the respondent has to act on the hypothesis (Shimp et al., 1991). Moreover, hypothesis guessing can result in random or systematic errors (Shimp et al., 1991).

6. The aim here is not to necessarily be consistent with the literature as much as to reconcile current findings with the literature and articulate reasons for differences. The key here is that existing literature not be ignored. Current findings need to be explained in light of the existing literature. This is not to assume that the current literature has to be taken as a given in terms of accuracy but rather to develop theories that are able to explain findings in a stream of research beyond the study in question.

7. The measurement framework is also very useful at the research design level in evaluating econometric models based on relationships between variables. For example, a model to predict catalogue purchases may use variables, such as timing of previous purchase, number of previous purchases, and amount of previous purchase, to predict timing of the next purchase. Such models are often designed to better predict events when compared to existing models, the aim being to use the model with the most predictive accuracy. This is usually demonstrated through greater predictive accuracy. However, other types of validity may be very relevant. Overlaying a measurement framework, convergent validity is, of course, shown through high associations with past measures or, in this case, past models. Convergent validity could be shown through convergence among predictions of two models. However, this may not be sufficient. The aim, after all, is to show the new "measure" to be better. Thus, predictive validity is important. But other types of validity are also germane. In fact, treating the model as a simple self-report measure can help generate additional tests. Several validity tests are implicit in such testing. For instance, predictive validity, or known-group predictive validity when there are different ratings between groups, is one test. Nomological validity through relationships with theoretically relevant variables is another test. Nomological validity translates to showing compatibility with existing knowledge. Discriminant validity through differential predictions of outcomes or through small or nonexistent associations with outcomes is another test. Discriminant validity translates to showing noninfluence of competing variables and explanations. Content validity is implicit in developing the rationale for the proposed model. Content validity here parallels the rationale developed in support of design choices.

Appendix 10.1

Basics of Survey Research Design

This appendix is intended for readers not familiar with survey research. In survey designs, several types of error in addition to measurement error have to be considered. These errors are all the more critical when the goal of research is to generate accurate absolute estimates. Such errors can be roughly categorized into frame error (error arising from mismatch between the lists used to represent the population and the population, such as inclusion of elements in the list not in the population or exclusion of elements from the list that are in the population), sampling error (error inherent in drawing estimates from samples rather than the entire population), nonrespondent or nonresponse error (where nonrespondents are systematically different from respondents); and response or measurement error (Appendix 10.1 Figure). The errors can be viewed as arising from a sequence of events in the method. First, a frame has to be chosen to represent the population, leading to frame error. Next, a sample of respondents has to be selected from the frame, leading to sampling error. In the course of selecting a sample, some individuals chosen to be in the sample may not respond, leading to nonresponse error. Finally, responses collected may deviate from true values, leading to measurement error.

Consider a survey of a sample of university students on binge drinking, wherein 50% of the respondents respond that they have been binge-drunk in the past 2 weeks. Frame error occurs to the extent that the list of students used to represent the population—say, a phone book—includes nonstudents or excludes current students. Nonresponse error is likely to point to a higher rate of binge drinking, assuming that nonrespondents may consist of a disproportionately higher number of frequent binge drinkers who do not want to reveal information about their behavior. In the U.S. presidential election in 2004, frame error in telephone polls may include U.S. citizens living abroad, newly registered voters, and voters who do not own land lines and use their cell phones exclusively. Nonresponse error is likely to occur for 1-day telephone polls that attempt to reach people once and do not afford the opportunity to call back at some other time. Such error may occur because of difficulty in reaching certain types of respondents, say, those with multiple jobs. To the extent that nonrespondents are systematically different from respondents, there is nonresponse or nonrespondent error. Nonresponse error may also occur because of refusal by potential respondents who are systematically different from respondents, say, on alienation from the political process.

target segment

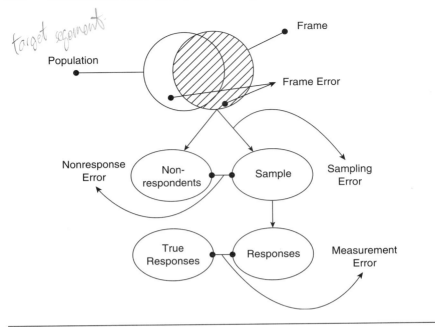

Appendix 10.1 Figure   Types of Error in Survey Designs

Similarly, in a survey on restaurant usage or TV viewing, nonrespondents, when compared to respondents, may be those who rarely visit restaurants or who watch TV infrequently, essentially being less interested in the topic and not participating. With customer satisfaction measurement used by hotels where patrons self-select into the sample, in addition to measurement error, nonresponse error is germane. People may complete the survey because they are very happy or very unhappy with their experience. Therefore, the hotel can seek out a representative sample through random sampling rather than allowing self-selection. Alternatively, the data can be put to appropriate use, not as being representative of all hotel consumers but in identifying problem areas and tracking them longitudinally. In other words, the data could be used as a source of ideas rather than as population estimates.

Nonrespondent and frame errors are akin to additive systematic error in causing bias in one direction. Sampling error is similar to random error in being in either direction. If sampling is probabilistic, then sampling error can be quantified. A key issue here is that measurement error may well be just one contributor to overall error or total error. Thus, focusing on measurement error while neglecting other types of error is an important concern. Nonresponse error or frame error may well overwhelm other types of error.

It should be noted that nonrespondent or nonresponse error and frame error do not relate to how a survey is administered to respondents; they relate to who the respondents are. Hence, these errors are conceptually distinct from measurement error. The latter includes the outcomes of everything done in the course of collecting data from selected respondents. Issues of nonresponse and frame are distinct from administration of surveys to selected respondents. As discussed in Chapter 5, however, the samples are relevant in validating measures across usage conditions, including distinct populations.

Appendix 10.2

Basics of Experimental Design

This appendix is intended for readers not familiar with experimental research. The following discussion borrows from the classic writings of Cook and Campbell (1979). A simple and poorly designed study is discussed to cover the basic terminology of experimental design.

Consider an organization that asks its salespeople to volunteer for 2 months of training in October and November of a year. Before and after the training, they complete a test of their sales knowledge. Their monthly sales before and after the training (i.e., in September and in December) are also monitored. Based on an increase in test scores and in their sales in December when compared to September, a causal inference is made that training caused higher sales and better performance on the test. This poorly designed experiment suffers from several alternative explanations or extraneous variables in addition to the presumed causal variable. It is affected by many factors that can be grouped into certain categories of extraneous variables. First, there is *history,* or events going on that are parallel to and external to the experiment, such as seasonal effects on sales. Second, there is *maturation,* or changes in the experimental units over time that would have happened anyway. Suppose that these salespeople were new employees. The two months of experience may have improved their sales performance merely because of the passage of time. Such a scenario may also occur in experiments where participants are asked twice about their liking for a brand-new product or a recent acquaintance, with an interval of a few months between evaluations. Maturation alone may explain improved ratings as the participants learn more about a product or a person. *Instrument variation* is another category that occurs because of changes in the measurement instrument before and after the training. In this case, if the price of the products being sold changed, then sales may not be comparable across time. If the administered tests differed across time, then the scores may not be comparable across time. *Experimental mortality* occurs when experimental units leave the experiment as it is conducted, say, if several salespeople left the training and the company. It may be impossible to ascertain how these salespeople would have performed if they had stayed through the training. *Selection bias* occurs because salespeople were allowed to volunteer. Relatively highly motivated salespeople may have volunteered. There are several forms of testing effects. The *main effect of testing* may occur if salespeople perform better on the second test, simply from having taken the test before and remembering it. Testing on the first occasion can affect responses to the same test on the second occasion. The *interactive effect of testing* occurs if salespeople, knowing they will be tested again, learn aspects of the training that will help them on the test. This effect constitutes an interaction between testing and treatment—the very act of completing a test affects behavior in the treatment group. Testing is used here to refer to any form of measurement and relates to the very act of measurement affecting subsequent measures or behavior in a treatment or control group. *Statistical regression* occurs if the salespeople are selected on extreme criteria, such as the lowest performing salespeople in September. Such an extreme may have been due to the combination of a variety of factors, and the next time they are measured, they are likely to improve just because of a regression toward their individual average. Interaction of several of these categories of factors, such as the interaction of selection with other factors, has been discussed in the literature.

Pure experiments have two main prescriptions: adding a control group and assigning experimental units randomly to the treatment versus the control group. Random assignment and large samples aim to address selection bias by attempting to make the two groups equivalent going into the experiment. Random assignment is not always possible, such as when studying households in different towns with different treatments or when studying the effects of smoking. Random assignment, of course, does not guarantee equivalence between groups. In combination with large samples, random assignment is expected to lead to equivalence. Often, quasi-experimental designs match experimental units on a number of relevant variables as a proxy for random assignment. For example, in a study of smokers versus nonsmokers, matching would occur on many characteristics, such as physical fitness and demographics. The logic of a control group is not, of course, to control all the extraneous factors; this is just not possible. Rather, it is to allow these factors to influence the control group in the same way as the treatment group, thereby accounting for these factors. A control group typically accounts for history, maturation, and the main effect of testing.

Important terminology relevant to experimentation includes *demand characteristics*, which are cues in an experiment that may suggest the hypothesis under study to respondents, and *demand artifacts*, which refer to the bias itself (Kruglanski, 1975; Shimp et al., 1991). For a respondent to be demand-biased, a demand characteristic has to be encoded; the correct hypothesis discerned; and the hypothesis acted on, leading to biased responses (Shimp et al., 1991). Within versus between designs refer to all participants being exposed to all levels of a manipulation versus distinct groups of participants being exposed to specific levels of a manipulation, respectively. Interactions occur when the effect of an independent variable on a dependent variable is contingent on levels of another variable. Studying interactions is important for several reasons. Interactions reflect naturally occurring phenomena, which are interactions between myriad variables. Interactions involve studying the joint effects of two or more variables and are therefore likely to lead to unique insights and counterintuitive hypotheses when compared to studying main effects (i.e., the effect of one variable). It may be more difficult to generate an alternative explanation for a hypothesized interaction, which is a relatively specific prediction about the joint effect of two variables when compared to a main effect.

Appendix 10.3

Validity of Research Designs

Whereas the earlier chapters discussed the validity of individual measures, validity is also central to the entire research design. In this regard, four types of validity of research designs have been discussed in the literature. The level of analysis here needs to be distinguished when interpreting the usage of the term *validity* for individual measures versus the entire research design. The literature on the validity of research designs has developed mainly within an experimental context; however, these issues are important for other types of research designs as well. The following discussion borrows from the classic writings of Cook and Campbell (1979).

Statistical conclusion validity, as the name suggests, deals with drawing accurate or valid statistical conclusions about covariations. Therefore, it assesses whether a study will detect an effect and its magnitude accurately. Ways of achieving this form of validity include power analyses. Threats to this form of validity relate to purely statistical issues (such as violation of assumptions, statistical power, and fishing and error rate problems) as well as measurement issues that bear on statistical error (such as reliability, randomness in experimental settings, and random heterogeneity in respondents).

Internal validity relates to *causal* relationships between operations *irrespective of what these operations represent in terms of underlying constructs*. Unlike statistical conclusion validity, which relates to statistical interpretations of covariation, internal validity relates to causation. Threats to internal validity relate to events that may *co-occur* with operations that may lead to alternative causal explanations (such as history, maturation, selection, testing, and mortality). Using control groups and randomization rules out several, but not all of, these threats.

Construct validity relates to the extent to which it is possible to generalize from the relationship between two variables at the operational level to the relationship between two constructs at the conceptual level (see Appendix 10.3 Figure). A set of threats to construct validity relates to the construct validity of individual measures of constructs—such as lack of explication of constructs, and mono-operation bias, or the use of a single operationalization—whereas other threats relate to the construct validity of *relationships*—such as using a single method, hypothesis guessing, evaluative apprehension (respondents being apprehensive and presenting themselves in positive light), experimenter expectancies, and improper calibration. Whereas construct

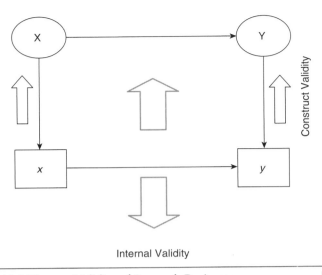

Appendix 10.3 Figure   Validity of Research Designs

validity relates to the relationship between the operational and the conceptual levels, internal validity relates to the operational level.

For the purposes of internal validity analyses, the operationalization is taken as capturing the intended construct, and all other variables are considered threats to internal validity. In experimental terms, any effect due to a variable other than the treatment is a threat to internal validity. Construct validity issues relate to what the operationalization purports to capture in terms of underlying constructs. For example, hypothesis guessing is a threat to construct validity, not internal validity. It represents an alternative explanation for the observed relationship rather than the constructs in question. The main effect of testing is a threat to internal validity because it represents a variable other than the treatment as operationalized. The interactive effect of testing is a threat to construct validity because it affects the operationalization itself in terms of manipulating the intended construct (i.e., the x [manipulation] – X [construct] link). Hence, threats to construct validity arise because of problems either in the operationalization of individual constructs or in generalizing from the relationship between measures or manipulations to the relationship between constructs (see Appendix 10.3 Figure). Each branch of the upward relationship between measures and constructs can threaten inferences about relationships between constructs (see Appendix 10.3 Figure).

Construct validity asks the question, Can the relationship between variables as operationalized be generalized to the relationship between constructs? Hence, multiple operationalizations of a single construct and multiple methods provide support for the construct validity of a relationship. Multiple, divergent methods that suggest a relationship provide strong evidence of construct validity. Well-designed samples and settings provide evidence of construct validity.

External validity has been used to refer to the validity of conclusions "drawn about the generalizability of a causal relationship to and across populations, of persons, settings, and times" (Cook & Campbell, 1979, p. 39). External validity asks the question, Does a theoretical relationship generalize to a variety of settings and samples? Hence, a variety of background factors come into play and moderate a relationship. In the course of assessing external validity, theoretical understanding of the relationship between constructs may be strengthened and theoretical explanations may be refined. Programs of research that assess relationships across methods strengthen the construct validity of theoretical relationships.

The meaning of external validity has been much debated elsewhere and discussed briefly here (Berkowitz & Donnerstein, 1982; Calder, Phillips, & Tybout, 1981; Lynch, 1982; Mook, 1983). External validity is often confused with the appearance of a method and reduced to whether it looks like reality. The term *ecological validity* (Mook, 1983) may be more appropriate for the degree to which a method reflects reality. In fact, a method that mimics reality may have less external validity than one that is artificial, yet captures the theoretical meaning of constructs involved. For instance, a similar argument has been made when comparing heterogeneous and homogeneous samples (Lynch, 1982). Neither type of sample per se leads to a superior design. In fact, homogeneous samples may be preferred over heterogeneous samples for a number of reasons in enhancing external validity. By choosing a homogeneous sample, other aspects of the research method can be adjusted to create an effective design. For example, a student sample can enable the appropriate choice of stimuli about which students are knowledgeable if this is necessary for the design of a study and test of a theory as well as for creating strong tests of hypotheses. For instance, using student samples with "light" attention may well lead to strong tests. However, whether the essence of the construct has been captured needs to be assessed. This line of reasoning is not intended as an excuse for any artificial approach that is convenient. The key is to capture the theoretical meaning of the constructs involved. Researchers have noted that the meaning that respondents assign to an experimental task is central to external validity (Berkowitz & Donnerstein, 1982). If light attention in a student sample affects the meaning that respondents assign to an experimental task, and therefore the degree to which underlying constructs are captured, it undermines the construct validity of the design. Considering an extreme (and absurd) scenario, in terms of the sample, children obviously cannot be respondents in a study of marital relationships because they lack the basic knowledge and experience required. The meaning they assign to the tasks in the study would not capture the intended meaning of the constructs being studied. But could graduate students be respondents in a study of managerial decision making? Perhaps, if they have sufficient experience and corresponding knowledge that enables the theoretical meaning of constructs to be conveyed. Again, the key is the correspondence between the theoretical constructs being assessed and the mix of sample, setting, stimuli, and administration procedures used to capture these constructs.

An important distinction can be made between findings and underlying theoretical explanations. Researchers have noted that what generalizes from a study is not so much the findings but the theoretical understanding (Calder et al., 1981; Lynch, 1982; Mook, 1983). Therefore, both construct validity and external validity ultimately pertain to the generalizability of theoretical understanding. Whereas construct validity relates to generalizability from operational results to theoretical relationships, external validity relates to the generalizability of theoretical understanding.

11

What Is the Role of Measurement in Science?

Overview

In this chapter, several issues germane to measurement and the conduct of science are discussed from a broad perspective. Issues discussed include basic assumptions in quantitative measurement. Qualitative research is also discussed and placed in perspective when compared to quantitative research and measurement. Physical versus psychological measurement is compared and contrasted to understand the conduct of the social sciences. Circles of thinking that occur by measuring the measurable and researching the researchable are discussed. The role of informal measurement in day-to-day life is discussed to highlight potential pitfalls for researchers. Finally, the role of ethics in measurement is discussed.

Assumptions of Measurement

Measure development procedures described in preceding chapters assume that a construct can be isolated and examined. By measuring or manipulating individual constructs, relationships between constructs are studied and substantive hypotheses about these relationships are tested. The very notion that numbers can be assigned to attributes of people, objects, or events is premised on being able to study attributes or constructs separate from other constructs. After all, measurement relates to rules for assigning numbers to *attributes* of people, objects, and events. As discussed below, this is not the case for many phenomena. A complex network of constructs may influence a phenomenon and may not be separable into individual constructs for purposes of measurement.

Quantitative research involves a basic assumption that constructs can be isolated and measured or manipulated. The basis for psychometric measurement is that a single construct is being measured. In fact, the very idea of quantitative measurement involves identification and definition of an isolated construct. Phenomena or sets of isolatable constructs are studied in an experimental or survey context. Note that these quantitative approaches ideally require such isolation. Controlled experiments and correlational studies aim for such isolation. Natural experiments are quasi-experiments in that constructs are not strictly isolated. Yet alternative explanations could be accounted for at a conceptual level. In correlational and experimental studies, conceptual arguments need to be made to isolate constructs and understand interrelationships. For instance, manipulations of constructs such as product status may involve potential confounds, requiring conceptual arguments in addition to empirical evidence against alternative explanations. In designing high, medium, or low levels of status of, say, a restaurant, several other variables, such as price or quality perceptions, may be manipulated. Are results then due to status levels, or price or quality differences? Some constructs may be difficult to isolate for manipulation. Others may be impossible to measure because of their level of abstraction. In such scenarios, conceptual arguments have to be made against possible alternative explanations for findings. For instance, in the example above, alternative explanations in terms of quality or price differences rather than status differences have to be countered.[1] A series of studies may need to be designed to show that the results can be uniquely explained by a variable, such as status, and by ruling out alternative explanations. For instance, the effect of status on a number of variables could be studied, or the effect of a number of variables on status could be studied.

A construct is also sometimes assumed to be unchanged in quantitative research; therefore, consistency is assessed over time. However, such an assumption does not hold if the phenomenon is changing. Consider a longitudinal study of a construct with a specific underlying dimensional structure. At a certain point in time, a scale may be shown to have internal consistency, stability, dimensionality, and validity. If the phenomenon in question changes over time, however, then several possibilities arise. Consider a scenario where an individual difference variable is being measured and may change over time (e.g., current mood). For such constructs, internal consistency, dimensionality, and validity can be assessed. However, stability is not germane because mood is transitory rather than enduring. Alternatively, the internal structure of a scale may change over time. Consider, for example, an individual trait of a social psychological nature, such as social identity, that changes over time. The internal structure in terms of the underlying dimensions may vary over time. The parallel here is with internal structures of constructs that vary across cultures. Constructs may be specific to cultures. Alternatively, measures may be specific to cultures with underlying constructs being identical in internal structure across cultures.

A key requirement for longitudinal studies where a construct is changing is a validated measure as a starting point. If anything, the procedures emphasized earlier in this book are extremely important. A starting frame of reference and point of comparison is provided by such measures. Thus, over time, changes in internal structure can be assessed, such as stronger relationships between dimensions of a construct, without added uncertainty about measurement to begin with. A similar argument applies in cross-cultural measurement. Well-developed measures of constructs in one culture provide a baseline or a comparison point for measure development in other cultures.

The assumption in quantitative research that a single construct can be isolated and measured or manipulated has important implications for conceptual and methodological issues. Can a single construct be isolated conceptually? Methodologically?[2] Quantitative measurement may not be a viable research method in many situations. Qualitative research offers an alternative in such situations. When constructs cannot be isolated and studied, the researcher serves as the measurement instrument in understanding a complex pattern of interrelationships between constructs. The assumptions underlying quantitative measurement should be noted, that there are isolatable constructs that can be studied. In fact, as discussed, some constructs cannot be easily isolated and manipulated. In such situations, conceptual arguments have to be made for one explanation versus another. Rather than completely isolating constructs in either a manipulation or a measurement, alternative arguments could be ruled out conceptually. Pushing this line of reasoning further, qualitative research is a viable approach for studying a number of interrelated constructs that cannot be isolated but have to be studied as complex relationships. Conceptualizations in qualitative research can be more organic in nature rather than of a strict linear, causal form.

Qualitative Versus Quantitative Research

The following discussion attempts to draw parallels between quantitative and qualitative research. It is not intended to suggest that the same criteria be used to assess qualitative research as is used in quantitative research. The discussion does not cover epistemological underpinnings of different types of research, which have been addressed in great depth elsewhere (e.g., Denzin & Lincoln, 2003; Strauss & Corbin, 1990).

Several parallels within quantitative research are useful in comparing quantitative and qualitative research. A parallel can be drawn between all objective and subjective measurement of constructs. For instance, consider a construct such as span of control, wherein the number of people at some level of an organization could be used as an indicator of span of control. On the other hand, subjective perceptions of span of control could be used as a measure. This subjective measure is more direct in terms of the respondent evaluating and rating span of control. The objective measure is more closely related to direct numerical data. This is somewhat similar to a researcher being the measurement instrument (i.e., self-reporting an interpretation) versus interpreting data collected from respondents on a measure. Another parallel is from projective measures discussed earlier, where inkblots and such tap into multiple constructs, subject to interpretation. As discussed, inconsistencies in administrations and scoring in projective tests cause unreliability. These tests are not usually assessing a single construct. Rather, results are used to infer levels of a variety of interrelated abstract concepts, such as alienation and depression. Another parallel is when conceptual arguments have to be used to argue against plausible alternative explanations for findings in quantitative research. This is common when dealing with abstract constructs; alternative explanations in terms of other constructs have to be countered. In this regard, researchers in quantitative research have argued for a comparative rather than a confirmatory approach to theory testing (Sternthal et al., 1987); the former emphasizes showing the superiority of one explanation over rival explanations, whereas the latter emphasizes using validated measures and multiple operationalizations.

Qualitative research may also be appropriate because it is the only methodologically viable means. An example is presented in Exhibit 11.1 using the study of low-literate consumers, a group that may be difficult to study with conventional quantitative approaches. In qualitative research, the researchers are the instruments. Thus, qualitative measurement involves rules for assigning words (i.e., qualities) to phenomena rather than numbers (i.e., quantities) to attributes. Whereas measurement is used to draw inferences about abstract concepts, this process is not mediated by numerical responses but by the researchers themselves.

(Text continues on page 358)

Exhibit 11.1   Qualitative Research on Low-Literate Consumers

Relevant abridged details of a qualitative research study (Viswanathan, Rosa, & Harris, in press) is provided for illustrative purposes.

Research Method

Given the inherent difficulties that functionally illiterate consumers have with standard research instruments (Wallendorf, 2001), we adopted a qualitative approach. We first describe the informants, followed by different elements of the method.

Informants

The informants were enrolled at adult education centers in the midwestern United States. Those enrolled in courses ranged in age from 16 to 90-plus years, and they were operationally divided into two groups, 0–4 grades and 5–12 grades, based on standardized grade-equivalent test scores in reading and math. Education at such centers is customized to student needs, focusing on skills applicable to everyday life. Some students acquire desired skills and leave the centers after a few months of training; others remain enrolled for several years. By studying students with 0–12 grade-equivalent scores, the aim was to gain understanding across a range of levels of functional literacy.

English as a Second Language (ESL) and poor literate consumers were included in the study to sharpen our understanding of functionally illiterate consumers. Our objective was to disentangle the effects of literacy from those of income or English-language difficulties. ESL students were recruited from classes offered at one of the adult education centers. They varied in their English-language skills between second- and sixth-grade levels, but all had one or more university degrees. Functionally literate poor adults were interviewed at a homeless shelter. Their education levels ranged from high school diplomas to postgraduate studies.

Method

We used interviews and observations of students. At the start of the process, two of the authors attended a training program for volunteer tutors and served as tutors at an adult education center, one for 150 hours over an 18-month period, and the other for 15 hours over a 2-month period. All interviews were unstructured, but recurring themes from early phases were interwoven as appropriate into later phases. Interviews ranged from 20 minutes to 2.5 hours, averaging about an hour. Teachers were also interviewed. All interviews were tape-recorded and transcribed. Observation took place during classroom activities, one-on-one tutoring sessions, and shopping trips. Notes and conversations were recorded during and immediately

(Continued)

(Continued)

after observation sessions, transcribed, and analyzed. The 0–4-level students were observed during classroom activities and on two of the shopping field trips regularly scheduled by one of the adult education centers. Shopping tasks (e.g., procuring items and spending within a budget) are regularly assigned as part of the shopping field trips. Students choose to complete shopping tasks either by themselves or in groups.

One-on-one shopping observations of 15 students were also conducted. These informants were asked to complete their typical shopping at a large chain store, and their personal funds were supplemented by $10 gift cards and two coupons. Consumers were primarily observed from a distance, occasionally being approached to ask clarification questions about products, prices, shelf displays, and purchases. Observations were followed by interviews. In total, data collection extended over 55 months and included 35 interviews with functionally illiterate consumers, 19 interviews with ESL and poor literate consumers, 15 one-on-one shopping observations, two shopping field trip observations involving 10 students each, and more than 150 hours of observation during tutoring.

Data Analysis

All authors analyzed interview and observation data independently, focusing attention on statements and behaviors that shed light on how functionally illiterate, ESL, and poor literate consumers assessed choices, made decisions, and engaged in coping behaviors, and on how they used information in making their decisions. Interviews were analyzed using guidelines for qualitative interviews (McCracken, 1988), by which commonalities and differences among informants are identified. In addition, critical evaluations of our findings were done by teachers at the adult education center, who found that the cognitive predilections, decision rules, trade-offs, and coping strategies we noted characterize functionally illiterate students they know. The findings were further validated by independent analyses conducted by 10 university students as a course assignment. Our findings are elaborated in the next section with quotes from the data, where informant identities have been disguised.

Findings

In general, we found that functionally illiterate consumers display cognitive predilections, decision rules, trade-offs, and coping behaviors in line with our expectations. In our discussion, we separate predilections, decision strategies, and trade-offs from coping behaviors, although the phenomena are clearly interrelated. The conceptual flow of the findings is illustrated in the figure. For purposes of illustration, one cognitive predilection, concrete thinking, is elaborated here.

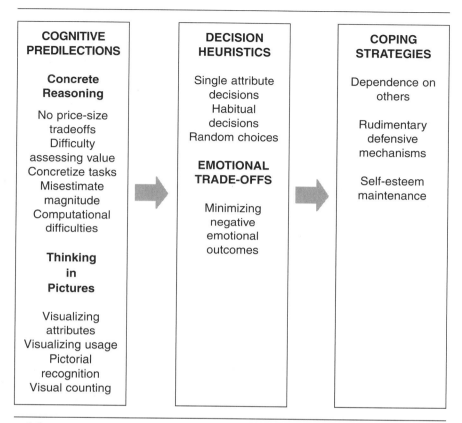

COGNITIVE PREDILECTIONS	DECISION HEURISTICS	COPING STRATEGIES
Concrete Reasoning	Single attribute decisions	Dependence on others
No price-size tradeoffs Difficulty assessing value Concretize tasks Misestimate magnitude Computational difficulties	Habitual decisions Random choices **EMOTIONAL TRADE-OFFS** Minimizing negative emotional outcomes	Rudimentary defensive mechanisms Self-esteem maintenance
Thinking in Pictures		
Visualizing attributes Visualizing usage Pictorial recognition Visual counting		

Exhibit 11.1 Figure   Conceptual Flow of Findings

Overview of Findings

Our observations of functionally illiterate consumers immediately made clear that they spend considerable effort on basic tasks. This was particularly true of those at the 0–4 reading level. In shopping trips, they labored over tasks such as locating products and price displays, reading prices, and translating volumes into purchase units (e.g., a total of 150 candles requiring boxes of 100 and 50). In general, computation was difficult for most functionally illiterate consumers. Computing the price of two units if the price of one was known, for example, often required paper-and-pencil calculations. Price displays often caused confusion because of the multiple prices presented, and many informants had trouble computing final prices based on percentage- or fraction-off signs. Cost and value estimations, which are forms of abstraction, were also difficult. Many functionally illiterate consumers struggled with computing the total cost of their goods basket prior to checkout. Instead of rounding cents to dollars, they rounded dollars to fives or tens of dollars and often made

(Continued)

(Continued)

significant errors. Allowing for taxes was a significant concern. Computing prices on percentage-off or fraction-off deals was effortful and often avoided. Magnitudes were not easily interpreted in terms of meaning; for instance, when given a task to buy six items while staying within a budget of $50, consumers who bought one item for approximately $2 computed the balance remaining rather than estimate the magnitude. We observed consumers inaccurately estimating the total cost of products in their cart (e.g., items costing $25–$30 were estimated to cost $10).

Cognitive Predilections—Concrete Reasoning

Functionally illiterate consumers display a predilection for what we call concrete reasoning—focusing on a single perceptible piece of information, such as a price, or a product attribute or ingredient, such as size, when engaged in shopping decisions. Concrete reasoning was manifest often when consumers struggled with trade-offs, such as between price and size. When considering size and price, many functionally illiterate consumers focused exclusively on only one dimension, as illustrated below:

Interviewer: Let's say you have a big bag that cost $2.50 versus a small bag that costs, say, ninety cents. How do you consider sizes? Do you look for that at all?

Rita: Yeah, I look and see if they've the big ones or do they have any smaller size. Just like in cereal. I buy like the . . . [pause]. They have the big kinds of cereals, then they have like, the smaller size. Just like the Raisin Bran, I look to see which costs the most and which costs the less, and so I just get the smaller one because they cost the less.

Furthermore, concrete reasoning was evident even when follow-up questions were more pointed.

Interviewer: Let's say you buy a packet of bread that's half the size. You are getting less bread for the money. How do you try to make sure it's cheapest in terms of how much you are getting also?

Naomi: I just look at the tag and see what's cheapest. I don't look by their sizes.

Many of the functionally illiterate consumers reported that they always buy "the cheapest." In terms of attribute trade-offs, some functionally illiterate consumers tended to fixate on one attribute. Teresa focused on sugar, reporting that she chooses higher sugar-content products consistently.

Teresa: I go down and we've got, like . . . some of them saying 14 grams, the other might say 46 grams of sugar. I get the one that got the most.

Concrete thinking was often employed after students had participated in adult education programs. Prior to the adult education experience, with its emphasis on life management skills, functionally illiterate consumers often followed the approach of buying whatever they wanted to without checking price.

There were several distinctions among consumers in this regard. Some consumers compared physical size of products on the shelf (i.e., including packaging) to derive an intuitive physical size-to-price ratio on which to base their decision. As noted, unit price was not understood or used, mostly likely because of its abstract nature. Some consumers claimed to check sizes and get the best deals, but these claims were not borne out in our observations. Functionally illiterate consumers also made errors in estimating the number of units in multiple-unit packs of products, such as soaps, while trading off size and price. Some consumers made accurate greater-than and less-than assessments of price, but the magnitude of the dollar value difference between the prices being compared escaped them (e.g., they had difficulty distinguishing between $2.00 and $3.50 price differences). Some consumers traded off a single attribute with price. Generally, active consideration of a set of product attributes was not reported. The value of a product was a confusing concept to articulate, often equated with a concrete price.

There are several reasons to buy the cheapest other than cognitive constraints, such as income constraints or even storage constraints. However, it was evident in probing through our interviews and observations that cognitive constraints were leading to such an approach for a number of functionally illiterate consumers. In contrast and without exception, ESL and poor literate consumers performed product attribute and price-size trade-offs easily and mentioned complex trade-offs that they go through during decision making. Unlike some functionally illiterate consumers, who did not grasp the notion of price-size trade-offs or did not articulate their thinking on this, ESL and poor literate consumers displayed a clear grasp of the issues. Often, it was pointless to continue with follow-up questions about specific trade-offs.

Mei Kim: If it's more cheaper, then I buy the large size. . . . For example, small size, two times the large size, but price is 1.5 times or something, I buy it large size.

ESL and poor literate informants immediately understood questions about price per unit and attribute trade-offs. They see such trade-offs as central elements to consider when shopping.

We found one study (Capon & Kuhn, 1982) that serves as another comparison basis with literate consumers studied in past consumer behavior. This study addressed price-size trade-offs among consumers and has some bearing on our findings on concrete reasoning. Capon and Kuhn (1982) presented shoppers with pairs of products with different price and size information, and asked them to choose one.

(Continued)

(Continued)

They classified the shoppers' verbal responses into six types in ascending order of sophistication: extraneous, task-extrinsic (i.e., nonuse of weight or price, such as, "I'd buy the small one; I'd never use the big one up"); extraneous, task-intrinsic (e.g., which is a better buy?); partial, noninferential (use of broad price/weight approximations); subtraction (e.g., computing weight and price differences); weight ratio diagnosis (e.g., "Well, almost twice as much for less than twice the price; the big one is cheaper"); and direct ratio. With the exception of extraneous, task-extrinsic processing, the other uses of information that Capon and Kuhn (1982) found among consumers were more complex than those generally exhibited by functionally illiterate consumers.

Concrete reasoning is consistent with Luria's (1976) findings based on a study of peasants in Central Asia in the early 1900s that low-literate people can perform some concrete operations on specific units, such as time, and tend to engage in concrete, situational thinking based on practical necessity. In the consumer realm, price appears to be a central unit along which concrete operations are performed. The necessities of handling money, the relative ease of availability of price information, and the relative ease of identifying the lower price (i.e., the lower number) are likely factors that influence concrete reasoning using price. Situational demands of handling money and transacting based on price may lead to the centrality of price in concrete, situational thinking. Combining attribute information in more complex decision making requires the use of abstract conditions in reasoning and deduction, the need to isolate abstract attributes such as value, and the need to use abstract symbolic information on attributes. Functionally illiterate consumers today may be more literate than Luria's informants, but the demands of the current marketplace are higher as well.

Within a consumer decision-making framework, functionally illiterate consumers appear to engage in a restricted, single-attribute, modified lexicographic strategy, typically using price as the focal attribute. This is consistent with the notion that lack of cognitive resources leads to simplified decision heuristics involving less effort (Payne, Bettman, & Johnson, 1993). Habitual choice and random choice strategies were also reported frequently. The notion of concrete reasoning is also consistent with the use of simplifying decision strategies in the face of negative emotions (Luce et al., 2001). Negative emotions associated with decision tasks stemming from a history of material and social costs by themselves may affect cognitive performance.

Functionally illiterate consumers often attempted to concretize their decision making in several ways. Naomi has learned, through instruction, to look at the dates for freshness. In this context, the date becomes a number that is concrete enough to be used.

Interviewer: Do you look for just one brand? You said you look at dates and stuff.

Naomi: Dates and stuff, yeah.

Interviewer: What are you looking for when you look at the dates?

Naomi: The dates are the numbers on 'em . . . expired or something like that.

Teachers also pointed to the importance of a concrete context in enabling adding.

Teacher : Some of the low-level math students, I start teaching in terms of
(0–4) money. Three take away from seven, they can't quite fit. And I say, well I give seven dollars, and you spend three of them . . . It worked.

As expected from prior research (Luria, 1976), and related to concrete thinking, functionally illiterate consumers had difficulty transferring knowledge across domains of experience. ESL and poor literate consumers, in contrast, did not exhibit the same levels of anxiety or confusion. Both groups welcomed opportunities to shop in novel environments and did not report difficulties performing shopping tasks when such opportunities did arise. Functionally illiterate consumers also exhibited difficulty transferring basic arithmetic skills across different domains. Otto, for example, reported not being able to give attention to prices while shopping before enrolling in adult education courses:

Interviewer: Okay, now, before you went to adult ed, would you check prices like you're checking now?

Otto: No, I'd just go in and get stuff and throw it in the basket and keep going.

Interviewer: Even though you could count very well?

Otto: Yeah, I'd just throw it in there and gone, not even worry about it, but now you see, you gotta look, be careful, you know.

Interviewer: So, before you would look for wheat bread and throw it or just any bread?

Otto: Just get it and throw it in there.

What is interesting about Otto is that his arithmetic skills for handling money in other contexts are quite good. Otto sold illegal drugs for several years before going to prison, a profession where being off at the end of a shift can result in a beating or worse. Otto could handle hundreds of dollars and make proper change on street corners, but he struggled with prices and running counts in grocery stores. A similar example comes from Esther, who joined the adult education center to learn to read in her early 80s. Although Esther has considerable difficulty with reading, writing, or

(Continued)

(Continued)

performing simple arithmetic in the abstract, she can keep a running total of what she has put in her cart while shopping, and compare it to whatever she has available to spend, based on relationships between currency types that she learned as a little girl.

In summary, some similarities and differences between quantitative and qualitative research are illustrated here. For instance, the approach of using comparison groups here was similar to setting up control groups in an experimental design. The flexibility in qualitative methods enables pointed follow-up questions as the situation demands.

Parallels between measure validation and research design discussed for quantitative research apply for qualitative research as well (Figure 11.1). Multiple methods were used to collect data from different sources paralleling convergent validity and consistency across methods. The time frame over which data were collected allowed for modifications in the research design over time, and for revisiting inferences drawn from data analysis paralleling stability or consistency across time. Providing evidence to support explanation of observed behavior in terms of literacy rather than income or other alternative explanations is akin to discriminant validity at the level of the research design. Placing current research in the context of past literature is akin to nomological validity at the level of the research design.

EXHIBIT SOURCE: Adapted from Viswanathan, M., Rosa, J. A., & Harris, J. (in press), Decision-making and coping by functionally illiterate consumers and some implications for marketing management, in *Journal of Marketing*. Published by the American Marketing Association. Reprinted with permission.

Parallels between measure validation and research design illustrated in Chapter 10 can be applied to qualitative research. Basic measurement issues apply to such designs at a more abstract level. In conducting in-depth interviews or observations, the notion of reliability could be translated to the notion of consistency for each researcher in his or her interpretations from each respondent or across respondents. Such reliability is not related to a strict correlational view as much as to the degree to which themes and interpretations are consistent. The unit of analysis is not responses provided by respondents but inferences made by researchers. Thus, researchers typically revisit the data over time, somewhat akin to stability, and revise their interpretations. This is an important procedure to allow interpretations to emerge over time. Themes may also be assessed across respondents, although not in a statistical sense, to achieve a parallel to internal consistency. Data from individual respondents may also be examined for internal consistency.

Checking specific items across different sources (referred to as triangulation) (Lincoln & Guba, 1985) is akin to convergent validity, as is convergence in interpretation across researchers or consistency across researchers (Figure 11.1 and Exhibit 11.1). Thus, multiple researchers who make independent judgments enhance such research and are akin to multiple measures. Convergence can also be achieved by a discussion of differences. In addition, referees can assist in the process of developing convergent validity, and participants can also be involved in this process. Note that the unit of analysis is not a single construct but an interrelated set of themes. Such themes may be developed from multiple methods. Lack of convergence can also be explained by instrument characteristics (i.e., researchers' unique perspectives), adding to understanding of the phenomena. Nomological validity and discriminant validity are relevant to individual themes as well as to the relationships between themes in a set. Discriminant validity corresponds to potential alternative explanations for data (Figure 11.1). Nomological validity corresponds to making sense of the proposed relationships in light of past research (Figure 11.1). For example, in Exhibit 11.1, concrete thinking and its rationale of cognitive constraints in buying the cheapest needs to be distinguished from an alternative explanation in terms of income constraints leading to a similar outcome, akin to discriminant validity. Similarly, developing explanations within the context of existing literature in Exhibit 11.1 is akin to nomological validity. Finally, similar to construct validity, the overall validity of a set of themes is relevant.[3]

Quantitative versus qualitative research involves measurement with or without mediation through numbers, respectively. Each type of research is appropriate for different types of phenomena or for different slices of phenomenon. Quantitative research involves separate numerical measurement or manipulation of each construct in a set of constructs. Qualitative research involves the study of a constellation of constructs.

Scientific research could be boiled down to the following over-simplification: that a verifiable research method rooted in relevant literature is employed. More than a generalization of what scientific research is, it is easier to specify some characteristics: (a) full disclosure to allow independent evaluation (and replication, if necessary) and (b) accurate measurement (whether in quantitative or qualitative research). Accurate measurement is a truism—who in scientific research would want inaccurate measurement? The point is to employ procedures in research methods that can be *demonstrated* to be accurate in light of what is known (i.e., past literature). Thus, the substance of scientific research is the methodology, whereas the form is the ethic of full disclosure. An oversimplification for quantitative research is that research should be replicable no matter who

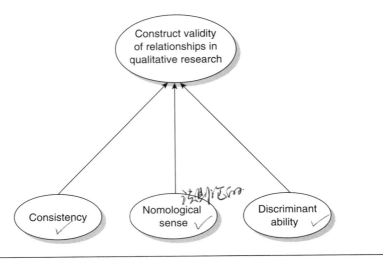

Figure 11.1   Construct Validity of Relationships in Qualitative Research

conducts the research, allowing, of course, for sampling variation. Not so with qualitative research, where the researcher is the measurement instrument, the research method is relatively unstructured, and phenomena are studied in context. Thus, replication across researchers is not applicable to the same degree. Nevertheless, accurate measurement is at the heart of scientific research.

Revisiting projective measures discussed earlier, such approaches can provide rich insights; however, quantitative measurement using such approaches requires appropriate modification and validation. When phenomena being researched involve a constellation of interrelated constructs that cannot be isolated, qualitative research is appropriate. The characteristics of phenomena studied roughly vary across disciplines from cognitive psychology to sociology and anthropology. From a quantitative measurement point of view, several phenomena do not meet the assumption of separable constructs and measures. Thus, the researcher is the measurement instrument in qualitative research without intervening numerical measurement. Such research may also be the appropriate methodological route when there are significant hurdles to the use of standard instruments, such as experiments and surveys, as may be the case with low-literate respondents or in anthropological studies in different cultures.

Force-fitting numerical measurement onto a purely qualitative approach may provide some solace to the quantitative researcher trained to look for demonstrable, "objective" evidence, but such numbers likely reflect poor measurement or trivial constructs or both. Consider providing a number count of instances of words repeated by low-literate consumers to quantify concrete thinking in excerpts shown in Exhibit 11.1. A number count of specific words likely taps into a very concrete construct at best and not an abstract construct. Hence, a theme such as concrete thinking may not be captured. Alternatively, the researcher could raise the level of the construct by identifying instances of concrete thinking. Here, the researcher, or judges, act as the respondent in the sense of providing numerical responses. This technique is employed in quantitative analyses of written protocols. For example, judges examine protocols to identify the number of phrases that are positive, negative, or neutral, converting statements into numerical scores. Clear definitions of what constitutes a single piece of information and appropriate ways to classify information are usually provided. The aim here is to facilitate consistent interpretation among independent judges and increase reliability. Frequencies are employed as numerical measures of constructs. Frequency of word occurrences is also examined in content analysis. In the case of concrete thinking, the theme emerged from qualitative analysis and represents a qualitatively distinct type of processing or thinking. Perhaps a quantitative study of the occurrence of concrete thinking vis-à-vis other distinct types of thinking could be conducted. But the theme itself emerged from qualitative analysis that is not readily reducible to quantitative data. Moreover, the data from which inferences are drawn are not restricted to self-reports but also to reports from others, observations in different settings, or a combination of these approaches.

Content analysis is a means of interpreting qualitative information, such as from people's descriptions of events, by classifying into categories. In identifying categories to be independent, it is important to clearly define each category. If multiple constructs are involved, each has to be defined to facilitate consistent interpretation by observers. This is akin to clearly defining a term in a question, such as *recreational activities* in a question on how much people spend on recreational activities. Just as all respondents need to interpret items consistently, all observers or judges need to interpret conceptual categories consistently. The unit of analysis (e.g., a phrase or a sentence) needs to be clearly defined, the issue again being consistency. A content analysis scale of perceived threat in clients' communications with therapists includes scale categories such as death (i.e., reference to death with such subcategories as self and animate others) and mutilation (Viney, 1993). Transcriptions of therapy sessions are checked for accuracy and divided into units (clauses). Then, content categories are applied (Viney, 1993). Reliability is computed through intersubjective agreement (Viney, 1993). However, such an approach may not be applicable when the construct or interrelated constructs in question are more abstract. For example, with concrete reasoning, in Exhibit 11.1, instances describing this theme have to be identified. Yet the abstract theme emerges from examining these instances rather than the reverse, another distinction between qualitative and quantitative research. Having emerged from qualitative analysis, the idea of confirming an instance numerically with the same data is circular reasoning. On the other hand, confirming it in a different sample may also be questionable. First, numerical measurement analysis requires statistical standing, thus suggesting large sample sizes. Second, and more importantly, a numerical count of instances of an underlying theme is, at best, a poor measure of qualitatively distinct phenomena, such as intensity of expressed emotion. In fact, the theme in question may be compromised in efforts to make it quantifiable. Third, an effort to confirm through numerical measures based on frequency distorts the qualitative research method into one of asking questions to confirm rather than allowing the respondent to be the informant, being intrusive in this regard. The notion that frequency of communication conveys a continuous measure of the content of communications is fraught with problems. It does not capture intensity. It does not account for interviewer effects, which could lead respondents. It does not account for differences in communicative ability. For example, a reticent informant can provide considerable insight about low-literate consumers, say, in terms of the relationship between illiteracy and verbal communication. It does not account for combining data from multiple sources, such as self-reports and observations. Therefore, numerical measures should not be force-fit where they lead to poor measurement, thus undercutting the very intent of reliable and valid numerical measurement. In a sense, qualitative research is similar to using naturally occurring events as items in quantitative research, as in the example in Chapter 8 on pace of life. The similarity is in using data that reflect multiple influences rather than self-reports on a single previously isolated construct. However, there are significant differences. Unlike quantitative research, numbers do not mediate the inferences drawn by qualitative researchers. Moreover, data may be used not just to draw inferences about constructs in isolation but also to draw inferences about an interrelated set of themes. Also, data from multiple sources, such as interviews and observations, may be combined to draw holistic inferences.

The notion that three or four out of five interviewees should be similar for an inference to hold or the approach of looking for similarities across a certain proportion of a small sample is ingrained in quantitative research approaches. However, in qualitative research, unique data from one informant in a small sample may provide insights into what *can* happen. This is similar to an artificial experiment that shows what *can* happen, even in artificial settings (Mook, 1983). In a sense, qualitative research can be like a lab experiment—it could show what can happen, but not necessarily the degree to which it happens. Artificial experiments are very similar, in this respect, to qualitative research. Milgram's studies, in which respondents were willing to administer electric shocks to other people, represent artificial experiments that showed what can happen (Mook, 1983). If anything, the artificiality may have strengthened the conclusions. More generally, academic research is not primarily about developing population estimates and the degree to which something occurs in the natural environment as much as it is about developing theories and testing them, such as through predictions that follow for specific settings.

The very issues that are central in quantitative research may be detrimental in qualitative research, such as structured procedures with a strict sequencing of questions in interviewing. Listening to stories often may be more effective than going over lists of questions in qualitative research. Statistical notions of drawing inferences across a set of respondents may well be misplaced. One respondent may provide insight into what can happen akin to an artificial experiment that shows what can happen in the lab. Leading or pointed questions may have a role as well, when they follow more open questions, although this is also true of quantitative research as well. However, unstructured, qualitative approaches are flexible and facilitate such questioning based on responses to earlier questions (as illustrated in the follow-up question about purchasing packages of bread in different sizes in Exhibit 11.1).

In this regard, it may be useful to carefully sequence these distinct approaches when designing data collection that involves both. Quantitative approaches to obtaining data would be open to multiple interpretations if the degree of structure in data collection is diluted through unstructured, qualitative approaches. Ideally, a structured approach could be used to collect data, followed by an unstructured, open-ended approach; otherwise, the latter is likely to influence responses to the former, which is more dependent on careful ordering. Sequencing is, of course, central to structured approaches, which in turn enables consistency and allows for interpretation and comparability of quantitative data.

This distinction suggests a black-and-white difference between quantitative and qualitative approaches. In reality, as discussed, a number of quantitative approaches involve somewhat unstructured data, such as thought listings or observations of natural occurrences. The key, though, is the use of procedures for reliable and valid quantitative measurement, whether it be through ratings by judges or otherwise. What is being referred to as qualitative here is analysis without the use of numbers and quantification.

Ultimately, science is about using clues to infer underlying relationships between abstract concepts. These clues may come in many forms, ranging from naturalistic observation to measurement using items. These clues, or data, could be quantitative or qualitative. Qualitative research provides a big-picture understanding that can lead to subsequent well-grounded quantitative research. More specifically, qualitative research can provide the basis for richer conceptualizations of constructs and their relationships, as well as improved measurement. This is the traditional but restrictive exploratory (qualitative) versus confirmatory (quantitative) view. Even if quantitative research is viable in a situation, all qualitative research may not have or need a confirmatory counterpart that is quantitative in nature. For instance, big-picture understanding from qualitative research may not be testable through quantitative research. The overall model shown in the figure in Exhibit 11.1 does not appear to have a logical quantitative counterpart to test it, nor is the purpose of such a test apparent. On the other hand, in-depth, specific quantitative studies could be conducted about elements of the model, such as identifying conditions under which one type of decision heuristic versus another is used or examining the effect of concrete thinking on memory as a function of literacy (see the figure in Exhibit 11.1). Qualitative and quantitative research often examine different slices of a phenomenon.

With quantitative research, a paper-and-pencil method may, in effect, restrict the phenomenon that is studied. Current paradigms and conventional theory may restrict what is studied. Such restrictive circles of substantive and methodological knowledge need to be constantly challenged to enable insights that are tangential to current conventional wisdom. This is particularly the case with methodological circles. Entire research streams may develop out of narrow methods that provide a sense of security. The security of quantification through narrowly construed measures is one example. Breaking thinking in circles requires new insights. For instance, a focus on research using certain narrow measures perpetuates itself, whereas a healthy dose of reality can infuse substance and improve measurement. Qualitative research can serve to infuse such reality.

Also noteworthy are a number of qualitative decisions that underlie quantitative data, starting from choosing a phenomenon to study and establishing its importance to defining constructs; delineating domains; generating items; using quantitative data to make qualitative decisions, such as the number of dimensions and labels for dimensions; hypothesizing effects in a specific direction after weighing arguments and counterarguments; deciding on the strength of manipulations; interpreting results in terms of magnitudes; ruling out alternative explanations based on conceptual arguments; and so forth. Clearly, quantitative data provide the empirical reality or correction to temper conceptual analysis as emphasized throughout the book in terms of the need for conducting conceptual and empirical analyses in conjunction. However, the underlying qualitative bases for quantitative data should be kept in perspective in interpreting research. Whereas numbers provide some security and precision, the latter may sometimes be illusory. Where the numbers came from (i.e., what was involved in collecting the numbers) and what they capture should be kept in perspective.

Measuring the "Measurable"

There is sometimes an understandable tendency in science to measure what is relatively easy to measure. Over time, these measures take on a life of their own to the point where they become the only things worth measuring. A case in point is some ability testing. With such tests, the emphasis is on demonstrating measurement properties that are relatively easy to demonstrate (i.e., reliability or consistency). This stands to reason because a reasonable level of consistency is necessary for further inquiry. But validity is a whole different story that requires fuller understanding of that thing being measured. Although predictive validity can be shown through the use of a criterion, such as grade point average in college, the criterion variable itself may suffer from the issue of measurability. Meaningful constructs of success or accomplishment are very difficult, often impossible to capture. The point to note is that empirically demonstrable psychometric properties such as reliability may often be the tail that wags the dog. So what is to be done? At a minimum, a clear understanding of that thing that is being measured is indispensable. If measurement drives the research, then the construct should be defined appropriately, resisting the temptation to use narrowly construed measures to represent broad constructs. At an extreme, each item can be construed as a measure of something—a very concrete construct. However, this is an inefficient way of conducting scientific research. Multiple items enhance reliability by averaging, but also by using items measuring slightly different things that covary with each other.

Rigorous scientific research is often associated with isolating constructs and studying them through specific methods. Such reductionism comes at a price—the inability to study the big picture.[4] The rigor and precision that are possible by isolating and studying specific constructs lead to a problem of measuring the measurable and researching the researchable. They are manifest in finding different ways to study narrow issues. Paradoxically, more sophisticated methods may be applied to study narrower and narrower issues. A variation on this notion is the use of a tried and tested research method to look for problems it can solve (somewhat like finding a hammer on a weekend at home and then looking for nails to pound in). All of this is part of the marketplace of ideas where different types of research compete with each other. The purpose here is not to pass judgment on different types of research or individual research projects as much as to make broader observations at the level of disciplines and methods. Researchers choose programs of research for a variety of reasons, including interest, and different types of research serve to build a picture.

Several points are noteworthy with regard to measuring the measurable, and therefore putting the measurement "cart" ahead of the construct "horse." Although a pragmatic consideration of what is measurable is, of course, relevant, it is sometimes the only consideration. Assumptions about what is measurable may need to be challenged. Innovative ways of measuring difficult constructs may need to be attempted. Innovation also extends to the conceptual level, where conceptually rich constructs and complex relationships between constructs are visualized. Although all such hypothesized relationships cannot be tested rigorously through quantitative measurement, they should nevertheless be conceptualized. Moreover, qualitative research provides a way of assessing a constellation of constructs wherein the researcher is the instrument. Such research requires a different kind of rigor. Rigor is often associated with certain quantitative, reductionist approaches. But a narrow view of rigor can result in narrow issues being studied. Different research questions require different types of research methods. Some complex phenomena require rigorous qualitative research; the alternative is to not research the phenomena at all. Perhaps rigor, which is sometimes used to refer exclusively to the use of a specific research method or a data analysis technique, should be extended to the nature of conceptual thinking as well as the fit between research objectives and research methods. The nature of evidence differs for different phenomena; establishing causality between smoking and cancer involves a different type of evidence than establishing causality between information processing goals and memory. Proof is different in the physical versus social sciences and so, too, within the social sciences. A narrow view of methodological rigor can lead to a narrow focus on narrow research questions.

Several metaphors could be used to characterize a narrow substantive or methodological approach: lenses or filters or mental compartments or more extreme paradigmatic straitjackets. A story about the elephant and the six men who could not see is one such metaphor. One version of the story relates how each man touched a different part of an elephant; one thought the tail was a piece of rope, another thought a leg was a tree trunk, and so on. If the elephant is the phenomenon under study, the aim is to see as much of the elephant as possible through substantive theories and methodologies, while realizing that many parts remain to be seen. A narrow substantive focus may narrow the methodological focus, which in turn may narrow substantive insights.

An approximate disciplinary circle is shown in Figure 11.2, although it is not meant to be interpreted strictly in the sequence presented. What is known influences what is looked for, which in turn influences how it is looked for (the method) and what is found. Substantive theories and specific methods often go hand in hand and are associated with specific disciplines, such as the type of experiments in cognitive psychology. A tangential intellectual force may move thinking out of the disciplinary circle and lead to new insights.

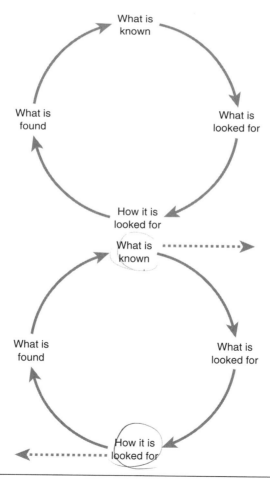

Figure 11.2   Disciplinary/Methodological Circles

Essentially, there are several domains in research: a theoretical domain with concepts, a methodological domain with methods, and the domain of phenomena (Figure 11.3). A narrow theoretical perspective may lead to the choice of a narrow method and narrow insight into phenomena, whereas a broader focus theoretically and methodologically may lead to broader insight. Such an approach requires an understanding of specific theories and methods while being open to different theoretical and methodological perspectives.

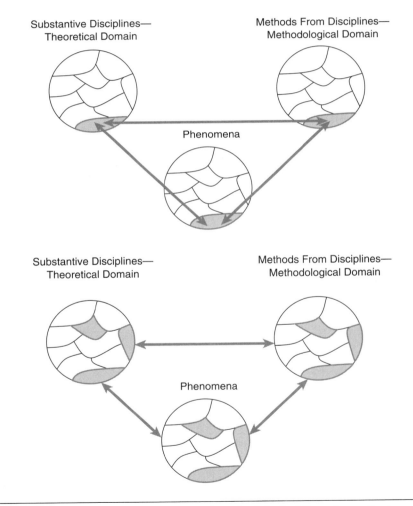

Figure 11.3   Choosing Theoretical and Methodological Domains to Study Phenomena

The goal of science is to understand phenomena being researched. There are many situations in research. In some situations, qualitative research could be used as a mode of discovery that is later justified using quantitative research. In other situations, quantitative research could be used in a preliminary study and subsequently followed by qualitative research. In some domains, it may not be appropriate to use one form of research (or the other). Similarly, both quantitative and qualitative questions and analyses could be used in a single study. Another benefit of being open to both methods is triangulation. A few things could be agreed, that scientific endeavor aims to develop abstract theory from concrete phenomena and aims to be methodical about it. What distinguishes science from nonscience is the use of the research method, whether quantitative or qualitative. The research method should fit the objectives, the design choices should be supported conceptually and empirically, and the validity of the research method should be demonstrated.

From a broad perspective, essential to research and research methods is a frame of mind that is open in several respects: to alternative theories, to different measures and methods, and to different interpretations of data. What characterizes the conduct of science is its research method, and central to conducting science is a mentality, a mind frame, a research ethic. Keeping an open mind and revisiting/reinterpreting the design and the data are central to the mind frame, or the mentality. Such a mind frame is also essential in learning from other research.

From Physical to Psychological Measurement

So what is measurement in the social sciences? How do the "soft" numbers in the social sciences compare to the "hard" numbers from measurement in the physical sciences? A brief journey through physical measurement of inanimate objects to physiological measurement, often coupled with physical measurement in this discussion, to psychological measurement is instructive. Measurement in the social sciences has similarities to measurement in these diverse disciplines. The discussion that follows oversimplifies distinctions and sweeps entire disciplines into clear-cut categories. Nevertheless, it is intended to stimulate thinking from a broader perspective. In fact, differences in measurement within the social sciences are quite large, reflecting characteristics of physical and physiological measurement to different degrees, as discussed in Chapter 8.

Considering the concept of length, the distance between the conceptual and the operational is minimal. Even here, the measurement of length is far from obvious with larger distances and, of course, with astronomical distances. In other words, the underlying construct is physically discernible, directly paralleling the measurement of the construct. Measurement involves calibrating a ruler or tape with equidistances based on conventional agreement. An external comparison standard is available. Reliability or consistency is likely to be affected by human error in reading. Through mechanization, such error can be reduced or even eliminated. Multiple readings are akin to multiple-item scales and enhance reliability. Test-retest reliability can be assessed by direct comparison of lengths. Thus, if a tape expands over time, it affects test-retest reliability. Because an absolute standard is available, reliability does not have to hinge on relative ordering. In fact, availability of an absolute standard is related to consistency in measurement of the phenomenon. The ratio scale property per se is not the key characteristic; it is the availability of an established external standard against which a measure can be assessed. The ratio scale property is not necessary, a temperature scale being an example. Time is similar to length in that the distance between the conceptual and the operational is small, at least in the past 300 years! Weight is perhaps more abstract than length—the construct is discernible through the sensory mode—but the correspondence between the construct and its measurement is not as apparent as for length. Again, an external standard is established and available that converts weight into calibrated intervals and presents symbols representing weights. Moreover, the measure follows from the conceptual definition, say, gravitational pull or how heavy an object is, but perhaps not as directly as length.

With physical properties, external measurement standards are available. Physical phenomena may appear more or less constant relative to psychological phenomena. However, many factors may impinge on physical measurement. For instance, the measurement of wind chill requires specifying measurement conditions, such as feet above the ground. As discussed in Chapter 8, the wind chill index represents a formative indicator of how cold air feels on human skin. It combines wind speed about 5 feet above the ground (human face level) with a calculation of heat transfer, skin tissue resistance, clear night sky conditions, and a calm wind threshold of 3 miles per hour. Although formed by precise observations and calculations, this measure requires certain assumptions, such as feet above the ground and wind at calm conditions. Administration conditions have to be specified for measurement. Extraneous factors may affect accurate measurement, say, wind conditions in measuring speed. Physical measurement is far from clear-cut as discussed because of variations in administration. Moreover, administration conditions need to be specified. Consider battery life measured through tests that simulate usage conditions in toys. Such specification necessarily incorporates some usage conditions while excluding others. Thus, some aspects of battery life are captured, and not others. Alternatively, the construct has to be redefined to be narrower. This is because "battery life" is an abstraction imposed by researchers. This example illustrates how physical constructs can be placed on a continuum where some involve abstractions, only slices of which are captured in measurement. Physical measurement is also based on assumptions about conditions, and about factors that lead to a phenomenon, with measurement procedures excluding some factors and including others. It is conceivable to form a summary measure that sums up items (or measurements) across different conditions somewhat like sampling from a domain of items.

Physiological measurement falls somewhere between physical measurement and psychological measurement. Here, human beings, rather than inanimate physical objects, are the focus. Although conscious control over physiological responses may be difficult, a variety of factors can lead to changes in readings. For example, blood pressure can be affected by posture or other factors. Yet external validation is available (i.e., absolute measurement that is not generated by respondents).

Considering constructs in the social sciences, responses are influenced by myriad psychological factors. Whereas physiological observations are not usually under conscious control, self-reports can be influenced by many factors, such as complex motivations for self-presentation. Also, external standards of measurement generally are not available. (A qualification is appropriate here because ability tests and other such measures are similar to physical measurement in many respects.) Rather, there are many metrics or units of measurement, usually relative rather than absolute. Thus, validation usually rests on relative rather than absolute criteria. Differences from absolute values are usually not meaningful because the notion of some precise absolute value is not available. An absolute standard is available when a narrow concrete physical/sensory dimension is captured. Alternatively, when a numerical scale, such as stock market performance or IQ, is agreed upon by convention, absolute differences are relevant.

Psychological attributes, of course, relate to the mind and necessarily involve abstract attributes. Thus, the distance between the conceptual and the operational is relatively large. Moreover, responses are provided by humans rather than merely recorded in the case of physical attributes. Complexities in human cognition and motivation influence responses, thus necessitating multiple nuanced items. Observations of human behavior, while involving only recording similar to physical measurement, typically purport to capture abstract psychological constructs. Measurement of constructs is usually indirect.

With physical measurement, different types of error can creep in through administration. Random error can occur because of, say, deviations in administering a measure. Either test-retest or multiple readings (i.e., very small time intervals) can be employed. Errors can occur in reading. A parallel here is with research associates or interviewers administering methods including observations. Say the observational method is employed to assess information search by recording the number of products examined in a store. Clear specification of the behavior to be recorded is needed, such as definition of an instance when products are removed from a shelf. In observations in physical measurement, the human element is involved in administering a measure and recording a reading. However, for psychological constructs, the observed element is an indicator of a latent construct. Moreover, the element needs clear definition, and measurement is subject to administration errors. Research associates who deviate from instructions can cause a variety of errors. But additionally, the measurement technique has inherent error in that the element of observation is an imperfect indicator of the underlying construct, say, information search (i.e., it is sampled from the domain of information search). This example captures the essence of the difference between physical and psychological measurement. Any item or measure is inherently imperfect in psychological measurement. Any item typically captures only a slice of an underlying construct. Moreover, there is error in the relationship between the item and the slice that it purports to capture. In a sense, the relationship between a construct and an item can be viewed as probabilistic in psychological measurement and deterministic in physical measurement.

Constructs in physical and physiological research are, of course, not necessarily concrete, narrow dimensions. Because abstract thinking is a part of the psychological makeup of human beings, psychological constructs that capture such thinking may be expected to be abstract, whereas physical and physiological constructs may be expected to be relatively concrete. However, when abstract thinking is applied to phenomena in the physical or physiological realm, abstract constructs are created. Consider medical research, where indications of narrow constructs, such as blood pressure, are then used to diagnose conditions. Levels of a variety of physiological indicators form or define conditions. Indicators of individual dimensions are combined to assess more abstract constructs. Such models (e.g., for disease diagnosis) could be considered as substantive relationships between constructs. However, they can also be viewed from a measurement perspective. Specific dimensions are combined to define a broader construct. Thus, certain symptoms in combination point to disease (i.e., formative indicators). For instance, cancer detection may involve looking for missing cells, reoriented cells, or sequencing of genetic codes.[5] However, a judgment has to be made by viewing these characteristics in the larger context of the patient's history; otherwise, a computer program rather than a pathologist would be able to make judgments. Paralleling the mind-body distinction, measurement involves psychological or physical characteristics. Physical attributes can be narrowly defined and translated on an available standard. They are discernible through sensory mechanisms or through symbolic representation (e.g., calories). The psychological element is manifest in human error, including bias in reading and administration; and in machine error. In physiological measurement, the psychological element is also manifest in the degree to which it influences the physiological, that is, in the degree to which the mind can be used to manipulate physiology. Abstracted constructs, such as diagnosis of diseases, involve the use of narrow indicators of physical characteristics to draw broader inferences. Note that the measurement of physical characteristics has error, sometimes considerable error, as well.

So, does the notion of a latent construct as used in the social sciences occur in physical or physiological measurement? If measures are observable, and each individual observation is of a slightly different aspect, then conditions or categories, such as diseases, are inferred from a combination of observations. Clearly, what underlies the symptoms is the disease. But each symptom is not an indicator of the disease as each item is a measure of a psychological construct. The item-as-measure model applies to abstract constructs capturing psychological phenomena. Here, the latent construct is an abstraction, and items are created to capture it in different ways. In physiological observations such as blood pressure, the parallel to multiple items is multiple readings. A different method to measure blood pressure would represent just that, and convergent validity would be germane. However, the notion in psychological constructs of developing a set of items rather than a single item to capture a latent construct is not paralleled for a relatively concrete physical or physiological measurement, that is, for a narrow construct that can be captured by a single item, such as weight or temperature. The measure is relatively close to the construct it captures. However, even a physical dimension such as battery life is an abstraction in the sense of covering a domain of applications or usage situations. As the distance between the conceptual and the operational increases, the potential for developing multiple measures of a construct increases. Restated, as distance decreases, the potential for developing multiple items as measures decreases. As the abstractness of constructs increases, multiple items are needed to cover the domain and to capture these constructs in different ways through different nuanced items. Dimensions are latent, and it is not fruitful to assign each item to be a different dimension. This could lead to countless dimensions, one for each item nuanced by wording—actually, an idiosyncratic combination of content and method. Thus, sets of items typically are used to represent single dimensions and cover the domain. Given the need to cover an abstract domain, dimensions or factors are not sliced narrowly but rather cover a sizable subdomain. For concrete measurement, different ways of measuring a concrete construct represent different measures rather than different items. Multiple repeated readings are the closest parallel to multiple items.

Note that the inherent nature of measurement is quite different in physical measurement—observing a physical reading versus some form of self-report or observation in psychological measurement. Hence, wording issues and the need for multiple items that are similar become critical in psychological measurement. Important here are different ways of capturing something while accounting for human differences in understanding items and generating responses. Moreover, the need to cover a domain, which does not rise to the level of multiple dimensions, is important. Thus, latency and abstractness of the construct and complexity in human self-reporting necessitate multiple-item scales.

The aim in psychological measurement is to approximate an abstract domain through a sampling of items (i.e., domain sampling) (Nunnally, 1978). The key word here is "approximate"—physical measurement that is relatively concrete could be captured by a single item. Psychological measurement and construct definition aim for some parsimony. Thus, constructs are approximated by a sampling of a domain. This is not purely deductive reasoning; it is both deductive and inductive. Conceptual or empirical analysis may suggest that a domain has to be split into dimensions. Such dimensions are then the unit of analysis approximated by a set of items. Carefully selected multiple items serve to enhance representation of the domain, an issue germane to validity. To the extent that items belong together, they enhance internal consistency reliability. Covariance across items enhances coefficient alpha.

Human error is involved in physical measurement. But this is often perceptual and sometimes motivational (say, in biased reading). The researcher, rather than the respondent, is involved in the recording of responses. A latent feeling is not being translated into a response to an item by a respondent or observer. Thus, in psychological measurement, uncertainty about capturing a domain because of distance between the conceptual and the operational, and uncertainty about human perception and response generation because of self-reports or observations by human beings, are two reasons to generate multiple items assuming an item-as-measure model. Another reason overlaps with multiple readings in physical measurement—the notion of averaging across error-filled trials. The notion of using multiple items for purposes of averaging is incomplete. It applies to physical measurement more than to psychological measurement. In psychological measurement, each item is also somewhat different, trying to capture different aspects of an abstract domain. Moreover, nuances in wording are used to elicit accurate responses from respondents. The latter is a way of assessing consistency across similar items, whereas the former is essentially getting at slightly different aspects of the domain.

Thus, physical measurement can involve aspects of psychological measurement, imperfect measurement of slices of constructs due to researcher-imposed abstractions, and various types of errors due to administration. In psychological measurement, the first issue is accentuated and qualitatively different, and the second issue involves some unique elements due to conscious responses being produced by human beings. Note that physiological measurement of attributes under human control fall on the margin between physical and psychological measurement. Thus, unique in psychological measurement is the human element in responses and the need for nuanced items. As noted earlier, sweeping distinctions between physical and psychological measurement are employed here for purposes of the discussion. However, differences in measurement within physical or within psychological measurement are vast. For instance, there are relatively concrete constructs in psychological research.

Another issue here is a type of measurement that falls along the continuum from physical to psychological measurement: the use of objective data on natural occurrences. As discussed in Chapter 8 and repeated here, when disparate concrete measures are studied to gain insight into a construct such as pace of life, a germane issue is whether these measures necessarily should converge if they are tapping into the same construct. Although the need for such convergence is evident when using an item-as-measure model and developing multiple items to tap into a construct, objective data from available sources do not fall into these neat categories. Rather, items aiming to measure pace of life, such as time taken for a transaction at the post office or pace of walking at a downtown area, are each idiosyncratic and naturally occurring, rather than responses to a carefully designed set of items. Such specific items are influenced by many factors in addition to the construct in question. The same is true of organizational indicators, such as R&D expenses or percentage of new products. In fact, each such concrete measure may provide some insight into the phenomenon, yet not be considered as measuring the same thing in terms of the degree of convergence among measures. Each different measure of, say, pace of life can in turn provide insight into different slices of a phenomenon, thus adding to understanding. In contrast, a self-report scale of pace of life summarizes it with all its implications into self-report items that are likely to covary. Measures formed from secondary data or natural observations do not fit into the category of a multiple-item scale and all the related criteria. The model of a latent construct measured by covarying items maps onto traditional self-reports on multiple items. But this model is not as easily transferable to items that are objective data on natural occurrences (Figure 11.4). Data based on natural occurrences have parallels with physical measurement of concrete things that are then accumulated into a broader construct, or physiological measurement, such as using physiological indicators to arrive at an overall diagnosis of a medical condition.

In a sense, the item-as-measure model of conceptualization corresponds to or maps onto a measurement process where respondents provide self-reports to items. The process of measurement corresponds to the nature of the relationship between items of a measure and the underlying construct. The measurement model suggests that levels of the underlying construct lead to responses on individual items. In actual measurement, the latent construct causes responses on items of a measure. Each item is capturing some aspect of the underlying construct. Each item is carefully constructed to capture primarily the construct, although it is subject to other influences. Although each item captures some different aspect of the domain of a construct, responses to items are expected to be correlated because they are caused by the same underlying construct. Objective data, on the other hand, are, in some sense, naturally occurring and subject to many influences, one of which is the construct in question (Figure 11.4). Rather than being carefully constructed items that primarily capture the construct in question, they are naturally occurring and also happen to (sometimes coincidentally or accidentally) provide data on a construct. Structured observations are somewhere in the middle, essentially the continuum being from self-reports on items to structured observations in response to carefully designed stimuli to naturally occurring events.

Informal Measurement

Humans are informal measurement experts in social lives, or so we may think. In daily life, inferences are drawn from a sample of information about abstract notions. Various types of errors occur with parallels in research. Noteworthy in social judgments is self-presentation, which represents some manifestation of underlying traits. It represents the generation of certain levels of variables akin to manipulations in experimental design. Individuals explore and interact with the environment by generating levels of underlying traits, sometimes inflated or disguised. Thus, individuals and events are stimuli that are "rated" by observers. The very act of being observed (measured)

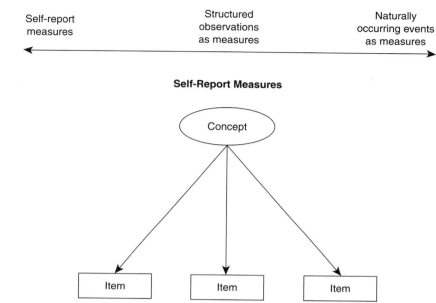

Self-report
measures

Structured
observations
as measures

Naturally
occurring events
as measures

Self-Report Measures

Concept

Item   Item   Item

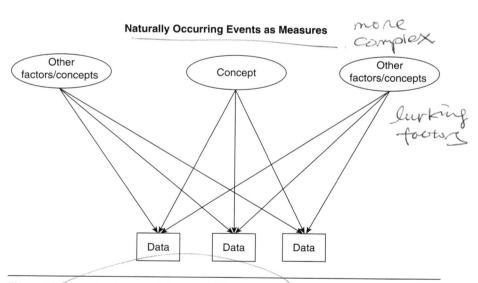

Naturally Occurring Events as Measures   *more complex*

Other
factors/concepts

Concept

Other
factors/concepts

lurking factors

Data   Data   Data

Figure 11.4   Continuum of Types of Measures

can change behavior (responses). Observers form impressions akin to measurement by researchers, although often forming judgments simultaneously on multiple dimensions. Once impressions are formed, subsequent data may be interpreted in light of these previous impressions. Avoiding biases in scientific research, in interpretation of the data, in the design of studies, and so on parallel similar biases in day-to-day life. Impressions formed from data may then be used to interpret subsequent data. As discussed in terms of circles of thinking, what is known influences what is looked for, how it is looked for, and what is found.

Focusing on day-to-day judgments by observers, a variety of errors can occur. Random error occurs because of factors such as the observer being distracted or ambiguity in the behavior being observed. Thus, a subsequent observation may have led to a different impression. Of course, such subsequent observation may never occur, fortunately or unfortunately. Similarly, additive systematic error can occur because the observer is biased one way or the other. Correlational systematic error occurs across measures in the extent to which relationships between different traits are overestimated or underestimated (i.e., the degree to which there is a halo effect in forming impressions on multiple traits). Thus, a "naive" measurement model is employed in day-to-day life. As per this model, the observer is the researcher. Single-person judgments rather than sample-based aggregate judgments are common. Correlational systematic error occurs for individual judgments rather than across individuals in a sample. Data collection is, of course, informal. Multiple items translate to multiple observations of behavior. Moreover, a single construct is not necessarily in focus for the observer. Rather, multiple constructs may be accessed or identified after the fact. Therefore, single pieces of data may not be associated with a specific construct. Constructs are sorted out by observers, data being occurrences akin to observational or secondary data, which may involve multiple constructs, or responses to specific questions akin to self-reports, which may involve one or more constructs. Thus, informal measurement is useful in understanding our roles in day-to-day lives as researchers. Researchers in a discovery mode often attempt to understand natural observations. The inferences they draw may suffer from problems similar to those in informal measurement. Such problems in informal measurement have parallels in qualitative research and in quantitative research, such as using natural occurrences as measures. These issues also point to the complexities involved in conducting research and drawing conclusions about phenomena.

Calibration is an essential aspect of measurement and experimental design. In physical measurement, calibration involves application of an external standard. In social judgments, however, calibration is a relative process based on prior experiences and cognitive styles. Consider any overall judgments of specific individuals in daily life. Calibration requires some comparative standard, such as other individuals in general or other individuals who are similar on some characteristics. In contrast, physical measurement may have an objective, "ruler-like" standard available. For social judgments, observers have to create their own rulers. These rulers may be based on other individuals, an aggregation of individuals, or the same individual based on past observations (i.e., across time). Each malleable ruler can lead to a different judgment. Perspective is relative, and broader or narrower perspectives lead to different rulers. Individuals may struggle with context. Incorporating context into judgments leads to variation in rulers. Thus, naive measurement models and naive psychometrics in day-to-day life involve judgments based on measurements or observations. Judgments of best and worst and everything in between are based on a ruler. Each ruler has inherent systematic error, either additive or correlational. Comparison to extreme standards leads to contrast effects. Assimilation can similarly cause error. Thus, from a naive measurement perspective, judgment errors can be categorized into formal categories of measurement error. Naive measurement models are also useful when assessing measurement through interviews and other qualitative research. Similar issues of calibration arise in research. Quantitative measurement aims for reliable and valid rulers that are usable across respondents. Calibration of magnitudes of effects is difficult, as is evaluating studies and their contexts. There is no precise ruler for many aspects of research, just as there is no ruler for day-to-day events. Importance of topics and variables, magnitudes of effects, calibrations of manipulations, argumentation against alternative explanations, and so on require qualitative insights gained from experience.

Constructs are also used by individuals from a philosophical or religious perspective. Sustaining beliefs that provide a means to negotiate day-to-day life are often tested by reality, in a sense similar to scientific testing. Such belief systems may well be the most abstract of construct networks, dealing with the human mind and its conception of existence, the meaning of life, and other such issues. Reality offers data on various measures all intertwined into events, which is then matched with belief systems. For researchers as well, broader guiding beliefs or philosophies, say, about the nature of human beings or of markets, and so on can influence more context-specific research. Awareness of and correction for these personal orientations are part of the necessary mind frame for the conduct of science.

The use or misuse of numbers in informal measurement also has parallels in research. Numbers provide precision in a complex environment, something to focus on, whether it be the Dow Jones Industrial Average, a company's ROI, the master points earned by a bridge player, the price of a product, or an individual's weight. Numbers are precise and concrete, providing what is often a false sense of certainty and, sometimes, a short-term focus reflecting the availability and time frame associated with numbers. Such a treatment of numbers is paralleled in research as well. A literal focus on narrow statistics and concrete rules is one symptom in research. Once collected, numbers may take on an aura, all the more so perhaps when analyzed through high-level statistics and presented with sophisticated graphics. Measures are sometimes equated with constructs, and numbers are assumed to represent constructs without error. Many measures based on secondary data or natural occurrences are used to draw inferences about one or more constructs. In summary, various types of errors that occur in informal measurement have parallels in research and point to potential pitfalls for researchers.

Ethics in Measurement

A brief note on ethics is relevant here when discussing issues relating to measurement and science. Generally, ethics is discussed in various disciplines as a distinct topic applied to specific situations. When it comes to research, though, good research and good ethics may often go hand in hand. The discussion of accuracy in measurement and the need for a mind frame that aims for accuracy has important ethical implications. Intellectual honesty and accuracy are really two sides of the same coin. At a broader level, if a researcher uses unethical means to achieve desired ends, the credibility of the research and the researcher is open to question on all fronts.

From the viewpoint of respondents, informed consent (e.g., disclosure of research method to respondents to the extent possible without contaminating a study in order to enable informed choice), reasonable demands on time and effort, appropriate debriefing, and confidentiality are important elements. Appropriate treatment of respondents is both good ethics and good research. If a respondent is informed that a study will take 15 minutes and it takes 30 minutes, the data collected in the last 15 minutes are questionable and may reflect justifiable anger. Often, the issue is not one of ethics as much as of making good judgments, but the outcome may be similar.

In both quantitative and qualitative research, ethical issues arise frequently. Ultimately, issues from the research viewpoint come down to striving to be accurate in measurement and presenting the data on measurement for what they are. When testing hypotheses in quantitative research and interpreting results, ethical issues arise in the need to maintain sufficient detachment despite investment in the research, the desire for specific results that will enable successful publication, and so forth. In qualitative research, sufficient detachment is needed, whether in reading too much in the data given the inherent desire to find something, or in collecting data slanted to confirm previous conclusions or at the expense of the informants' privacy or psychological state (e.g., questions that exploit weaknesses in research on low-literate consumers). To summarize, in both quantitative and qualitative research, good ethics and good research design may often go hand in hand.

Summary

Accurate measurement is central to the conduct of science. Several basic assumptions are involved in quantitative measurement. When these assumptions do not hold, qualitative research is a viable alternative. Physical versus psychological measurement can be compared and contrasted to understand the conduct of the social sciences. Circles of thinking may occur by measuring the measurable and researching the researchable, suggesting the need to infuse new insights and perspectives into the research. Informal measurement in day-to-day life has parallels with measurement in science and points to potential pitfalls for researchers. And finally, good research and good ethics may often go hand in hand, honesty and accuracy really being two sides of the same coin.

Notes

1. In this regard, researchers in quantitative research have argued for a comparative rather than a confirmatory approach to theory testing (Sternthal, Tybout, & Calder, 1987); the former emphasizes showing the superiority of one explanation over rival explanations, whereas the latter emphasizes using validated measures and multiple operationalizations.

2. The distinction between "quantitative" and "qualitative" research methods is itself quite ambiguous (Hammersley, 1996). In the terminology employed here, quantitative research is characterized by numbers being assigned to levels of variables. Quantitative versus qualitative research involves measurement with or without mediation through numbers, respectively.

3. Whether criteria such as reliability and validity are relevant in qualitative research is open to debate (Merrick, 1999). Reliability, as in consistency, is not readily applicable to qualitative studies. Researchers have enumerated parallel criteria, such as dependability to parallel reliability, credibility to parallel internal validity, and transferability to parallel external validity (Lincoln & Guba, 1985). Dependability could be shown through an inquiry audit where the process and findings of the research are evaluated (Lincoln & Guba, 1985). Credibility can be shown through sustained engagement; triangulation, where accuracy of data

is checked using multiple sources; peer debriefing; negative case analysis, where hypotheses are revised with additional findings; and member checking, where findings are checked with informants (Lincoln & Guba, 1985). Trustworthiness is another criterion discussed by qualitative researchers and includes disclosures about the researcher's biases, engagement with the material, sustained observation, triangulation, and discussion with others (Stiles, 1993).

4. Nisbett (2003) makes this point in comparing cross-cultural differences in research. He argues for an analytical versus holistic difference in research in the United States versus Europe.

5. Thanks to Dr. Ramesh Ramanathan for educating me about cancer detection in the course of researching for this book.

12

What Are the Principles and Guiding Orientations of This Book?

Overview

This chapter summarizes some of the key issues discussed in this book. The concluding chapter is as good a place as any to discuss the orientation that underlies the material covered in this book. Following a summary of chapters and implications for measurement and methodology, the guiding principles or orientations that underlie the material in this book are summarized. This concluding discussion to the book at the end of the chapter puts the material covered in perspective.

Summary of Chapters

There are two basic types of measurement error in all of scientific research—random error and systematic error—related to reliability and validity. The measure development process consists of a series of steps to develop reliable and valid measures. Rather than proceed directly from an abstract construct to its concrete measurement, the distance between the conceptual and the operational has to be traversed carefully and iteratively. Measure development ideally should combine empirical assessment with conceptual examination.

Random and systematic error can be further categorized into subtypes: idiosyncratic and generic random error, and additive (constant and partial) and correlational systematic error within and across measures. Various sources of error lead to different types of error, which are reflected in response patterns that are assessed through empirical procedures. A detailed examination of this interplay provides the foundation for this book. Many sources can cause each of the types of measurement error described. By understanding what causes error, these sources can be minimized in the design of items and measures. These sources can be roughly categorized into individual-related sources of errors (idiosyncratic and generic) and method-related sources of errors, with the latter being separated into item content, response format, and administration issues. Empirical procedures commonly employed during measure development—specifically, internal consistency, test-retest reliability, and factor analyses—capture a wider set of errors than intended. A low correlation between an item and the total score could be caused by several errors other than random error.

A three-step process is presented for identifying and correcting for measurement error at each stage of measure development: (a) assessing diagnostics from traditional psychometric procedures, design characteristics of psychometric tests, and conditions of future usage; (b) identifying specific types of error using these diagnostics; and (c) correcting for error. Recommendations are made at five different levels: item (e.g., changes in wording of items), measure (i.e., the aggregate set of items that comprises the measure, such as changes to response scales, changes in sequencing of items, short forms, and use of filler items from other measures between items), administration (i.e., aspects of a method at a more aggregate level than a single measure, such as sequencing of measures of multiple constructs, procedures, settings, and samples), data analysis (e.g., specifying method factors), and construct (i.e., reassessing the construct conceptually, such as rethinking its dimensionality).

Implications from understanding measurement error at a conceptual level include innovative design and analyses that can be used to identify measurement error in both measure development and research design. Insight into the nature of measurement error during measure development can be gained using internal consistency and test-retest reliability in conjunction, using correlations across item-level correlations, and assessing the effects of item ordering. These unique approaches can help reduce error in the development of items, measures, and methods.

Measures differ in fundamental ways with implications for their development, validation, and usage. For instance, measures can be categorized as stimulus-centered versus respondent-centered scales. Measures can also be categorized as formative versus reflective; many prescriptions in earlier chapters apply to the latter. Formative indicators predefine the measure of the construct, and the issue of internal consistency does not arise, nor do some other issues germane to reflective indicators.

An examination of scales across different disciplines provides stimulating examples of creative design. Rather than restrict consideration to self-report measures of agreement with statements, researchers can be creative in designing scales that capture the construct of interest by considering a variety of approaches and formats from different disciplines. At one end of what is really a continuum are purely relative scales that aim to order events, objects, or individuals. At the other end are physical scales with a clear external standard and one-to-one correspondence (e.g., length or time). Cross-cultural measurement raises a host of challenging issues relating to whether a construct exists in a different culture, whether similar dimensions exist, whether measures are valid across cultures, and so on.

An understanding of measurement error has implications for the use of existing measures in research methods, for the use of structural equation modeling (SEM), and for measurement in applied research. The framework of error and error sources is central in evaluating and using existing measures with or without modification. The proposed framework can provide a robust set of items for SEM to begin with as well as sufficient preliminary work and theoretical justification for measurement models in SEM. Many of the issues discussed in this book are as important for applied research as for basic research.

Understanding the measurement or manipulation of many things and the entire design has been the theme throughout this book. The nuanced discussions of error, including across-measure systematic error, and error sources, including administration factors and data collection on measures of multiple constructs in a research design, are examples of this orientation. The principles described in measuring one thing are used in the measurement and manipulation of multiple things (i.e., in the design of an entire method: different types of designs, strength of tests of hypotheses, methodological replications, and a broader discussion of the application of measurement principles to the entire research method).

Accurate measurement is central to the conduct of science. Several basic assumptions are involved in quantitative measurement. When these assumptions do not hold, qualitative research is a viable alternative. Physical versus psychological measurement can be compared and contrasted to understand the conduct of the social sciences. Circles of thinking may occur by measuring the measurable and researching the researchable, suggesting the need to infuse new insights and perspectives into the research. Informal measurement in day-to-day life has parallels with measurement in science and points to potential pitfalls for researchers. And finally, good research and good ethics may often go hand in hand.

Implications for Measurement and Research Design

A central theme of this book is that measurement error should be understood in each stage of developing measures and in their use. Another central theme is that errors in developing and using measures are closely interrelated: Understanding error in one requires understanding error in the other. These dual themes motivate the guidelines to identify and correct for error in developing and using measures. By pursuing these guidelines, researchers can conduct substantive studies in extended research programs with improved methodological design and interpretation of results. The suggestion here is not that all measurement errors can be eliminated—this is clearly impossible. However, it is possible to use a fuller understanding of measurement error in designing research, analyzing and interpreting data, and acknowledging limitations, all of which are essential to sound empirical research.

This book examines the concepts of random and systematic error. Important conceptual distinctions are drawn between idiosyncratic and generic random error (within and across administrations), additive systematic error (constant and partial), within-measure correlational systematic error (due to a common method factor and due to different traits/specific method factors), and across-measure systematic error. This book also examines how these types of error have been operationalized in traditional measure development procedures. The level of correspondence between fundamental measurement concepts and their operationalization in traditional empirical procedures leads to important considerations during measure development and validation. Whereas past research has addressed many of these issues in different ways, the primary contribution here is in subjecting measurement error to an examination of conceptual meaning and operationalization. Hence, measurement error involved in assessing measurement error is the focus.

This analysis leads to a framework within which to view measurement error in measure development and methodological design. Whereas more specific implications have been discussed throughout the book, at a broader level, this book emphasizes the importance of conceptual examination of measurement error in conjunction with empirical analyses employing indicators of measurement error. Analyses based purely on empirical results may be incomplete, and examination of the nature of error involved is important using the conceptual distinctions in measurement error developed here. For example, for internal consistency procedures, low item-to-correlation, an indicator of random error, may be the result of a variety of conceptually distinct errors: idiosyncratic random error, suggesting sufficient sample sizes; generic random error, suggesting item deletion or modification of administration procedures; additive systematic error, suggesting directions for item editing (toning up or down) or item generation; and correlational systematic error, suggesting confirmatory factor analysis, empirical examination of measure characteristics, and content analysis for redundancy. Similar implications are drawn for test-retest reliability, factor analysis, internal consistency and test-retest reliability in conjunction, and validity tests.

During measure development, internal consistency and test-retest procedures can be used in conjunction to identify the nature of measurement error that is influencing item response. Empirical analyses illustrated earlier can provide insight into the types of error that may be driving item response. The line of reasoning developed here also emphasizes the importance of multiple administrations of internal consistency procedures across different settings where a measure is likely to be employed, with test-retest procedures being used for strict replication to assess item wording issues. In this regard, generalizability studies offer a comprehensive approach to understanding the nature of measurement error across items and occasions. Empirical tests designed to assess measure characteristics, such as item ordering, may also be useful. Another important implication is the use of measure assessment procedures that mimic future usage of scales and the specification of conditions for usage of measures in substantive studies. Because scales can benefit from correlational systematic error within measures, the use of modified forms of scales or the use of fillers in substantive studies requires separate measure assessment and validation procedures. Measure assessment cannot be accomplished at the item level, the implicit assumption in varying item ordering during methodological design from conditions under testing. Rather, assessment necessarily has to be at the level of the method, which includes items, sequencing, and instructions. In a sense, what is validated is not the measure itself but its use, and construct measurement involves a "trait-method union" (Campbell & Fiske, 1959, p. 81; Finn & Kayande, 1997).

For validity tests, key concerns relate to across-measure systematic error due to related traits or methods. An understanding of the nature and direction of likely systematic error can guide design and interpretation of validity tests. Depending on the direction of hypothesized relationships and the direction of systematic error, strong tests of validity can be designed. Across-measure correlational systematic error should be addressed explicitly in the design of specific validity tests through grouping or separation of central variables and consideration of alternatives, such as randomization of item order and the use of multiple methods for different variables.

Underlying many of the prescriptions discussed here is the issue of content validity. The development of items with content validity is at the beginning of the process of measure development. Whereas the thrust of the implications is on identifying the nature of measurement error in conjunction with empirical procedures, adhering to procedures that facilitate the development of items with content validity "before the fact" can reduce both random and systematic error. Researchers have documented a host of issues that need to be addressed in developing content-valid items (DeVellis, 1991; Haynes et al., 1995). Through careful attention to crucial steps in developing content validity, such as specification of the domain and dimensions of a construct, item generation, and item editing, many of the errors discussed above can be minimized. For example, careful item wording and editing can decrease generic random error, as well as additive systematic error (through proper toning of items), and careful representation of the domain of a construct can minimize within-measure correlational systematic error. An examination of the taxonomy of error sources presented in Chapter 3 suggests that a host of errors can be minimized through careful attention to procedures for establishing content validity.

The issues discussed in this book have important implications for the methodological design of substantive studies, such as experimental and nonexperimental (correlational) designs. Validated measures that are employed under untested conditions (i.e., a change in the order of items or in interviewer instructions or in differences in setting) may involve systematic error pertaining to related methods and traits. Additional assessment is needed to evaluate the measures under untested conditions. Scales that have not been validated in prior work may tap into related traits/methods, which are sources of systematic error that may inflate or deflate correlations. Multiple interpretations can be made from data collected under such conditions involving confounded methodological and substantive factors.

These issues are also of importance to the reliability and validity of dependent variables in experiments and have been well documented in the literature (Cook & Campbell, 1979). Procedures to minimize random and systematic error also play a role in the reliability and validity of treatment manipulations, in developing measures for checking manipulations (Perdue & Summers, 1986), in developing treatments wherein random error in manipulations may lead to unreliability and additive systematic error may lead to floor and ceiling effects, and in placing manipulation checks within a set of measures in the context of an administration. In addition, experimental design issues are different in that causal variables take precedence and involve generating certain levels of dimensions rather than measuring them. Systematic error between a manipulated independent variable and a dependent variable may result from factors such as demand characteristics. Independent and dependent variables can be administered in several ways to avoid systematic error, such as separation of central dependent variables, dual administration, and randomization of the order of items tapping various dependent variables. Whereas the requirement of obtaining a clean inference on the central dependent variable suggests that no other fillers or dependent variables precede it, the need to minimize systematic error may suggest otherwise, leading to a trade-off between internal validity and construct validity. Separation of independent and dependent variables is important for the construct validity of the design, as in the case of correlational designs. When multiple dependent variables are used in experimental designs, the issues discussed for correlational designs are relevant.

This book prescribes explicit conceptual examination of measurement error in conjunction with empirical analyses employing indicators of measurement error, as well as the design of specific studies to assess measure characteristics, to enhance measure development and methodological design. An examination of research in the social sciences suggests several areas where the prescriptions developed here may be relevant. Measurement has made many strides, yet measure development and methodological design procedures should extend beyond the use of appropriate empirical techniques to conceptual examination and thorough explication of the nature of measurement error involved. An often-neglected aspect of measure validation and methodological design is explicit consideration of systematic error. This book echoes and reinforces classic work from past research that has emphasized the importance of construct validation and the lack of attention to method variance (Campbell, 1996) and emphasizes the importance of conceptual examination of measurement error in measure validation and methodological design. Measurement error occurs in the operationalization of the concepts of measurement error with important implications for measure development and methodological design in scholarly research in the social sciences.

The issues discussed in this book have numerous implications for future research. For instance, future research should examine the relative influence of such generic factors as sequencing, the use of fillers, and unique instructions on the psychometric properties of measures and the consequent estimation of relationships between variables. Research on the effects of a variety of factors on responses in survey research, with its focus on estimating accurate means (Sudman et al., 1996), provides a noteworthy parallel. Examples such as research demonstrating higher reliability of later items are available for academic research on psychometrics. However, such a research stream can be envisioned and pursued more formally using the categories of errors described here. Rather than assuming that measures are not sensitive to methodological factors, what is required is a prioritization of methodological factors through conceptual reasoning and empirical evidence. For example, differential ordering of items may not be as important as using fillers between items or using measures in vastly different populations. Unless these factors are systematically examined, many aspects of research methodology will remain largely implicit and without explication. Future research should examine the relationship between sources of error and types of measurement error (e.g., the sources of idiosyncratic random error). An understanding of why and when specific types of measurement errors occur will facilitate the methodological design of studies.

Summary of Orientations

Several guiding principles, or orientations, that underlie the material in this book are discussed to put the material covered in perspective.

Measurement-Related Issues

Some issues relate specifically to measurement. One key point made here is the importance of examining measures both conceptually and empirically. Understanding of measurement error in considerable depth can lead to improved design of items, measures, and methods. Related to this issue is the need to understand measurement at an intuitive level in terms of what error is and what causes it rather than at a purely statistical level, which may create a distance in terms of understanding. In many ways, as discussed in Chapter 11 on measurement in daily life, researchers may be susceptible to the same misuse of numbers as anyone else. Measurement involves rules for assigning numbers. Numbers can be precise and concrete, and therefore illusive to researchers. Where these numbers came from should be kept in perspective. And approximate accuracy may be preferable to illusory precision.

Another issue is that the use of a measure has to be understood in order to develop it. Validity and reliability are not characteristics of a measure but of how it is used—that is, essentially everything that is done to collect the data. Reliability and validity relate to particular uses of a measure, and these usage conditions need to be articulated and validated. Users of measures should develop conceptual and empirical support for using short forms and making other modifications to existing measures.

Measures can be developed with much creativity and thinking outside the box. They do not have to be restricted to self-reports and agree/disagree scales. Creativity has to be coupled with efforts to demonstrate validity, a scientific necessity. But creative measures may actually elicit more interest on the part of the respondent and may increase reliability and validity. This is akin to having an interesting conversation, a parallel that has been drawn in relation to questionnaire design (Sudman & Bradburn, 1982).

Considerable preliminary work is essential before using structural equation modeling in a confirmatory fashion. Such work that improves items and measures can provide the basis to interpret the results of structural equation modeling. Rather than put all the eggs into a basket and invest in a single study, preliminary measurement work can improve the measurement model and lead to improved design of substantive tests of hypotheses.

Generic Issues in Research Methodology

Some issues relate to methodology in general. The method is really everything that is done to collect data. Although there is no convenient and detailed categorization of everything that is done, it can be divided roughly into measures and manipulations, settings, samples, and administration procedures; in other words, who provides the data (sample), where they provide the data (setting), on what they provide the data (measures and manipulations), and how they provide the data (administration procedures).

As discussed, treatment of measurement and methodological issues at an intuitive level is one orientation in this book. Intuitive treatment enables understanding of methodological procedures. Rather than view statistical procedures in distant terms, the aim here is to make them accessible by examining what all these numbers mean and from where they come.

Another orientation is that both research methods and statistical analyses are a means to an end rather than an end in themselves. The end is to gain understanding about phenomena. Rather than look for literal rules and be guided exclusively by stringent empirical criteria, it may be fruitful to keep the end in perspective. Scientific disciplines and orientations are, in a sense, similar to distinct, narrow compartments. For example, a narrow compartment could be characterized by a narrow statistical orientation.

Two guidelines that can be followed in empirical research are careful design before the fact and interpretation of findings in light of limitations after the fact. Sophisticated analyses may not be able to overcome poor design. For instance, if related measures are placed next to each other and lead to a strong hypothesized relationship, alternative methodological explanations loom, which may be extremely difficult, perhaps impossible, to account for through data analyses. If a measure has poor reliability, the onus should be on the researcher to improve it rather than to depend on an attenuation formula. There is usually no substitute for sound design.

The measurement framework can be moved up a level in unit of analysis to assess experimental and correlational designs, and even qualitative designs. Experimental manipulations involve generating levels of constructs along continua. At the core here is reliability, which transfers to strict replicability; convergent validity, which transfers to multiple operationalizations and conceptual replicability; nomological validity, which transfers to making theoretical sense out of findings; and discriminant validity, which transfers to ruling out alternative explanations.

Researchers may be restricted by narrow circles of measuring the measurable and researching the researchable. What they know (theory) can determine what they look for and how they look for it (method), as well as what they find (that is, how they interpret the data), which in turn determines what they know. Tangential intellectual forces are needed to broaden out of such circles of thinking. Ultimately, research requires a frame of mind or a mentality to be genuinely open to unexpected outcomes and to pursue accurate measurement.

Quantitative measurement should be contrasted with qualitative research, where the researcher is the measurement instrument. The very rules that are central to quantitative research, in terms of using a structured process that emphasizes consistent procedures and facilitates comparisons, are deliberately and appropriately broken in qualitative research. The researcher—the measurement instrument—directly draws inferences about relationships between constructs rather than isolating each construct and studying it.

It is only fitting to close with a note on ethics, which is generally discussed in various disciplines as a distinct topic. When it comes to research, though, good research and good ethics may often go hand in hand. Honesty and accuracy are really two sides of the same coin.

References

Achenbach, T. M. (1992). *Manual for the Child Behavior Checklist/2–3 and 1992 profile*. Burlington: University of Vermont Press.

Aiken, L. R. (1974). Two scales of attitude toward mathematics. *Journal for Research in Mathematics Education, 5*(3), 67–71.

Aiken, L. R. (1998). *Tests and examinations: Measuring abilities and performance*. New York: Wiley.

Alfonso, V. C. (1995). Measures of quality of life, subjective well-being and satisfaction with life. In D. B. Allison (Ed.), *Handbook of assessment methods for eating behavior and weight-related problems: Measures, theory, and research* (pp. 23–80). Thousand Oaks, CA: Sage.

Alliger, G. M., & Williams, K. J. (1992). Relating the internal consistency of scales to rater response tendencies. *Educational and Psychological Measurement, 52*, 337–343.

Allison, D. B. (1995). *Handbook of assessment methods for eating behaviors and weight-related problems: Measures, theory, and research*. Thousand Oaks, CA: Sage.

Anderson, J. C. (1985). A measurement model to assess measure-specific factors in multiple-informant research. *Journal of Marketing Research, 22*, 86–92.

Anderson, J. C., & Gerbing, D. W. (1984). The effect of sampling error on convergence, improper solutions, and goodness-of-fit indices for maximum likelihood confirmatory factor analysis. *Psychometrika, 49*, 155–173.

Anderson, J. C., & Gerbing, D. W. (1988). Structural equation modeling in practice: A review and recommended two step approach. *Psychological Bulletin, 103*, 411–423.

Andrews, F. M. (1984). Construct validity and error components of survey measures: A structural modeling approach. *Public Opinion Quarterly, 48*, 409–442.

Bachman, J. G., & O'Malley, P. M. (1984). Yea-saying, nay-saying, and going to extremes: Black-white differences in response styles. *Public Opinion Quarterly, 48*, 491–509.

Bagozzi, R. P. (1980). *Causal models in marketing*. New York: Wiley.

Bagozzi, R. P. (1983). Issues in the application of covariance structure analysis: A further comment. *Journal of Consumer Research, 9*, 449–450.

Bagozzi, R. P. (1984, Winter). A prospectus for theory construction in marketing. *Journal of Marketing, 48*, 11–29.

Bagozzi, R. P. (1991). Further thoughts on the validity of measures of elation, gladness, and joy. *Journal of Personality and Social Psychology, 61,* 98–104.

Bagozzi, R. P. (1993). Assessing construct validity in personality research: Applications to measures of self-esteem. *Journal of Research in Personality, 27,* 49–87.

Bagozzi, R. P., & Edwards, J. R. (1998). A general approach to representing constructs in organizational research. *Organizational Research Methods, 1*(1), 45–87.

Bagozzi, R. P., & Heatherton, T. F. (1994). A general approach to representing multifaceted personality constructs: Application to state self-esteem. *Structural Equation Modeling, 1*(1), 35–67.

Bagozzi, R. P., & Yi, Y. (1988). On the evaluation of structural equation models. *Journal of the Academy of Marketing Science, 16*(1), 74–94.

Bagozzi, R. P., & Yi, Y. (1991). Multitrait-multimethod matrices in consumer research. *Journal of Consumer Research, 17*(3), 426–439.

Bagozzi, R. P., & Yi, Y. (1992). Testing hypotheses about methods, traits, and commonalities in the direct-product model. *Applied Psychological Measurement, 16*(4), 373–380.

Bagozzi, R. P., & Yi, Y. (1994). Advanced topics in structural equation models. In R. P. Bagozzi (Ed.), *Advanced methods of marketing research* (pp. 1–51). Cambridge, MA: Basil Blackwell.

Bagozzi, R. P., Yi, Y., & Phillips, L. W. (1991). Assessing construct validity in organizational research. *Administrative Science Quarterly, 36,* 421–458.

Bardo, J. W., Yeager, S. J., & Klingsporn, M. J. (1982). Preliminary assessment of format-specific central tendency and leniency error in summated rating scales. *Perceptual and Motor Skills, 54,* 227–234.

Baumgartner, H., & Steenkamp, J. B. (2001). Response styles in marketing research: A cross-national investigation. *Journal of Marketing Research, 38*(2), 143–156.

Bearden, W. O., & Netemeyer, R. G. (1999). *Handbook of marketing scales: Multi-item measures for marketing and consumer behavior research* (2nd ed.). Thousand Oaks, CA: Sage.

Bearden, W. O., Netemeyer, R. G., & Teel, J. E. (1989). Measurement of consumer susceptibility to interpersonal influence. *Journal of Consumer Research, 15,* 473–481.

Beere, C. A. (1990). *Sex and gender issues: A handbook of tests and measures.* Westport, CT: Greenwood.

Bendig, A. W. (1954). Reliability and the number of rating scale categories. *Journal of Applied Psychology, 38*(1), 38–40.

Bentler, P. M. (1969). Semantic space is (approximately) bipolar. *Journal of Psychology, 71,* 33–40.

Bentler, P. M. (1990). Comparative fit indices in structural models. *Psychological Bulletin, 107*(2), 238–246.

Bentler, P. M., & Bonnett, D. G. (1980). Significance tests and goodness of fit in the analysis of covariance structures. *Psychological Bulletin, 88,* 588–606.

Berkowitz, L., & Donnerstein, E. (1982). External validity is more than skin deep: Some answers to criticisms of laboratory experiments. *American Psychologist, 37*(3), 245–257.

Berscheid, E., Snyder, M., & Omoto, A. M. (1989). The Relationship Closeness Inventory: Assessing the closeness of interpersonal relationships. *Journal of Personality and Social Psychology, 57,* 792–807.

Bollen, K. A. (1986). Sample size and Bentler and Bonnett's nonnormed fit index. *Psychometrika, 51*(3), 375–377.

Bollen, K. A. (1989). *Structural equations with latent variables.* New York: Wiley.

Bollen, K. A., & Lennox, R. (1991). Conventional wisdom on measurement: A structural equation perspective. *Psychological Bulletin, 110*(2), 305–314.

Boomsma, A. (1982). Robustness of LISREL against small sample sizes in factor analysis models. In K. G. Jöreskog & H. Wold (Eds.), *Systems under indirect observation: Causality, structure, prediction* (Vol. 1, pp. 149–173). Amsterdam: North Holland.

Braucht, N. G. (1972). Analysis and reduction of components of systematic error in ratings. *Multivariate Behavioral Research, 7*(2), 203–222.

Brazelton, T. B. (1973). *Neonatal Behavioral Assessment Scale.* Philadelphia, PA: Lippincott.

Brennan, R. L., & Prediger, D. J. (1981). Coefficient Kappa: Some uses, misuses, and alternatives. *Educational and Psychological Measurement, 41,* 687–99.

Briggs, S. R., & Cheek, J. M. (1988). On the nature of self-monitoring: Problems with assessment, problems with validity. *Journal of Personality and Social Psychology, 54*(4), 663–678.

Britt, T. W. (1993). Metatraits: Evidence relevant to the validity of the construct and its implications. *Journal of Personality and Social Psychology, 65*(3), 554–562.

Bruner, G. C., II, & Hensel, P. J. (1992). *Marketing scales handbook: A compilation of multi-item measures.* Chicago: American Marketing Association.

Buck, R. (1976). A test of nonverbal receiving ability: Preliminary studies. *Human Communication Research, 2,* 162–71.

Burdock, E. I., & Hardesty, A. S. (1967). *Children's Behavior Inventory.* New York: Springer.

Cacioppo, J. T., & Petty, R. E. (1982). The need for cognition. *Journal of Personality and Social Psychology, 42*(1), 116–131.

Cacioppo, J. T., Petty, R. E., & Kao, C. F. (1984). The efficient assessment of need for cognition. *Journal of Personality Assessment, 48*(3), 306–307.

Cain, L. F., Levine, S., & Elzey, F. F. (1963). *Manual for the Cain-Levin Social Competency Scale.* Palo Alto, CA: Consulting Psychologists Press.

Calder, B. J., Phillips, L. W., & Tybout, A. M. (1981). Designing research for application. *Journal of Consumer Research, 8,* 197–207.

Campbell, D. P. (1974). *Manual for the SVIB-SCII Strong-Campbell Interest Inventory.* (2nd ed.), Stanford, CA: Stanford University Press.

Campbell, D. P., Hyne, S. A., & Nilsen, D. (1992). *Manual for the Campbell interest and skill survey.* Minneapolis, MN: National Computer Systems.

Campbell, D. T. (1996). Unresolved issues in measurement validity: An auto-biographical overview. *Psychological Assessment, 8*(4), 363–368.

Campbell, D. T., & Fiske, D. W. (1959). Convergent and discriminant validation by the multitrait-multimethod matrix. *Psychological Bulletin, 56*(3), 100–122.

Campbell, D. T., & O'Connell, E. J. (1967). Method factors in multivariate-multimethod matrices: Multiplicative rather than additive? *Multivariate Behavioral Research, 2*, 409–426.

Campbell, D. T., & O'Connell, E. J. (1982). Methods as diluting trait relationships rather than adding irrelevant systematic variance. *New Directions for Methodology of Social & Behavioral Science, 12*, 93–111.

Capon, N., & Kuhn, D. (1982). Can consumers calculate best buys? *Journal of Consumer Research, 8*(4), 449–453.

Casagrande, J. (1954). The ends of translation. *International Journal of American Linguistics, 20*, 335–340.

Cattel, R. B. (1950). *Personality: A systematic theoretical and factual study.* New York: McGraw-Hill.

Chen, C., Lee, S., & Stevenson, H. W. (1995). Response style and cross-cultural comparisons of rating scales among East Asian and North American students. *Psychological Science, 6*, 170–175.

Christensen, A. L. (1979). *Luria's neuropsychological investigation* (2nd ed.). Copenhagen: Monksgaard.

Church, T. A. (2000). Culture and personality: Toward an integrated cultural trait psychology. *Journal of Personality, 68*(4), 651–703.

Church, T. A. (2001). Personality measurement in cross-cultural perspective. *Journal of Personality, 69*(6), 979–1006.

Church, T. A., & Katigbak, M. S. (1988). The emic strategy in the identification and assessment of personality dimensions in a non-Western culture: Rationale, steps, and a Philippine illustration. *Journal of Cross-Cultural Psychology, 19*(2), 140–163.

Churchill, G. A., Jr. (1979). A paradigm for developing better measures of marketing constructs. *Journal of Marketing Research, 16*(2), 64–73.

Churchill, G. A., Jr., & Iacobucci, D. (2004). *Marketing research: Methodological foundations* (9th ed.). Mason, OH: Thomson/South-Western.

Cohen, J. (1960). A coefficient of agreement for nominal scales. *Educational and Psychological Measurement, 20*, 37–46.

Cohen, J. (1968). Weighted Kappa: Nominal scale agreement with provision for scaled disagreement or partial credit. *Psychological Bulletin, 70*(4), 213–220.

Comrey, A. L. (1978). Common methodological problems in factor analytic studies. *Journal of Consulting and Clinical Psychology, 46*, 648–659.

Comrey, A. L., & Lee, H. B. (1992). *A first course in factor analysis* (2nd ed.). Hillsdale, NJ: Lawrence Erlbaum.

Converse, J. M., & Presser, S. (1986). *Survey questions: Handcrafting the standardized questionnaire.* Beverly Hills, CA: Sage.

Cook, T. D., & Campbell, D. T. (1979). *Quasi-experimentation: Design and analysis issues for field settings.* Chicago: Rand McNally.

Couch, A. S., & Keniston, K. (1960). Yea sayers and nay sayers: Agreeing response set as a personality variable. *Journal of Abnormal and Social Psychology, 60,* 151–174.

Cox, E. (1980). The optimal number of response alternatives in a scale: A review. *Journal of Marketing Research, 17,* 407–422.

Cronbach, L. J. (1946). Response sets and test validity. *Educational and Psychological Measurement, 6,* 475–494.

Cronbach, L. J. (1951). Coefficient alpha and the internal structure of tests. *Psychometrika, 16*(9), 297–334.

Cronbach, L. J., & Furby, L. (1970). How we should measure change—Or should we? *Psychological Bulletin, 74,* 68–80.

Cronbach, L. J., & Meehl, P. E. (1955). Construct validity in psychological tests. *Psychological Bulletin, 52*(7), 281–302.

Cronbach, L. J., Rajaratnam, N., & Gleser, G. C. (1963). Theory of generalizability: A liberalization of reliability theory. *British Journal of Psychology, 16*(11), 137–163.

Crowne, D. P., & Marlowe, D. (1964). *The approval motive.* New York: Wiley.

Cushman, W. H. (1986). Reading from microfiche, a VDT, and the printed page: Subjective fatigue and performance. *Human Factors, 28*(1), 63–73.

Dehaene, S. (1997). *The number sense: How the mind creates mathematics.* New York: Oxford University Press.

Delis, D. C., Kramer, J. H., Kaplan, E., & Ober, B. A. (1987). *The California verbal learning test* (research ed.). San Diego, CA: Harcourt Brace Jovanovich.

Denzin, N. K., & Lincoln, Y. S. (2003). *The landscape of qualitative research: Theories and issues.* Thousand Oaks, CA: Sage.

DePaulo, B. M., & Friedman, H. S. (1998). Nonverbal communication. In D. T. Gilbert, S. T. Fiske, & G. Lindzey (Eds.), *The handbook of social psychology* (Vol. 2). New York: Oxford University Press.

DeShon, R. P. (1998). A cautionary note on measurement error corrections in structural equation models. *Psychological Methods, 3*(4), 412–423.

DeVellis, R. F. (1991). *Scale development: Theory and applications.* Newbury Park, CA: Sage.

Diamantopoulos, A., & Winklhofer, H. M. (2001). Index construction with formative indicators: An alternative to scale development. *Journal of Marketing Research, 38*(2), 269–277.

Dowd, D. J., & West, S. C. (1969). An inventory of measurement of affective behavior. In W. H. Beatty (Ed.), *Improving educational assessment and an inventory of measures of affective behavior.* Washington, DC: Association for Supervision and Curriculum Development.

Duda, J. L., & Hayashi, C. T. (1998). Measurement issues in cross-cultural research within sport and exercise psychology. In J. L. Duda (Ed.), *Advances in sport and exercise psychology measurement.* Morgantown, WV: Fitness Information Technology.

Ebel, R. L. (1951). Estimation of the reliability of ratings. *Psychometrika, 16,* 407–424.

Ebel, R., & Frisbie, D. (1986). *Essentials of educational measurement* (4th ed.). Englewood Cliffs, NJ: Prentice Hall.

Edwards, A. L. (1957). *The social desirability variable in personality assessment and research*. New York: Dryden.

Edwards, J. R., & Bagozzi, R. P. (2000). On the nature and direction of relationships between constructs and measures. *Psychological Methods, 5*(2), 155–174.

Elder, G. H., Jr., Pavalko, E. K., & Clipp, E. C. (1993). *Working with archival data: Studying lives* (Sage University Papers Series on Quantitative Applications in the Social Sciences, series no. 07–088). Newbury Park, CA: Sage.

Ellsworth, P. C. (1977). From abstract ideas to concrete instances: Some guidelines for choosing natural research settings. *American Psychologist, 32*(8), 604–615.

Epstein, S. (1983). Aggregation and beyond: Some basic issues on the prediction of behavior. *Journal of Personality, 51*, 360–392.

Faber, R. J., & O'Guinn, T. C. (1992). A clinical screener for compulsive buying. *Journal of Consumer Research, 19*, 459–469.

Fairburn, C. G., & Cooper, Z. (1993). The eating disorder examination. In C. G. Fairburn & G. T. Wilson (Eds.), *Binge eating: Nature, assessment, and treatment* (12th ed., pp. 317–332). New York: Guilford.

Feldman, J. M., & Lynch, J. G., Jr. (1988). Self-generated validity: Effects of measurement on belief, attitude, intention, and behavior. *Journal of Applied Psychology, 73*, 421–435.

Ferreira, A. J., & Winter, W. D. (1963). The palmar sweat print: A methodological study. *Psychosomatic Medicine, 25*, 377–384.

Finn, A., & Kayande, U. (1997). Reliability assessment and optimization of marketing measurement. *Journal of Marketing Research, 34*(5), 262–275.

Fishbein, M., & Ajzen, I. (1975). *Belief, attitude, intention and behavior: An introduction to theory and research*. Reading, MA: Addison-Wesley.

Fisher, R. J. (1993). Social desirability bias and the validity of indirect questioning. *Journal of Consumer Research, 20*(2), 303–315.

Fiske, D. W. (1971). *Measuring the concepts of personality*. Chicago: University of Chicago Press.

Fiske, D. (1982). Convergent-discriminant validation in measurements and research strategies. In D. Brinberg & L. Kidder (Eds.), *Forms of validity in research* (pp. 77–92). San Francisco: Jossey-Bass.

Fornell, C. (1983). Issues in the application of covariance structure analysis: A comment. *Journal of Consumer Research, 9*, 443–447.

Fornell, C., & Larcker, D. F. (1981). Evaluating structural equation models with unobserved variables and measurement error. *Journal of Marketing Research, 18*, 39–50.

Fowler, F. (1993). Designing questions to be good measures. In *Survey research methods* (2nd ed., pp. 69–93). Newbury Park, CA: Sage.

Franzen, M. D. (1989). *Reliability and validity in neuropsychological assessment*. New York: Plenum.

Frisch, M. B., Cornell, J. E., Villanueva, M., & Retzlaff, P. J. (1992). Clinical validation of the Quality of Life Inventory: A measure of life satisfaction for use in treatment planning and outcome assessment. *Psychological Assessment, 4,* 92–101.

Furnham, A. (1986). Response bias, social desirability, and dissimulation. *Personality and Individual Differences, 7,* 385–400.

Gardner, W. (1995). On the reliability of sequential data: Measurement, meaning, and correction. In J. M. Gottman (Ed.), *The analysis of change.* Mahwah, NJ: Lawrence Erlbaum.

Gates, S. (1993). *101 business ratios: A manager's handbook of definitions, equations, and computer algorithm.* Scottsdale, AZ: McLane.

Gawron, V. J. (2000). *Human performance measures handbook.* Mahwah, NJ: Lawrence Erlbaum.

Gelmers, H. J., Gorter, K., Weerdt, C. J., & Wiezer, H. J. A. (1988). Assessment of interobserver variability in a Dutch multicenter study on acute ischemic stroke. *Stroke, 19,* 709–711.

Gerbing, D. W., & Anderson, J. C. (1984). On the meaning of within-factor correlated measurement errors. *Journal of Consumer Research, 11*(6), 572–580.

Gerbing, D. W., & Anderson, J. C. (1988). An updated paradigm for scale development incorporating unidimensionality and its assessment. *Journal of Marketing Research, 25*(5), 186–192.

Gesell, A., Halverson, H. M., Thompson, H., Ilg, F. L., Castner, B. M., Ames, L. B., & Amatruda, C. S. (1940). *The first five years of life: A guide to the study of the preschool child.* New York: Harper and Row.

Ghiselli, E. E. (1964). *Theory of psychological measurement.* New York: McGraw Hill.

Ghiselli, E. E., Campbell, J. P., & Zedeck, S. (1981). *Measurement theory for the behavioral sciences.* San Francisco: Freeman.

Gielen, U. P., & Markoulis, D. C. (2001). Preference for principled moral reasoning: A developmental and cross-cultural perspective. In *Cross-cultural topics in psychology* (2nd ed., pp. 81–102). Westport, CT: Praeger.

Golden, C. J. (1978). *Stroop color and word test: A manual for clinical and experimental uses.* Wood Dale, IL: Stoelting.

Grayson, C. E., Schwarz, N., & Hippler, H. J. (1995, May). *The numeric values of rating scales may affect scale meaning.* Paper presented at the annual meeting of the Midwestern Psychological Association, Chicago.

Greenleaf, E. A. (1992a). Improving rating scale measures by detecting and correcting bias components in some response styles. *Journal of Marketing Research, 29*(5), 176–188.

Greenleaf, E. A. (1992b). Measuring extreme response style. *Public Opinion Quarterly, 56*(3), 328–351.

Grice, J. W. (2001). Computing and evaluating factor scores. *Psychological Methods, 6*(4), 430–450.

Grimm, S. D., & Church, A. T. (1999). A cross-cultural investigation of response biases in personality. *Journal of Research in Personality, 33,* 415–441.

Groves, R. M. (1991). Measurement error across disciplines. In P. P. Biemer, R. M. Groves, L. E. Lyberg, N. A. Mathiowetz, & S. Sudman (Eds.), *Measurement error in surveys* (pp. 1–25). New York: Wiley.

Guadagnoli, E., & Velicer, W. F. (1988). Relation of sample size to the stability of component patterns. *Psychological Bulletin, 103,* 265–275.

Guilford, J. P. (1954). *Psychometric methods.* New York: McGraw-Hill.

Gulliksen, H. (1950). *Theory of mental tests.* New York: Wiley.

Hair, J. F., Anderson, R. E., Tatham, R. L., & Black, W. C. (1998). *Multivariate data analysis* (5th ed.). Upper Saddle River, NJ: Prentice Hall.

Haladyna, T. M. (1999). *Developing and validating multiple-choice test items.* Mahwah, NJ: Lawrence Erlbaum.

Hambleton, R. K., Swaminathan, H., & Rogers, H. J. (1991). *Fundamentals of item response theory.* Newbury Park, CA: Sage.

Hamilton, D. L. (1968). Personality attributes associated with extreme response style. *Psychological Bulletin, 69*(3), 192–203.

Hammersley, M. (1996). The relationship between qualitative and quantitative research: Paradigm loyalty versus methodological eclecticism. In J. T. E. Richardson (Ed.), *Handbook of qualitative research methods for psychology and the social sciences* (Vol. 12, pp. 159–174). Leicester, UK: British Psychological Society.

Hampton, J., & Gardner, M. (1983). Measures of internal category structure: A correlational analysis of normative data. *British Journal of Psychology, 74*(11), 491–516.

Hawkins, R. C., II, & Clement, P. F. (1980). Development and construct validation of a self-report measure of binge eating tendencies. *Addictive Behaviors, 5,* 219–226.

Haynes, S. N., Richard, D. C. S., & Kubany, E. S. (1995). Content validity in psychological assessment: A functional approach to concepts and methods. *Psychological Assessment, 7*(3), 238–247.

Heine, S. J., Lehman, D. R., Peng, K., & Greenholtz, J. (2002). What's wrong with cross-cultural comparisons of subjective Likert scales? The reference-group effect. *Journal of Personality & Social Psychology, 82*(6), 903–918.

Helms, J. E. (1992). Why is there no study of cultural equivalence in standardized cognitive ability testing? *American Psychologist, 47,* 1083–1101.

Herman, C. P., & Polivy, J. (1975). Anxiety, restraint, and eating behavior. *Journal of Abnormal Psychology, 84,* 666–672.

Herndon, R. M. (1997). *Handbook of neurologic rating scales.* New York: Demos Vermande.

Hertzog, C., & Schear, J. M. (1989). Psychometric considerations in testing the older person. In T. Hunt & C. J. Lindley (Eds.), *Testing older adults: A reference guide for geropsychological assessments* (pp. 24–50). Austin, TX: Pro-Ed.

Hill, N., & Alexander, J. (2000). *Handbook of customer satisfaction and loyalty measurement.* Bodmin, UK: MPG.

Hocevar, D., & Bachelor, P. (1989). A taxonomy and critique of measurements used in the study of creativity. In J. A. Glover, R. R. Ronning, & C. R. Reynolds (Eds.), *Handbook of creativity* (pp. 53–75). New York: Plenum.

Holland, J. L. (1975). *Manual for the Vocational Preference Inventory*. Palo Alto, CA: Consulting Psychologists Press.

Hu, L., & Bentler, P. M. (1998). Fit indices in covariance structure modeling: Sensitivity to underparameterized model misspecification. *Psychological Methods, 3*, 424–453.

Hui, C. H., & Triandis, H. C. (1985). The instability of response sets. *Public Opinion Quarterly, 49*(2), 253–260.

Hurt, H. T., Joseph, K., & Cook, C. D. (1977). Scales for the measurement of innovativeness. *Human Communication Research, 4*, 58–65.

Iacobucci, D. (1994). Analysis of experimental data. In R. P. Bagozzi (Ed.), *Principles of marketing research*. Cambridge, MA: Blackwell Business.

Irvine, S. H. (1973). Tests as inadvertent sources of discrimination in personnel decisions. In P. Watson (Ed.), *Psychology and race* (pp. 453–466). London: Penguin.

Irvine, S. H., & Carroll, W. K. (1980). Testing and assessment across cultures: Issues in methodology and theory. In H. C. Triandis & J. W. Berry (Eds.), *Handbook of cross-cultural psychology: Methodology* (Vol. 2, pp. 181–244). Boston: Allyn & Bacon.

ITU-T Recommendation. (1994). *Telephone transmission quality subjective opinion tests: Methods for subjective determination of transmission quality*. Geneva: International Telecommunication Union.

Jackson, C. (1996). *Understanding psychological testing*. Leicester, UK: British Psychological Society.

Jacob, H. (1984). *Using published data: Errors and remedies* (Sage University Papers Series on Quantitative Applications in the Social Sciences, series no. 07-042). Beverly Hills, CA: Sage.

James, L. R. (1982). Aggregation bias in estimates of perceptual agreement. *Journal of Applied Psychology, 67*, 219–229.

Jarvis, C. B., MacKenzie, S. B., & Podsakoff, P. M. (2003). A critical review of construct indicators and measurement model misspecification in marketing and consumer research. *Journal of Consumer Research, 30*(2), 199–218.

Johnston, R. D. (1996). Beyond intelligibility: The performance of text-to-speech synthesisers. *BT Technical Journal, 14*, 100–111.

Jones, R. L. (1996). Handbook of tests and measurements for black populations: Introduction and overview. In R. L. Jones (Ed.), *Handbook of tests and measurements for black populations* (Vol. 2, pp. 1–18). Hampton, VA: Cobb and Henry.

Judd, C. M., Jessor, R., & Donovan, J. E. (1986). Structural equation models and personality research. *Journal of Personality, 54*(1), 149–198.

Kahle, L. R. (1983). *Social values and social change: Adaptation to life in America*. New York: Praeger.

Kaplan, D. (2000). *Structural equation modeling*. Thousand Oaks, CA: Sage.

Kaplan, R. M., & Saccuzzo, D. P. (2001). *Psychological testing: Principles, applications, and issues*. Stamford, CT: Wadsworth.

Kassarjian, W. M. (1962). A study of Riesman's theory of social character. *Sociometry, 25,* 213–230.

Katz, E. R. (1982). Behavioral approaches to pain and distress in children with cancer. In *Western State Conference on Cancer Rehabilitation Conference Proceedings*. Palo Alto, CA: Bull.

Kaufman, A. S., & Kaufman, N. L. (1983). *K-ABC administration and scoring manual*. Circle Pine, MN: American Guidance Service.

Keefe, F. J. (2000). Self-report of pain: Issues and opportunities. In A. A. Stone, J. S. Turkkan, C. A. Bachrach, J. B. Jobe, H. S. Kurtzman, & V. S. Cain (Eds.), *The science of self-report: Implications for research and practice* (pp. 317–338). Mahwah, NJ: Lawrence Erlbaum.

Kellerman, H. (1989). Projective measures of emotion. In R. Plutchik & H. Kellerman (Eds.), *Emotion: Theory, research, and experience. Vol. 4, The measurement of emotions* (pp. 187–203). San Diego, CA: Academic Press.

Kerlinger, F. N. (1986). Constructs, variables, and definitions. In *Foundations of behavioral research* (3rd ed., pp. 26–44). New York: Holt, Rinehart and Winston.

Kim, J. O., & Mueller, C. (1978). *Factor analysis: Statistical methods and practical issues* (Sage University Papers Series on Quantitative Applications in the Social Sciences, series no. 07–014). Beverly Hills, CA: Sage

Kishton, J. M., & Widaman, K. F. (1994). Unidimensional versus domain representative parceling of questionnaire items: An empirical example. *Educational and Psychological Measurement, 54*(3), 757–765.

Klein-Walker, D. (1973). *Socioemotional measures for preschool and kindergarten children*. San Francisco: Jossey-Bass.

Knowles, E. S. (1988). Item context effects on personality scales: Measuring changes the measure. *Journal of Personality and Social Psychology, 55,* 312–320.

Knowles, E. S., & Byers, B. (1996). Reliability shifts in measurement reactivity: Driven by content engagement or self-engagement? *Journal of Personality and Social Psychology, 70*(5), 1080–1090.

Knowles, E. S., & Nathan, K. T. (1997). Acquiescent responding in self-reports: Cognitive style or social concern? *Journal of Research in Personality, 31*(2), 293–301.

Kolko, D. J. (1985). The heterosocial assessment inventory for women: A psychometric and behavioral evaluation. *Journal of Psychopathology and Behavioral Assessment, 7,* 49–64.

Kolko, D. J., & Milan, M. A. (1985). A woman's heterosocial skill observational rating system. *Behavior Modification, 9,* 165–193.

Korgaonkar, P. K., & Moschis, G. P. (1982). An experimental study of cognitive dissonance, product involvement, expectations, performance and consumer judgment of product performance. *Journal of Advertising, 11*(3), 32–44.

Kraft, V., & Portele, T. (1995). Quality evaluation of five German speech synthesis systems. *Acta Acustica, 3,* 351–365.

Krippendorff, K. (1980). *Content analysis: An introduction to its methodology.* Beverly Hills, CA: Sage.

Kruglanski, A. W. (1975). The human subject in the psychological experiment: Fact and artifact. In L. Berkowitz (Ed.), *Advances in experimental social psychology* (Vol. 8, pp. 101–147). Orlando, FL: Academic Press.

Kumar, N., Stern, L. W., & Anderson, J. C. (1993). Conducting interorganization research using key informants. *Academy of Management Journal, 36*(6), 1633–1651.

Lance, C. E., LaPointe, J. A., & Stewart, A. M. (1994). A test of the context dependency of three causal models of halo rater error. *Journal of Applied Psychology, 79*(3), 332–340.

Lawler, E. E., III, Porter, L. W., & Tennenbaum, A. (1968). Managers' attitudes toward interaction episodes. *Journal of Applied Psychology, 52*(12), 432–439.

Lennox, R. D., & Dennis, M. L. (1994). Measurement error issues in substance abuse services research: Lessons from structural equation modeling and psychometric theory. *Evaluation and Program Planning, 17*(4), 399–407.

Lester, P. E., & Bishop, L. K. (2000). *Handbook of tests and measurement in education and the social sciences.* Lanham, MD: Scarecrow.

Levine, R. (1997). *A geography of time.* New York: HarperCollins.

Levine, S., & Elzey, F. F. (1968). *San Francisco Vocational Competence Scale.* New York: Psychological Corporation.

Lewis, J. R. (2001). *The revised Mean Opinion Scale (MOS-R): Preliminary psychometric evaluation* (IBM Technical Report TR 29.3414). West Palm Beach, FL: IBM Voice Systems.

Lichtenstein, D. R., Ridgway, N. M., & Netemeyer, R. G. (1993). Price perceptions and consumer shopping behavior: A field study. *Journal of Marketing Research, 30,* 234–245.

Lincoln, Y. S., & Guba, E. (1985). *Naturalistic inquiry.* Beverly Hills, CA: Sage.

Loken, B., & Ward, J. (1990). Alternative approaches to understanding the determinants of typicality. *Journal of Consumer Research, 17*(9), 111–126.

Long, J. S. (1983). *Covariance structure models: An introduction to LISREL.* Beverly Hills, CA: Sage.

Lorr, M. (1989). Models and methods for measurement of mood. In R. Plutchik & H. Kellerman (Eds.), *Emotion: Theory, research, and experience. Vol. 4, The measurement of emotions.* San Diego, CA: Academic Press.

Luce, M. F., Bettman, J. R., & Payne, J. W. (2001). Emotional decisions: Trade-off difficulty and coping in consumer choice. *Monographs of the Journal of Consumer Research, 1.*

Luria, A. R. (1976). *Cognitive development: Its cultural and social foundations.* Cambridge, MA: Harvard University Press.

Lyerly, S. B. (1973). *Handbook of psychometric rating scales.* Rockville, MD: National Institute of Mental Health.

Lynch, J. G., Jr. (1982). On the external validity of experiments in consumer research. *Journal of Consumer Research, 9,* 225–239.

MacCallum, R. C., & Austin, J. T. (2000). Applications of structural equations modeling in psychological research. *Annual Review of Psychology, 51*(1), 201–226.

MacCallum, R. C., Widaman, K. F., Zhang, S., & Hong, S. (1999). Sample size in factor analysis. *Psychological Methods, 4*(1), 84–99.

Mandler, G., & Sarason, S. B. (1952). A study of anxiety and learning. *Journal of Abnormal and Social Psychology, 47,* 166–173.

Manning, K. C., Bearden, W. O., & Madden, T. J. (1995). Consumer innovativeness and the adoption process. *Journal of Consumer Psychology, 4*(4), 329–345.

Marsh, H. W. (1987). *The Self-Description Questionnaire I: Manual and research monograph.* San Antonio, TX: Psychological Corporation.

Martin, J. (1964). Acquiescence: Measurement and theory. *British Journal of Social & Clinical Psychology, 3*(3), 216–225.

McCracken, G. (1988). *The long interview.* Newbury Park, CA: Sage.

McCrae, R. R. (2001). Trait psychology and culture: Exploring intercultural comparisons. *Journal of Personality, 69*(6), 819–846.

McGee, R. K. (1967). Response set in relation to personality: An orientation. In I. A. Berg (Ed.), *Response set in personality assessment* (pp. 1–31). Chicago: Aldine.

McKeown, B., & Thomas, D. (1988). *Q methodology* (Sage University Papers Series on Quantitative Applications in the Social Sciences, series no. 07–066). Newbury Park, CA: Sage.

Meehl, P. E., & Hathaway, S. R. (1946). The K factor as a suppressor variable in the MMPI. *Journal of Applied Psychology, 30,* 526–564.

Mendoza, J. L., Stafford, K. L., & Stauffer, J. M. (2000). Large-sample confidence intervals for validity and reliability coefficients. *Psychological Methods, 5*(3), 356–369.

Merrick, E. (1999). An exploration of quality in qualitative research: Are "reliability" and "validity" relevant? In M. Kopala & L. A. Suzuki (Eds.), *Using qualitative methods in psychology* (pp. 25–36). Thousand Oaks, CA: Sage.

Messick, S. (1967). The psychology of acquiescence: An interpretation of research evidence. In I. A. Berg (Ed.), *Response set in personality assessment* (pp. 115–145). Chicago: Aldine.

Messick, S. (1968). Response sets. In D. L. Sills (Ed.), *International encyclopedia of the social sciences* (Vol. 13, pp. 492–496). New York: Macmillan.

Messick, S. (1991). Psychology and methodology of response styles. In R. E. Snow & D. E. Wiley (Eds.), *Improving inquiry in social science: A volume in honor of Lee J. Cronbach* (pp. 161–200). Hillsdale, NJ: Lawrence Erlbaum.

Michell, J. (1999). *Measurement in psychology.* Cambridge, UK: Cambridge University Press.

Miller, D. C. (1991). *Handbook of research design and social measurement.* Newbury Park, CA: Sage.

Miller, D. C., & Salkind, J. S. (2002). *Handbook of research design and social measurement* (6th ed.). Thousand Oaks, CA: Sage.

Molloy, D. W., Alemayehu, E., & Roberts, R. (1991). Standardized mini-mental state examination (SMMSE): Its reliability compared to the traditional mini-mental state examination (MMSE). *American Journal of Psychiatry, 148*, 102–105.

Mook, D. G. (1983). In defense of external validity. *American Psychologist, 38*(4), 379–387.

Moreno, J. L. (1934). *Who shall survive? A new approach to the problem of human relationships.* Beacon, NY: Beacon House.

Morley, E., Bryant, S. P., & Hatry, H. P. (2001). *Comparative performance measurement.* Washington, DC: Urban Institute Press.

Mulaik, S. A., James, L. R., Alstine, J. V., Bennett, N., Lind, S., & Stilwell, C. D. (1989). Evaluation of goodness-of-fit indices for structural equation models. *Psychological Bulletin, 105*(3), 430–445.

Murray, H. A. (1938). *Explorations in personality.* New York: Oxford University Press.

Mutran, E. J., Danis, M., Bratton, K. A., Sudha, S., & Hanson, L. (1997). Attitudes of the critically ill toward prolonging life: The role of social support. *Gerontologist, 37*, 192–199.

Naglieri, J. (1999). *Essentials of CAS assessment.* New York: Wiley.

National Adult Literacy Survey. (1993). *Adult literacy in America: A first look at the results of the National Adult Literacy Survey.* Executive Summary, Educational Testing Service (Facts Line Doc. No. 05001).

Neter, J., Kutner, M. H., Nachsteim, C. J., & Wasserman, W. (1996). *Applied linear statistical models: Regression, analysis of variance, and experimental designs* (4th ed.). Homewood, IL: Irwin.

Newcomb, T. (1931). An experiment designed to test the validity of a rating technique. *Journal of Educational Psychology, 22*, 279–289.

Nguyen, L., & John, D. R. (2003). *Materialism in children and adolescents: The role of the developing self-concept.* Working paper.

Nisbett, R. E. (2003). *The geography of thought: How Asians and Westerners think differently . . . and why.* New York: Free Press.

Norton, R. W. (1975). Measurement of ambiguity tolerance. *Journal of Personality Assessment, 39*(6), 607–619.

Nunnally, J. C. (1978). *Psychometric theory* (2nd ed.). New York: McGraw-Hill.

Nunnally, J. C., & Bernstein, I. H. (1994). Introduction. In *Psychometric theory.* New York: McGraw-Hill.

O'Donovan, D. (1965). Rating extremity: Pathology or meaningfulness? *Psychological Review, 72*(5), 358–372.

Osgood, C. E., Suci, G. J., & Tannenbaum, P. H. (1957). *The measurement of meaning.* Urbana: University of Illinois Press.

Osterlind, S. J. (1998). *Constructing test items: Multiple-choice, constructed response, performance and other formats* (2nd ed.). Norwell, MA: Kluwer.

Overall, J. E., & Gorham, D. R. (1962). The Brief Psychiatric Rating Scale. *Psychological Reports, 10*, 799–812.

Parameswaran, R., Greenberg, B. A., Bellenger, D. N., & Robertson, D. H. (1979). Measuring reliability: A comparison of alternative techniques. *Journal of Marketing Research, 16,* 18–25.

Parasuraman, A., Zeithaml, V. A., & Berry, L. L. (1988). SERVQUAL: A multi-item scale for measuring consumer perceptions of service quality. *Journal of Retailing, 64,* 12–40.

Parten, M. (1932). Social participation among preschool children. *Journal of Abnormal and Social Psychology, 27,* 243–270.

Paulhus, D. L. (1991). Measurement and control of response bias. In J. P. Robinson, P. R. Shaver, & L. S. Wrightsman (Eds.), *Measures of personality and social psychological attitudes* (pp. 17–59). San Diego, CA: Academic Press.

Payne, J. W., Bettman, J. R., & Johnson, E. L. (1993). *The adaptive decision maker.* Cambridge, UK: Cambridge University Press.

Perdue, B. C., & Summers, J. O. (1986). Checking the success of manipulations in marketing experiments. *Journal of Marketing Research, 23*(11), 317–326.

Perreault, W. D., Jr., & Leigh, L. E. (1989). Reliability of nominal data based on qualitative judgments. *Journal of Marketing Research, 26,* 135–148.

Perri, M., & Wolfgang, A. P. (1988). A modified measure of need for cognition. *Psychological Reports, 62,* 955–957.

Peter, J. P. (1979). Reliability: A review of psychometric basics and recent marketing practices. *Journal of Marketing Research, 16*(2), 6–17.

Peter, J. P., Churchill, G. A., Jr., & Brown, T. J. (1993). Caution in the use of difference scores in consumer research. *Journal of Consumer Research, 19,* 655–662.

Peterson, R. (1994). A meta-analysis of Cronbach's coefficient alpha. *Journal of Consumer Research, 21*(9), 381–391.

Phillips, L. W. (1981). Assessing measurement error in key informant reports. A methodological note on organizational analysis in marketing. *Journal of Marketing Research, 18,* 395–415.

Pike, K. M., Loeb, K., & Walsh, B. T. (1995). Binge eating and purging. In D. B. Allison (Ed.), *Handbook of assessment methods for eating behaviors and weight-related problems* (pp. 303–346). Thousand Oaks, CA: Sage.

Plutchik, R. (1989). Measuring emotions and their derivatives. In R. Plutchik & H. Kellerman (Eds.), *Emotion: Theory, research, and experience. Vol. 4, The measurement of emotions* (pp. 1–35). San Diego, CA: Academic Press.

Podsakoff, P. M., MacKenzie, S. B., Lee, J. Y., & Podsakoff, N. P. (2003). Common method biases in behavioral research: A critical review of the literature and recommended remedies. *Journal of Applied Psychology, 88*(5), 879–903.

Price, J. L. (1972). *Handbook of organizational measurement.* Lexington, MA: D. C. Heath.

Rand, C. S. (2000). "I took the medicine like you told me, Doctor": Self-report of adherence with medical regimens. In A. A. Stone, J. S. Turkkan, C. A. Bachrach, J. B. Jobe, H. S. Kurtzman, & V. S. Cain (Eds.), *The science of self-report: Implications for research and practice* (pp. 257–276). Mahwah, NJ: Lawrence Erlbaum.

Ray, J. J. (1983). Reviving the problem of acquiescent response bias. *Journal of Social Psychology, 121*(1), 81–96.

Redman, B. K. (2002). *Measurement instruments in clinical ethics.* Thousand Oaks, CA: Sage.

Rentz, J. O. (1987). Generalizability theory: A comprehensive method for assessing and improving the dependability of marketing measures. *Journal of Marketing Research, 24*(2), 19–28.

Rest, J. (1979). *Development in judging moral issues.* Minneapolis: University of Minnesota Press.

Richins, M. L., & Dawson, S. (1992). Materialism as a consumer value: Measure development and validation. *Journal of Consumer Research, 19,* 303–316.

Rodrogue, J. R., Geffken, G. R., & Streisand, R. M. (2000). *Child health assessment: A handbook of measurement techniques.* Boston: Allyn & Bacon.

Rokeach, M. (1968). *Beliefs, attitudes and values.* San Francisco: Jossey-Bass.

Rorer, L. G. (1965). The great response-style myth. *Psychological Bulletin, 63,* 129–156.

Rorschach, H. (1942). *Psychodiagnostics.* New York: Greene and Stratton.

Rosch, E. (1973). On the internal structure of perceptual and semantic categories. In T. M. Moore (Ed.), *Cognitive development and the acquisition of language.* New York: Academic Press.

Rosch, E., & Mervis, C. (1975). Family resemblances: Studies in the internal structure of categories. *Cognitive Psychology, 7,* 573–605.

Rosenthal, R., Hall, J. A., DiMatteo, M. R., Rogers, P. L., & Archer, D. (1979). *Sensitivity to nonverbal communication: The PONS test.* Baltimore, MD: Johns Hopkins University Press.

Rossiter, J. R. (2002). The C-OAR-SE procedure for scale development in marketing. *International Journal of Research in Marketing, 19,* 305–335.

Rotter, J. B., & Rafferty, J. E. (1950). *Manual: The Rotter incomplete sentence blank.* New York: Psychological Corporation.

Russell, J. A. (1989). Measures of emotion. In R. Plutchik & H. Kellerman (Eds.), *Emotion: Theory, research, and experience. Vol. 4, The measurement of emotions.* San Diego, CA: Academic Press.

Russell, J. A., Weiss, A., & Mendelsohn, G. A. (1989). Affect grid: A single-item scale of pleasure and arousal. *Journal of Personality and Social Psychology, 57*(3), 493–502.

Rust, J., & Golombok, S. (1999). *Modern psychometrics.* New York: Routledge.

Rust, R. T., & Cooil, B. (1994). Reliability measures for qualitative data: Theory and applications. *Journal of Marketing Research, 31,* 1–14.

Sarason, I. G. (1975). Test anxiety, attention, and the general problem of anxiety. In C. D. Spielberger & I. G. Sarason (Eds.), *Stress and anxiety* (Vol. 1). New York: Halsted.

Sawyer, A. G. (1975). Demand artifacts in laboratory experiments in consumer research. *Journal of Consumer Research, 1,* 20–30.

Scherer, K. R. (1989). Vocal measurement of emotion. In R. Plutchik & H. Kellerman (Eds.), *Emotion: Theory, research, and experience. Vol. 4, The measurement of emotions.* San Diego, CA: Academic Press.

Schlundt, D. G. (1995). Assessment of specific eating behaviors and eating style. In D. B. Allison (Ed.), *Handbook of assessment methods for eating behavior and weight-related problems: Measures, theory, and research* (pp. 241–302). Thousand Oaks, CA: Sage.

Schlundt, D. G., & Zimering, R. T. (1988). The dieter's inventory of eating temptations: A measure of weight control competence. *Addictive Behavior, 13*, 151–164.

Schmidt, F. L., & Hunter, J. E. (1996). Measurement error in psychological research: Lessons from 26 research scenarios. *Psychological Methods, 1*(2), 199–223.

Schuman, H., & Presser, S. (1981). *Questions and answers in attitude surveys.* New York: Academic Press.

Schutz, R. W. (1998). Assessing the stability of psychological traits and measures. In J. L. Duda (Ed.), *Advances in sport and exercise psychology measurement* (pp. 393–408). Morgantown, WV: Fitness Information Technology.

Schwarz, N., & Hippler, H. J. (1991). Response alternatives: The impact of their choice and presentation order. In P. P. Biemer, R. M. Groves, L. E. Lyberg, N. A. Mathiowetz, & S. Sudman (Eds.), *Measurement errors in surveys* (pp. 41–56). New York: Wiley.

Schwarz, N., Knauper, B., Hippler, H. J., Noelle-Neumann, E., & Clark, F. (1991). Rating scales: Numeric values may change the meaning of scale labels. *Public Opinion Quarterly, 55*, 618–630.

Shavelson, R. J., & Webb, N. M. (1991). *Generalizability theory: A primer.* Newbury Park, CA: Sage.

Shelton, M. L., & Klesges, R. C. (1995). Measures of physical activity and exercise. In D. B. Allison (Ed.), *Handbook of assessment methods for eating behaviors and weight-related problems* (pp. 185–214). Thousand Oaks, CA: Sage.

Shimp, T. A., Hyatt, E. M., & Snyder, D. J. (1991). A critical appraisal of demand artifacts in consumer research. *Journal of Consumer Research, 18*, 273–283.

Shimp, T. A., & Sharma, S. (1987). Consumer ethnocentrism: Construction and validation of the CETSCALE. *Journal of Marketing Research, 24*, 280–289.

Shindell, S. (1989). Assessing the older adult with visual impairment. In T. Hunt & C. J. Lindley (Eds.), *Testing older adults: A reference guide for geropsychological assessments* (pp. 135–149). Austin, TX: Pro-Ed.

Shulman, A. (1973). A comparison of two scales on extremity response bias. *Public Opinion Quarterly, 37*, 407–412.

Simmons, C. J., Bickart, B. A., & Lynch, J. G., Jr. (1993). Capturing and creating public opinion in survey research. *Journal of Consumer Research, 20*(2), 316–329.

Sirotnik, K. A. (1980). Psychometric implications of the unit-of-analysis problem (with examples from the measurement of organizational climate). *Journal of Educational Measurement, 17*(4), 245–282.

Slade, P. D., & Russell, G. F. M. (1973). Awareness of body dimensions in anorexia nervosa. *Psychological Medicine, 3*, 188–199.

Smith, M. C., & Thelen, M. H. (1984). Development and validation of a test for bulimia. *Journal of Consulting and Clinical Psychology, 52*, 863–872.

Snyder, M. (1974). Self-monitoring of expressive behavior. *Journal of Personality and Social Psychology, 30*(4), 526–537.

Sonntag, G. P., Portele, T., Haas, F., & Kohler, J. (1999). Comparative evaluation of six German TTS systems. *Proceedings of the ESCA Eurospeech '99 6th European Conference on Speech Communication and Technology* (pp. 251–254). Budapest, Hungary.

Spanier, G., & Filsinger, E. E. (1983). The Dyadic Adjustment Scale. In E. E. Filsinger (Ed.), *Marriage and family assessment: A source book for family therapy.* Beverly Hills, CA: Sage.

Spielberger, C. D., Gorush, J., & Lushene, H. (1970). *Manual for the State-Trait Anxiety Inventory.* Palo Alto, CA: Consulting Psychologists Press.

Steele, C. M. (1997). A threat in the air: How stereotypes shape intellectual identity and performance. *American Psychologist, 52*(6), 613–629.

Stening, B. W., & Everett, J. E. (1984). Response styles in a cross-cultural managerial study. *Journal of Social Psychology, 122*(2), 151–156.

Sternthal, B., Tybout, A. M., & Calder, B. J. (1987). Confirmatory versus comparative approaches to judging theory tests. *Journal of Consumer Research, 14*(6), 114–125.

Stiles, W. B. (1993). Quality control in qualitative research. *Clinical Psychology Review, 13,* 593–618.

Stockford, L., & Bissell, H. S. (1949). Factors involved in establishing a merit rating scale. *Personnel, 26,* 94–118.

Stotland, S., Zuroff, D. C., & Roy, M. (1991). Situational dieting self-efficacy and short-term regulation of eating. *Appetite, 17,* 81–90.

Strauss, A., & Corbin, J. (1990). *Basics of qualitative research: Grounded theory procedures and techniques.* Newbury Park, CA: Sage.

Strong, E. K., Jr., & Campbell, D. P. (1966). *Manual for strong vocational interest blank.* Stanford, CA: Stanford University Press.

Sudman, S., & Bradburn, N. M. (1982). *Asking questions: A practical guide to questionnaire design.* San Francisco: Jossey-Bass.

Sudman, S., Bradburn, N., & Schwarz, N. (1996). *Thinking about answers: The application of cognitive processes to survey methodology.* San Francisco: Jossey-Bass.

Takooshian, H., Mrinal, N. R., & Mrinal, U. S. (2001). Research methods for studies in the field. In L. L. Adler & U. P. Gielen (Eds.), *Cross-cultural topics in psychology* (2nd ed., pp. 29–46). Westport, CT: Praeger.

Taylor, R. L. (1997). *Assessment of exceptional students: Educational and psychological procedures.* Needham Heights, MA: Allyn & Bacon.

Thompson, J. K. (1995). Body image: Extent of disturbance, associated features, theoretical models, assessment methodologies, intervention strategies, and a proposal for a new DSM IV diagnostic category—body image disorder. *Progress in Behavior Modification, 28,* 3–54.

Thorndike, E. L. (1920). A constant error in psychological ratings. *Journal of Applied Psychology, 4,* 25–29.

Thorndike, R. L., Hagen, E. P., & Sattler, J. M. (1986). *Technical manual: Stanford-Binet Intelligence Scale* (4th ed.). Chicago: Riverside.

Tucker, L. A. (1982). Relationship between somatotype and body cathexis of college males. *Psychological Reports, 50,* 983–989.

Tucker, L. R., & Lewis, C. (1973). A reliability coefficient for maximum likelihood factor analysis. *Psychometrika, 38,* 1–10.

Van deVijver, F., & Tanzer, N. K. (1997). Bias and equivalence in cross-cultural assessment: An overview. *European Review of Applied Psychology, 47,* 263–279.

Vernon, M. (1989). Assessment of older persons with hearing disabilities. In T. Hunt & C. J. Lindley (Eds.), *Testing older adults: A reference guide for geropsychological assessments* (pp. 150–162). Austin, TX: Pro-Ed.

Viney, L. L. (1993). Listening to what my clients and I say: Content analysis categories and scales. In G. J. Neimeyer (Ed.), *Constructivist assessment: A casebook* (pp. 104–142). Newbury Park, CA: Sage.

Viswanathan, M. (1993). Measurement of individual differences in preference for numerical information. *Journal of Applied Psychology, 78*(5), 741–752.

Viswanathan, M. (1994). On the test-retest reliability of the Preference for Numerical Information Scale. *Psychological Reports, 75,* 285–286.

Viswanathan, M. (1997). Individual differences in need for precision. *Personality and Social Psychology Bulletin, 23*(7), 717–735.

Viswanathan, M., & Childers, T. L. (1999). Understanding how product attributes influence product categorization: Development and validation of fuzzy set based measures of gradedness in product categories. *Journal of Marketing Research, 36*(1), 75–94.

Viswanathan, M., Rosa, J. A., & Harris, J. (in press). Decision-making and coping by functionally illiterate consumers and some implications for marketing management. *Journal of Marketing.*

Viswanathan, M., Sudman, S., & Johnson, M. (2004). Maximum versus meaningful discrimination in scale response: Implications for validity of measurement of consumer perceptions about products. *Journal of Business Research, 57*(2), 108–124.

Viswanathan, M., & Viswanathan, M. (2005). Measuring speech quality for text-to-speech systems: Development and assessment of a modified mean opinion score (MOS) scale. *Computer Speech and Language, 19*(1), 55–83.

Wallendorf, M. (2001). Literally literacy. *Journal of Consumer Research, 27*(4), 505–512.

Watkins, D., & Cheung, S. (1995). Culture, gender, and response bias: An analysis of responses to the Self-Description Questionnaire. *Journal of Cross-Cultural Psychology, 26*(5), 490–504.

Weber, R. P. (1985). *Basic content analysis* (Sage University Papers Series on Quantitative Applications in the Social Sciences, series no. 07-049). Beverly Hills, CA: Sage.

Weiss, D. J., & Kingsbury, G. G. (1985). Application of computerized adaptive testing to educational problems. *Journal of Educational Measurement, 21*(4), 361–375.

Wilkie, W. L., & Pessemier, E. A. (1973). Issues in marketing's use of multi-attribute attitude models. *Journal of Marketing Research, 10,* 428–441.

Williams, J. E., & Roberson, J. K. (1967). A method of assessing racial attitudes in preschool children. *Educational and Psychological Measurement, 27,* 671–689.

Wise, S. L. (1985). The development and validation of a scale measuring attitudes toward statistics. *Educational and Psychological Measurement, 45,* 401–405.

Wyer, R. S. (1969). The effects of general response style on measurement of own attitude and the interpretation of attitude-relevant messages. *British Journal of Social and Clinical Psychology, 8*(2), 105–115.

Zuckerman, M. (1979). *Sensation seeking: Beyond the optimal level of arousal.* Hillsdale, NJ: Lawrence Erlbaum.

Index

Page references marked *t* are tables. Page references marked *f* are figures.

About the Author

Madhu Viswanathan is Associate Professor of Marketing in the Department of Business Administration within the College of Business at the University of Illinois, Urbana-Champaign, where he has been on the faculty since 1990. He holds a PhD in business administration (marketing) from the University of Minnesota and a Bachelor of Technology in mechanical engineering from the Indian Institute of Technology, Madras.

He teaches a course on measurement and research methods to PhD students and courses on marketing research to undergraduate and MBA students. He has been listed several times as an excellent instructor at the University of Illinois.

His research has appeared in journals such as *Journal of Applied Psychology; Journal of Consumer Psychology; Journal of Marketing Research; Personality and Social Psychology Bulletin;* and *Computer, Speech, and Language.* His research is in two areas: measurement and research methodology, and low-literate buyer and seller behavior. His work on literacy has been supported by grants from the National Science Foundation and the Illinois Center for International Business Education and Research.

He serves on the editorial boards of *Journal of Consumer Psychology, Journal of Consumer Research,* and *Psychology and Marketing.* He has served as the secretary-treasurer for the Society for Consumer Psychology and as the chair of the Consumer Behavior Special Interest Group of the American Marketing Association. He also chaired national conferences for the American Marketing Association and the Society for Consumer Psychology.

He directs the Marketplace Literacy Project (www.marketplaceliteracy .org), a nonprofit organization that aims to disseminate knowledge about low-literate buyer and seller behavior. Its activities include the development and distribution of educational materials for adult education, nutrition, and other programs targeted at low-literate consumers in the United States, and the development and provision of business and consumer literacy training for low-literate, low-income adults in India and other similar contexts.

He lives in Champaign, Illinois, with his wife and 10-year-old son.